Growing up
COMMUNIST and **JEWISH**
in Bondi

JOHN DOCKER is a writer and cultural historian who lives in Sydney with his wife the historian Ann Curthoys. He researches and writes in a number of fields, including Australian literature in international contexts, Jewish identity and diaspora, genocide and massacre studies. In exploring cultural theory, he has written on Edward Said, Gandhi, Derrida, Mikhail Bakhtin and Walter Benjamin. He contributes essays to the *Journal of Holy Land and Palestine Studies*. With Ann Curthoys he published *Is History Fiction?* (2005, 2010) as well as essays in genocide studies and cultural studies, for example, 'Stuart Hall and Cultural Studies, circa 1983' (2017). He is currently writing a book entitled *Sheer Folly and Derangement: Disorienting Europe and the West, from the Enlightenment to Modernity*.

VOLUMES IN THIS WORK:
Volume 1: My Father, Ted Docker
Volume 2: My Mother, Elsie Levy
Volume 3: I am Born

ALSO BY JOHN DOCKER
Australian Cultural Elites: Intellectual Traditions in Sydney and Melbourne, Angus and Robertson, 1974
In a Critical Condition, Penguin Books, 1984
The Nervous Nineties, Oxford University Press, 1991
Postmodernism and Popular Culture: A Cultural History, Cambridge University Press, 1994
1492: The Poetics of Diaspora, Continuum, 2001
The Origins of Violence: Religion, History and Genocide, UNSW Press, 2008
Race, Colour and Identity in Australia and New Zealand, edited with Gerhard Fischer, UNSW Press, 2000
Rethinking Gandhi and Nonviolent Relationality: Global Perspectives, edited with Debjani Ganguly, Routledge, 2007

Growing up COMMUNIST and JEWISH in Bondi

An Ego Histoire, a Dictionary of Modernity, an Autobiography, a Romance

I am Born
Volume 3

JOHN DOCKER

KERR
Melbourne, Victoria

First published 2020
Kerr Publishing Pty Ltd
Melbourne, Victoria
ABN 64 124 219 638

© 2020 John Docker

This book is copyright. Apart from fair dealing for the purpose of private study, research, criticism or review, or under Copyright Agency Ltd rules of recording, no part may be reproduced by any means.
The moral right of the author has been asserted.

ISBN (volume 3) 978-1-875703-35-7 (Print on Demand, PoD)
ISBN (set)   978-1-875703-32-6 (Print on Demand, PoD)
ISBN (volume 3) 978-1-875703-39-5 (eBook)
ISBN (set)   978-1-875703-36-4 (eBook)

BIC Category: Biography & Autobiography
BISAC Category 1:   BIO006000 BIOGRAPHY & AUTOBIOGRAPHY/
                    Cultural, Ethnic & Regional/General
BISAC Category 2:   BIO006000/Historical; BIO037000/Jewish; BIO10000/
                    Political
BISAC Category 3:   HIS004000/Australia & New Zealand

Cover photograph: Ted, Elsie and John Docker

Cover and book design: Paul Taylder of Xigrafix Media & Design
Typeset in Verdigris MVB Pro Text 10.5/14pt

Print-on-Demand and eBook distribution: ebookalchemy.com.au

National Library of Australia PrePublication Data Service:

 A catalogue record for this book is available from the National Library of Australia

For Ann, Ned, Shino and Leo

Contents

29	I Am Born	1
30	Primary and High School Years	27
31	Stray Thoughts on My Undergraduate Years	57
32	How I Became a Teenage Leavisite and Lived to Tell the Tale	69
33	1970: A Campaign Against Censorship, and a Scandalous Festival of Banned Works	85
34	1970: Interlude – a Socialist Scholars Conference, Without its Invited Main Speaker	157
35	1971-2: A Tribute to Henry Mayer – Inspiring Mentor, Intellectual Trickster, a non-Jewish Jew, a Diasporic Consciousness, the Stranger Who Stayed	169
36	1973: Hippie Trail through South East Asia – Bali, Jogjakarta, Jakarta, Singapore, Malacca, Kuala Lumpur, Penang	223
37	1973: Hippie Trail through Burma, India, Kathmandu	259
38	1973-4: Ann and John in London	289
39	Men and Women's Liberation 1974	331
40	The Chorizo and Genocide: Travel Notes on Barcelona, Granada, Cordoba, and Portbou, June-July 2005	355
41	Prostate Politics: A Personal Memoir, 2017	363
	Epilogue: father and son, a conversation with Ned Curthoys	379

I am Born
Volume 3

29

I Am Born

While working on this ego histoire over the many years it is taking to write, friends and acquaintances would often smile and say, 'When will you be born, John?' or 'Is this going to be' – smiling as well, I sometimes finish the sentence for them – 'something like Sterne's *Tristram Shandy*?' In 1945, 8 October, I emerged into the world: an Antipodean spring baby, a Red Diaper baby, a post-World War II Baby-Boom baby, destined to be spoilt as the youngest child, and the only boy, with two older sisters. When Ann and I got married on 3 July 1971 in the Registry Office opposite Sydney's Hyde Park, my elder sibling, at the reception afterwards at the Sydney Teachers Club, confided at speech time to the assembled Curthoys and Docker and Levy families ranged around a long table, that John her little brother was so spoilt as a child that he had his own jar of strawberry jam, kept in a cupboard, only he could have it.

Tristram Shandy like, I do recall my mother's favourite stories recalling the circumstances of my being conceived and born.

My mother said her mother, my grandmother one day said, 'If you fall now the baby will be a boy.'

'You were almost born in a taxi between Bondi and Crown Street Women's Hospital. You were the third baby, everything was happening too quickly. "Driver," I said, 'you'd better hurry or I will give birth to the baby in your cab." When you were born, you came out red in the face looking angry. The doctor said you would have a lifelong bad temper.'

⚜

I can also peruse a record of some of my earliest sentient moments. In the second of the two large notebooks of notes I took in 2010 of Ann and my papers in Mitchell Library in Sydney, I see that I took notes from a folder entitled 'Letters 1983'. This contained information of an intimate kind, in particular, an envelope with one's baby hair, golden, in a tiny cotton sock. There is also a small booklet with a grey cover concerning advice, circa 1945–6, given out to mothers by the Australian Mothercraft Society on how to follow the Truby King System: *Truby King Nurse's Advice to Mothers by Courtesy of the late Sir F. Truby King*. The booklet is a record of my mother's visits to the Baby Clinic at 1 Bondi Road, Bondi Junction, phone FW 1022.

On the first page there is a call To Mothers!

> The most loving act a mother can do is to nurse her baby.
> Nothing can ever replace the milk and the heart of a mother.
> Old French Proverb

Name of child: John Docker
Name of parent: Mrs E. J. Docker
Address: 48 Edward St. Bondi

[third page] When first seen by Nurse 8.11.45

Date of birth   8.10.45
Present Age   4 3/7 weeks
Weight at Birth 7 lbs 10 oz.
Present Length   22"

… Feed Baby regularly every four hours, five feeds a day, no night feed.
Give baby one to two ounces of cool, boiled water some time during the day.

[Another page] Best food – Mother's milk.

Best substitute – Modified Cow's Milk, suitably graded.
Bathing – bath and dress very quickly in a cosy corner. No dawdling.
Regularity of all habits. Regularity of feeding, with proper interval and no food between meals. Regularity of exercise, sleep, etc. Regularity of the bowels. Secure at least one motion every day.

1-7 – 46 – 4 feeds – omit 10am breast feed.

Date 8 – 7 – 46 Age 9 mths – Omit 6pm breast feed. [This, dear reader, is the last entry of the booklet.]

Ann has told me that her mother also adopted the Truby King System, which, when our son Ned was born in 1974, seemed like ancient history, quaint and bizarre. Bringing up Ned I don't think we followed any system though we did visit a clinic where a nurse checked on weight and so on. Ann remembers that we occasionally consulted Dr Spock.

⁓⋆⁓

Curious, I look up what is known of a system of early child rearing that likely shaped the collective psyche of the post-World War II Baby Boom generation, whether inducing lifelong notions of an ordered life, or equally a lifelong rebelliousness against such relentless regularity of body and mind. I look up the entry on Truby King, written by historian Barbara Brookes, in the *New*

Zealand Dictionary of Biography, which tells us that Frederic Truby King, born in 1858, grew up in a family of New Plymouth settlers in Taranaki, who had a sizeable farm holding as well as trading and political interests. In his early twenties, he decided to embark on a career in medicine; he left New Zealand in August 1880 to train at the University of Edinburgh like so many New Zealand doctors of his time, first visiting Paris where he witnessed Jean-Martin Charcot demonstrating a case of hysteria.

On 26 October 1887, at Edinburgh, he married Isabella Cockburn Millar; Bella was dux of the Edinburgh Educational Institution for Young Ladies and a prize-winner in the examinations offered by the Edinburgh Association for the University Education of Women. The month after their marriage, Truby King took a post as ship's surgeon on the *Selembria*, and he and Bella sailed to New Zealand. In 1889, he was appointed medical superintendent of Seacliff Lunatic Asylum, and lecturer in mental diseases and examiner in public health and medical jurisprudence at the University of Otago.

From 1894 the Kings made periodic visits to the UK, and King was admitted as a member of the Psychological Association, London. In 1904 they set off for a six-month visit to Japan. Truby King was particularly impressed by the physical fitness of the Japanese and by the custom of extended breast feeding.

Back in New Zealand, Truby King became interested in the feeding and care of infants and what advice might be given to mothers. Fellow medical men were unenthusiastic about this intrusion on their domain, so King turned for support to prominent women in the community. On 14 May 1907 he addressed a public meeting on the promotion of health of women and children, and out of this meeting the Society for the Promotion of Women and Children was born. The Society came to be known as the Plunket Society after Lady Victoria Plunket, the wife of the governor, and she became an ardent supporter. The Society inspired a movement promoting breastfeeding and infant welfare; clinics were opened throughout New Zealand.

Training mothers for breastfeeding was very much a joint cause for Truby King and Bella King. Truby King's 1913 book *Feeding and Care of Baby* became extremely influential, while Bella wrote a popular column 'Our Babies' which, by 1914, appeared in 50 newspapers throughout New Zealand. In 1917 Truby King was invited to Britain by the founders of the Babies of the Empire Society to advise on training at their Mothercraft Training Centre.

Bella King died in 1927. Truby King died in 1938, and was the first private citizen to be honoured by a state funeral.

I wonder what happened to the Truby King System. The Wikipedia entry observes that King's babycare method continued in popularity, finding favour in post-war Britain at least until the 1950s. The 1960s became associated with Benjamin Spock, who influenced parents to be more flexible and affectionate with their children, and to treat them as individuals.

In 2007 a British reality TV program *Bringing Up Baby* was made by Channel 4, causing an uproar. In the *Guardian* 7 October 2007 columnist Leo Hickman wrote an opinion piece registering his response to a mother and father dramatising what he referred to as the 'military routine' prescribed in Truby King's 1913 book *Feeding and Care of Baby*. Hickman was frankly repelled by Truby King's teachings: 'the advice appears so austere and lacking in empathy that, for me at least, it felt that it verged on being almost abusive of the babies' emotional and physical needs.' He found watching 'a set of twins being subjected to this regime' to be 'utterly heartbreaking'. Hickman reports that at the time of writing, the Office of Communications 'has received 580 complaints about the programme'.[1]

In our street in south Bondi, Edward Street, the apartment block was well situated; all along the windows side, scented honeysuckle grew on the neighbours' wire fence. My mother recalled that when Japanese baby submarines bombed Bondi during the war (on 8 June 1942), many people left for the Blue Mountains to the west of Sydney. My father, who must have been away somewhere travelling for the Communist Party, said, quick, start renting one of these flats. Not far from Edward Street, in the direction of the city, was Simpson Street, where, my mother once said, one of the Japanese shells had landed, it looked like there had been a huge hole in the road. Occasionally I would go there with my mother because one of the comrades – a house painter, she said – in the Bondi branch of the Party lived in Simpson Street in an apartment block, and my mother would visit and give him a copy of *Tribune*, the Party's newspaper.

There was a Fair Rent Act in operation, which must have kept rents quite low in our apartment building. Because our flat looked north it received sun all winter, serving me as a rule in life: when looking for a house or apartment to live in, always try to get one looking north; a southern aspect would be darker and colder. (And later in life after Ann and I began to travel I realised the reverse was true for the northern hemisphere.)

The northern aspect occasionally got us children, so careless usually of consequences as children can be, into scrapes. The apartment block seemed full of elderly single people, including an old lady with a rich Scottish accent who gardened outside her apartment, next to us, and she would offer us biscuits. Upstairs, on the southern side, lived a man who apparently had been in New Guinea, maybe during World War II; once he showed us his collection of long spears that he'd brought back. He liked to sit outside our front window, on a patch of grass, back against the wall, maybe reading, soaking up the sun, which was unfortunate because occasionally we kids, having bread to eat, would throw our crusts out the window, presumably raining down on or near his head. There must have been a protest, because my father said very firmly laid down a do-not-throw-crusts-out-of-the-window rule.

Bread proved a problem for me. Occasionally the landlord upstairs, who seemed fearfully old, would ask my mother to send her boy up Imperial Avenue, the street at right angles to Edward Street, to Bondi Road where all the shops were. I was to buy and bring back for him a kind of square oblong of white bread in two halves, and I would find myself eating little bits from the soft end; trouble ensued, I was not to do it again, though I think I found it very hard not to do it, as I walked down Imperial Avenue taking tiny bits, maybe he won't notice this time.

How should a Communist family bring up their children? I think my parents decided that they would freely talk politics in front of us, whether we could understand what was being said or not. Party members of the Bondi Branch, my parents were in would hold meetings in our living room; these were good-humoured affairs. We kids would talk to the branch members before the meeting began. Also, the branch would sometimes drive down for a picnic in the National Park, south of Sydney; my parents didn't own a car, so we drove down with a Party member who lived not too far away who did have one. Sometimes the Bronte branch had parties in the house of Peter and Betty Bloch, which overlooked Bronte beach, two beaches south of Bondi (in between was Tamarama Beach; south of Bronte was Coogee and then South Coogee); my mother and Betty Bloch were friends; sometimes I would go with my mother and Betty for lunch somewhere, and at the end of the meal my mother and Betty would squabble over who was to pay. Betty, who had variously lived in Lithuania, Russia and Germany, had come to Sydney as a refugee in 1939.[2]

The family income must have been modest. My father until

1949 was a paid functionary of the Communist Party, but after the Coal Strike of 1949, which proved disastrous for the Party, he returned to working full time as a carpenter. My mother, perhaps as the children went to school, did paid housework in people's homes (as had her mother after the family came to Sydney). She was also an excellent cook, and I have a vague memory she helped out in a motel restaurant on O'Brien Street near where my grandparents lived. She also worked in the kitchen in some kind of institutional home. I remember visiting her there, near the top of Wellington Street Bondi, opposite the primary school we three children attended. (It was high on the hill on Wellington Street; my father would always say that somehow the Catholics in Sydney grabbed the hills for their churches and schools, look at St Mary's Cathedral opposite Hyde Park in the city, how did they get that prime spot?)

Sometimes, after dinner, I went with my mother, walking through dark streets, to deliver *Tribune* the Party newspaper to Bondi branch members; we would walk in one direction to Simpson Street to the house painter's flat, at other times in another direction, much closer to the beach, to the flat of her friends Stan and Debbie. Stan was a Polish Jew. (Once, much later, after Ann and I got together, I visited Stan and Debbie's flat to borrow a cap, I had to go with my mother to a synagogue for an occasion involving one of her London kin living in Sydney.)

Sometimes the family would walk on a peace march, perhaps a Hiroshima anti-bomb march, along Bondi Road and Oxford Street to a park in the city to hear speeches. (I still have a certain dread of listening to political speeches.)

As a Communist, my mother believed in local action; she was active in the Mothers Club at our Wellington Street primary school, and I think was once given some sort of civic award by the local council in recognition of her work; later, when I went to Randwick High School in 1958, she was active in the school's

Parents and Citizens group; she was also very active in helping organise for a public library for Bondi, which was part of Waverley municipality; until then, the closest public library was in Paddington Town Hall, some distance from Bondi along the Oxford Street tram route. My memory is that the new library began life in an old arts school on Bondi Road, next door to a Masonic hall. According to the online publication 'Waverley Library celebrates 50 years!', in 1964 Waverley Council decided to support a free public library, and bought 12 000 books which were first housed in two rooms upstairs in the Bondi Pavilion at the beach; when it opened on 26 September 1964 as Waverley Municipal Library, its books variously included the history of the Australian press, tapeworms in animals, orchid growing and Cretan mythology.

'Being active' was a favourite term for Communists, perhaps worldwide; in her memoir *A Fine Old Conflict*, Jessica Mitford amusingly recalls a visit in 1950 by her sister Debo, now a Duchess, to Oakland California, where Jessica lived with her family, Jessica by then in the American Communist Party. The Oakland Party comrades 'craved to meet Debo' and a dinner was held in her honour: 'We introduced them CP fashion, in which one indicates the area of a person's political work: 'This is Andy Johnson, he's active in the Youth Movement. Phyllis Mander, active in the Peace Committee. Dr Pierson, active in the CRC, and so on.' Jessica recalls that in the following Christmas, Debo sent a 'card with an official-looking photograph of herself and Andrew, dressed in their ducal robes as for a coronation, garlanded with orders, chains, jewels, staring stonily ahead. Under the photo she had written: "Andrew & me being active."'[3]

In Chapter 6, 'CRC Secretary', of *A Fine Old Conflict* Jessica relates that she became executive secretary of the East Bay CRC, the Civil Rights Congress, which was under black Party leadership. She recalls a visit from William L Patterson, a leader of the CRC nationally, who would often come out from New York to meet local chapters; he had presented the 'CRC petition "We Charge Genocide: The Crime of Government Against the Negro People" at a United Nations meeting in Paris'. The East Bay branch of the CRC mainly engaged in 'local campaigns' which revealed 'the Party's genius for organization'.[4]

Local actions, being active, and a genius for organisation, we can observe, were universal features of Communist Parties everywhere.

An added note here: in our essay 'Defining Genocide' in *The Historiography of Genocide* (2010), Ann and I discuss the CRC petition to the UN *We Charge Genocide* as a momentous event in American and African-American history; in December 1951, it was presented by William L Patterson to the UN General Assembly in Paris, and by Paul Robeson to the UN Secretariat in New York, only 11 months after the 1948 UN Genocide Convention went into effect; the petitioners included W E B DuBois and Jessica Mitford.[5] I can also admit here that Ann and I are Jessica Mitford tragics.

The Australian Communist Party had a youth wing called the EYL, the Eureka Youth League, which held summer camps at various locations outside of Sydney; we all stayed in tents. I recall at one of these gatherings I glimpsed Ann for the first time.

The organisers in charge of the camp must have wanted everyone to join in activities; I remember, for example, looking on as a play was staged in the evening on one occasion, perhaps the only time I went to an EYL camp, in any case this is the only one that comes to mind, because of a certain incident. I think one morning I didn't want to leave the tent I was assigned to; after a while, an organiser came in, asked me why didn't I want to join in what everyone else was doing? I said I just didn't want to join in, I wanted to stay where I was, in the tent. He finally went away, puzzled. I think that I was revealing what became an odd if permanent character trait: I don't like joining in, I'm not a joiner.

<hr>

Undoubtedly, little boys have a death wish. This threatens their continuing existence on this earth, one reason being they were allowed a freedom to roam denied to their sisters; I think of my uncles Lew and Jock in their reminiscences of their childhood in the East End in London roaming far and wide, which their sister, my mother, I don't think was allowed to do. Jock recalled that Lew couldn't have been more than eight or nine, Jock couldn't have been more than five or six, 'yet we wandered around I should imagine Clapham area and Stepney area so we were always on our own'.[6] Like my uncles, I wandered at a young age.

I think my mother perhaps tried to rein in my wanderings. They often led to some kind of disaster. There was an occasion when for some reason I was left alone in the flat under strict instructions not to leave. However, I jumped out the front verandah window and ran down Edward Street and then Francis Street, along and parallel to Bondi Road, to explore – for unknown reasons – among the rocks on the southern headland. Here I managed to cut myself on the wrist on a broken bottle, rather life-threateningly, the artery showing. I think I washed the blood under a tap belonging to a nearby apartment block. I then must have run home, and my mother, who had meanwhile come home, took me up Imperial Avenue to the doctor on Bondi Road. The jagged scar is still visible, and I occasionally proudly show it to friends when relating this episode.

Another time, running around a playground some distance away, I ran into the metal corner of a slippery dip. I somehow limped home, and my mother took me to a chemist on Bondi Road; I can still see the scar, above the knee.

I'm sure I must have been a very irritating, sort of lawless child; out the front of the apartment block was a white-painted railing, below it a sort of cliff face and then the road. I took to attempting to walk along the whole length, which I think I accomplished, because I can't remember ever falling. I did however fall over a wall next to our apartment block, landing on the concrete below, then finding myself in hospital; all I can remember is eating soft sweet junket – or maybe it was custard.

I'm also certain I was a horrible child. When we played cricket outside a row of garages just along from where we lived, on the opposite side of the road, if I was bowled out, I refused to leave the crease and the game had to be abandoned.

How should a Communist family bring up their children in terms of knowing about religion?

It must have been worked out between my parents that in a Communist family we children should grow up without any religion (though on Sunday mornings, I recall, we were sent to Sunday School, situated a block or so along Edward Street going towards the beach, I think on a corner; maybe that involved some religion, listening to biblical stories or some such, in any case perhaps also an opportunity for one's parents to relax). Yet it was hard to avoid knowing that other people, other families, did practise religion of various kinds. I know my mother got to know a Mizrahi (Oriental) Jewish family in an apartment block round the corner in Imperial Avenue, they'd migrated from Israel, and she would occasionally help them out with preparing food for festive occasions; one time visiting the Mizrahi family, they had shown her how to make grilled eggplant slices with garlic on top. She got me to taste one, and I still make my own version of it.[7] There's also a version featured on the cover of Yotam Ottolenghi's *Plenty*, I've just looked at it among our cookery books: an eggplant is roasted, sliced and topped with buttermilk and Greek yoghurt sauce flavoured with crushed garlic and with pomegranate seeds sprinkled on top.

Some kind of religious temptation emanated from the apartment block next door, the one I'd fallen into. We didn't seem to relate to anyone there. All I knew was my mother telling me that a well-known professional wrestler, a huge man with a Polish name, lived there. There were stories about him in the papers: he challenged all comers. However, I got to talking to a boy lived there who was a little older than me, and he told me he had just gone to hear Billy Graham – in Australia to gather converts – speak at some kind of Christian revivalist meeting. Graham made his first crusading visit to Sydney in 1959, my second year of high school. The neighbouring boy asked did I want to come along, he had gone out the front at the meeting to be converted. I must have said no, because I can't remember going and I'm sure my parents would have disapproved.

Nonetheless, every year our family celebrated Christmas. There was a Christmas tree and great excitement about presents. I got some kind of tricycle one year, and I rode it furiously along the pavement. Also, I've just checked with Ann: her Communist family also celebrated Christmas.

Yet if we were brought up without any formal religion, I always knew I was somehow Jewish. I knew my mother was Jewish, and that one was Jewish through one's mother. My mother could explain Jewish things to me. Across the road from us lived a Jewish family who ran a delicatessen in Six Ways. Sometimes a little Jewish man with a long beard and black coat walked by, always barked at furiously by a dog belonging to an Anglo-Australian family also living opposite us. I asked my mother who the man was and she said he was the *shohet* who supervised the killing of animals in the proper way.[8]

I knew my grandparents were Jewish, from London's East End. The family would always shout at Phil, my grandfather don't fast, you're too old. Next door to their semi-detached house in O'Brien Street lived a friend of the family, Esther I think, and as a child I would pick up that the women in my family were hostile to her husband because he was violent towards her. My grandfather was tall, and when he walked along O'Brien Street, he would lift his hat to ladies he passed. My grandmother Rose was very short, and she was beloved by the family; my memory is that she provided the kindliness and warmth that suffused the house. My mother, I recall, called her 'Rose', not 'Mum'; we children called her Nan. The final words of the concluding mosaic of my *1492: The Poetics of Diaspora* are 'Nan was a great cook of beautiful large round apple pies. But when Nan buttered the matzos, we kids would say more, more on that corner, that bit, Nan.'[9] In winter, we would play dominoes in front of the coal fire. Sometimes uncle Jock and auntie Awky would visit, and there were loud political arguments I couldn't understand. They may have related to 1956 when the Soviet Union sent tanks to crush the revolt in Hungary, the time when Communist Parties around the world lost most of their intelligentsia – though not my mother and father, who always remained loyal to the Soviet Union.

My memory is that my grandparents were poor. There was old lino on all the floors. Rose was a brilliant cook, rolling flour on a board and making pastry, then baking the apple pies in a huge black stove. Also, their semi-detached house was fortunately on the side of O'Brien Street looking north, and maybe that was why my mother chose the flat in Edward Street. Rose and Phil would sit outside on the verandah on an old sofa enjoying the warm sun. In the patch of grass out the front was a frangipani tree with white flowers.

When my grandmother Rose died, my mother in our flat in Edward Street cried for days. When we went to the Jewish funeral centre opposite Centennial Park, my mother cried out in anguish, 'Mother, there's mother.'[10] When we got to the Jewish section of Rookwood Cemetery my grandfather looked down on the plot where his wife lay, she who he'd married so many decades before in London, in the plot next to hers destined for him. I think I was then about 16, and I wrote a poem about it.

<hr />

When I was about 9 or 10 or 11, I was obsessed with tennis, and would walk along Edward Street to Wellington Street and then proceed down the hill holding my precious racquet; I would cross over O'Brien Street and come to the clay courts, quite a number of them. Here, I was coached by the head coach Mr Ferguson, who it was said had once played or nearly played Davis Cup for Australia with Adrian Quist. I would then play for hours with the other kids similarly obsessed, and then, as evening came, helped to sweep the courts with a huge broom. Mr Ferguson was to be respected, held in awe. For some reason, I had a good backhand which impressed the coach, and once I visited Mr Ferguson with my mother. He lived near the courts, behind O'Brien Street, in a street that curved round towards Six Ways. Mr Ferguson said I had a very good backhand, and could undertake intensive coaching for a future in tennis. My mother said no, we would like him to concentrate on his schooling.

I'm not sure why she said this. I'd ever shown the slightest interest in reading anything, except, I vaguely recall, English comics about Manchester United, I knew there was a newsagent in Six Ways which stocked them and I would go down there to see if the next comic had arrived; why I was interested in Manchester United, I have no idea. And I hope this memory is true, that I am not making it up.

Embarrassing to recall, there was a period about then when I would sleep with my racquet on the top bunk of the verandah room.

During late 2017 or early 2018, I read an article in the *Guardian* online by an American writer concerning her fear of dogs; she explained that when she was a child growing up in a large house occupied by a number of families, there was a fierce dog which would attack you if you ever ventured into the backyard; it left her with a recurring fear of dogs so that she found it hard to negotiate open spaces or streets she'd never been in before, until, finally, she overcame her fear and now has a lovely friendly cuddly little dog of her own. Apart from the redemptive ending, this graphically told story reminded me of my lifelong fear of dogs.

When Ann and I holidayed in Lisbon in early June 2019, we learned of José Saramago, the Portuguese writer who was awarded the Nobel Prize for Literature in 1998. We immediately read some of his translated works in Lisbon's Ler Davagar Bookshop, where we could buy them and sit reading over coffee. Ann read *Blindness* and then embarked on his *Small Memories: A Memoir*, about his childhood, and came across some early pages where Saramago tells of his lifelong fear of dogs. He had once been attacked by the neighbours' Alsatian: 'The fear – which even today, and despite recent happy experiences, I can barely control when face to face with an unfamiliar representative of the canine species – comes, I am sure, from the utter panic I felt as a seven-year-old, when, one night as darkness was falling and the street-lamps were already lit and just as I was about to go into the house on Rua Fernão Lopes, in the Saldanha district of Lisbon, where we lived along with two other families, the street door burst open and through it… came the neighbours' Alsatian dog, which immediately began to pursue me, filling the air with its furious, thunderous barking.'[11]

Just along from where we lived in Edward Street was a Russian Jewish family in a large freestanding white double-storey house, whose son, Henry I will call him, I was friends with. We were roughly the same age, maybe he was a little older. Next door was a Polish-Jewish family. The two families intensely disliked each other. The Polish family had a vile dog, from memory a pale cur, which attacked anyone who walked along the street, including the other side of the road. Whenever I walked to tennis, on the opposite side, the dog would rush across the road and try to bite my legs. I would swish it with my racquet and run.

Eventually, it wasn't around when I walked along there. There must have been increasingly urgent complaints and action taken. But my fear of dogs has never left me, though of course friends have sweet cuddly little dogs they're devoted to, and are very friendly when you visit.

In those childhood days, in the early 1950s, it was a different world from today; dog owners now, incessantly walking their dogs, have to keep them on a leash and scoop up their poo in plastic bags provided by the local council. In the early 1950s there were hardly any cars coming along Edward Street, and large packs of dogs would gather on the road, in bizarre formations, stuck to each others' anuses it would appear from a distance. (Wondering about this memory, I've just googled, and it does appear that such a phenomenon can occur during dog copulation.) Beside the road, the grass was usually littered with slimy dog shit, and more than once one would have to try to scrape it off one's sandal or bare foot.

Naturally the corollary of my fear of dogs is a lifelong liking for cats, or at least the idea of cats. (Ann and I have owned cats, I especially recall a placid tabby and a cantankerous marmalade cat, but travel makes cat owning difficult; on one occasion we took our tabby around to a friend to look after, and it promptly disappeared up the chimney, never to be seen again.) I admire cats, they're not needy like dogs, which whimper at night when their owners dare to be out. I feel cats have inherited the wry wisdom of the ages; having observed humanity for millennia, nothing humans do can surprise them; and they carefully bury their poo. (As I write this, I'm reminded of the cat in Virginia Woolf's *A Room of One's Own* crossing a lawn outside a Cambridge University college: the cat signified waywardness, eccentricity and indifference to Cambridge's ridiculous rules.)

Ann has just asked if there were any cats in the block of flats I grew up in in Edward Street; I said I don't think so, maybe no pets were allowed. I remember there was a cat across the road, next to a lane which led to Francis Street, it belonged to a family who lived in a house next to the lane. I got into trouble once: I was supposed to feed the cat, who I had made friends with. I think the family had gone away on holidays, but I think I got scared of going into their backyard by myself, perhaps I was supposed to feed the cat at dusk. I got into trouble when they got back and was scolded by them: why didn't you feed our cat, you love the cat… I'm haunted by this memory, how badly it reflects on me.

I don't know how little boys in that era survived billy carts. My father must have made one for me; there must have been some kind of crude stopping device, which I didn't always use. I recall racing at breakneck speed down a very steep street parallel to Wellington Street, then somehow turning at the bottom into Edward Street, where fortunately cars were rare. There were other streets too, on the way to my grandparents' place where I would rattle downhill in the middle of the road. I'm now closing my eyes; I don't want to think about how dangerous it was.

Yet I was also a notable mummy's boy. When my mother made the marital bed, I would lie on it and she would make the bed over me, first the sheet, then blanket, then eiderdown. Also, I would lie next to her and cuddle her soft arm. Visitors would say what a mummy's boy you are. (A friend of ours recalls that her twin boys would do the same with her; also, our little grandson does the same with Ann's arm.) There must be a male oddity here (though

Ann says she loved it when her mother also made the bed over her; we talked it over, maybe it's an obvious Freudian thing about reliving the warmth and cosiness of the womb).

Henry and I got into trouble. It was with Henry that I would really wander afar. One time, Henry said he didn't want to go home, and let's go to the golf course. The course at North Bondi, was quite a long way from Edward Street, so we would sleep the night there. We found some bushes next to Military Road, and slept there all night. When we got home, this was not appreciated by either family.

Then, for some reason, in a different direction, on a corner of Rose Bay golf course and Old South Head Road, we decided to throw stones at passing cars. From memory, we were apprehended by the police, and there must have followed a conference of the two families where Henry and I were told we could never see each other again, and indeed we never did.

Curiously, many decades later, Ann and I lived on Military Road, in a small block of apartments just north of the North Bondi golf course, on the other side of the road, and while walking down for coffee at the nearby bus depot shops I pointed out the bushes and related the episode, my friendship with Henry and never seeing him again to her.

At dusk or early evening, older Anglo-Australian boys in the street played hide and seek, the generally car-less road making it safe to run around; they asked me to play as well. These bigger boys also taught me to catch waves at the beach at Bondi; however, I have a lifelong fear of putting my face in the water, so I can't really do swimming by breathing as in freestyle (which Ann can very capably do). I would have to catch waves by standing in the surf, though I would also use a flipper to go into deep water, diving under waves to get out there. I unfairly blame my English mother for imparting to me a fear of the water: though she didn't live far from the beach, she never to my knowledge went near it.

I was small for my age. Once a family in the street in an apartment block across the road and down a bit, found themselves locked out, and a call went out. 'Doc (my street nickname) can do it, he can climb through the breadbox'; the family watched as I threaded myself through their bread box and opened their front door for them.

Occasionally a car would come along the street; there were also visits by the ice man delivering blocks of ice to people's fridges, including ours; and maybe the baker delivering bread, though that must have stopped if the landlord upstairs would ask my mother to send me up to Bondi Road to buy a loaf for him.

The occasional car would usually be chased by dogs desperate to bite their tyres (or something, I'm not sure what they were trying to do). Once, I remember, a very young neighbourhood dog tried to chase a car and was hit by it; the dog lay on the side of the road, distressed, breathing hard, there was blood, it was dying.

I've told this anecdote before, also involving a bread box.[12] Along Edward Street going towards the beach, in the next block to ours, lived a Catholic family, hostile to us as a Communist family. Their eldest boy, a teenager much older than me, I think his name was Robert, would taunt me as a Communist kid and would threaten to bash me. I told my parents. They said the next time he chases you into the flats, grab a hammer we'll put in our breadbox, and chase him out again. Which I recall on one occasion doing. Things must have been turning ugly for us, because on another occasion my father, then quite elderly, chased this boy, who was shouting insults at us from the street, back towards his own home. Yet there must have been some sort of reconciliation between the two families, because later I recall Robert and I would of an evening look together in trees for rare black cicadas, rather than the more common green cicadas. (I've just googled concerning this memory: black cicadas, it appears, are not rare at all, they live all along the eastern Australian coast and are known as black princes; they are to be distinguished from the green-coloured cicada, commonly called the green grocer, these inhabit the coastal regions of southeastern Australia and are one of the loudest insects in the world, they can deafen whole communities who have the misfortune to live nearby.)

I've also told the following anecdote before. Along Edward Street towards Wellington Street lived a White Russian family who were hostile to my Communist parents. When I visited there with the older boys, I was met with venomous hostility from the boy of the house, your parents are Communist, aren't they? I told my parents, who said, next time, say your mum and dad vote for the Labor Party.[13]

※

Something about my childhood puzzles Ann. Whenever she mentions a children's story from her childhood, I have to confess complete ignorance, I've never heard of it. We try to work it out. I said I couldn't remember ever reading, or being read to, children's stories. Are you sure? Yes, I can't remember anything like that. Ann said her mum always read to her lots of stories, such as those in the Golden Books and A A Milne's *Wind in the Willows*. Her mum loved A A Milne and would recite passages from his poems, James James Morrison Morrison Weatherby George Dupree/ took great care of his mother though he was only three… When Ann could read, she moved on to Enid Blyton in a big way.

Perhaps, I said, my mother didn't read children's stories to me because her mother hadn't read children's stories to her. I was thinking about something that my uncle Lew said when he and uncle Jock were reminiscing about their early upbringing in London: 'what stays in my mind is that these two people, my mother and father, were just barely literate. Words seemed to overwhelm them and that had quite a significant effect on my later adult life.'[14]

If a significant effect on my mother's later life was that she couldn't tell me children's stories, it makes me wonder: did this lack or absence harm me in some way? Did it irretrievably stunt my imagination at a crucial age? Or, to the contrary, did it have a different, a positive, consequence?

After Ann and I started to live together in 1969 in Balmain in Sydney, I tried belatedly to catch up a little, with Ann's help, as if to begin life again. Ann said, start with Enid Blyton's *Famous Five*. As a child she very much liked the character of the girl called George. She thought most girls who read *The Famous Five* stories liked George because she was so tomboyish, she was the daring one in the Five's escapades and adventures. This did lead to one odd moment. I was in the Malaya, a café in George Street in Sydney near Central Railway, perhaps our favourite for its sambals, their particularly hot curries, and this is where our subculture went to for Nyonya food, Chinese-Indian-Malayan, in 1969 or 1970. I was sitting there by myself, reading a book as one does when eating alone, when a literary critic I vaguely knew – he'd also done English at Sydney University – came over on his way out. He asked what I was reading, looked down at *The Famous Five*, and could not conceal that he was completely appalled. But I was not to be deterred. Another time, for example, I read with pleasure (and tears, when Mathew dies) *Anne of Green Gables*, another favourite of Ann's childhood.

When our son Ned was little we read children's stories to him as much as we could, stories such as *The Very Hungry Caterpillar* and *In the Night Kitchen*, and Dr Seuss's *Green Eggs and Ham*.

We encouraged Ned's reading when he was older. In the northern summer of 1982, we went to North America on Ann's study leave, ending up in Montreal, where Ann attended a Women's Studies conference, held in the hotel we were staying in. Ned and I amused ourselves in the hotel or wandering about the underground city. Somewhere in the hotel there were Archie comics on sale, and Ned was immediately enchanted with Archie, Betty, Veronica and Reggie. I think for the first time he began to really enjoy reading and was launched into a lifetime of reading. As part of Ann continuing her study leave, we flew to London and stayed near Hampstead Heath in a bizarrely tiny basement flat for short-term renters. The flat was on Tanza Road down from Parliament Hill, near the bottom of the street. We were able to enroll Ned in a nearby school, Fleet Primary on Fleet Road, and we would pick him up at the end of the school day and, as we walked home, we would go into a corner shop and buy English comics, *Beano* and maybe also *Dandy*. It is *Beano* I remember Ned hugely enjoying. (I have to confess to also reading and enjoying them.)

We watched a lot of TV with Ned as a child, children's and adult shows. I think of *Monkey*, *Dr Who*, *I Dream of Jeannie*, *Bewitched* and a little later *Prisoner*. I was writing opinion pieces on TV for what was then the *Sydney Morning Herald*'s pink TV Guide, and in one I mentioned that Ann, Ned and I would curl up on the sofa and watch *Prisoner* (also known as *Cell Block H*, it went from 1979 to 1986; decades later, in 2013, it was revived on TV as *Wentworth*). It was rather notorious for its tough female characters. Writing about *Prisoner* got Ann's mother Barbara into a spot of bother; Barbara was rung by socialist friends who said Ann and John watching *Prisoner* with her little grandson was dreadful – she had to do something. (Actually, all she did was tell us this had happened; we were quite amused.)

Catching up on children's stories as an adult and discussing them with Ann helped get me interested, in the early 1980s, in going out there and defending popular culture, perhaps a trifle provocatively since popular culture and especially popular television, it is fair to say, were generally regarded with a kind of settled contempt by the left, who viewed them as a major means by which the mass of people were secured for social conformity and passivity. As I explain in my Introduction, I became part of a Sydney-based discussion group on media and popular culture, and we subsequently published essays in the Melbourne based journal *Arena* in 1982. My essay was entitled 'In Defence of Popular Culture', which led to a lifelong interest in Walter Benjamin's cultural theory. Here, I heretically interpreted Benjamin's famous mid-1930s essay 'The Work of Art in the Age of Mechanical Reproduction' to suggest that Benjamin returns a positive verdict on the relationship between film, mass audience response and psychoanalysis, where popular audiences enjoy media such as photographs and films in their own way, as a collective experience, leading to a deepening of what he calls apperception, the combining of enjoyment and conscious discrimination. Benjamin, I was proposing, was opposing the critics of his own time, in the 1930s, who despised the new medium of film and its mass audiences.

My general understanding of popular culture in 'In Defence of Popular Culture', however, was inchoate and preliminary. All I could think of to say was that popular culture is dominated not by a socially binding social realism – for which I have a lifelong aversion – but by fantasy, myth and symbolism; social exploration; and populism.[15]

Ann and I decided we must be more historical in our approach to popular culture. We began to think about long cultural histories of carnival and World Upside Down by which to situate and explain contemporary popular culture; we were particularly fascinated by Natalie Zemon Davis's wonderful essay, 'Women on Top' in her *Society and Culture in Early Modern France* (1975), discussing strong female figures in carnival festivity and art of early modern Europe, We had begun reading Russian literary and cultural theorist Mikhail Bakhtin on carnival and carnivalesque and World Upside Down in early modern Europe.

Ann and I (and Ned!) continued to enjoy *Prisoner*. In July 1983 Ann and I gave a paper, ironically entitled '"Nothing but nasty people behaving nastily in a nasty situation": A Discussion of *Prisoner*', to the Australian Communication Association Conference held in Sydney where we began to apply the concepts we were finding in Benjamin, Bakhtin and Natalie Zemon Davis.[16] The response to the paper met with startling almost violent hostility, so much so that over the years we are still drawn to reflect on it.[17]

My uncle Lew wrote that his parents' difficulty with reading and words influenced his later life; I'm not sure what he meant by that intriguing statement, though it could have inspired my uncles and my mother to participate so enthusiastically in the Sydney Jewish Youth Theatre they helped create in the 1930s, and to seek out knowledge so intensely, as a way of redressing their upbringing.

My interest in popular culture began with a wondering question from Ann: how is it that I didn't know any children's stories? And then Ann suggesting *The Famous Five* as my entry point into children's literature, helping to inspire a decades-long appreciation, a relishing, of popular culture as a realm of theatricality, flamboyance, extravagance, excess, parody self-parody.

In this journey, Benjamin, Bakhtin and Natalie Zemon Davis became abiding heroes of mine, as is apparent in this ego histoire.

26 Growing Up Communist and Jewish in Bondi

1. Leo Hickman, 'The Verity of childrearing', *Guardian*, 7 October 2007.
2. See obituaries on Betty Bloch's full and interesting life by her daughters Paula and Cathy for Australian Society for the Study of Labour History http://www.labourhistory.org.au/hummer/vol-3-no-8/paula-bloch/ http://www.labourhistory.org.au/hummer/vol-3-no-8/cathy-bloch/
3. Jessica Mitford, *A Fine Old Conflict* (Vintage Books, New York, 1978), pp.158–9.
4. Jessica Mitford, *A Fine Old Conflict*, pp.120, 127, 128.
5. Ann Curthoys and John Docker, 'Defining Genocide', in Dan Stone (ed,), *The Historiography of Genocide* (Palgrave Macmillan, London and New York, 2010), pp.15–21.
6. John Docker, *1492: The Poetics of Diaspora*, p.154.
7. John Docker, 'Troubled reflections on my father', in Ann Curthoys and Joy Damousi (eds), *What Did You Do in the Cold War, Daddy? Personal Stories from a Troubled Time* (NewSouth, Sydney, 2014), p.110.
8. John Docker, 'Troubled reflections on my father', p.109.
9. John Docker, *1492: The Poetics of Diaspora*, p.264.
10. John Docker, 'A Space for Self-Fashioning: An Antipodean Red-Diaper Baby Goes to University in the Sixties', p.60.
11. José Saramago, *Small Memories: A Memoir*, translated by Margaret Jull Costa (Vintage Books, London, 2010), pp.17–19.
12. John Docker, 'Troubled reflections on my father', p.109.
13. John Docker, 'Troubled reflections on my father', p.109.
14. John Docker, *1492: The Poetics of Diaspora*, p.153.
15. John Docker, 'In Defence of Popular Culture', *Arena* 60, 1982, pp.72–87.
16. See Ann Curthoys and John Docker, 'In Praise of *Prisoner*', in John Tulloch and Graeme Turner (eds), *Australian Television: Programs, Pleasures and Politics* (Allen and Unwin, Sydney, 1989), pp.52–71; Ann Curthoys and John Docker, 'Melodrama in Action: Prisoner, or Cell Block H', chapter nineteen of John Docker, *Postmodernism and Popular Culture: A Cultural History* (Cambridge University Press, Melbourne, 1994), pp.260–72.
17. Docker, *Postmodernism and Popular Culture*, p.159; Ann Curthoys and John Docker, 'Stuart Hall and Cultural Studies, circa 1983', *Cultural Studies Review*, Vol.23, no.2, 2017, p.166.

30

Primary and High School Years

It is so obviously difficult to recover in memory one's early years. To call on Walter Benjamin, when images from the past flash up for a moment you have to quickly try to grasp them, don't let them slip away.

Here I try to grasp images of my early primary school years in what could be described as the southern part of Bondi, some distance away from the beach.

The Bondi Wellington Street Public School was situated at the top of Wellington Street at its steepest, a block away from Bondi Road and its shops and trams. Across the road was a Catholic school, and I can't remember any interactions with it ever; next to the Catholic school, at the corner of Wellington Street and Bondi Road, was a Catholic church, a forbidding dark brick structure.

From memory, the public primary school was made of sandstone, with large windows; it was divided in half, girls on one side, boys on the other; in the playground next to the road, there was a dividing fence between the boys and girls. The only time the boys and girls mingled, I think, was on certain ceremonial occasions when in the playground area at the back of the school, we all stood to attention and maybe a flag was raised to the glory of the British Empire (I think we were celebrating the British Empire). Then we all broke for the nearby tuck shop.

I can't remember anything about kindergarten at all, but when I turned old enough to go to my first primary class, on the first day I ran home, down Wellington Street, then I would have turned right into Edward Street and ran to our flat, Flat 2, 48 Edward Street. There my mother cooked me egg and chips for lunch, and came back with me to the class. Actually, quite often at lunch times I ran home for lunch and my mother would make me egg and chips, still a childhood food I make for myself when Ann is away interstate at a seminar or conference.

I can't remember pretty well anything about the early years of primary school, except a few images that have suddenly flashed up. At some time in the morning, free milk provided by the government would be delivered and the bottles would sit in the sun for an hour or two, going sour; then we had to drink it; quite often kids, including me, started immediately vomiting.

At playtimes, we boys often played marbles in our section of the playground, and oddly, for a shortsighted boy, I was good at it. My school nickname was, rather predictably, Doc – 'Good one, Doc' – though sometimes I was banned from playing. I'd won too many of the other kids' marbles.

My increasing short sight got me into some difficulty. I found it hard to see the blackboard from the back of the class, so would move to the front. Then I started looking at the workbook of the kid next to me, and got accused by the teacher of cheating. The upshot was that my mother and I went into town to the government eye clinic, and I was fitted with glasses.

In those years my reading must have expanded a little. We would all have to read stories in school magazines given out to all the schools, but I can't remember any of them.

Male teachers – they were all male in the boys' school – liked to be violent. They were all armed with long canes and practised in telling an offending boy, lift your arm up, stretch your hand, then, pausing for a long moment, delivering from a great height six of the best.

In the great theorist Michel Foucault's terms, it was a spectacle of punishment directed at the body in order to intimidate the class to behave, though Foucault, perhaps too hastily, argued that violence to the body was really a feature only of early modern Europe. In the modern world it was the mind that was to be disciplined; unfortunately, no one told the teachers at Wellington Street Primary School that they should focus only on disciplining the minds of their pupils.

Teachers in those years were actors, and they must have enjoyed the theatre of it all, the teacher on the stage at the front with cane raised, the audience of boys staring.

Images of two incidents involving the cane appear before me.

The first is quite mysterious; perhaps the teacher concerned had been reading too much Dickens. For a reason I certainly can't recall, I and another boy in our older class were asked by our teacher to go to the classroom of a younger class, and tell its teacher something. We walked along the hallway in the handsome sandstone building to the class room we were told to go to, and stood in front of the class and delivered our message. However, we must have smirked or sniggered in our delivery. The teacher of the younger class immediately became enraged; we were insulting his class, this could not be borne, I will make an example of you, he produced his cane, and in front of the little boys, littler anyway than we were, he gave us his six of the best, then finished up with, see boys what we do to bigger boys who come here and are rude to us. Perhaps a little bewildered and with hands hurting and trying not to show it, we went back to our class.

The next incident was also a little mysterious, perhaps a little demented, certainly extravagant on the teacher's part. It occurred in the fifth year, the penultimate year, of primary school. Usually my handwriting was very good, very neat, noticed as such by the teacher, a little man called Mr McClennan. On one occasion, however, I turned in some sloppy work, I don't know why. The teacher became enraged, come out here, come out the front (to the stage), the cane was produced, stretch out your arm, stretch out your hand, and he then produced a fairly vicious six of the best. At the end of the day, as we walked down Wellington Street to play touch football in the park, I couldn't conceal my tears of pain and humiliation from the other boys.

Talking it over with Ann and our friend Rosemary Pringle, Rosemary suggested the teachers' behaviour might have something to do with World War II, that cut across, not too long before, their lives in traumatic ways.

In this class, it became apparent I could spell well, when the class was tested with words by this teacher, I was often the last one standing.

So, at this stage of my primary schooling, I was good at three things: marbles, spelling and handwriting (with one egregious exception).

༺༻

Over afternoon coffee, after a hard day's writing of these reminiscences, I was telling Ann what I'd written about primary school, and we then had a conversation about how different girls' experience of primary school might have been. I asked her to write down her memories.

> I didn't experience the kind of violence John did; my understanding is that girls couldn't be caned. You could get a slap with a ruler on the back of the legs though, which I did once, and still remember what I thought was the injustice of it. But overall my primary school days were happy, except for a few months in fifth class, when my teacher, Mrs Westwood, took against me (possibly my parents' Communist politics, but no other teacher throughout my school years did that), and my grades plummeted. Thankfully, she was replaced after a few months by the gentle

Mrs Collins and all was well again.

My school, like John's, had separate boys and girls sections, to meet only over folk-dancing which we didn't like at all. Us being with boys seemed weird, it was unfamiliar, we felt we didn't know how to behave, and neither did they; it was unsettling.

We girls played lots of games, like tunnel ball, and other ball games. During my primary school years I read Enid Blyton obsessively – the Famous Five, the Secret Seven, the Magic Faraway Tree, and a little later perhaps, the Malory Towers books. I enjoyed learning, and remember classes about Aboriginal people – piccaninnies, coolamons, weapons, gunyahs, with no idea that there were Aboriginal people around me; it all seemed exotic and far away. Near the end of primary school, though, I did attend in school holidays an Awabakal Canare, a festival for children celebrating local Awabakal culture, which looking back seems quite progressive for 1957.

Ann, out of curiosity, did some googling and up came some visual images: her primary school in Newcastle appeared quite huge, and recently built, boys downstairs, girls upstairs; Wellington Street Bondi school by contrast appeared small and much older.

I'm trying to remember sixth class in 1957, the final year of primary school. It was taken by the headmaster. The atmosphere was completely different. I can't remember any caning at all. He was quite an emotional and eccentric figure. Two images flare up before me.

The headmaster on one occasion had a kind of breakdown in the class, began to talk about the cruelty of the Japanese in the last war, then cried.

The other image was more like a comical anecdote revealing his eccentricity. He would often keep his glasses on top of his head.

On one occasion, he said he couldn't find his glasses, he must have left them at the milk bar on the corner of Wellington Street and Bondi Road, John (I think he called me John, not 'Docker', actually, not sure) could you go down there and get them. I ran down, but the milk bar said they weren't there. When I got back the teacher explained that they were on the top of his head the whole time.

Sixth year was notable for me for an event that influenced my life and still in a way does: my IQ Fiasco.

I must have done well in sixth class lessons, though I can't remember anything at all about them or what we were supposed to have learned. It turned out that at the end of the year I came first, or equal first with another boy, I can't remember. This might have augured well for whatever high school I was then to go to; but, it turned out, whatever high school one went to wasn't based on one's school results or the work one had been doing all year or, for that matter, the opinion of the teacher who had been teaching one all year. No, it all turned on a kind of sudden-death IQ test administered by the Education Department – who were spectacularly uninterested in how well you went in your school work, which one might have thought would be of interest to something calling itself the education department. The same department was also sublimely indifferent to the sordid history of IQ tests, which a moment's research would have disclosed; a history emerging from late nineteenth-century racism and eugenics which has never quite been abandoned by its practitioners, and it periodically resurges with great relish and insistence. Psychologists and psychiatrists have every reason to continue providing IQ tests because they guarantee so much employment for their profession, which is at its most dubious, most dangerous when it claims to be that ridiculous chimera: a science of the mind.

In sixth class, then, in 1957, presumably at the end of the year after I'd shared first place in the school, I and all the other pupils had to sit for an IQ test; here boys, there's something we want you to do, an IQ test, we know you've never heard of it in all the years of your schooling which you thought was about learning about the world but just answer the required questions, it won't take long.

I have told this story elsewhere, in a memoir essay, 'A Space for Self-Fashioning: An Antipodean Red-Diaper Baby Goes to University in the Sixties'.[1] I went very badly in the IQ test. I simply couldn't do the test, which seemed to involve trains going at different speeds with apples and pears on board. My parents must have been informed, that because of my low IQ score, I would have to enroll at Randwick Boys' High, presumably held to be an inferior high school. My father was particularly upset as a nephew of his had gone to Sydney Boys' High, the superior state high school in our part of Sydney, and he had been hoping I could go there too.

My parents must have protested to the Education Department, pointing out my end-of-year results. One might have thought that the Education Department could have decided to go with the end-of-year results and what the teachers at that primary school thought about this lad, let's go by their judgement, they're our teachers. But no, I was then told I was to sit for another IQ test, which I did, and fared just as badly, if not worse, than before. My parents were then told I must go to the Randwick school. My parents must have protested again, because a few weeks after starting schooling at Randwick Boys' High my parents told me I could go to Sydney Boys' High after all. My parents said, 'It's up to you. Do you want to change schools?' I said no, I'm settling in at the new school.

My subsequent life proceeded through the decades on its course, hopefully at every stage exploring knowledge as an adventure of ideas. For decades I barely if ever gave the long-ago IQ Fiasco a fleeting half thought, and then suddenly, in Sydney in 2016, my mind turned to it. I registered what had happened most of a lifetime before, as a matter of acute anxiety, repetitively telling Ann and our friend Rosemary about it at our weekly breakfasts at Sonoma breadshop in Bondi after our early-morning weekend swims, railing against its injustice, venting my anger at psychologists and psychiatrists. This episode I think that can be recognised as a long-delayed Post Traumatic Stress Disorder. After a few weeks I came out of it, the miasma. I told my son Ned Curthoys about it, he quite rightly pointed out that if I had gone to Sydney Boys' High I might have become a different sort of person, perhaps a prig, and would never later have met Ann his mother and he wouldn't exist. Ann and Rosemary, perhaps wistfully recalling Bondi breakfasts where we'd talked about something else, pointed out that I've always pursued writing about anything I want to in any way I want to.

Looking back, I'm very proud that I performed so spectacularly badly in the two IQ tests in 1957.

One other thing I've thought about is psychology and psychiatry's claim – and psychoanalysis, as we saw with Freud's 'Dora' – that as disciplines they represent a science of the human mind conceived as universal. But there is no universal human mind.

In my essay 'A Space for Self-Fashioning' I write that humanity should rejoice in its diversity of minds, adding that the longer one lives, the more one realises that what is most noteworthy about our minds is their differences, and what is most valuable for interesting thinking is eccentricity and idiosyncrasy.[2] While writing these last phrases, I had in mind the final chapter 'Is a History of Humanity Possible?' of Ann and my book *Is History Fiction?* (the revised edition of 2010). Here Ann and I refer to the world historian Janet Abu-Lughod, suggesting that significant historical narrative will have a number of qualities: it will include a 'private vision', an element that is extremely personal; 'synthetic imagination or vision' is also to be valued, as is a capacity for 'reflexivity and self-conscious awareness'; above all, she feels, eccentricity and idiosyncrasy are important as sources of new vision, inspiring 'many of the major transformations in how we think about the world'.[3]

Maybe we can say this: the moronic notion of a single universal mind is centripetal, it flattens out the mind, draws it into a single thing. The recognition of the mind's diversity, possible eccentricity and idiosyncrasy of it, is centrifugal – in their unpredictability minds fly off in all directions.

I have a modest proposal for the whole excrescent tribe of psychologists and psychiatrists devoted to managing IQ tests; drunk with a power that society should never have accorded them, they should be immediately divested of it. They can then hang out their shingle in the far corners of failing shopping centres next to flat-earth-society shops among dust and cigarette butts. O how the mighty would then have fallen!

From 1958 to 1962 I attended Randwick Boys' High for a fairly uneventful five years. (Oddly, it was in 1962 that, responding to the Wyndham Report, six years of high schooling were introduced into NSW secondary schools). Each morning, leaving my parents' flat, in school uniform, having learned to tie a Windsor knot for my tie, I walked across Edward Street and proceeded down a narrow lane to Francis Street, turned left, then right along a street whose name I can't remember (where I occasionally used to go on a billycart as a child), to O'Brien Street, to catch a school bus to Randwick Boys'. However, I shared an unfortunate trait with my mother: I was congenitally late. So sometimes I walked up Imperial Avenue to Bondi Road and caught an ordinary bus to Bondi Junction, went round the corner and caught a little bus, 314, that went to Coogee, getting off at The Spot, a group of shops, then walking to school, hoping just to make it before classes started.

Again, I'll have to grasp at images before they slip away. The school was situated on a very long street, Avoca Street, starting from one side of a large park, Queen's Park, then proceeding past Randwick Girls' High (which had been attended for a while by my elder sister), going past on the right the large Prince of Wales Hospital, then proceeding along until Avoca Street met a street I think called Rainbow Avenue; the school was on this corner. Randwick Boys' appeared to be a series of long makeshift barracks-like huts, perhaps left over from World War II, as there was an army base not too far south of it. The school's buildings could once have been part of it. In any case, the huts looked like they were meant to be temporary, except for a new assembly hall, built not too long after I began schooling there.

Before the assembly hall was built, the headmaster would have to conduct school assembly in the open air, in the playground between the huts and the gym. I recall once that the boys sitting in the front would face him wearing bright fluoro socks, and were duly reprimanded. These were not to be worn again.

On another occasion, the headmaster told the assembly that he was being bothered by a woman, a mother of one of you boys, who would ring to see if her little boy could be reminded that he had to go to the dentist that afternoon after school; whoever you are, he said, looking out at us, could you remind your mother this is a school, not a messenger service.

This was acutely embarrassingly, as I'm sure it was my mother who'd rung the headmaster, given that for years I nearly always forgot to go to a dentist appointment after school. I sat there turning various shades of extreme red.

Eventually the school hall was built, which enabled acting groups to form and put on plays, exams could be sat for there, and so on. Sometimes a school dance was held in the evening. We were all told we must go, and, frighteningly, girls would be there. We little boys hung around outside.

I was quite good at, and enjoyed doing, algebra, odd since I can barely count now. I also developed a squint in my first year or two of high school, as did a friend I made, Johnny Hogg, who lived not too far away from us. We would sit together, squinting. When my mother came to meet-the-teachers at the end of the year, the maths teacher told her how disconcerting it was to have two little boys sitting together staring at him, continuously squinting. My mother relayed the story to me, and indeed I did strive after that to bring squinting to a halt.

Some things didn't change. I continued to play marbles at playtime; I was still called 'Doc'.

Scripture classes were held. I asked my parents what should I do, and they said attend the group for non-religious kids, which I did; whoever took them told stories from the Bible.

Male teacher violence was not confined to primary school, and is not easily forgotten. Male teachers seemed to wander the school looking to mete out discipline to anyone doing anything they shouldn't, perhaps concentrating their energies on the junior kids. I recall one occasion when outside the school waiting for the school bus to arrive, I had taken off my tie, prematurely. We probably took our ties off on the bus when we got to the upper deck as it rattled off back to Bondi. A teacher, a wandering enforcer, saw me waiting tieless, suddenly leapt on me, and dragged me back into the school gym and roughed me up, shouting never take your tie off again. (Thinking about it now, the teacher could have taken an entirely different approach to this boy without a tie, waiting next to the road for the school bus: hello, what is your name – Docker, sir – well Docker, even though you are outside the school fence, next to the road, you still must observe the school rule, which is that your tie must be worn at all times in order to uphold the high reputation of our school in the community; it appears that you have forgotten that obligation, but try to remember it next time, OK?)

On another occasion, I had been sent to wait outside a classroom door. Maybe I had been talking too much. I confess to being something of a prankster at high school, perhaps a release of the repressed, at home with two older sisters about I rarely said a word. As I was standing there, a teacher enforcer walked past, pounced on me, so you've been sent outside the classroom have you, and immediately began shouting and violently shaking me, I'll teach you not to do whatever you did. (This teacher could also have taken an entirely different approach: he could have simply walked by, assuming that his colleague inside the class room was in control and knew what he was doing, and, after all, it was his class.)

There was another occasion of teacher violence, the most extreme of my whole school experience. I enjoyed Latin very much, and did well in it. But once, when the Latin class was taken by the head Latin teacher, a cantankerous hobgoblin called Mr Kresner, he became angry at my work. He called me to his desk out the front, shouted at me, ripped off my glasses, slapped my face and threw the glasses out the window. I then had to go outside to retrieve them. Naturally, memory of this episode never left me. It could be said to be searing.

※

Still, I kept on doing and enjoying Latin with the usual teacher until classes in it came to an abrupt halt. Numbers taking Latin must have been declining; at the end of third year, a small group of us went to see the headmaster or more probably deputy head, and asked for Latin to be continued to be taught for our final years; he said the school could only now afford one Latin teacher, who wouldn't be able to take later-year classes. Sorry, boys.

Disappointed, disconsolate, we trudged away down the

corridor, young keen students eager to learn, missing out on something we really wanted to do.

Here my IQ Fiasco did make a difference to my school life. If I had gone to Sydney Boys High, I could, I'm sure, have taken Latin through the later years, and taken Greek. This became important when Ann and I started writing our *Is History Fiction?* in the early 2000s; we decided we must discuss Herodotus' *Histories* and Thucydides' *History of the Peloponnesian War* as foundational to modern historical writing. It would be good to know classical Greek in a hopefully inward way, or at least the beginnings of an inward way, but neither of us had done Greek at school. I then took introductory Greek for a semester at ANU as an auditor, and very much enjoyed it, and I think a certain familiarity with Greek, however painfully slow I was compared to the bright quick young students also doing it, did help when we wrote the Herodotus and Thucydides chapters of *Is History Fiction?* and when I later wrote about the classical world in my *The Origins of Violence* in relation to group violence and genocide.

⚜

So, these were the first few years of my high-school life. I was good at: marbles, squinting, algebra (briefly), Latin (until it was brutally terminated) and arriving late. I was also physically assaulted, though not by any school bullies. I can't remember any school bullies in my high-school years, nor, for that matter, in my primary years. I was assaulted by teachers.

⚜

I now snatch at images as they flash past of later high-school years.

One was particularly humiliating. I decided to try my hand at debating It shouldn't be too hard, you stand before everyone and debate some point; debates were held in the school library; when on one occasion it was my turn to defend or articulate a position

I stood there, froze, my mind shut down, couldn't speak, went bright red, and then decided to do the only proper and honourable thing: I started walking. I walked out of the library into the Valley of Ignominy.

Another image is perhaps revealing of the gender attitudes of male teachers in the 1950s and into the 1960s. One day some young girls suddenly appeared like apparitions, in the uniform of Randwick Girls' High School back up Avoca Street; a teacher told us that the girls had come down to take physics and chemistry classes; the teacher then warned us boys, a little enigmatically, don't you go near those girls, talk to them and next thing you know you'll be married.

Now I wonder what these girls felt, having to go for science subjects to a boys' school down the road in a set of huts; did they, for example, see wandering teacher enforcers shouting at and roughing up young boys in the corridors? They were clearly determined and courageous.

I knew Ann had done physics and chemistry at her high school in Newcastle, and asked her about her experience. Ann writes:

> At my school, we didn't go to the boys' school to do science subjects, we had them ourselves. Though we only gained the full suite of possible science subjects in 1961, when I was in what was then called Fourth Year. In my last two years of high school, 1961 and 1962, I studied both Physics and Chemistry, as separate subjects. (I also studied both Maths I and Maths II, along with English and History; it was a very maths – and science-oriented set of subjects.) We were the first cohort at Newcastle Girls High School to whom Physics as a full subject had been offered as an option; my understanding is that the only other all-girls school at the time to offer stand-alone Physics was St George Girls' High in southern Sydney. Offering science subjects to girls where they had not been offered before was, I think, part of a wave of rethinking science education in the

West as a response to the Russian success with Sputnik in 1957. (I vividly remember standing in the back yard with my father who pointed out Sputnik, which you could see, moving in the night sky.) One reason we girls at NGHS benefited was, I have always thought, a result somehow of pressure placed by Dr Beryl Nashar, then Associate Professor of Geology at Newcastle University College, who had been a student at our school. I do remember that although we were an all-girls school, with largely female teachers, our maths and science teachers were all male. I remember our Chemistry teacher well, Mr Anderberg, who inspired in us an enthusiasm for Chemistry. I can't remember the Physics teacher's name; he was younger, and, let's say, not very effective. I don't remember much about what I learnt in Physics, though there was a lot about pulleys and forces. When our results came out, I was appalled to learn I had only a B in Physics. I later found out that in our class of about 17, one girl had got Bs for both Physics and Chemistry, one had achieved honours in both, and the rest of the class had done exactly as I had, gained an A in Chemistry and a B in Physics. Although I went into the humanities at university, mainly studying English and History, I've never regretted doing such a heavy maths and science program for the Leaving Certificate. It gave me at least an inkling of how the sciences and humanities differ, and also, how they are almost the same.

Somehow, around this time, inspired by one particular teacher, Mr Head I think was his name, I began to go well in English. Perhaps too well, as I gained a minor reputation, the word must have gone around, Doc's good at English, and sometimes boys asked me if I could write their essays for them.

I was becoming more and more interested in literature, and dreaming of being a poet, and indeed I managed to write some truly appalling poems.[4]

I did play tennis in school teams in my high school years, though my feeling is that I was losing interest compared to primary school when I was so obsessed I as it were slept with my racquet at night (though much later in life I enjoyed occasional social tennis).

Then I got to know a Hungarian boy called Thomas Hardy, whose family had presumably come to Australia after the Soviet invasion of Hungary in 1956. For anyone surprised by his name, we can recall that quite a few Europeans escaping Europe when at its violent worst, took names from English authors or the names of characters in Jane Austen novels. Thomas Hardy lived in a small apartment in King's Cross, historically densely populated, perhaps the most 'European' part of Sydney. I would visit and there we would study together our school work.

I was also, I think, becoming fascinated by King's Cross.

I'll depart from seizing images of the past to reporting on some archival research, some digging in past documents, which I now think of as the Pegasus Files. What emerges is a great deal of additional information to be pondered and played with, leading me to think that my memory-only writing heretofore in this chapter is perhaps a trifle too harsh, or at least needs complicating.

For some months in 2011, in preparation for this ego histoire, I looked through and took notes from the boxes of material that Ann and I had donated in the early 1990s to Mitchell Library in one box, Box (4/6), there were copies of *Pegasus*: magazine of the Randwick Boys' High School, on its cover the school motto, *Labore et Honore*. There were five copies, from 1958 to 1962. I took them out of the box, the earliest, 1958, was Vol.12, No.1, so *Pegasus* had been going since 1946, indicating that Randwick Boys' High was fairly new, a postwar school trying to make its way in the world.

Primary and High School Years   43

Opening the 1958 issue, I starting transcribing items and taking notes on what might be possibly interesting to write about. The headmaster was a Mr A E Johnstone BA. There was a listing of teaching departments, and for the Department of Language I noted the name of the Latin teacher, Mr H Kresner MA. There were lots of pages on the school's sporting activities. On p. 27 boys could read the school song, I'll quote two of the verses, the second being peculiarly martial:

> Hasten, Randwick, to the call,
> Seniors, Juniors, schoolboys all.
> Work your hardest, play your best,
> Meet life's challenge full of zest,
> Raise the Green and White on high,
> Labore et honore, Labore et Honore.

> Though the task be stark and grim,
> And our chance of winning dim,
> Let us play with all our might,
> To the fray with courage bright,
> Let us keep in mind for aye,
> Labore et honore, Labore et Honore.

[I googled *Labore et honore*, and it appears lots of schools adopted this as their motto.]

The school was divided into a number of 'houses', House Notes on pp. 25–27 listing Blaxland – Lawson – Macquarie – Wentworth. [So, three white settler-colonial explorers Blaxland, Lawson and Wentworth, and Governor Macquarie, a complex figure, usually very honoured though recent historical enquiry is asking lots of questions of Macquarie, as a massacrist of Indigenous people.]

On p. 28 there is a riveting description of the school uniform:

> The Headmaster requires all boys to wear the school uniform, which is as follows:
> A clerical grey coat and trousers (short trousers and long socks for junior boys):
> A light grey shirt (nylon shirts allowed).
> A grey pullover with green stripes in the neck, cuffs and basque; Black shoes;
> A grey felt hat with school hatband (optional)
> A school pocket on the coat;
> Socks: For junior boys – grey socks with green stripes at the top; for senior boys – matching grey or green socks. Bright colours are not allowed.
> In summer time boys are not required to wear the coat. A school blazer may be worn.
> Next year (1959), the Prefects will be entitled to wear a special blazer. This will have no white braid, but the word 'Prefect' will be added.
> A specially designed grey zip-up jacket with the school colours and pocket has been approved.

On p. 29 there is a report, written by Peter M McCallum, 5B, on the Film and Photographic Society:

> Since its establishment last year, the Film and Photographic Society has increased in popularity and now our quarters are, even more, a centre of activity. We usually show our films to packed 'houses' (we seat only forty) for there is a big demand to see films such as that which showed the historic climb of Mt Everest.
>
> A photographic exhibition was held and some striking entries were submitted… Boys and their teachers joined in an exhibition of colour slides.

On pp. 35–6 there were reports on Debating, Junior and Senior. On pp. 41–8 there were Football reports, on Rugby Union, and here's a surprise, a photo for Sixth Grade Rugby, and in the back row, there's a tiny figure, with glasses: J Docker! (Could I have attempted to play rugby in first year? I could run fast, like my father before me, and I had played rugby league in primary school, but I was also small and skinny, not to say miniscule.) There was a kindly note attached to Sixth Grade rugby: 'Sixth Grade, although only winning two matches and drawing one, were unlucky in some games when a reliable goalkicker could have made up the leeway, as most games were keenly contested.'

There were further pages of reports on cricket, soccer, water polo, swimming, basketball, tennis and athletics. Then from pages 73 to 106, there were stories and essays, including – and I have absolutely no memory of this, no trace of an image to be snatched at – a short story, 'A Dingo Hunt' by John Docker, 1A, which refers to the Australian countryside in the far west of NSW, to which I most certainly had never been. I've just read it, and it seems to be a sympathetic story about a dingo. Please indulge me, I'll quote the first few sentences:

> It was early dusk, as Barooka glided swiftly and silently through the scrub and mulga, her body a passing shadow on the landscape.
>
> Far behind, she heard the low menacing growls of the fierce cattle and sheep dogs, as straining on their leashes, they followed her scent.
>
> It was a long, dry summer, and Barooka was forced to leave the sparse scrubland west of Bourke.
>
> She had crossed the Darling River and journeyed eastward to the sheepland around Cobar.
>
> Compelled by acute hunger, she had entered the sheep pens, but the taste of blood drove her berserk, and she had killed seventy sheep in two nights.

The owner of the sheep station had organized a dingo hunt, with every man available.

Barooka, though exhausted, evades capture by wading along a stream for 'one hundred and fifty yards', the chasing dogs losing her scent: 'the station owner realized that Barooka had been too clever, and cancelled the hunt'. Barooka travels back to 'her native country', crossing the swollen Darling, and was 'greeted by vast green pastures, and an abundance of beautiful wild flowers'.

Reading this now, I think, where did all this come from? Surely I knew nothing of towns like Bourke and Cobar, let alone the Darling River. It's obviously derivative of something, but I don't know where John Docker, 1A, got it all from. Perhaps the sympathy for the hunted dingo is of mild interest, and that the hero of the story is female not male.

On pp.90–91 there is a long, informative and witty essay, by Gareth Hurst, 5A, 'Sydney's New Society', evoking Expresso Coffee Shops:

> A new society has formed in our city – that of the Expresso Coffee Shop. We find that a new type of person has emerged from the 'wilds' of the Cross to take his or her place with the other inhabitants of Sydney. This is the type of person who spends much of his spare time in dimly-lit or bright coffee shops savouring black, white, or indeterminate coffee.
>
> The society to which he belongs came to our shores from far-off Austria and Italy with the introduction of Italy's 'greatest invention', the Expresso Coffee Machine. Beginning with a few shops at King's Cross, the society, or rather the haunts of the society, have spread to the city proper and have invaded many country towns…
>
> Let us look at a cross section of this society.
>
> To begin with we have the true member of the society. He or

Primary and High School Years   47

she is usually seen in small, exotic coffee shops most nights of the week. This member is usually attired in duffel coats or 'ski-jackets' and corduroy trousers or tight black slacks and often squints from being too long in bad light. The haunts of this member have such names as 'El Rocco', 'Kashmir', 'Cha Cha', 'Brazil' and 'Mambo'…

There we have our new society, and if you are not already a member drop into a coffee shop some time, order a cup of coffee, and you will embark upon a new existence which you never before thought possible.

Names like El Rocco and Cha Cha and so on sound more like names of nightclubs than European-style coffee shops, a bit puzzling; in the 1950s, in the city but some distance from the Cross, was Lorenzini's in lower Elizabeth Street and Repin's in King Street. Yet perhaps reading 'Sydney's New Society' as a wide eyed first-year boy stimulated my own later interest in King's Cross as bespeaking a kind of 'European' cosmopolitanism in postwar Sydney, and led me to imagining, in my final school years, that I had actually been to a coffee shop in King's Cross – which I probably hadn't because, as the article by Gareth Hurst, 5A, suggests, the true denizen of Sydney's New Society would have to go there at night time, not something a boy living at home in Bondi could readily do.

On p. 105 there is a short story by John Docker, 1A, whose mind now had taken to the sea, beginning:

> The dawning sun glistened on the silver expanse of ocean as the 'S.S. Essentio' sliced through the Pacific. [O, no: 'glistened', now one of my banned words that I list on my fridge.]
>
> Leaning against the rail of the great liner, I looked around at the distant horizon, and, except for a small black dot in the east, nothing but endless sea was visible… [then follows a description of 'a tropical island on which was an extinct volcano']
>
> [Last par:] Once again my observations were interrupted by

the clanging of the bell, this time for afternoon tea. When, half an hour later, I went back to the deck, I saw the island becoming a dot in the west.

On p. 107, there is a roll call of 1958 students, and there is 'Docker, J. E.' So, in first year high school, I had already picked up a male fondness for initials.

Pegasus 1959, my second year. On p. 117 I am in Class 2A, and the class teacher is Mr G Hill, and I wonder if the teacher I remember as Mr Head is actually Mr Hill. Merit Certificates for Latin were awarded to J Docker and J Hogg. The indefatigable John Docker, 2A, on p.90, provided for the Literary Section a pagelong description of a wild storm, and was also sighted playing Junior Tennis.

On p. 8 it was announced that the new Assembly Hall has been built, and to mark its completion there was a flurry of theatrical activity: 'Eight plays were presented during the day on Friday, 14 August'. Class 2A – though I have absolutely no memory of this – presented 'The Fable of Baghdad' and its 'effects and stage work were very good. The large audiences showed marked appreciation for this play and all actors are to be commended for their work.' One of the plays by older boys provided an interesting thread in 1959 and 1960, revealing considerable interaction with girls' schools, both Sydney Girls' High and Randwick Girls' High.

> [*Pegasus* 1959 p.8:] The School Dramatic Society attempted an ambitious project in presenting the first act of 'The Teahouse of the August Moon' and the success of the play was a fitting reward for the boys who had rehearsed most thoroughly… Special mention is given to H. Szeps, P. Savelieff, J. Johnstone, T. Shepherd and G. Podinonsky in the leading parts…

Primary and High School Years 49

In *Pegasus* 1960, pp. 25–6, we learn that in this year on 16 and 17 March the 'boys of Randwick Boys High School, with the assistance of four guest players from Sydney Girls High School, presented "The Tea-house of the August Moon" – the first major dramatic performance to be staged in the W M Gollan Assembly Hall'.

> The play is set in Okinawa, an island near Japan, and shows the nature of the American occupation at the conclusion of World War II in the village of Tobiki. In particular, it concentrates on the erection of a tea-house which the natives [sic] have set their heart on building and which they finally succeed in getting through the machinations of the wily interpreter Sahini.
>
> … Henri Szeps, as Sahini, deserves special mention, for on him rested the responsibility of narration and the preservation of the spirit of the play, not to mention a good deal of its humour. All this he did with admirable success.

So, maybe here was launched the notable theatrical, film and television career of Henri Szeps. We also now learn more detail about the contribution of Sydney Girls' High School:

> Most hearts went out to Wendy Golding, our female lead from Sydney Girls' High School, whose grace of movement and deportment would have done credit to a much more experienced actress. She was ably supported in the dancing scenes by Diane Burns, Julia Tandlich and Kay Miller.

Hhhmmm, I think, I've seen the name Wendy Golding before, I remember the name from Ann's book *Freedom Ride: A Freedom Rider Remembers*. Wendy Golding was on the 1965 Freedom Ride.

More was to come from this cooperation between a boys' school and a girls' school. On p. 26 we read that the crowning glory of the staging of *The Tea-house of the August Moon* was when on 24 and 25 March the 'play was presented at the Elizabethan Theatre during the Annual Secondary Schools' Drama Festival'. On p.26, *Pegasus* included an extract from *The Education Gazette* dated 1 June 1960: '"Tea-house of the August Moon" is a play for entertainment, but it is rather more than that. It is a good example of the development of the modern comedy of entertainment towards comment on contemporary things and is full of ironic implications and self-criticism by the Americans of their own blunders in civilising [sic] Okinawa.'

From *Pegasus* 1960 I transcribed a story on p. 87 called 'Meditations' by John Docker, 3A, pleased that Sydney is not a planned city like Adelaide or Melbourne because it has King's Cross, 'the famous Cross, the immortal Cross', even if, the story cautions the Reader, 'how drab, how disappointing, how dead it is in daytime'. (I have a vague memory of going to the Cross to have my hair cut, for unknown reasons. I would also see the Cross in daytime when visiting Thomas Hardy to do homework.)

⁓※⁓

Pegasus 1961, my penultimate year. On pp. 6–7, there are two photos of the Assembly Hall, obviously the school's pride and glory.

On p. 53, for the Annual Play Day of 18 August, there was a staging of *Trial by Jury*:

> The large cast for the 'Trial' was augmented by our guests from Randwick Girls' High and to them we express our thanks for their co-operation and assistance.

[A little googling indicates that this was a Gilbert and Sullivan one-act operetta, a courtroom farce, first staged in 1875 at London's Royalty Theatre.]

Primary and High School Years

I must have been still brooding about what visiting a King's Cross coffee shop at night time might be like. In the Literary Section of *Pegasus* 1961 there is a short story, or rather a kind of prose poem, 'In the Mood' by John Docker, 4A. This might be the literary effort that in memory I think of as my night time King's Cross Coffee Shop poem, yet having to confess that I had never been near the Cross and its coffee shops at night. I hope the reader will indulge me if I reproduce this rather hectic effusion:

> The room was black, except for a cigarette which pinpricked the darkness with its flickering glow. Smoke poured white from its end and was suddenly lost. On a radiogram in the corner a jazz record spun. Its notes were cool and vibrant. They throbbed through the blackness and merged with the harsh rhythm of the man playing a bongo drum somewhere in the centre of the room. His hands beat remorselessly. Occasionally they seemed to work up to a frenzy, beating madly. Then they would slow down as if he were matching the cool of the jazz. Or, the man's mood was changing as the beating of his hands; as if the drum was an emotional outlet, onto which he outpoured his feelings. The beat seemed to change from love, remorse, to hatred and tingling anger at the world. He banged hard and strong as if he wanted to fight the world and he was slow and dragging as if wanting to resign to his fate, reluctant to stand up, fight, take it, but to run away, a defeated man.
>
> He beat on, his hands moving as his mood. The cigarette faded. The jazz came hot and then cool; inspiring, kicking, ecstatic, wallowing in the atmosphere. But it was overshadowed by the drum beats. The mood of this man was overpowering. His thought dominated the room; a man completely immersed in a sea of emotion, hammering it out, beat after beat, with jazz and his thoughts his only companions.

In my 2011 notes I wrote 'not bad?! – maybe much more promise re writing prose than poetry??'. Now I think: maybe the indefatigable J Docker was here revealing a yearning to belong to some kind of bohemian New Society as evoked by Gareth Hurst, 5A, in his 1958 contribution to *Pegasus*, evoking Expresso Coffee Shops in King's Cross; even a kind of Outsiders Society as evoked by Virginia Woolf in her 1938 essay *Three Guineas*. Perhaps writing 'In the Mood' was a counterpart to what I recall, that in my later school years I did quietly stage a short-lived insurrection. I decided I was surrounded at the school by provincial barbarians, and sat in an empty classroom and refused to move; I told a teacher who happened to walk past and asked me what I thought I was doing, that I wanted to be considered separate from the rest of the school; this minor insurrection, which perhaps lasted for half an hour or so, was met with no response at all.[5]

Pegasus 1962, my final year.

For all my desire to be an Outsider, it is clear from the Pegasus Files that I was enmeshed in the school in quite conventional ways.

On pp. 16–17 there is a group photo of prefects for that year, with Tom Hardy and J Hogg there, and also, second last in the second row, J Docker; I do remember that when I became a prefect I vowed never to put anyone on detention, and I never did.

I notice I am wearing large black glasses. Indeed, I was the only boy with glasses: how can that be? Was I the only boy in the whole school wearing glasses?

Nonetheless, on p.37 there is a group photo of the Senior Debating Team, composed of L Sawicki, T Purvis, R Gridiger, S David, V Berger, and I'm pleased to see that four out of the five are wearing glasses, otherwise the school seemed to be a glasses-free zone.

On p. 45, I see that J Docker has earned Best Contribution to School Magazine (Senior), and actually I remember receiving the prize, on some kind of ceremonial occasion, in the Great Hall, a copy of *Phoenix: The Posthumous Papers of D. H. Lawrence*. The deputy head I think it was, presented it to me, asking why I had chosen Lawrence, and I think I stumbled out some kind of answer; I think I had to buy the book myself, maybe I was given a coupon, and I still have it on my shelves after all these years, going slightly yellow; opening it now, I see that *Phoenix* was first published in 1936 and reprinted in 1961, and I purchased it at Dymocks Book Arcade in the city, there's a little Dymocks sticker on the inside cover. On the second inside cover page, I see that pasted in was a note, under *Labore et Honore*, of this award to J Docker for Senior Literary Award for Contribution to School Magazine, signed A E Johnstone, Headmaster, per J Harrison, presumably the deputy head.

On p. 76, there is a photo of the 1st Grade Tennis team, its regular members listed as J Docker, J Meaney, G Davies, D Parr; J Docker is still wearing his big black glasses, the only boy in glasses.

In the literary section for 1962 J Docker and his friends J Hogg and T Hardy of class 5A seem gripped by melancholy concerning fate and love. The contribution on p. 87 by the indefatigable J Docker, 'A Winternight', opens with 'The cold crouches on the window pane', an outrageous steal of images from Eliot's 'The Love Song of J. Alfred Prufrock' ('The yellow fog that rubs its back upon the window-panes, The yellow smoke that rubs its muzzle on the window panes'), unless, shouldn't I be more generous, it's a deliberate allusion. O no, I can see a 'glittering' here: 'The lamppole leans on the night/ And is repulsed by the stars' glittering stares'; there's some phrasing that is not half-bad, referring to 'the silver sea striding between/The horizon's dark silhouettes'. Then comes the final three melancholy lines:

> A mournful whistling runs along the streets
> And Night and Winter kiss and smirk
> In triumphant union.

At the very least, then, it would appear that I was at this time reading some T S Eliot and D H Lawrence, maybe they were being discussed in class by the perhaps mythical inspiring teacher Mr Head.

My fellow literary contributors from class 5A share this sombre mood, in relation to the perfidy of love, as in, on p. 88, 'Lament' by J Hogg, perhaps drawing on Metaphysical poetry, or more likely Keats' *La Belle Dame Sans Merci*, these also could have been taught in 1962 English. Opening with 'Oh untrue love!', 'Lament' ends with:

> Oh frigid state!
> Thy icy ocean doth encumber
> In waves of wretched wrath,
> A lover lost, a love forlorn,
> A life that hath no dawn.

On p. 89 T Hardy in his poem entitled 'Contemplation on Love' protests Love's fatal unkindness:

> Well, Love, you enemy of mankind,
> Who is to be your next victim?
> What heart will you seize? What hopes instil
> How long will the effect of your bliss last
> Only to be followed by hate? For you and
> Your brother, Hate, are like spring and summer
> That follow in each other's footsteps eternally.

On p. 90, there is another poem by the indefatigable J Docker,

'Dark Oppression', with lots of images of nightmare and claustrophobia, and, again, too much drawing on 'Prufrock', though, I noted in 2011, a slight touch of hope at the end, with one line we might have wished that the young J Docker had hastily revised:

> The wind stuttered in the gutter
> With the suspended chat[t]er of children
> Whose sounds of joy lingered
> In the lanes and led me
> Away.

So ends my evocation and interpretation of the notes I took in 2011 of *Pegasus* 1958–62.

There was, however, another item in Box (4/6) in Mitchell Library, that surprised me. This was the *Randwick Review*, a monthly magazine of the Randwick Boys' High School Parents and Citizens. In the box was Vol. I, No.1, December 1961. It opens with a 'Message from P & C President', E M Crawford: 'Some means of publicizing the activities of this association had been needed for many years, especially for those parents who rarely meet.' Also on p. 1 is a statement headed 'To Parents and Friends: Some of the reasons for the introduction of our P &C Association periodical are obvious. We aim to give you a regular, informed bulletin of news concerning your school. We shall try to stimulate, perhaps even to provoke you.'

The authors of this statement are listed as E Docker (my mother!), R Brien, and A L Head.

I did manage to scrape together enough As in the Leaving Certificate at the end of 1962 to gain a Commonwealth

Scholarship, and looked forward to doing English literature at Sydney University in 1963.

I never saw my friends in fifth year again, except for one drunken reunion some decades later.

1 John Docker, 'A Space for Self-Fashioning: An Antipodean Red Diaper Baby Goes to University in the Sixties', in Dee Michell, Jacqueline Z. Wilson and Verity Archer (eds), *Bread and Roses: Voices of Australian Academics from the Working Class* (Sense Publishers, Rotterdam, 2015), pp.62–3.

2 John Docker, 'A Space for Self-Fashioning: An Antipodean Red Diaper Baby Goes to University in the Sixties', p.62.

3 Ann Curthoys and John Docker, *Is History Fiction?* revised edition (University of Michigan Press, Ann Arbor, 2010), pp.248–9.

4 John Docker, 'Troubled reflections on my father', in Ann Curthoys and Joy Damousi (eds), *What Did You Do in the Cold War, Daddy? Personal Stories from a Troubled Time* (NewSouth, Sydney, 2014), p.112.

5 Docker, 'A Space for Self-Fashioning: An Antipodean Red Diaper Baby Goes to University in the Sixties', p.64.

31

Stray Thoughts on My Undergraduate Years

My first year or two at university were quite lonely. I didn't consciously think to myself, I am not a joiner, it simply never crossed my mind to join any political clubs, which would have been leftwing clubs, given my Communist Party family background. At lunch I would sit by myself in a small garden just below the large sandstone building (the quad), or go to the men's union building. Once or twice, I struck up a conversation with a student who was a little older, I think a theology student of some kind, and we would discuss the curious whereabouts of the soul; he said God had given everyone a soul. I said I'm not sure about that, where is this soul; he said in the body; I said where in the body; these were fleeting, cordial, conversations, and no definite conclusions were reached.

In my undergraduate years I experienced various parallel existences only tangentially related to the university.

Because I had grown up in a Communist Party family and was still somehow part of it, I became in my second and third years, part of a Communist Party student branch at the university; I'll check my memory here with Ann, she was also in it. We were a small group, and meetings were held in the office in the physics building of Dick Makinson, who looked quite elderly though we must have appeared to him as impossibly young. Groupuscules formed within the group. I was apparently aligned in one groupuscule, Ann was in another, but I never knew what the differences were. Nonetheless, an older student, a history postgraduate, took me aside and warned me to stay away from the other groupuscules, they were ideologically wrong, be careful.

On Friday nights, I was also part of another parallel life. The Communist Party had a youth wing, the Eureka Youth League, and growing up in the Party one was willy-nilly in it. The Eureka Youth League itself had a wing, a kind of bohemian grouplet centred in postgraduates at the university, and on Friday nights I would go with them downtown to the Royal George hotel near the docks next to the city, the Royal George being home to Sydney's libertarian Push, or at least one of their haunts. Here, coming from an ascetic teetotaller family (my father didn't drink, smoke or swear), I unfortunately learned to drink, and drink too much, though I couldn't spend too much of my scholarship money, I had to spare some money for a taxi ride home, often arriving at our Bondi flat and collapsing asleep in the doorway, there to be found by my father, an early riser.

I also recall attending a kind of off-campus group of would-be poets, I can't remember how I knew about them, where a young man, the eldest there, would intone, when we write, we mustn't be precious, we mustn't be precious.

※

In my second and third year, doing honours I came to know some of the other honours students in the Leavisite stream, so university life was becoming less lonely, or at least more peopled, for me.

I was still living at home in the Bondi flat (my sisters had left home), though sadly falling into seemingly compulsive arguments about the horrors of Stalin's Soviet Union with my father. I'll quote here from an essay 'Father and Son: From Old Left to New' I wrote for *Island Magazine* in 1984, the year after my father died, in a special feature devoted to Growing Up in Australia (based, I see, I'm looking at my copy of the journal now, it's in a state of disrepair, it's falling apart, on a series of talks presented at the 3rd Salamanca Arts Festival in Hobart on 26 November 1983). I begin the essay in the way I must have begun the Salamanca talk, by relating that my father, Ted Docker, until then the last surviving founding member of the Australian Communist Party, had died early in 1983, and that I hoped to explore how, as a young student at Sydney University living at home, my father and I found ourselves conflicting sharply over questions of left politics, and that such conflict, blatantly Oedipal as it was on my part, nonetheless shed light on the vast unintended consequences of education in shaping class consciousness and identity.[1]

My father was in his quiet way delighted that I was attending university. I remember him saying that I had to learn to be a good 'speaker'. He had spoken at large rallies in the Sydney Domain – Sydney's Hyde Park corner – and that he knew I had to learn what they were teaching me at university and to pass my exams, for one day I would turn this knowledge to good account to aid the progressive movement, to help the revolution, be able to defeat the bourgeoisie with its own intellectual weapons. I would still see myself as working class and would be helping the working class as a supportive intellectual.

However, the New Left which I was becoming part of, was shaped by an altogether different orientation to class and class consciousness, constituting itself as a movement by assuming that the 'traditional' working class (regarded by the 'old left' Communist Party as the heirs of history) was dead, defunct, inflected with all the ideological features – sexism, racism, anti-homosexuality, anti-hedonism; acceptance of industrial society, social rules, hierarchy and work discipline – that the New Left was keen to oppose. The New Left saw itself as an intelligentsia wishing to unite not with the 'working class' but with the marginal in society, with women, blacks, gays, the unemployed and the oppressed Third World. Looking back, it perhaps wasn't so strange that I was reading with equal enthusiasm both American radical sociologist C Wright Mills and British literary critic F R Leavis. For C Wright Mills, following Frankfurt School theorists like Adorno, Horkheimer and Marcuse, was arguing that the working class had sunk into the decay of 'mass culture'; a dislike, we can see, he shared with Leavis even if Mills and Leavis didn't recognise this themselves. It followed that only the intelligentsia could be the carrier of true values. For Mills this meant being in a minority culture of radical intellectuals supporting movements of the non-working-class oppressed; for the New Left in general, the 'traditional' working class was in complicity with this oppression because it accepted dominant ideological values; the working class had become part of the enemy in history.

Perhaps, then, conflict between father and son, Old Left and New Left, was inevitable, as in an historical allegory.

My father and I would be sitting in the parental flat at Bondi. Suddenly an Oedipal squall would burst upon us. I'd accuse my father of complicity with 'Stalinism'. I'd say Stalin put people in forced labour camps, and I'd scream 'Stalin *killed* people! How can you defend someone who killed people?' My father would respond by talking about the greatness of the Russian Revolution, about how the Soviet Union had been invaded by 14 armies, about how the Revolution had changed the course of history (the first revolution to wrest power from capitalism), and about how easy it is to be misled by the capitalist press. My mother would try to intervene and say 'Don't argue with your father. Why do you do it?' as if the Oedipal drive could be stopped. Our arguments were long and bitter and grinding. I remember once my father suggested that I leave home. He also accused me of using my university education against him, of throwing names at him he didn't know.

Often, I've thought of these Oedipal conflicts. It distresses me that I shouted at my father and probably did use my tertiary education against him as a self-taught man. I know in my writing I keep coming back to this conflict, with changing views on it. In my essay 'Troubled reflections on my father' in Ann Curthoys and Joy Damousi's collection *What Did You Do in the Cold War, Daddy?* (2014), I revisit my 1984 *Island Magazine* article with more searching questions in mind than I expressed there, by referring to the entwined histories of the families of Ann and Ann's mother Barbara Curthoys, our friend and Ann's fellow historian Lyndall Ryan, and Ted Docker. These family and political histories turn on the years 1930 and 1931, when Lyndall's father Jack Ryan, along with Jack Kavanagh, then leading figures in the Australian Communist Party, were expelled for what at that time the Comintern in Moscow deemed 'social fascism': that is, for practising a kind of inclusive radical politics that involved open discussion and amicable relations with social democrats. A newly ascendant group, closed aligned to the Comintern and demanding unswerving dedication to the new line, a group that included my father, had assumed control within the Party's structures and would be powerful for the next couple of decades.[2]

This is a story movingly told by Barbara Curthoys in a 1993 essay entitled 'The Comintern, the CPA, and the Impact of Harry Wicks'. Wicks was a Comintern agent who visited Australia at this time (he was also known as Herbert Moore, and turned out to be some kind of double agent, serving both the Comintern and hidden right-wing masters).[3] Barbara's essay is sympathetic to Ryan and Kavanagh, based on research she conducted in Moscow in 1990 in the then newly released Comintern Archives. Barbara writes that in the late 1920s and early 1930s Ted Docker chose to adopt the new Comintern position required of the Australian Communist Party, with its harshness towards dissenters, a harshness signaled in the expulsion of Ryan and Kavanagh. Whereas before this Ted Docker's political writings were relaxed and continued the insouciance that characterised the oppositional culture of the syndicalist IWW that he belonged to before 1920 when the Communist Party was formed, it seems all too clear, Barbara observes, that he now exercised a new sensibility: stern, authoritarian and denunciatory. The Party then followed Stalin's notions of democratic centralism where more and more power was invested in the Central Committee and the Central Executive. Such, Barbara suggests, became the form of organisation that was to last in the Party for many years, making it forbidding, centralised, dogmatic and ever more closely tied to the organisational practices, image and reputation of Stalin's Soviet Union.[4]

In 'The Comintern, the CPA, and the Impact of Harry Wicks', Barbara Curthoys evokes the brutal expulsion by the Central Committee of Jack Ryan, who was told of his expulsion just as he was boarding a train to Melbourne to attend the 1930 ACTU Congress. In her warm portrait of Jack Ryan, he emerges as a very impressive figure, an able journalist and orator who spoke against the White Australia policy, and was prominent in an international trade union body established by the Comintern in 1921 to coordinate trade unions in countries bordering the Pacific, such as China, India, Russia, Japan, Canada, the US and Australia; when he was expelled in 1930, he also lost his job as acting editor of the *Pan-Pacific Worker* (for which my father had written articles in syndicalist spirit only a few years before).[5]

In my 'Troubled reflections on my father', I tell how shaken I feel by Barbara's essay and its revelations about what occurred in 1930. In my essay in *Island Magazine* I say that 'my father benefited a great deal from his life in the Communist Party. It gave him friendships, social life and eventually marriage. As a full-time functionary he travelled constantly around Australia and New Zealand', as well as journeying to England and then to Moscow for the Communist International's Seventh Congress.[6] Now, the image is etched into my mind of Jack Ryan being so peremptorily expelled – as Barbara Curthoys says, the 'case for Jack Ryan's expulsion was so weak that today it appears absurd' – by the newly ascendant group that included my father.[7]

Barbara Curthoys herself was expelled from the Australian Communist Party in 1970, and we can see her essay as a critical exploration of the culture and trauma of expulsion all too characteristic of radical political parties and movements, usually associated with a new line, often a complete reversal, that had to be obeyed. My father participated in this culture. In different generations Jack Ryan and Barbara Curthoys, among many others, were victims of it.[8]

My two autobiographical essays, 30 years apart no less – for *Island Magazine* in 1984 and in Ann and Joy's 2014 collection *What Did You Do in the Cold War, Daddy?* – now exist in my mind in an uneasy conversation. I end 'Father and Son: From Old Left to New' on an affectionate note. My father had died the year before, I was still upset by his death; I write of my father as having in his lifetime

> participated in stirring events, for example those that thwarted Menzies' policy of sending 'pig iron' to Japan... he was at times jailed and ordered out of towns by police. He never wavered in his belief in revolution; he never owned a house and never owned a car. In his minor role in the history of the Communist Party he may be seen as a stern, unrelenting Stalinist. I see him as someone who, when I was growing up, was never petty or nasty, who was loyal to his family, who had a mischievous sense of humour and was always making jokes.

Throughout his adult life he was unwaveringly radical. In my adult life I've tried in my own way to follow him.[9]

My final paragraph in my 2014 essay is much more disturbed and agitated.

> I never ceased to feel affectionate towards my father. I admire my father for being in the IWW; I was delighted to read, courtesy of Lyndall Ryan, his 1926 *Labour Monthly* articles which I feel continue the élan of the IWW; I admire his courage in 1934 in opposing the racism of the Anglo-Australian miners in Kalgoorlie and wonder if I could ever have done anything like that. Yet, in thinking about the expulsion of Jack Ryan in 1930 and Barbara Curthoys's impassioned essay, I also feel deeply unsettled, to the point of misery and nausea.[10]

I remain deeply unsettled.

※

Despite the arguments over Stalinism with my father, I continued to live at home in the Bondi flat. While during the week attending university, I was increasingly absorbed in the English novels and poems favoured by the Leavisites, on Friday nights I would go to the Royal George and drink too much. Such led to attendance at various parties and much drunken sort-of dancing, I think to Rolling Stones records.

At the end of each year, I took to travelling. With M, a particular Eureka Youth League friend, we drove – or rather, he drove, I didn't know how to drive – to the far north of Queensland and back to Sydney. Another time we decided to hitch-hike across to Perth. On the way across the Nullabor, we hitched a ride in the back of a ute with two guys who appeared to be friends, but who fell out just before we reached Kalgoorlie, and one of them got out a rifle and shot the other in the arm; we went with them to the hospital.

When M and I reached Perth I rang the venerable Australian writer Katharine Susannah Prichard. My father had said to do this. They had known each other from the very early days of the formation of the Communist Party, in the early 1920s; I also knew that there was mention of my father in Prichard's novel *Winged Seeds*, it was part of family lore. We went out to her home, and I recall sitting under a grapevine in the shade. She was gracious and kindly, and asked what I was studying. Forwarding a lifetime, when Ann and I came to Perth in 2016 to help Ned and Shino look after our grandson Leo, we joined a wheatbelt tour with the UWA English department colleague Tony D'Aeth which began by assembling at KSP's old home. Ann asked if I could remember where the grapevine was, and I said no, I can't.

At the end of another undergraduate year, I went with two new friends, students in science at Sydney University who I met at the Royal George, and, young urban students with long hair, decided to travel to Darwin, hitchhiking. Somehow we got to the Riverina and came to a small town, and decided to try to earn some money by doing agricultural work, it shouldn't be too hard. We went to an employment office, they gave as hoes and said go out to a certain farm and chip weeds away from the rows of cotton; it was very hot, we lasted about half an hour, when suddenly we realised at the same moment that we were already exhausted. We left our hoes and ran to a kind of water channel at the end of the rows of cotton, plunged our faces in the channel and sucked in water, mud and insects. Somehow, we made our way back to town and the employment office, and asked to be paid for our half hour's work. Maybe we were paid, I can't remember. Then we kept hitchhiking west to South Australia, until we intersected with a train station where we caught the Ghan. Not the spruced up Ghan you see now on the famous *Slow TV* program going from Adelaide to Darwin, passengers drinking wine and so on, but an old Ghan, paint peeling, bumping along, long hard planks on either side of the carriage for seats; maybe there were other passengers, I don't know, we didn't see any; it seemed to end somewhere in the desert, and then we made our own slow journey, hitchhiking in trucks going north until we reached Darwin, where we stayed in some kind of lodging house, full of bizarre happenings I don't want to talk about. Mostly we walked around the streets, staring into shops, sometimes laughing manically. After a week or two I ran out of money and contacted my mother to send money for the airfare back home.

Looking back, John the mummy's boy had abandoned his friends, without a thought.

For another end-of-year journey I decided to hitchhike around Tasmania by myself. When I got to Melbourne, I visited the writer Judah Waten. My father had asked me to contact him, I'm not sure why, he said he once had to expel Waten from the Communist Party decades before.[11] Then I took a ferry across to and started hitchhiking around Tasmania, beginning in Hobart. Clearly worried, my father had given me a penknife with a wooden handle to have by me at all times, I've still got it among one's little store of bric-a-brac which always goes with you in life. I recall staying for a couple of days at a hotel in a tiny town on the east coast; in the morning, the hotel people asked me to eat breakfast in the kitchen rather than in the formal dining room. I was the only guest. In the evening I sat in the bar while the locals became dementedly drunk, as in a phantasmogria, as in a scene from *Wake in Fright*, that most frightening of films for urbanites to watch.[12] When they learned I was a student, they accused me of feeling superior to them: you're a student, you've got a future, you'll go back to Sydney.

❦

When I returned from hitchhiking in Tasmania, my father was visibly moved to see me; he was also pleased and proud of his son's exam results, given that like many of my generation I was the first in the family to go to university.[13]

In 1966, my final honours year in English, I stayed home all year studying, I never went out, I knew I had to try to get a postgraduate scholarship, which I fortunately did, and decided to move to Melbourne. The Leavisites had retreated south, its Goldbergite wing was back at the University of Melbourne. I would follow them down there. What could go wrong?[14]

1   John Docker, 'Father and Son: From Old Left to New', *Island Magazine*, Vol.18–19, 1984, pp.77–80.
2   John Docker, 'Troubled reflections on my father', in Ann Curthoys and Joy Damousi (eds), *What Did You Do in the Cold War, Daddy? Personal Stories from a Troubled Time* (NewSouth, Sydney, 2014), p.88.
3   Barbara Curthoys, 'The Comintern, the CPA, and the Impact of Harry Wicks', *Australian Journal of Politics and History*, vol.39, 1993, pp.23–36.
4   John Docker, 'Troubled reflections on my father', pp.88, 99–101.
5   John Docker, 'Troubled reflections on my father', pp.103–4.
6   John Docker, 'Father and Son: From Old Left to New', *Island Magazine*, p.80.
7   Barbara Curthoys, 'The Comintern, the CPA, and the Impact of Harry Wicks', p.25.
8   John Docker, 'Troubled reflections on my father', pp.104–5.
9   John Docker, 'Father and Son: From Old Left to New', p.80.
10 John Docker, 'Troubled reflections on my father', p.113.
11 John Docker, 'Troubled reflections on my father', p.102.
12 John Docker, 'Epistemological vertigo and allegory: thoughts on massacres, actual, surrogate, and averted – Beersheba, *Wake in Fright*, *Australia*', in Frances Peters-Little, Ann Curthoys, John Docker (eds), *Passionate Histories: myth, memory and Indigenous Australia* (ANU E Press, Canberra, 2010), pp.62–5.
13 John Docker, 'Troubled reflections on my father', p.113.
14 John Docker, 'A Space for Self-Fashioning: An Antipodean Red-Diaper Baby Goes to University in the Sixties', in Dee Michel, Jacqueline Z. Wilson and Verity Archer (eds), *Bread and Roses: Voices of Australian Academics from the Working Class* (Sense Publishers, Rotterdam, 2015), p.66.

32

How I Became a Teenage Leavisite and Lived to Tell the Tale

Sydney University was, and is, a rather grand sandstone structure built in the mid part of the nineteenth century on the top of a hill not far from the city. From our Bondi flat, I would walk up Imperial Avenue to Bondi Road and catch the 380 double decker bus (I think it was the 380) into the city, to Railway Square, and then either catch another bus or walk up Broadway which turns into Parramatta Road to the university.

In my first year, 1963, I took English literature, anthropology and French; but French was held early, at 9 o'clock, and, being always slow to leave home, I struggled to arrive there by nine; after a few weeks, I decided dropping French was preferable to getting up earlier. I had in any case done five years of French at high school with the same uninspiring teacher. I did well enough in English in first year, and – this was good – doing honours counted as a subject in itself. So, in second year, I could do pass English, honours English and anthropology, which I rather liked but expended little energy on. I decided to just mosey along; much later, after we got together in the late 1960s, Ann and I worked out that, unbeknown to each other, we both had done anthropology in 1963, but Ann had done much better than I had. I did anthropology for three years, always with interest – it still interests me – but never an obsessive interest, as English literature was.

Just how obsessive it was I will try to explain, if one can explain from what in this distance in my life looks rather like lunacy.

In my second, third and fourth years, I became a Leavisite. As a student, one knows very little of what is happening in the world of the academic staff, but it appears that the English department was splitting into two camps, the Leavisite and the anti-Leavisite. As an accident of history, as a student I fell into the Leavisite camp because the tutors I had happened to be Leavisites. Somewhat later I wrote an essay, 'How I Became a Teenage Leavisite and Lived to Tell the Tale', which I will now reprise as it may be of minor historical interest, and I have talked before in this ego histoire of F R Leavis and Q D Leavis and T S Eliot and suchlike.

The essay was first published in *Meanjin* in 1981, and then appeared as the prologue in my 1984 book *In a Critical Condition*; I will type out the essay as it first appeared in *Meanjin*, doing some abridging as I go along.[1]

Departments of English must often have been a baffling and frustrating experience to the generations of students who have passed through them since the enlargement of universities after the Second World War. The secrets and rituals of the mysterious activity called literary criticism are certainly transmitted to honours students in their senior years, mainly because most honours students are favoured by staff resources and attention. For most pass students – let alone for non-university people – the mystery remains, as a kind of vague irritant.

The dominant assumptions of a department are usually presented to its students as if they are universal, as if all teachers in whatever area in all departments in all universities all over 'know' their subject in the same way. One sign of this is that departments, for example, of English or History, rarely offer to students in early years courses in theory or methodology which will raise basic questions about the variety and contingency of intellectual approaches; usually courses like this might be given only to fourth-year honours students.

All university departments of anything have of course their own distinctive character, though many might seem peculiarly characterless and ghostly, composed of staff who are noticed mainly as they disappear into their rooms, or nod at each other in corridors, or chat in the tea-room. Most teaching departments are not very interested in holding staff-postgraduate seminars, and even when they're held most staff don't turn up. Staff will publish for a variety of reasons, particularly in the competitive atmosphere created by demands for promotion,[2] but rarely will acknowledge each other's work. (It's almost a convention that staff don't say to each other, Oh, I've seen your latest publication and it's very interesting and stimulating and sure to create a stir in Spenser or something studies.) Nevertheless, despite this fragmentation and the fleeting quality of personal relations in the corridors – and despite that other phenomenon, amazing mutual hatreds and hostilities between this or that staff member – departments usually (but not always) teach within a uniform conceptual framework, a common paradigm or problematic.

Sometimes, however, sharp intellectual rather than personal differences are present in departments, and students can be faced with choosing sides. The Philosophy department at Sydney University has been the arena of one such struggle. The Sydney English department in the early 1960s also saw remarkable scenes of internecine bitterness and hostility, made even more dramatic because one side was warring within itself while trying to ward off the common rival. An analysis of this struggle might help illuminate something of the mystery of English departments; for once, unstated assumptions were forced out into the cold fresh air. In any case, I was, as a 19-year-old student, caught up in it myself.

The Sydney English department troubles began when S L ('Sam') Goldberg came up from Melbourne University, with various trusted lieutenants, to become professor of English. Goldberg and his troops were followers of the English critic F R Leavis, himself given to vigorous public brawling, as in his famous controversy with C P Snow over the relative virtues of positivist science as against literary culture.

F R Leavis is undoubtedly a monumental figure in the development of twentieth century literary criticism. Born in 1895 in Cambridge, he became a teacher there, influencing many to take up his concerns and to shape themselves in his aggressive mould. In books like *New Bearings in English Poetry* (1932) and in essays in the journal *Scrutiny*, which he edited from 1932 to 1953 – essays which later formed the basis of famous books like *The Common Pursuit*, *Revaluation* and *The Great Tradition* – Leavis tried to redraw the maps of received criticism. On one front he took up arms against an older conservative orthodoxy that was established in the universities in the 1920s and 1930s, an orthodoxy that still favoured weakly sentimental verse of a late-Victorian cast. Instead, Leavis pointed to the excitement of the new poetry of the age such as that of Gerard Manly Hopkins, Ezra Pound, and T S Eliot, and argued that its force and verve demanded new criteria and standards not only for twentieth century poetry but for the whole development of English poetry since the sixteenth century. As Leavis acknowledged, he was in part applying the insights of T S Eliot's critical essays in *The Sacred Wood* (1920), particularly the stress on poetry as fusing intellect and emotion. Pre-nineteenth century poets like Donne and Marvell (the 'line of wit'), Dryden and Pope could now be restored, poets whose merits had been slighted by nineteenth-century critics like Matthew Arnold for being too rational or cerebral.

In these terms Leavis can be seen as a courageous pioneer of modernism in university criticism, applied first to poetry then to the novel, as in Conrad, George Eliot, James and Lawrence. Certainly, he received little encouragement from the critical establishment he took on at the time. Academic preferment came niggardly in his direction, and his followers often had to pick up what must have seemed like minor posts in colonies on which the sun was setting fast – a vast diaspora of prickly Leavisites.

Leavis fought as well on another front, against the prevailing Marxist approaches to criticism and cultural history, in some ways, however, meeting Marxism on a common ground. Leavis and the Leavisites agreed with Marxists that a purely internal approach to literary criticism was not desirable – though such an approach was the staple of their teaching method – and produced their own kind of cultural history, one that brought into primary focus an apocalyptic concern for the plight of civilisation. Civilisation was being destroyed by industrialism and a narrow Benthamite utilitarian ethos, creating a debased 'mass civilisation' which only a dwindling 'minority culture' could do something about saving. Criticism, in departments of English, was the central agency of preservation. Critics could develop in themselves the values of responsiveness, vitality, fineness, intelligence, vigour, subtlety, and wit that are created in the best literature. At the same time they would need to have a scalpel-like sense of which literature and which criticism don't realise such values. How urgent, then, were the tasks of the true critics! How contemptible were those who were thwarting them – who were indeed helping to hasten the decay of civilisation!

Given this sense of historical occasion, it's not difficult now to remember why Leavisism seemed so attractive. The doctrine gave a sense of great power and authority to being a critic as such. The critic was not a mere follower of writers, penning commentaries in their wake, nor but a writer *manqué*. Now the critic was taking the initiative by saving civilisation itself, keeping alive its traditions and vitalities. Again, Leavisism was a method and a vocabulary which offered keys to the understanding of all literature. The greats of literary history were no longer inaccessible, they were all available now for analysis and value judgement. Henry James could be judged subtle and fine, but lacking – compared to George Eliot – in vigour. Leavisites were always constructing hierarchies, judging writers against an implicit scale of which writer maximized – 'realised' – which and how many possibilities of life, a calculus of possibilities which ranged from talismanic terms like fineness to vitality. Further, Leavisism allowed entry into analysis of poetry, that seemingly most opaque of literary arts. A poem had to be a unified whole; its explicit meanings, however, could be modified or contradicted by other elements in this whole, by its tone or rhythm. The explicit urgings of the poem might be embodied in weak or notional or unconvinced or febrile rhythms, so that its real meanings lay in those parts more forcibly or intensely created.

It certainly wasn't an unpleasant feeling to regard oneself as part of civilisation's needed creative minority. This kind of elitism gave Leavisites the confidence, if not outright arrogance, to decide on any literature that ever came before them, and on any other piece of criticism – or piece of critic – they felt was inadequate and so endangered the historical mission of criticism: not unlike the harshness with which many left-wing groups judge each other. (Interestingly, some later abandoned Leavisism to become Trotskyists; they didn't have far to go.)

Many of the Leavisites were fervent students in their early twenties, and excited enough because some staff had bothered to get to know them, let alone invite them to join the chosen. This was a rare thing at Sydney University, traditionally remote towards its students.

Leavis's influence on his many admirers was not a simple one, and there could be different Leavisite strands and outposts, each equally truculent and all guns blazing. In his three to four years at Sydney University Professor Goldberg was opposed by various dissident Leavisites, mainly quite young staff and some students, who felt his peculiarly Melbourne stress on metaphysical rather than moral values was precious, that Goldberg liked James Joyce too much, that more tough-minded writers like Thomas Hardy should be made more central, and so on. Goldberg's *Melbourne Critical Review* (to be changed to *The Critical Review*) was opposed by the dissident Leavisites in their own journals, like *Harpoon* and, later, *Chauntecleer*.

For the young Leavisites, dissident and non-dissident, these were heady days. The doctrine had to be lived. They were to foster complexity and vitality, both in seminar and extra-seminar discussion (seminars would often repair for tea and coffee after) and by non-university activities, for example, by imagining themselves like Birkin and Gerald in Lawrence's *Women in Love*, and having life-enhancing wrestling matches on the floor at parties. There was also a Leavisite wedding, where passages were read out from *Women in Love* – obviously a key text – and the young couple were left after to consummate their relationship in a way befitting the novel's chief characters. People fervently liked each other and just as fervently might distrust the sensibility of another in the various grouplets and fall out. All was intensity and tension.

At the same time the Leavisites as a whole clashed badly with the older Sydney members of the department. The elitism of the Leavisites blended in well with pre-existent Melbourne cultural traditions stressing the social function of knowledge and the educative role of intellectuals, the assumptions of a journal like *Meanjin*.[3] But these attitudes didn't at all go down well in Sydney when Professor Goldberg brought them along for display and dissemination. The older Sydney lot felt aggrieved at the confidence of the new group, and how, as they saw it, it was dominating key areas of teaching and making them marginal. They also felt that the Sydney English department had its own traditions, descending from former giants like Mungo MacCallum and le Gay Brereton and Waldock, in 17th century English studies and in Australian literature, which shouldn't be scorned. They also discovered that these Sydney traditions were wonderfully pluralist, and didn't allow of moralizing and forcing people to accept great traditions and strict canons of literary worth. In their eyes, to relate literature to 'life' was importing non-literary (contextual) standards: criticism was rather a matter of describing strictly literary qualities, and everything that moved the Leavisites, they judged not to be literary and so no business of the critic. The Sydney critics historically aligned themselves with an unexalted empiricism and supposed high standards of scholarship. Their ideal critic was one who went to Oxford and collated a minor seventeenth-century text, or went to London University to study the concerns of a nineteenth-century novelist: but usually nothing spectacular, rarely any original theorising, since this would be rude in a colonial; the Sydney scholars were to help tidy up the margins of knowledge.

At the same time, in a journal like *Balcony*, which sprang into existence fully-armed in March 1965 to combat the Leavisites, the links between this kind of empiricism in Sydney literary criticism and Sydney philosophic traditions were dusted and brought forward for use, especially Andersonian pluralism and its offshoot Libertarianism: in particular the Andersonian and Libertarian opposition to elites setting values for the rest of society, the sins of solidarism and moralism.

As it happened, the older Sydney members could muster more friends higher-up in the university power structure than the intruders from Melbourne. The English department split into Leavisite versus anti-Leavisite groups, and thence into offering alternative A and B courses to students.

The drama drew to a close, mainly because its chief player, Professor Goldberg, probably with some joy, took up a chair in the

Melbourne English department; he and his lieutenants trooped back there. The strident young anti-Goldbergite Leavisites also took themselves off south, mainly to La Trobe, where they were to regroup, join hands with other non-Goldbergite Leavisites still in captivity in Sydney, and in 1970 began to produce *Chauntecleer*, a journal which hoped to show that the correct Leavisite approach could cope with all the demands and challenges of the barbaric contemporary world in which they found themselves.

A little shaken, the Sydney English department resumed its time-honoured course. In terms of basic challenges to its ruling critical concepts, the Sydney department was probably more lastingly affected by the politicization of intellectuals during the Vietnam War. Staff members like Stephen Knight, Michael Wilding and Terry Sturm desired to teach courses which try to discover the shaping effect of political and ideological assumptions on literature, though Knight and Wilding were also drawn by the strong pull of Sydney Libertarianism, which suspects any attempt at wide-ranging theories of being monistic.

I experienced these years of comedy and trauma personally, since I enrolled in the Sydney English department as an undergraduate in 1963, just as Professor Goldberg was beginning to compete for the hearts and minds of first-year students by introducing new courses and insisting on more frequent tutorials and close study of texts. I also became quite a fervent Leavisite, and in seminars would enter into the debates with whatever passion I could muster. I was so convinced that I followed Professor Goldberg to Australia's Leavisite heartland, the Melbourne English department.

This was a remarkable shock in every way. I was, undoubtedly, like all my kind, arrogant and abrasive, but I was also, to say the least, young, shy, naïve and socially inept. While I had been a Friday night drunk at various pubs for a number of years, including the Royal George, the site of the Push and various libertarian excitements, I had in fact lived the usual suburban student's life at home with my parents in Bondi. My mother deemed me so young that when I caught the Melbourne train she cried on the platform. In Melbourne, in Carlton, opposite the cemetery and in the shadow of the huge blocks of flats, I established a household with a fellow ex-Sydney postgraduate and Goldbergite. Here we tried to live, with rudimentary-to-nil notions of relating and housekeeping, and I would go from our semi-detached to the University, to begin an MA on T S Eliot's super-difficult *Four Quartets*, and to offer fine and subtle perceptions to my students in the part-time tutoring I was doing.

I found nothing in Melbourne's intellectual culture that was not alien. Everything seemed too genteel. Professor Goldberg and Jock Tomlinson and Maggie Tomlinson and the other Goldbergites (actually I'm not sure if there were any other Goldbergites) were certainly very kind; there was sherry most afternoons at five, where everyone seemed nervous and tense, although a courteous atmosphere reigned. I was struck by the men standing conspicuously for any woman who entered the room. There was University House, and a civilized lunch with members of the department, where everything they considered amusing, witty, funny, adroit and droll I found dull and simple; everything they felt was a stimulating thing to say about literature I thought marginal and uninteresting. Further, the department, it didn't take long to realise, was fairly split (with one or two notable exceptions perhaps, like Chris Wallace-Crabbe) by an almost ethnic level of tension, between the Goldbergites and Professor Vincent Buckley and his followers, who were or wanted to be Irish, went in for creative writing, were interested in contemporary Australian and American poetry, and were very political in a kind of throwback Cold War way. The Goldbergites tended to be critics only, and felt that literature revealed truths far more important than the passing shows of politics.

The young Buckleyites also, I felt, quickly made it known that we young postgraduate boatpeople should have stayed in Sydney with the other battered (in so far as any Leavisite's confidence can be disturbed) remnants there of Goldberg's original landing party and colony. We were gross visitors to the higher south. It was criminal of Sam to bring us down; we should have been shoved off the fleeing ship.

Another shock was the discovery that departments of the same thing could have radically different teaching methods in different universities. One young Buckleyite postgraduate, almost shaking with the intensity of his calling, invited me to sit in on one of his tutorials, and unselfconsciously put on a most remarkably authoritarian performance as a teacher. He would commence a point, a statement, ask if anyone disagreed or had any problem with it, then make his next point, and so on. Teaching methods at Sydney University had been more Socratic, based on discussion.

Starting with incidents like these I soon began to swim in a deep pool of nostalgia and idealization, for mother Sydney (or perhaps my Sydney mother), its intellectual sub-cultures were refreshingly cynical – 'know more about life' – I would bitterly feel, than all this self-proclaimed and slightly revolting high-minded intensity, this posturing and exhibition of sensibility.

By the end of the first year of my MA I was disillusioned with the Melbourne Leavisites, and in general in a bad way – altogether less than happy, getting very drunk too often, flaking on (disapproving) people's floors, fond of imagining suicide on a disused pier near where I was then living at Albert Park and finding in the most unlikely places lines about soft and easeful death, and then given to rushing to Sydney during vacations to bore my Sydney friends silly by getting hopelessly drunk and claiming I was unintense and unhighminded and 'flexible' about all things. The terrors and fatuities of exile…

My friend and fellow Sydney exile Ian Lennie and I set about trying to work out the bases of the Leavisite scheme.[4] The whole project seemed based on 'practical criticism', the close study of the inner workings of a text. But that text was also alleged to represent something about the period or age it was written in: it might, like Marvell's witty verse, indicate the fineness of early seventeenth-century civilization; or George Eliot and D H Lawrence might reveal persisting values and virtues in non-industrial rural English society. So that before you knew it the Leavisite critic was not talking about the text at all, but about something else, about qualities of vitality or energy or fineness which were held to characterise the best in an age's spirit. A disliked text, however, would show that a period or phase of society was but vulgar or thin or coarse. Texts became symptoms.[5]

The Leavisite analysis of a text, that is, was always dissolving into a version of cultural history and the evaluation of culture. It struck me as a theory very much influenced by a post-World War One apocalyptic mood about the decline of civilisation, shared by Pound and Eliot and Yeats as well as by Leavis, a thought which I also tried to work out, in a rough and rudimentary way, in my MA thesis. The notion of a writer or work representing an age seemed the most absurd of all the Leavisite propositions. How could one writer or work represent a whole society? In particular, because the Leavisites seemed habitually to idealise the past, what of all the features of pre-modern society that indicate social misery?

The notion of literature being an index of the quality or lack of quality of a period was also hopelessly circular. The critic perceives certain qualities in a work which reveal the essence of a society: we know the essence of a society because we can perceive it in the literary work. Left out of this equation is any actual historical knowledge, the remotest knowledge about the economic, political and ideological modes of the society some such work was supposedly representing and illuminating. And the notion of a unified essential spirit of a culture or period also seemed hopeless. Why couldn't different works reveal quite different – perhaps contradictory – aspects of a culture? Another thought was that the Leavisites tried to apply their terminology – stultifyingly repetitive as it was – to all literature. But terms like vitality and energy seemed very much rooted in the English romantic movement. The whole Leavisite project was based on assumptions which its practitioners showed every sign of not knowing were assumptions, believing them to be universally true. They were not only ignorant of history, but philosophically ignorant of themselves. They were unprepared to see their own critical concepts as themselves historically formed and contingent.

From all this I decided to become more and more historical in my own approach, to see literary criticism as well as literature as always part of broader contexts, of cultural history, the history of ideas, the impact of ideology. In particular I felt that 'tradition' was a necessary and crucial concept: you shouldn't, in analyzing a work, go straight from the text to the society. Rather, you try to work out how a text is part of a certain tradition: for example, how the ruling ideas that structure Lawrence's fiction also belong to, are shaped by, the romantic tradition with its stress on natural vitality (including sexuality) and its frequent identification of women with the natural world. One could then work out something of why romanticism was so attractive a tradition – for example, in its anti-industrialism – and how particular writers were always altering and reshaping this tradition in response to contemporary situations through which they were living.

In this way I was regaining contact with an inherited Marxism, while wishing to retain the strength of the Leavisite critical method. An original attraction of the Leavisite approach was that it promised to make available what Marxists so far had been unable to provide, at least in so far as I'd perceived Marxist attempts at aesthetics in the Communist tradition. Leavisites could analyse (it appeared) the details and detailed movement of a text, its very tone and rhythm, its ironies and ambiguities and the way it functioned as a self-sufficient whole. In particular, Leavisites were very good (it seemed) at analyzing poetry, while Marxists are usually fairly hopeless at poetry and tend to race to the novel or drama for analysis and as the basis for their generalisations.

So that when I arrived back in Sydney in the summer of 1968–69, I wasn't too shattered, the pieces were coming together again. I took up residence (shared a house) in Balmain and pondered on the whole Leavisite episode, which now seemed a very contradictory experience. I'd worked through from the Leavisite position to my own approach (text-based and contextual), and could now try and apply it to the predominant challenges of Sydney intellectual life: the Libertarianism (and behind it, Andersonianism) of many of my drinking companions at the Forth and Clyde in Balmain and the Newcastle near the Quay; the development of the counter-culture, drawing upon the romantic tradition for key notions, like closeness to nature and natural instincts and feelings, dislike of rationalism and utilitarianism, interest in subconscious states of experience; and the theories associated with the new liberation movements that sprang up during the Vietnam War. The Leavisite had been the Oedipal stage, but the later Vietnam War years provided the real intellectual apprenticeship: of particular importance was to be the Socialist Scholars Conference, held in 1970.

To go ahead and implement my new approach, however, I had to learn one thing the Leavisites neglected to teach, that is, methods of research. Why do research when it was exhausting enough responding to a text with all your sensitivities and intelligence at full bore? My friend Ann Curthoys was invaluable here; as an historian she was puzzled and pained by my lack of even the most rudimentary skills at research, and had almost to take me by the hand and show me around Mitchell Library. A typical conversation.

> 'Do you know how to take proper notes?'
> 'Yes, of course I do... Well, what do you mean, proper notes?'
> 'Proper notes. You know, take notes of what you're reading.'
> 'Yes, well of course I know that.'
> (Jesus. Gulp. Sounds like hard work. Why don't I stay a Leavisite?)
> 'Do you know how to use a card system?'
> 'Yeah. Bibliography cards.'
> 'No. A proper card system.'
> 'No I don't.'
> (Hate getting grilled.)
> 'Jesus. What do you bloody critics do?'
> (What is all this? Wouldn't know real research if he fell over it. Probably just bloody lazy. Moron literary critic.)
> How the friendship survived early encounters of this scholarly kind one puzzles to think.

One conviction I did bring away from life and fanciful death in the unsunny south was how different were the intellectual cultures of Melbourne and Sydney. I didn't think too coherently about this difference until I began giving tutorials in Australian literature at Macquarie University. For the session on Kenneth Slessor I read his prose essays, and was struck by the similarities between the social and political theory of Norman Lindsay as Slessor describes it, and the theories of the Sydney Libertarians whom I'd got to know at the Forth and Clyde and the Newcastle; and how different again was this kind of social thought from Melbourne's intellectual traditions. I wrote an article comparing Lindsay's and the Libertarians' thought, but neither *Australian Literary Studies* nor *Politics* felt able to chance either the politics or literary side of it, and it was then that it was suggested to me that

I should write what became *Australian Cultural Elites* as the only way of developing the argument in the one place. It would also give me room to develop ideas and approaches suggested by the whole problem of Sydney/Melbourne differences, in particular, that these differences, while not blanket, were so sharp that all the cultural history that usually went on as if you could talk about all Australian culture in one breath was nonsensical. Australian culture was not unified, it displayed conflict and diversity that had to be explained in part by the different histories of its two major cities. There was, I thought, a general principle here also: that culture is always a drama, a drama of differences, conflicts, contradictions, tensions, antagonisms.

In 1972 I resigned from Macquarie University to write *Australia Cultural Elites*. A brilliant career was behind me.

1   John Docker, 'How I Became a Teenage Leavisite and Lived to Tell the Tale', *Meanjin*, Vol.40, no.4, 1981, pp.411–22; John Docker, *In a Critical Condition* (Penguin Books, Melbourne, 1984), pp.l-14.
2   Here I footnoted Pierre van den Berghe, *Academic Gamesmanship* (Abelard-Schuman, New York, 1970).
3   Here I footnoted my first book: John Docker, *Australian Cultural Elites* (Angus and Robertson, Sydney, 1974), chapters on *Meanjin* and *Southerly*.
4   Here I footnoted: This bore fruit in Ian Lennie's superb article, 'English Studies in Australia', *Arena* 20, 1969.
5   Here I footnoted: René Wellek, 'Concepts of Form and Structure in Twentieth Century Criticism', *Concepts of Criticism* (Yale University Press, New Haven and London, 1963), p.59.

33

1970: A Campaign Against Censorship, and a Scandalous Festival of Banned Works

In late 1968, as soon as I could, I left Melbourne to return to live in Sydney. I stayed for a short while with my family in Bondi, then teamed up with Ann Curthoys. What we call our Living Together Date was 10 January 1969. I said to Ann, how do you remember that; Ann said, I just do.

In 1968, during the times I had rushed back from Melbourne at vacation times, Ann and I got to know each other properly, as it were, at the Forth and Clyde Hotel in Balmain, down near what had once been a busy dockyard in Sydney Harbour history; especially on weekends, the Forth and Clyde was a haunt of the Sydney Libertarians, the Push, a hotel with a single bar where women and men freely mixed, a bohemia, with Ann and I on its outer edge.

Now, at the beginning of 1969, Ann and I moved in to a house in Church Street, Balmain, with the Sydney University historian Ken McNab. It was once a corner shop, with large plate windows next to the street, at a slightly odd angle. Ann was researching for her doctoral thesis on race relations in colonial NSW in the latter part of the nineteenth century, going in every day to Mitchell Library.

Ann could recognise a lost and bruised soul when she saw one. I had come back from Melbourne with little or no life skills, though before leaving home for Melbourne in late 1966 or early 1967 I had asked my mother to teach me how to cook some dishes, and fortunately where I lived in Carlton I was near the Italian shops in Lygon Street, including an excellent butcher, the beginnings of a lifelong food obsession. I had no sense of any future. Ann said, what are you going to do now? I said, I don't know. Ann said, well, let's think: what about getting some kind of job, and finishing your thesis (I'd come back without having completed my MA on Eliot's *Four Quartets*), you've already written a lot of it, then we'll get it bound and sent off to the Melbourne English department. First, Ann said, a job, an academic position. How, what do I do? Well, be direct, go to the English department and ask if you can do some tutoring. I swallowed. I caught the 433 bus from Balmain to Parramatta Road, proceeded to the entrance to Sydney University opposite Glebe's Derwent Street, moved up the hill past Fisher Library, got to the quadrangle, found the English department, and walked into the office of Mr Ron Dunlop, who looked like an old army man, he was acting head of the English department while its professor, G A Wilkes, was away somewhere. He said, what can I do for you? I said, I've been doing an MA in the English department at Melbourne, could I do some tutoring. He said OK, you can have an office down below the Fisher stacks building, that's where the other tutors are. That, it would appear, was how things were done then.

So, in 1969 I tutored in the Sydney English department, though I can't remember anything I taught. At the same time, I must have spent time writing and finishing the thesis, then got it bound at a printer in Bondi Junction, though I got the numbering wrong, and had it numbered again, which meant every page showed two numbers. I have the thesis before me; the cover is red, the title simple, *T S Eliot: Four Quartets*, its author J Docker, accompanied by the information that the thesis was sent to the University of Melbourne in October 1969. I felt compelled to add an Errata slip: 'The pagination inadvertently was begun at Page 2 of the Introduction. There is also an internal numbering within chapters which should be disregarded.' I forlornly hoped that the examiners might forgive this rather bizarre presentation.

If I can't remember what I taught in the Sydney English department, I do remember giving a seminar paper on Dickens' *Hard Times* and F R Leavis, offering, as a recent ex-Leavisite still working his way out of it, a fairly excoriating account of Leavis's liking for Dickens and *Hard Times* in particular; sitting in the circle, I noticed G A Wilkes, which was a little unnerving, as I was reading out the scribbled paper, I thought, am I being checked up on?

Perhaps I was, because at the end of 1969 or early 1970 I found myself applying for a tutorship in the English department at Macquarie University, out in the north western suburbs, the Bible belt; this I got, only to find that like the other tutors I had to spend three weeks teaching the same poem, that is, 18 tutorials on the same text, then the three-week cycle would start again on another poem, a fairly deranging experience. I think Ann could attest to this.

Ann, whose memory is far better than mine, suggests that one poem I was teaching was a Gerard Manley Hopkins; in any case, by the 18th, or perhaps the 8th time, I was going slightly insane.

Near the end of 1969, or beginning of 1970, Ann and I left Ken McNab's house and moved to a tiny stone cottage at the border of Balmain and Rozelle the next suburb, at the corner of Evans Street and Carrington Street. This was our second home together; many more were to come; Ann and I once calculated that in the space of a few years we moved rental places 14 times. I recall that Ann's mum Barbara came to stay for a couple of days, bringing much needed kitchen equipment, especially a yellow frying pan, a Le Creuset, that we kept for decades, until its wooden handle came off and we reluctantly had to say goodbye to it; my carpenter father also visited and built some book shelves for us, and also a lovely wooden coffee table; new friends visited, I especially remember that the English department critic Terry Sturm would drop by on his way home, and we would put our feet up on the coffee table and talk, sipping tea. We hosted a number of gigantic Balmain cockroaches, also a Clint Eastwood poster on the kitchen wall, from one of his 1960s spaghetti westerns.

In May 1970, news came through about the fate of my MA thesis. Among my papers in Mitchell Library that I looked at in 2011, I came across a letter from Sam Goldberg, University of Melbourne department of English, 4 May, 1970, informing me that my MA had passed; he added that I couldn't know who the examiners were, nor could I see the reports in full. He ended the letter: 'Glad to hear you've got a job, though sorry that Macquarie doesn't seem very stimulating. Still, all very best wishes, Yours, Sam.' (I must have written to my Melbourne MA supervisor, Jock Tomlinson, about how boring Macquarie English was and telling the tale of how we tutors had to spend three weeks repeating the same tutorial on the one poem.) I looked at the anonymous examiner's report, it commented that Mr Docker's 'prose is, if not on the face of it lively, continuously alert and intelligent... Sometimes his logical progression is uncertain, sometimes his "plain man" bias strikes me as over-done and he can be over-solemn about literary echoes and antecedents.'

In the Mitchell papers I looked at in 2011 is a photo of J Docker in a cap and gown, with huge black spectacles, taken in Melbourne at the graduation ceremony at the university for my MA. I must have travelled to Melbourne with my mother, who wore a very smart suit for the occasion; my memory is that my mother and I stayed in the outer reaches of the city at the home of Geoff Sharp and Nonie Sharp, key figures in the Melbourne-based radical journal *Arena*. Embarrassingly, I recall that when I had a shower in the morning, I placed the plastic curtain outside the cubicle so that water went all over the floor.

Geoff and Nonie became lifelong friends for both Ann and me, and publishing in *Arena* became very important for us, permitting writing that was not conventional, that could be adventurous; it also meant that while I wished to live in what I fondly imagined to be bohemian cynical Sydney, I also had a very strong Melbourne connection through *Arena*, a lifelong double consciousness. I recall meeting Geoff in a hotel in Parkville, near the university, he was one of those editors always looking for the new and controversial; later, in Sydney, when I met Henry Mayer – more on Henry, as he was always known as, soon – I recognised the same kind of tricksterish desire. I've just looked on my shelves and found early contributions to *Arena* in 1968, 1969 and 1970 by Ann and me and also our Sydney friend Ian Lennie who was, like me, doing an MA in the Melbourne English department; new young full-of-confidence New Left intellectuals starting out.

In *Arena* number 17, summer 1968–9, irritated by conventional left disapproval of popular film and incomprehension in how to read texts, I contributed 'A Note on Bonnie and Clyde', its first sentence '*Bonnie and Clyde* is a very careful and thoughtful film – precise in all its effects', then offering an energetic critique of the dismissal of the film in *Arena* 16 by Max Teichmann, a politics lecturer, who had argued that the film was a symptom of all that was wrong with Western society, because of its 'idealization of a particularly odious pair of mass murderers'. I mildly pointed out that Teichmann does not observe the 'distinction between the material of a film, and the film's attitude to its material', that the film is not identifying with the actions of Bonnie and Clyde and may also be critical of them, ironic towards them. With some hauteur reminiscent of the Leavisites he was supposedly leaving behind, Docker then accuses 'non-critics – social scientists, historians etc', of a clear inability to analyse texts as texts.

In the same issue of *Arena* Ian Lennie, in 'Leftists and the Arts: A New Aestheticism?', also has a sprightly critique of recent contributions in *Arena* and in other contemporary radical publications, opening with, 'When it comes to the arts Marxists and leftists generally are frequently simpleminded and sentimental', they 'tend to *reduce* art to the social system which produces it', they approach art 'as though it were really a political or social message in disguise', yet when they see art as supporting 'something vaguely like General Human Values' they 'fall prey to the worst sentimentality'.

In *Arena* number 20, 1969, there are essays by Ian Lennie, 'English Studies in Australia', and John Docker, 'T. S. Eliot and Modern Criticism', and an essay by Ann Curthoys, 'The End of the Free U?', a searching examination of how the late 1960s Free U in Sydney came about, its achievements and limitations over the two years of its existence so far.

Ann notes that much of the Free U's inspiration came from the American anarchist educator Paul Goodman, who in July 1967 (in a collection of essays, *The Dialectics of Liberation*, edited by David Cooper) had discussed the American Free U movement. Ann records that in October 1967 the Sydney University student newspaper *Honi Soit* published two articles critiquing the 'mass universities', one by Terry Irving (a historian of working-class radicals who found a home in politics at Sydney University), and another by The Committee for a Free University; these articles suggested that the mass university had ceased to consider the purpose of the professional training it offered, and proposed that a radical experiment, an alternative Free University, should be established off-campus, consisting of a group of staff and students drawn from existing universities, who can study in small groups and who do not pay teachers, examine students or offer degrees; when reform from within seems hopeless, reform through a utopian alternative might succeed, the Free U carrying on a tradition of learning as a good in itself, a tradition of questioning which the mass universities had forgotten.

Response from hundreds of students, and some staff, was immediate. In December 1967 premises were rented in Darlington, near Sydney University, and enrolments at $5 each were made. Ann discerned a number of different strands of interest. One strand was in the spirit of liberal reform, focusing on issues of social concern, with the holding of a conference on poverty in 1968, and a later interest in Aboriginal children in the nearby Redfern area. Another strand was sociological, partly a reflection of the lack of sociology at Sydney University and other Australian universities, itself an inheritance of a British anti-sociological tradition. Courses were set up on Class and Power in Australia, Social Movements in Poor Countries, Culture and The Mass Media, and Race Relations, and in the absence of university sociology the convenors and students came from allied disciplines like history, political science and psychology. Those in the physical sciences were also interested in these courses; they were acutely aware of the technological nature of their training, and came to the Free U as a source of analysis of society.

Another strand was the setting up of a Creative Arts Course, which, Ann observed, gave the Free U a non-academic content which its founders had not expected.

Another strand was to prove its most radical, the anti-authoritarian attitude of its participants, and here, Ann thought, the Free U was important and original; the philosophy of its founders involved the breaking down of the distinctions between teacher and student, and the existence of groups which were small and self-directing. Courses were instigated on the basis of interest, either by a person who was relatively an expert, or by a group of equally inexpert students; members of the course decided at the beginning, and as they went, the topics and procedures of the weekly meeting. However, Ann commented, many felt the courses were a failure, nearly all petered out after two or three months, and Ann herself found them flat, unenthusiastic, lacking in initiative or original thinking, and the ideal of university level research, or group research, was rarely attained. Ann felt this was regrettable, and that she liked the idea that a group of people with a common interest can 'follow their nose' in an intellectual pursuit, that an open-ended course rather than a pre-structured one is possible. The strength of the Free U, the flexibility and feeling of equality in the courses, stemmed from this basic method.

The desire to be interdisciplinary, Ann suggested, to cut across boundaries between compartmentalised disciplines, had its limitations. Ann felt that the rejection of disciplines, old or new, as any kind of starting point, meant the rejection of any attempt to master a particular mode of attacking problems; members of the Free U tended to identify the very notion of disciplines with the particularly segmented nature of the study of society current in universities; yet disciplines, Ann pointed out, can be seen merely as a methodological necessity enabling deeper study, which does not prevent the claims of any one discipline to reach insights and conclusions of more general interest and importance.

By the second year, courses were less sociological; most of the sociologically-oriented courses, except for those on Research on Aborigines, and The Radical Tradition, faded quickly. On the other hand, the creative courses expanded, and 'participation' was exemplified in courses on Human Potential, Male-Female Relationships, Research and Action Projects.

Nonetheless, Ann's feeling was that by the end of the second year the Free U was on the verge of collapse, though she still wished that the 'real value of Free U, the experiment with the open-ended, freely moving seminar', could inspire a radical program in universities, could act as a challenge to conventional teaching, could inspire radical course content and new teaching methods.

⋙ ✤ ⋘

When I returned from Melbourne in late 1968 and Ann and I started living together, the Sydney Free U was still going. I remember – though Ann is not sure of this memory – that one day Ann set off, her wild hair going everywhere tightly drawn back, to give a talk at the Free U. Ann can't remember what she talked about, are you sure, I keep asking; also, I didn't go with her, I don't know why, why didn't I, at the beginning of our relationship, take a keen interest in what she wanted to talk about; this doesn't look good.

However, I did take an interest in a course being put on by the film and general screen enthusiast John Flaus. Ann suggested we go. She was already urging me to become interested, as she was at Sydney University, in the French New Wave cinema, Godard, Truffaut and so on. We went to Flaus's talk and liked it very much. (So, J Docker, you wouldn't go to hear Ann talk, but showed no hesitation in going along to hear someone else.)

I've now asked Ann what she thinks of the long-ago Free U, and she has agreed to re-read her *Arena* essay and see what she thinks.

⋙ ✤ ⋘

ANN: I hadn't re-read this essay for decades, and can barely remember it, or why I wrote it. Did I volunteer it to *Arena*, or did they invite me to write it? – I don't know. So, at John's insistence, I read it again, this time as if it were written by someone else, and as if I'd never read it before. I was surprised at how critical it was of the Free U, especially the emphasis on the failure of courses, and the suggestions of 'dilettantism'.[1]

In fact, I have pleasant memories of the Free U and attending a few of their courses, though none of them very consistently. I have little flashes of memory, like seeing the novelist and playwright Dorothy Hewett there, with long frizzy hair and a bevy of young female admirers; another flash of going to a course run by the anthropologist, Ian Bedford, on Peasant Society; and especially, like John, going to a session by John Flaus where he conducted a detailed analysis of *F Troop*. I had never heard anyone take a popular television show seriously before, and it influenced both of us I think in the way we understood television thereafter.

I've always regretted not taking John Fisher's course on Male-Female relationships more seriously. At the time, I thought it was an odd thing to talk about in a university context, and didn't go, but now I think, hey, this was just before the emergence of Women's Liberation in Australia, and he was truly ahead of his time.

What strikes me now is the strength of the critique that radical staff and students were making of the modern university in 1968. And how similar these critiques are to the ones people make now of the corporate university. I quote an article in *Honi Soit* that concludes that 'the universities at present splutter as centres of research, fail as means of education, and march backwards as agents of social change'. At another point, I suggest that the drive to create a free university off campus came in part from its founders' 'feeling of the massive intractability of the University', again surely a common feeling today among disgruntled academics, especially those struggling in casual positions or on the lower rungs of the academic hierarchy.

And yet, it's complicated, as one can't help feeling that the radical hostility to universities expressed in 1968, and now, must surely be tempered by a recognition that universities have supported excellent research, valuable education and have even, over time, supported positive social change. And when they have done so, the activities of educational radicals, like those at the Free U, have helped shape university culture, teaching practices, and experience more than they, or I in my essay, could have known.

Thinking about the Free U being based in Sydney, I wonder now why there wasn't also an equivalent Melbourne Free U. Yet perhaps there very much was: *Arena* and everything associated with it, what we can call the Arena project, was sort of Melbourne's Free U, but in a very distinctive and for that matter energetically continuing way.

Perhaps inevitably, Sydney-Melbourne differences played a shaping hand.

I've written about the Arena project before, though not in relation to Sydney's Free U. In *Arena* 99/100, 1992 I wrote an essay 'The Sydney Connection: A Reflection on *Arena*'.[2] I had been asked by the editors, I explain to the reader, to try to give some kind of historical appreciation of the journal, and I begin: 'It is with great pleasure I pay tribute to *Arena* on its one hundredth issue, and gratitude, since *Arena* gave me my start in intellectual life, way back in the late sixties.' I relate that I always appreciated *Arena*'s openness to discussion and disagreement, leading to its 'generous, eclectic, pluralistic editorial policy', a platform for the 'new and different and emerging in radical intellectual life'; a 'maverick of a journal, a trickster even, always escaping the hangman, the stifling grip of usual academic genres and conventions and guarded disciplinary borders'. Then I note that 'trickster' sounds not quite right to my fanciful 'Sydney' sensibility, if trickster suggests carnivalesque mocking humour, playfulness, parody and self-parody. *Arena* has always struck me, I said, as 'very characteristically "Melbourne" in its sense of the importance of intellectuals and intellectual activity' to political and cultural life;

in tone it tended to be 'unwaveringly intense, serious, solemn'.

The intensity, I suggested, emerged from certain philosophical beliefs, a kind of metaphysics. The Arena project assumes that modern society is laid waste by alienation, anomie, impersonality, fatally abstracted social relations. What is threatened by modernity are the face-to-face relations that characterise pre-modern and non-modern societies. Yet here is a profound ambivalence for the Arena project: *Arena* itself, the journal, relies on rationality, on an intellectual mode which is necessarily a form of abstraction, life mediated and distanced by ideas, hence creating relations that are not face-to-face.

The Arena people set themselves the task of creating a 'transitional' practice, involving the creation in Victoria of a rural community, a practical community involving face-to-face relationships, which was yet financially assisted by small businesses like *Arena*'s printing press, as well as by contributions from those in the group employed as teachers in universities; Arena as a publishing project has always tried to be self-sufficient in not relying on subsidies from government, from the state, and in Arena people printing the journal themselves.

The Arena project, then, does not present itself as a pessimistic or aloof avant garde. There are affinities with the Frankfurt School, with its critiques of modernity and its demonising of the media, mass culture, the culture industry. Yet there are appreciable differences as well. For the Frankfurt School, the only forces that can stand apart from and negate a fallen modern world are high modernist art and high intellectuals themselves; since the working class has succumbed to the social conformity induced by capitalism's mass culture, there can no longer be any historical agency or 'subject' that can be the basis of hope and progress in history; all we can now pursue as the true way is an art and intellectual life directed to criticism and negation.

By contrast, for the Arena project, history is a devolution

from a paradisiac past of face-to-face community, but that past community can still perhaps be historically recovered in their utopian, or at least semi-utopian, project. Traditional non-western communities existing now are to be defended against western modernity, reminders in the present that western abstraction has not universally succeeded; Aboriginal and Melanesian communities, though so tragically threatened, continue to speak their world-historical alternative being. The Arena project's belief in its historical project of recovery of *communitas* has continuously inspired the intellectuals who come into contact with it and participate in its various activities and collectives.

The Arena project, I conclude, is an intellectual, cultural and social movement of an unusually enduring and successful kind in Australia, a tribute to the vision, energy and persistence of its founders and the vision, energy and persistence of those who have associated with and contributed to it.

I did edge in a personal note, whimsically reflecting that the Arena project's combining of intellectual activity and manual skill, brain and hand, recalls a particular English romantic and utopian tradition associated with William Morris, adding in a parenthesis: 'I am rather grateful, having a technological IQ of minus, as someone once kindly said to me, that I am a far-off Sydney contributor'.

<hr />

In Sydney together, from late 1968, Ann and I engaged in another kind of double consciousness: not only Sydney/Melbourne, but New Left/Sydney Libertarian, with varieties of anarchism the common thread. We were part of a new generation, a New Left generation, anarchistic in its own way, with no interest in any kind of hierarchical or over-arching political organisation, given to direct non-violent action in a long tradition inspired by Mahatma Gandhi and Martin Luther King Jr, and highly confident – we sometimes later wondered, where did our generation's confidence come from, why did we think we could create history anew? Yet as Sydneysiders we were also drawn to another tradition of anarchism, embodied in 1950s and 1960s Sydney Libertarian pub life and associated philosophical ideas of pluralism (reaching back to the Sydney University philosopher John Anderson in the 1930s) and especially, as we shall see, its dislike of state-imposed censorship.[3] The closest we ever came to the Libertarians, indeed to joining them, or rather being asked to join them because of this closeness, was in 1970, a fairly momentous year as it turned out, the time of the CAAC protests in Australia against film censorship, and other kinds of proliferating censorship as well; in general, protest against Australia as a censorship society.

☙ ❦ ❧

CAAC stood for Campaign for Action Against Censorship. Among my and Ann's papers that I looked in 2011 was a large oblong school project scrap book, beautifully put together by Ann, which assembled leaflets CAAC put out as part of the campaign, along with many press cuttings; the campaign immediately attracted a great deal of press attention and commentary, much of it very supportive, some, especially in the tabloid newspapers, rather hilariously not. The campaign was part of a wider movement that was becoming extremely irritated by the direct censorship of films and books that had been practised by Australian governments for decades and which intellectuals, writers, film makers and enthusiasts, publishers, journalists, booksellers, artists and galleries, theatre producers and actors, viewers and audiences, and readers felt was unnecessary and insulting, was making Australia a world laughing stock, was denying to Australia any status as an adult sophisticated society, was helping to or trying to keep it insular and isolated. As for film censorship, it could be ended by simply bringing in a classification system telling viewers if such and such a film was for adults rather than children. While

1970: A Campaign Against Censorship

CAAC was part of a much wider movement, even an insurgency, of general fury and protest, its distinctiveness lay in marrying Libertarian anti-censorship ideals with New Left non-violent direct action; also, Ann and I were directly involved in helping start CAAC. From 1968 onwards, the gathering protests across the society against censorship became increasingly intense, and by mid-1970 were successful.

Talking about it now, trying to remember so far back, Ann and I think that Campaign for Action Against Censorship came out of a conversation with Kit Guyatt, a young documentary film maker who lived in Short Street in Balmain, a long street not too far from where we lived in Carrington Street, a very short street, a cul de sac. We felt angry at continuing censorship in Australia of films we wanted to see uncut, to see whole, what can we do about it, let's do something, what about a meeting, what about a manifesto, also what about books as well as films, what about everything, what kind of society are we living in that allows this to happen.

And, it would be fair to say, the campaign immediately launched itself into almost frenzied action; as the clichés go, it hit the ground running, off to a flying start.

Item 1: Opening Ann's scrap book, the first item is indeed a kind of CAAC manifesto, referring to a plan to hold a meeting; I have absolutely no memory of how we publicised it. At this date I have no idea who knew about the Boilermakers' Hall as a place to hold meetings, and how they were contacted. It begins:

> Censorship of books and films in Australia is so extreme, so inconsistent, arbitrary, bureaucratic and inaccessible, so puritanic and parochial, and shows so little sign of reform from within, that only direct action can now be effective. For years

arguments and facts about censorship have been publicized; very recently there have been many letters of protest to newspapers. But we feel that dramatic action is necessary, particularly by the use of demonstrations and other methods of direct confrontation.

Specific suggestions are the picketing of cinemas, using placards stating to what degree the film being shown has been cut (how many minutes, etc), asking for the cut parts to be in black, and stating the responsibility of the cinema owners and distributors in the censorship system. The placards would be detailed statements; we would also be prepared to argue with cinema-goers. We hope to point out to cinema-goers the effect of censorship on the film they are about to see, and also to show how common censorship is – that it doesn't merely affect a few films, or just films at Festivals. In very bad cases, such as *100 Rifles* or *Secret Ceremony*, we could wage a boycott campaign to affect distributors economically. Demonstrations should also be staged at censors' offices.

Support for publishers and booksellers, artists and galleries, theatre producers and actors facing censorship actions, could also be expressed by various means of direct action.

Our intention is not to propose alternative forms of censorship, but to focus the public's attention on the nature and extent of the present restrictions on free expression in Australia.

A meeting will be held on Thursday 12 February to gauge support for our aims, to consider the above ideas, to gather expert information, and to discuss various forms of action. The meeting will be held at the Boilermakers Hall, 232 Castlereagh St, 7.30 pm. Very soon after, a demonstration, probably outside a cinema, will be held.

Yours sincerely, John Docker, Kit Guyatt, Julie Docker, Ann Curthoys, Pat and Ian Lennie.

Item 2: a cutting from *The Age*, 7 February 1970, in a column entitled 'Cinema' by Colin Bennett, evidently part of a newspaper campaign against film censorship and in support of an R or X classification system for adults. Bennett appeals to 'Australia's ever-growing band of mature and selective film lovers'. beginning:

> Ninety per cent of the 100 films listed above will be mutilated or banned by the Australian censor this year.
>
> This is the prediction by men in the film trade I consulted this week.

The listed films include *Bob and Carol and Ted and Alice*, *Catch 22*, *De Sade*, *Easy Rider*, *Myra Breckinridge*, *Tropic of Cancer*, *Women in Love*, *Woodstock*, and *Zabriskie Point*. Ann reminds me, she has just looked it up, that Bennett had commented earlier, in the *Age* 20 September 1969, on what he considered was a brutal act of censorship: Joseph Losey's 1968 *Secret Ceremony*, starring Elizabeth Taylor and Mia Farrow, was first banned, then released with 10 minutes hacked so the film became incomprehensible.

Item 3: CAAC, 2 Carrington Street, Balmain, 2041 NSW.

> [Two contact telephone numbers are listed, of John Docker and Julie Docker.]
>
> The first meeting of the Campaign for Action Against Censorship (C.A.A.C.) was held on Thursday 12th February at the Boilermakers' Hall. About 35 people attended. The meeting was enthusiastic and anxious to demonstrate its opposition to censorship as soon as the appropriate circumstances arose. Accordingly, the following activities have been organized.
> 1. Friday 20th February, 6 p.m. Meeting at the Boilermakers' Hall 232 Castlereagh Street, Sydney (opposite Fire Station, near Bathurst Street) to make placards and collect leaflets for:
> 2. FIRST SPECTACULAR DEMONSTRATION at

PREMIERE SCREENING of MEDIUM COOL
A film of the Chicago riots by the cameraman on *Who's Afraid of Virginia Woolf*. The 'latest piece of the Australian Film Censor's lunacy'. FRIDAY 20th February 7.15 pm outside the State Theatrette, Market St., Sydney.

3. Monday 23rd February 9.30 am. DEMONSTRATION outside court action against bookseller following police seizure of Aubrey Beardsley and Michelangelo's David posters, at the central court, Liverpool St., Sydney (near George St.).

Placards, copies of seized posters, and leaflets will be available at the demonstration. Please also try to bring your own!

4. Thursday, 26 February, 7.30 pm. GENERAL MEETING at the Boilermakers Hall to discuss past and organise future activities.

Antonioni's *Zabriskie Point* and *Easy Rider* and other likely censored films will be opening March and April.

WE ARE ASSURED OF SUPPORT AND MASS PUBLICITY. PLEASE JOIN US!

John Docker Julie Docker Michael Thornhill Anne [sic] Curthoys Ian Lennie Kit Guyatt George Molnar Frank Moorhouse Jill Roe

Item 4: This is a cutting from *Financial Review* Feb 12, 1970, under the heading of Theatre, an article by John Edwards, 'Direct protest at the cinema', much of it quotes our initial manifesto leaflet and what was said at the first meeting; Edwards, it must be confessed, was part of our drinking scene. The article, rather amused, begins:

Techniques of direct action learned in the student revolt are now, it seems, to be applied in the cultural field.

An anti-censorship group is to be established in Sydney

based on an impatient group of young writers, film producers, academics and students dissatisfied with the slow pace of liberalization in censorship and 'appalled' by what they feel to be the conservative attitudes of the new Federal Minister for Customs, Mr Don Chipp.

The group includes a young film producer, Mr Kit Guyatt and young English literature academics Mr John Docker and Mr Ian Lennie.

It is also reported to have support from emerging cultural leaders like Michael Thornhill and the experimental short-story writer, Frank Moorhouse.

Item 5: small cutting from Martin Collins Page, *Australian*, Feb, 1970 (this was when Rupert Murdoch's *Australian* was still a liberal newspaper), article headed 'Blue pencils again':

> I saw the latest piece of the Australian film censor's lunacy the other night. It was the preview of *Medium Cool* a new movie about the Chicago riots, at which the censor has had heavy hacks.
>
> Every now and then there are jumps in the film – one sequence is leaping about the screen like a firecracker as a result – where the censor has made 'language cuts'. These, I am assured by someone who saw the film in America, have excised mild swearwords.
>
> The censor has also cut the only nude scene. That is a terrible shame, because before censorship got at it, *Medium Cool* was obviously a beautiful little film.

Item 6: this must have been the leaflet we handed out at the screening, our first direct action:

> ### MEDIUM COOL
> The film you are about to see has been censored. The cuts are:
> 1. A nude-scene between the hero and his best girl-friend, where

he chases her naked round the bedroom.
2. Numerous words like 'fuck' and 'shit' are cut, making the film disjointed.

Martin Collins of *The Australian* has called the censorship of *Medium Cool* the 'latest piece of the Australian Censor's lunacy'.

Authorised by John Docker, Julie Docker, Kit Guyatt, Anne [sic] Curthoys, Ian Lennie, Michael Thornhill, George Molnar, Frank Moorhouse, Jill Roe.

Item 7: small cutting from *Sydney Morning Herald*, Sat. Feb 21 1970:

> About 35 demonstrators last night protested against censorship outside the State Theatrette, which is showing the film *Medium Cool*.
> Moviegoers were handed a sheet which listed deleted scenes and words in the film. Police attended but there were no incidents. The demonstration was the first of a series planned by a newly formed group, the Campaign for Action Against Censorship.

Item 8: cutting from *Arena*, Macquarie University's student newspaper until a name change in the early 2000s; it's a review, undated, of *Medium Cool* by Mark Butler, who had come to attend the showing of the film; the review begins:

> Incredible, here are two fat cops looking like vegetarians at a barbecue, standing in the exit door of this dingy little theatrette while I'm watching their American Big Brothers beat the living shit out of people like me in *Medium Cool*. The cops were there to 'supervise' a protest of the newly-formed Campaign for Action Against Censorship outside the theatre, the whole freaking bit, so they weren't a paranoic hallucination as I had feared.

Item 9: a one-page leaflet, quite dense, explaining CAAC's positions, opens:

> Censorship of films, books and theatre is a main form of restriction on free expression in Australia. The argument for censorship is that the community has to be protected against itself. But this argument is illusory and authoritarian. Anyone who doesn't want to see a film can stay away or walk out. Anyone who doesn't want to read a book, need not borrow or buy it. To deny anyone's freedom of choice is to deny a basic political right of the individual. Australia's insistence on forcing everyone to see and read only what has been approved by the Government, puts it in line with totalitarian countries. Books and films are censored by a central authority, which makes all its decisions in secret. The details of these decisions are not freely available to the public: willful and arbitrary decisions are handed down as edicts to be obeyed. Just as with a totalitarian country, the basic aim behind censorship is to prevent ideas coming into Australia from overseas.
>
> [After a few paragraphs:] Books, magazines and posters locally produced are subject to punitive raids by the State Vice Squads on orders from bureaucratic officials. Recently a poster of Michelangelo's David was seized from a bookshop although an enormous statue of David had been on display for weeks in David Jones [Sydney's venerable department store]. That this stupidity can be arbitrarily imposed on the community is intolerable.
>
> [Final sentence:] The Campaign for Action Against Censorship was begun in order to draw public attention to the ever-encroaching repression of Australian censorship, with the aim of immediately changing it.

Item 10: article by Michael Thornhill, Films, *The Australian*, Tuesday 24 Feb 1970:

Last week I recommended, with reservations, Haskell Wexler's movie, *Medium Cool*, about a television cameraman caught up in the 1968 Chicago riots.

In Sydney, the newly-formed Campaign for Action Against Censorship (CAAC) demonstrated outside the State Theatrette on Friday and Saturday nights as the film opened its season there.

The demonstrations were peaceful and the only incidents were the photographing of the demonstrators on Friday and the seizure on Saturday of pamphlets detailing cuts in *Medium Cool*.

The senior constable who carried out the operation said, when challenged by a lawyer who was present, that the material was obscene and he wouldn't want his teenage daughter to read it.

The distributor of *Medium Cool*, Paramount Pictures, might feel that it has been singled out unfairly… They have, through the Motion Picture Distributors Association, supported the call by Mr Chipp, the Federal Minister for Customs, for the States to introduce the 'R' certificate, which would prohibit children from seeing adult films and drastically reduce the amount of cutting and banning.

The convenor of the CAAC, a young English department academic, John Docker, wanted to begin demonstrations against film censorship immediately. He put it to the first meeting on Thursday, February 12, and *Medium Cool* was chosen, somewhat arbitrarily, as the first target.

Apart from informing the cinema-going public, the CAAC's main target was the exhibitor, Greater Union Theatres. With other cinema proprietors – except the Melbourne-based Village group – Greater Union is happy with the present state of censorship.

At present, when the censor classifies a movie as Suitable Only for Adults, most exhibitors profit by allowing in children – and charging them adult prices.

Many people are, no doubt, bored by the censorship debate, but the CAAC is determined to keep the issue before the public by continuing with demonstrations. It hopes like-minded people in Melbourne will follow suit.

Item 11: Henry Mayer, 'Speaking Freely', his regular column in *The Australian*, 26 Febuary 1970, 'The private right to have lustful thoughts'. Mayer, who had been deported from Britain along with many other exiles from Nazism on the *Dunera* in 1940 as an enemy alien, had later become well-known for his provocative pluralism; he was in the politics department at the University of Sydney. I present an abridged version here:

> To me the key issue is much simpler, basic, and in one sense cruder: I believe that I have a right to choose whether I shall be corrupted, a right to have lustful thoughts, a right to watch 'dirt' if my fancy takes me so.
>
> The case for freedom must always be argued on what you dislike most; on what, in your view, has no value whatsoever. Hence, I have always defended, and will continue to defend, what I personally object to.
>
> The reasoning behind this type of position goes back to Milton: If there is such a thing as good and evil, one must have a chance of knowledgeable choice between them. And that means a right to see and taste the 'evil' bit after you've been forewarned that someone thinks you ought to avoid it.
>
> It's good to hear that the anti-censors are now trying a bit of direct action, and that the new Campaign for Action Against Censorship (CAAC) is going in for demonstrations. They had one last week in Sydney demonstrating against cuts in the film *Medium Cool*, which deals with the Chicago riots. It's good news that a couple of filmgoers, on leaving the theatre and seeing the leaflets listing the cuts, joined the demonstrators.

CAAC is composed of young film critics, writers and academics. Let's hope it spreads from Sydney all over Australia. You can get on its mailing list by sending 50c, for postage expenses, to 2 Carrington Street, Balmain, 2041, NSW.

There is, of course, no room for extremists like myself in the day-to-day campaign: Our support would be, in practical terms, counter-productive. But there's a wide range of other activities and arguments, from the Dutton-Harris book [*Australia's Censorship Crisis*, 1970] to CAAC which proceed in a more pragmatic and less politically absurd way.

I wish all of them the best of luck. In the meantime, I don't kid myself for a moment that my position will ever win over many people.

But there it is, for better or worse.

Item 12: Ann had cut out and inserted a regular feature of the tabloid newspaper the *Mirror* 3 March 1970, a column where people asked 'Suzy' a question; a photo of Suzy accompanied the column; on this date, Suzy was in conversation with D N of Epping, in north-west Sydney, under the heading 'They're not Vandals – just smug':

[D N's letter to Suzy:]
How can I contact the Campaign for Action Against Censorship group?

I have just heard that the film *Easy Rider* has had two minutes cut. In New Zealand it has passed through uncut.

Are we less intelligent than they are, or less mature?

It all sounds crazy. Censors must be vandals at heart.

D N, Epping

[Suzy's crisp advice was in bold:]
Impossible.

They are smug wowsers with tiny minds – they have no heart.

If you send 50c for postage expenses to 2 Carrington St. Balmain 2041 this will get you on to the mailing list of the CAAC.

Item 13: cutting of an article by Chris Pritchard, 'Campaign on Film Cuts', *Sun Herald* 1 March 1970:

> A militant anti-censorship group in Sydney plans 'direct action' against films which are cut before being shown in Australia.
>
> Members of the Campaign for Action Against Censorship will consider standing up during cinema performances to announce which film segments have been cut.
>
> They will also step up their campaign outside cinemas where cut films are shown, and of giving audiences leaflets explaining what cuts have been made.
>
> Audiences attending some performances of *Medium Cool* have been given leaflets by anti-censorship campaigners.
>
> One of the convenors of the Campaign for Action Against Censorship, Mr John Docker, said this:
>
> 'Our efforts at *Medium Cool* were rather hurried.
>
> 'Our first big campaign will take place at Easter when *Easy Rider*, minus several cuts, will open in Sydney.
>
> 'We shall demonstrate outside the cinema and hope to persuade the exhibitor to show a slide saying "censored" wherever cuts have been made.
>
> 'More direct action – such as standing up and describing the cut scenes – is being considered.'
>
> Mr Docker, a university lecturer in English literature, said the group would also protest against book censorship.
>
> 'Readings from banned books will be held on university campuses.'
>
> He said the Australian 'censorship crisis' warranted a body to deal specifically with the question.

'That is why the Campaign for Action Against Censorship was formed this month.'

Looking back, I don't think anyone stood up in the cinemas during films, but maybe some CAAC people did; my memory is that we stood outside handing out the leaflets.

Item 14: Sandra Hall, *The Bulletin*, 7 March 1970, in section CUTTING EDGE. I've abridged the article:

> ... The Campaign for Action Against Censorship made a modestly impressive debut last week by changing the minds of about 20 people who were on their way in to see the film *Medium Cool* at Sydney's State Theatrette. At least the demonstrators say they counted 20 people who read one of their leaflets listing the censor's cuts in *Medium Cool*, and then decided not to go into the cinema, after all. They add that it was then that the cinema manager, who was following their activities with interest, began to look worried.
>
> CAAC picketed *Medium Cool*... on two successive nights. On the first, the police merely made sure they stood in a straight line along one wall of the cinema, but on the next night, several leaflets, which listed, among other things, the excised pieces of dialogue, were confiscated and the names of two of CAAC's members taken.
>
> This, however, is only the beginning, since March and April threaten to be lively months in the film censorship business in Sydney – with the possible arrival of the trimmed versions of *Easy Rider* and the Western *The Wild Bunch*, which has been showing in Melbourne. But CAAC's big project is a demonstration against the censorship of Antonioni's film *Zabriskie Point*, which is already rumoured to be sustaining very heavy cuts.
>
> CAAC's spokesman John Docker says that they decided

on demonstrations because they wanted to use a direct form of protest. 'I don't think the kind of indirect pressure the Humanists and the Council for Civil Liberties have been applying for years is working. And a demonstration outside a cinema is very visible. We want particularly to inform the public about the pact of secrecy between the censor and the distributor. And cinema goers do seem receptive to the idea, especially as a lot of box-office successes are being cut now, not just art films.'

CAAC was formed some weeks ago, when a group, including several academics, students, a writer, and two freelance filmmakers were discussing their mutual anger over the bans on *Portnoy's Complaint* and *Easy Rider* and the censors' clumsy cutting of the film *Secret Ceremony*. In addition to the cinema distributors, they're hoping to hold discussions and readings of banned books.

Item 15: Michael Thornhill, column 'Films', *The Australian*, 3 March 1970. Most of the column reviews Woody Allen's *Take the Money and Run*. In an additional note:

> In the past 18 months, near to 50 films have been banned outright... But... the figures often lie. Many a banned film is re-submitted after heavy cutting by the distributor, or is sent back to Hollywood for complete re-editing, or else to have some scenes replaced by tamer ones.
>
> The following films were banned, then later passed in 'reconstructed' versions (mostly, they have been emasculated): *Twisted Nerve*, *The Killing of Sister George*, *The Detective*, *100 Rifles*, *Three in the Attic* (19 minutes missing), *The Desperadoes*, *Bob and Carol Ted and Alice*, *That Cold Day in the Park*, *Dutchman*, *Masculin Feminin* [Godard]. *Secret Ceremony* may have been banned – anyway, there are sixteen minutes missing.
>
> The texts of the cuts... [are] available in *Cinema Papers*, number four, January of this year.

Banned outright: Otto Preminger's *Skidoo*, *Angel, Angel Down We Go* (starring Jennifer Jones), *Last Summer*, *Psych Out*, *Five Ashore in Singapore*, Pier Paolo Pasolini's *Teorema* (with Terence Stamp), *Girl on a Motorcycle*, *The Libertine*, *Pretty Poison* (New York critics' best screenplay award in 1969), *The Incident*, *Bofors Gun*, *The Night of the Following Day* (starring Marlon Brando), *I Love, You Love*, *Seventeen*, *Birds Come to Die in Peru* and *Navajo Joe*.

There have been numerous requests from readers about censorship reform and the local film tabloid, *Cinema Papers* [then Thornhill gives information how to be put on CAAC's mailing list, and the postal address, in North Carlton in Melbourne, of *Cinema Papers*, published twice monthly.]

Item 16: Letter to the Editor in *Cinema Papers*, St Kilda, Melbourne, 2 March 1970 concerning Project X begins:

> For many years the Australian cinema-going public has been subjected to one of the most severe and ridiculous censorship systems that exists anywhere in the civilized world.
>
> One fight will be for the introduction of the 'X' certificate in this country. This means that any film bearing the classification cannot, by law, be shown to anyone under a predetermined age.
>
> The working title of our group will be 'Project X' and we plan to picket the exhibitors who remain the main stumbling block to the introduction of this much needed piece of legislation. There will be other activities, but these will evolve as the group grows. What we need at this time is people. We need to swell our ranks to a couple of hundred (or even thousands)...
>
> We have the backing of top people in every field connected with cinema in Australia, but what we want now is the man on the street.

Item 17: *Honi Soit* 5 March 1970 reprints CAAC leaflet with its general statement on censorship of films, books and theatre as a main form of restriction on free expression in Australia in 'Censorship Campaign Commences':

> The Campaign comprises a cross section of intellectuals, radicals and people associated with the Arts: – Kit Guyatt, film director; Michael Thornhill, film reviewer; Bruce and Barrett Hodgson, film-niks; Ian McPherson and Ross Tzannes from the Sydney Film Festival; University Department Academics, George Molnar, John Docker, Jill Roe, and Michael Wilding.

Item 18: *Cinema Papers* No.8 16 March 1970 'Action Against Censorship' from Frank Moorhouse in Sydney; reproduces CAAC leaflet distributed at *Medium Cool* demonstration.

Item 19: I might interpolate something here about how we knew about the cuts. I visited David Stratton, at this time Director of the Sydney Film Festival, later a well-known film critic with Margaret Pomeranz on an SBS TV show. I think I had to go to an upper-floor office of a tall building at or near the corner of George and Market streets in the centre of Sydney's retail area, and David Stratton would tell me of the exact length of the cuts to a film we were about to stand outside, and the nature of the scene or scenes that had been cut; this was utterly invaluable information, it gave precision to what we could say on our placards and leaflets. CAAC newsletter 18 March 1970; the newsletter is entitled 'Calendar', and is three pages long:

> At the last meeting on Thursday 26 February, it was decided that our initial demonstrations outside *Medium Cool* had been successful, and that now we could prepare for bigger demonstrations. Three demonstrations are planned: for *Easy Rider*, *Zabriskie Point*, *Three in an Attic*. The biggest will be outside

Zabriskie Point and *Easy Rider*. A Festival of Banned Works at Sydney University is also planned.

The technique we have evolved so far at our four demonstrations (two outside *Medium Cool* and two outside *That Cold Day in the Park*) is to stand outside the cinema with placards, referring either to censorship in general, or to the specific film, and also to hand out leaflets. These leaflets have carried a general anti-censorship argument and explanation of what CAAC is about on one side, and a history of the length and nature of the cuts in that film on the other. We intend to continue this technique for future cut films.

The meeting also discussed again the effectiveness, apropos both the public and the exhibitors and distributors. Firstly, the public: at the *Medium Cool* demonstrations there was a remarkable lack of hostility to the demonstrators by the public and passers-by. Twenty people on the Saturday night decided not to go in after reading our leaflet. We had a similar experience at *That Cold Day in the Park* demonstrations. As a general principle regarding demonstrations, we felt that while people can be against demonstrations as such (most are), they can nevertheless be influenced by them in so far as they are forced to realize that censorship is a contentious issue. Secondly, our effectiveness will be in putting economic and political pressure on the exhibitors (cinema owners), who in turn can put pressure on the distributors (owners of the films), to put pressure on the censors.

It was also discussed whether we should have a united stand as a group. We concluded that all views in opposition to censorship can be accommodated: the one necessary unifying factor is action against censorship. This does not mean, however, that discussion concerning the whole range of anti-censorship positions will not proceed. As the organisation grows, all sorts of meetings and forums on censorship may be held. But the discussions should be seen as being for interest and education, rather than with a view to arriving at a unified campaign policy.

As a result of three press references we have received support – 120 letters at the time of writing – from all over Australia. We are hoping, therefore, to promote similar action groups in other states. Already, other groups have begun or are beginning, at Sydney University and the University of New South Wales. At the inaugural meeting of the Sydney University group, Thursday 10 March, 60 people attended. The Sydney Uni group and downtown CAAC cooperated in a demonstration against the cutting of *That Cold Day in the Park* (cut 8 minutes) on Friday 13 March.

For all the following demonstrations, bring your own placards, although some placards and also leaflets will be available at the cinema.

1. Demonstration outside *Easy Rider*, Saturday 28 March, 4.30 and 7.30 pm at the Gala, Pitt Street. A crucial scene involving discussion of drugs has been cut. We will meet between times at 6.30 p.m. Boilermakers' Hall, 232 Pitt Street, near Bathurst Street. For further enquiries, contact Kit Guyatt, 31 Short Street, Balmain, 82–0350 (home) or 46–3241 (work).
2. Glorious week-long demonstration outside *Zabriskie Point* at the Liberty, Pitt Street, adjoining the Gala… There will also be a march from Sydney University on the first day of opening, starting at 3.45 pm to the Liberty Theatre in Pitt Street. For further details contact Kit Guyatt (see above).
3. *Three in an Attic*. 15 ½ minutes cut; including love-making scenes of black woman and white man. Again, see papers for opening: we will demonstrate the first Friday night. Film is on at the Roma, George Street. Contact Jill Roe, 88–9316.
4. Gala Evening: Festival of Banned Works on Wednesday 8 April at 8pm at Sydney University. Discussions and examples of banned novels, records, magazines, etc. It is planned that there will be more than one evening. If you are interested in

participating, contact SUCAAC at the SRC Office, Sydney University.

So far our interest has centred on film censorship. This does not mean that we are not interested in all forms of censorship. The SUCAAC has begun preparing information on book censorship, and the proposed Festival of Banned Works is aimed at all forms of censorship. In the near future, we may have to consider supporting student newspapers, coming under attack.

For Interstate Correspondents

About half of those who wrote to us after our address was published by Henry Mayer live outside Sydney. As you can see from above, we are concentrating on local action. Therefore we suggest the best thing is for people in each area to form their own groups.

QLD. Write to Queensland University Committee on Censorship, c/– English Department, Queensland University, St. Lucia, Brisbane. Another group, more interested in direct action, may be formed later.

TAS. Write to Ross Johns, 31 Silwood Avenue, Howrah, 7018.

NEWCASTLE, A.C.T., W.A., SA. There have been replies from all these areas. We are now in the process of finding someone in each state prepared to convene an initial meeting. We will then send our list of interested people to that person…

Other publications and information

1. Student newspapers.
2. Censorship News: published by Queensland Uni. Committee on Censorship.
3. The Council for Civil Liberties, 363 Pitt Street, Sydney.

4. *Australia's Censorship Crisis*, ed. Dutton and Harris, Sun Books.
5. Michael Thornhill's regular column in *The Australian*.
6. *Cinema Papers* (246 Richardson St. Nth Carlton, 3054).
7. *Australasian Book Review* eds. Harris and Wighton (27 Park Road, Kensington Park, SA. 5068).

Item 20: *The Australian* Friday, 20 March 1970 had an article by Kenneth Randall, protesting at the censorship of Easy Rider after he had seen the uncut version in San Francisco, and Michael Thornhill, 'Easy Censor', *The Australian* Friday, 20 March 1970:

> ... late last year the Film Censorship Board banned it. [Columbia Pictures appealed, and 'the appeal censor, after a couple of cliff-hanging months, released *Easy Rider*, with cuts, in February'.]

Item 21: *Sydney Morning Herald* 23 March 1970 'Censor cuts 25 films' Letter to the Editor from David J Stratton, Director, Sydney Film Festival:

> SIR, – I was extremely surprised to read A. R. Payne's letter (March 16) on the cutting of the film *100 Rifles*.
>
> Mr Payne says the version of the film released in Australia running 108 minutes has not had 'a large portion deleted by the censor', since the original American running time was 110 minutes. I will argue that two minutes cut from the film does represent a large deletion; but worse than that, Mr Payne's information is totally incorrect. When I saw *100 Rifles* earlier this year in a Sydney theatre I timed it with a stopwatch to a running time of exactly 100 minutes, which thus represents a massive 10-minute deletion.
>
> Since January 1 this year I have seen 37 feature films on first release either in Sydney or Melbourne. I timed each one, and compared the times with American or English film trade

information. Twenty-five had been cut – from a matter of two or three seconds in one film to an alarming 15 minutes in another. The average length of cuts was approximately four minutes.

Every film of serious intent has suffered cuts. The films to escape unscathed were such films as *Squeeze a Flower*, *The Brain*, *The Italian Job* and *On her Majesty's Secret Service*.

Item 22: *The Australian* 28 March 1970, small item by Greg Lentham, 'Kindly leave when depravity sets in':

Perhaps the activities of the militant students on the battlements of Sydney University were diversionary tactics aimed at screening more serious business.

While that rumpus was going on, down below in the corridors of the SRC offices 'A Night of Banned Works' was being planned by the SUCAAC, the Sydney University arm of the downtown Campaign for Action Against Censorship.

On the blue night – Wednesday night – the admission-free entertainment will include pornographic slides, a Lesbian scene from the Italian play *Venetian Things*, revue sketches, and readings from banned works graduated 'in order of shock value', from Noddy upwards. (Noddy books, you may remember, were banned by a Melbourne Municipal Library.)

'The readings have to be from photostats, otherwise the works could be seized as prohibited imports', explains one of the organizers.

'We don't want any seizures. We're not inviting prosecution or trying to test the law. The evening is an excursion into democracy, an experiment with the notion of self-censorship.'

The audience at the university's Wallace Theatre will be 'warned' about the nature of the material being presented and be invited to leave whenever they feel themselves in imminent danger of becoming depraved or corrupted.

The Vice Squad permitting, the group is prepared to organise other similar nights. 'But then perhaps we won't have to. Perhaps we'll find out we don't really like this sort of stuff.'

... the CAAC group has written to the Minister for Customs, Mr Chipp, and the 249 people on its mailing list, inviting them to join two demonstrations tonight.

The demonstrations will be held outside the Sydney theatres showing *Easy Rider* and *Zabriskie Point*, in protest against the cuts made to the films.

Item 23: two leaflets concerning *Easy Rider* and *Zabriskie Point*, and general CAAC and SUCAAC aims, all in block letters, were handed out outside cinemas. The first:

Easy Rider was initially banned outright by the Australian censor. After appeal it has now been cut by about four minutes. Two sequences have been cut 'significantly'. One is a lesson in marijuana smoking to a young alcoholic lawyer by the two easy riders, making the point that 'one man's poison is not necessarily another's'. 'Without the emphasis it had in the uncensored version, the sequence overall is less amusing, even a little tedious. The second series of cuts has done some unfortunate things to the 'trip' sequence in a New Orleans graveyard (where the riders) with two girls from the city's plushest brothel freak out on L.S.D.' One of the girl's 'first reactions is to take off all her clothes (giving) an underlying eroticism to the fear and desperation'. This girl 'has disappeared from the entire sequence, except for two fleeting, murky and quite incomprehensible shots'.

From: 'Easy Censor' by Kenneth Randall, who saw the uncut version in San Francisco.(*The Australian* Friday March 20, 1970)

Zabriskie Point is one of very few films which the distributor has admitted has been cut in Australia. According to MGM 'the censor cut certain close-ups of threesomes engaged in a sexual orgy. No dialogue was cut at all.' It is also significant that the word 'fuck', never before heard in a film sound track in Australia, has not been censored. Again, according to the distributor, 'only 62 seconds have been cut overall'. But why has the film been cut at all? And how do we know whether the distributor is even telling the truth, when no official details of censorship action are made public?

These demonstrations will continue at 7 every night up to and including Saturday, 4th April.

Wednesday, 8th April, 8 p.m. Wallace Theatre, Sydney University. Festival of Banned Works. A discussion of censorship with presentation of banned literature and photographs. The programme will be arranged in order of 'ascending shock value' so that the audience may censor themselves by leaving after they have been sufficiently offended. Admission free.

Second leaflet, also in block letters, handed out on same occasion:

... As overseas standards are liberalised, the Australian censor has been forced into censoring and banning so many books and films that the essential stupidity is becoming more and more apparent.
... Books are similarly subject to authoritarian restrictions. Imported books – including Australian books printed in Hong Kong – are banned in secret by customs clerks... Books, magazines and posters locally produced are subject to punitive raids by the state vice squads on orders from bureaucratic officials.

Please Join Us.

Item 24: *Daily Telegraph* Tuesday, 31 March 1970 'Protests on Censor's Film Cuts':

> Demonstrators yesterday afternoon protested outside two city cinemas about cuts in the films *Zabriskie Point* and *Easy Rider*.
> ... The Leader of the Opposition in the Senate (Senator Murphy) and his wife were among the crowd outside the theatre.
> Demonstrators handed pamphlets on censorship to people in the crowd.
> ... At yesterday's demonstration members of CAAC held placards reading 'Sex-Starved-Scissor-Happy-Censor', and 'You will not be depraved inside this cinema'.
> 'CAAC does not have a policy of its own, but provides a catalyst for all people opposed to censorship', Mr K. Guyatt, a freelance film-maker and spokesman for the group, said.
> ... The Sydney University CAAC group plans a 'Festival of Banned Works' at the Wallace Theatre, Sydney University, next week.
> Organisers hope people will bring their own material to the festival.
> This is expected to include selections from Rochester's *The Imperfect Enjoyment*, Norman Mailer's *Why Are We in Vietnam?* and the ballad *Eskimo Nell*.
> Other items are *Flossie, A Venus of Fifteen*, *Portnoy's Complaint*, and extracts from the Marquis de Sade.

Item 25: *The Australian* Monday, 30 March 1970, with photo of young people holding up placards reading CENSORED WHY?, 'You are paying to see a censored film!' and 'This film has been emasculated'. Caption to photo: Some Demonstrators of the Campaign for Action Against Censorship carried placards outside two Sydney picture theatres on Saturday night, picture by Peter Levy. Article by Michael Thornhill, '60 demonstrate over censor's cuts at 2 cinemas':

About 60 people from the Campaign for Action Against Censorship demonstrated outside the Sydney screenings of *Zabriskie Point* and *Easy Rider* on Saturday evening.

... The demonstrators carried placards with slogans like 'You are paying to see a censored film', '*Easy Rider* – the totalitarian censor has cut 4 minutes', 'Don't alow [sic] the censor to rob you of your individual rights' and 'Why allow a clerk in the Customs Department to dictate what you may see?'

COMPENSATION

The demonstrators handed out leaflets detailing cuts from both films. Many cinema patrons stopped to read them.

The most vocal protesters were Mr M. Syme, a barrister, and Mr F. Moorhouse, a short-story writer. Both suggested that movie-goers ask for a reduction in admission prices to compensate for the cuts.

... Next door at the Liberty cinema the management looked more worried. Although business was brisk most patrons knew that *Zabriskie Point* had been cut before they bought their tickets.

Item 26: 'Distributors are as bad as censors, says Phil', *The Australian* 4 April 1970, article accompanied by a photo of a young bearded 'Mr Phil Noyce'. We can picture here a very young Phil Noyce, the future director of *Rabbit Proof Fence* and Hollywood films like *Patriot Games*:

> According to Phil Noyce of the Sydney University Campaign for Action Against Censorship (SUCAAC), the film distributors... are the agents of the censors because they suppress information about the cuts made in films, he said.
>
> ... However, while the Sydney University group is actively involved in protests against film censorship, their interests cover a much wider field.

Through sub-committees composed of both staff and students, SUCAAC is also investigating political and literary censorship.

... Their preliminary findings are being published in *Honi Soit* each week.

[Phil Noyce:] '...do the students at Sydney University know that a Customs clerk makes regular visits to check on the books in Fisher Library?'

... *Honi Soit* is threatened with legal action over the publication of an article on incest.

Mere mention of the incident made Phil's hackles rise.

[Phil Noyce:] '*Honi Soit* was criticized in Parliament because of a word used in an article on incest. The author, Patsi Dunn, was threatened with a summons.

'Yet anyone in Sydney can go and hear the word being used in the film *Zabriskie Point*.

The Festival of Banned Works

Item 27: *Sunday Mirror* 5 April 1970 'Pornography Show at Uni – Letting public judge':]

Pornographic film slides and reading from prohibited books will be featured in a Festival of Banned Works at Sydney University next Wednesday night.

... Spokesmen for the festival organisers said this week that pornographic slides from Scandinavian countries would be shown.

... Students might act out scenes from a banned French play.

Item 28: *Arena*, Macquarie University student magazine, 7 April 1970 'Porno for the people':

This [the Festival of Banned Works] will be the first of many such evenings... which in the words of John Docker, one of the founders of the group (and a staff member at Macquarie) 'will get more and more pornographic as the night progresses'. They hope to have soirées such as this at all universities, and 'if Macquarie gets a group we'll all get to indulge in some porn…'

Item 29: *Sydney Morning Herald* Thursday, 9 April 1970 '2,500 at banned books festival'. This is the first report, but very much not the last, of the instantly notorious evening, which we might say turned out to be carnivalesque, creating a chaos of values, interpretations and experiences:

> A surging crowd of 2,500 crammed the Wallace Theatre at the University of Sydney last night for a Festival of Pornography.
> … The program included readings from banned books and the screening of banned slides.
> Two women fainted and were carried out of a screaming, shouting crowd which pushed into the already packed auditorium.
> Inside the theatre even the stage was covered with people, mostly students.
>
> THE SMITHS
>
> The readers of extracts from banned literature were introduced as 'Alphonse Smith', 'Oscar Smith', and so on.
> As the contents of the program steadily mounted in pornographic intensity the audience was advised to leave if they wished to. All it did was laugh.
> The first of banned excerpts to be presented on photostatted sheets, was one from the Marquis de Sade's writings.
> Next, after some disturbance in the crowd, came a reading from Norman Mailer's *The American Dream*.
> A reading of a sado-masochistic work, 'Image', followed.
> This was greeted with general applause and one loud cry of 'Ugh'.

Item 30: *Sun*, 9 April 1970. The *Sun* along with the *Mirror* were the two daily tabloids in Sydney. The article was accompanied by a photo, of young people, including young women, smiling and laughing:

A Dirty Night at Sydney University
More than 2,500 Sydney University students last night attended a 'festival of pornography' held in the Wallace Theatre.

... Highlight of the 'festival', if judged on applause, was a series of filthy Scandinavian colour slides.

These depicted nude young girls and men performing acts of depravity and closeups of male and female sexual organs.

They also featured an exhibition by two lesbians.

A series of readings which graduated from fairly mild pornography to hard-core filth were well received by the audience.

2 FAINTED

Students whistled, clapped and yelled for more.

One reader of a bawdy poem was accorded a standing ovation.

Descriptions of every kind of sexual depravity were read.

Young girls formed about 40 per cent of the audience. [Ann and I doubt very much that so many young women were in the audience.]

Few seemed shocked by what they saw and heard, but two girls fainted and were carried out.

Throughout the readings there were continual interruptions as cat-calling students turned the affair into a display of vulgarity and filth.

Eventually the students became bored by the continual recital of debaucheries and began a slow handclap.

This stopped when the organisers began showing the imported colour slides.

For more than an hour and a half four members of the Vice

Squad sat motionless in the theatre.

They made no attempt to intervene.

The students themselves seemed surprised that the detectives took no action.

Item 31: *Mirror*, 9 April 1970:

> ... more than 1500 people were crowded into the theatre, which has a normal capacity of 800.
>
> ... A senior lecturer in philosophy at the university... 'We want you to make your own decisions' [to leave at any time] he said.
>
> ...Masochism, sadism, four letter words, lesbianism, homosexuality, torture and sexual fetishes were dealt with in great detail by readers who all seemed to share the common name of Smith.
>
> ... The Chief Secretary, Mr Willis, said today no members of his department were at the theatre.
>
> The matter was not a public entertainment and need not necessarily concern him, he said.

Item 32: *Sydney Morning Herald*, 10 April 1970: 'No action planned on Uni display'. By John O'Hara:

> The Chief Secretary, Mr E.A. Willis, is planning no action against the Festival of Pornography at Sydney University.
>
> ... Mr Willis said no member of his department – which is responsible for policing the laws governing obscenity and indecency – was present at the festival in an official capacity.
>
> Four members of the C.I.B. Vice Squad attended the festival. It is understood they made copious notes, and are working on a report for the chief of the C.I.B., Detective Super-intendent R. Lendrum.

Item 33: Front page *Sun*. 10 April 1970 DIRTY FILMS AT UNI. Charges Likely: The article mentions that the Vice-Chancellor of Sydney University is Professor Bruce Williams:

> As many as 50 students may be suspended by Sydney University for their part in last month's siege. [this must refer to some kind of student action independent of the censorship campaign]
> Several others who organized an exhibition of pornographic film slides at the university on Wednesday night might face prosecution by the police.

Item 34: Article by Mungo MacCallum in *The Australian*, 11 April 1970 scornful of the Customs Minister Mr Chipp holding a 'small screening at the National Library of the things he feels would offend current community standards'. Chipp had invited members of parliament, the parliamentary press gallery, a few film critics, some film distributors and exhibitors, 'and – inevitably – church authorities'.

Item 35: *Sydney Morning Herald*, 14 April 1970, reported that at the showing of censored scenes at the National Library, Mr Chipp had said: 'I believe that censorship as a philosophical concept is undesirable.' Evan Williams in 'Mr Chipps's little show', wrote that Chipp was attempting to demonstrate that censorship is a 'necessary evil'. 'If the evening proved anything it proved the absolute and pressing need for a system of 'R' or 'X' certificates which would restrict certain films to people over 18.'

Item 36: undated letter from Jill Hellyer, secretary of the Australian Society of Authors, protesting that the Australian Broadcasting Commission had cancelled a radio program, a speech by Anthony Burgess on censorship: 'The refusal of the ABC to broadcast a public talk on censorship bears out the widely expressed view of visiting authors and intellectuals that our censorship makes us the laughing stock of the world.'

Item 37: *The Australian* 15 April 1970, news report 'Chipp Will Reconsider Film Cuts':

> The Minister for Customs, Mr Chipp, will reconsider his department's decision to cut two overseas experimental films bought by the National Library... after receiving a petition of protest signed by about 60 film students.
> ... Mr A. S. Cantrill, who presented the petition, said last night that Mr Chipp was reconsidering the censor's verdict.
> Mr Cantrill has a creative arts fellowship at the Australian National University in Canberra. He and his wife recommended a list of avant-garde films to the National Library.

Item 38: [two items in *The Australian* Wednesday April 15 1970, by Katharine Brisbane and Michael Thornhill]

[Katharine Brisbane, Theatre column, 'Does it shock the judge?', expresses concern that charges of obscenity are being directed at a stage performance in Melbourne]

> The *Boys in the Band* case, with three actors on the same charge, finally ended on March 23 with their conviction being upheld on appeal. And this despite any complaint from the public...
> It is now unlikely that *Hair* will visit Melbourne unless some way of circumventing arrest is found.
> The *Oh, Calcutta!* case was equally badly managed by the law. The production proceeded almost to opening night before legal action was taken and the show was condemned unseen on the basis of the New York script.

[Michael Thornhill, 'The censor shows his hand', reflects on Chipp's showing of the censor's cuts to a select audience in Canberra]

> ... Mr Chipp boxed himself into a corner when he said that films shouldn't offend 'average community standards'...
> Part of the difficulty here is that serious works of art often set out to offend 'average community standards'.
> [Thornhill is pessimistic that despite noises about reform within the Customs Department, nothing is changing: '... the censors' cuts in *Zabriskie Point*, *Satyricon*, the new Harold Robbins' movie *The Adventurers* and *Last Summer* suggest that it is snip go the shears as before.']

Item 39: *Honi Soit* report 16 April 1970, 'Pornography in Wallace Theatre' by David Hare:

> ... the show got under way a few minutes after eight when the redoubtable George Molnar emerged from the wings, waded through a morass of bodies on the stage... The first reader, a delightful frail girl in black, announced as 'Genevieve Smith', read the dedication from de Sade's *Philosophy in the Bedroom* (urging the reader to aspire and realize the supreme heights of lust and lubricity), followed by another member of the 'Smith' family, who boomed out a majestic passage from Mailer's *American Dream*.
> The high point of the night was one 'Alphonse Smith' who read, in an immaculate, fruity Dylan Thomas voice, and with the bell-like, impeccably enunciated tones of a parent telling its child a fairy-tale, an incredibly lascivious piece from an anthology of Victorian underground porno called *The Pearl*, spicing his reading with some of the most pregnant pauses heard on a Sydney stage in many years.
> [There were 'raucously vocal exclamations of delight'.]

[Also: readings of Genet's 'beautiful Our Lady of the Flowers', Sade's *Justine*, *Last Exit to Brooklyn*, *The Image*, dirty poems, a playlet from *Oh! Calcutta!* and other erotic treasures.]

… the audience appeared to relish a night of genuinely dirty stuff (the wildly exotic Scandinavian colour slides laid them in the aisles, metaphorically if not physically)…

One wishes Mr Chipp had been there. (He was issued an invitation by the organizer, C.A.A.C., but failed to reply).

Item 40: *The Bulletin* 18 April 1970 report on Wallace Theatre Festival of Pornography, 'Four-letter words in living colour':

'I wish there were more girls here', one of the organisers of Sydney's Festival of Pornography was saying with rather understated apprehension. 'There seems to be a number of ape-like young men around.'

He was speaking from the stage of the University of Sydney's Wallace Theatre, which, at that point, was holding a swelling, swaying crowd of 2000… It now looked as if departure before the end of the show was a physical impossibility.

There was a bit of Mailer, passages from *Why Are We in Vietnam?* which is banned outright in Australia, and a few more from the American edition of *American Dream* (we're allowed to read only the English [edition] one). Alphonse Smith (who looked suspiciously like short-story writer Frank Moorhouse) entered with a case of Tooth's [beer], from which he took occasional pulls between his reading of some Grove Press sado-masochism.

… the hit of this part of the program was a tutor in Adult Education who was introduced as Marmaduke Smith and read an extract from the Victorian underground magazine called *Pearl*. The episode involved two ladies, one gentleman and a dildo, and Mr Smith read it in a nicely fastidious Victorian manner. 'What delightful sensations I experienced', was one line.

Audience interest seemed to flag after that, although a full-blooded extract from Henry Miller's *Sexus* was popular, as was an Australian bush ballad called 'The Bastard from the Bush'.

... the evening's *pièce de resistance* [was] some Scandinavian colour slides in clinical close-up....

Those scheduled to read directly before the slides didn't fare too well against a sudden burst of hissing and slow hand-clapping, as anticipation built up again – just as it had at the start of the show. But once the slides began, the same thing happened – excitement turned into amusement or a kind of dispassionate interest.

Item 41: leaflet in yellow by CAAC 20th April 1970:

Recent activities of the Campaign for Action Against Censorship have been:-

1. Demonstrations outside *That Cold Day in the Park*. Many people were turned away, it worried the Liberty.
2. Week long demonstrations from March 28 to April 4 outside *Easy Rider* and *Zabriskie Point*, at the adjacent Gala and Liberty theatres in Pitt Street. 5000 leaflets were handed out explaining the details and effects of the cuts... There was favourable TV, radio and press coverage.
3. Festival of Banned Works, Sydney University, April 8. 2,500 attended readings of banned works, and banned pornographic slides. Again, there was considerable mass media coverage.

FUTURE PLANS

1. Meeting
   CAAC has arrived at a point where there is considerable discussion and some disagreement over what should be done next... We are searching for new ideas... Should we be considering political censorship, and if so, how? How can we support editors liable to prosecution?

These ideas will be discussed at a general meeting of all people interested in C.A.A.C. on Thursday 14 May, at the Boilermakers Hall, 232 Castlereagh St....

Meanwhile the following activities are already being planned.

2. High School Leafletting
The recent authoritarian action by headmasters in suppressing debate [in] high schools over Vietnam has highlighted the way censorship operates in the education system. We have therefore decided to leaflet a number of high schools this Friday, 24 April. Contact John Docker, phone 889373. Leaflets will be available at 2 Carrington Street, Balmain, on Thursday night.

3. Lunchtime Demonstration
On first Friday of *Three in the Attic* outside censor's office, Imperial Arcade, 1–2 pm.

4. Cinema Picketing
Friday night outside *Three in the Attic*, Roma Theatre, George Street. 7pm.

5. Festival of Banned Works at University of N.S.W. For information contact S.U.C. at University of N.S.W.

6. A C.A.A.C. group has been established at the University of New South Wales. Contact Andrew Jakubowicz, Sociology Dept.

7. A Centre for information re book censorship has been established at Sydney University by George Molnar, Philosophy Dept.

8. Frank Pacey, 1 Hazelwood Place, Epping, is establishing a debating and discussion group on Censorship. Write or ring 865841 after 6pm.

OUTSIDE SYDNEY

1. Melbourne

 Mr and Mrs C.A. Burgess (Unit 3, 10 Auburn Grove, Hawthorn, 3122) have said they are willing to establish a C.A.A.C. group in Melbourne.

2. Brisbane

 An action group may also be forming in Queensland. Queensland readers could contact Trevor Wilson, Hon. Sec. Uni of Queensland Film Group.

Item 42: Julie Docker, *Union Recorder*, 22 April 1970:

HELP THE SMITH FAMILY [play on name of a well-known Australian charity]

What a night! The Festival of Banned Works on Wednesday, 8th April...

I pushed myself in by the side-door and climbed behind the curtains on the stage. The scene was tremendous! Thousands of bodies everywhere and all to listen to some readings and look at a few slides – there were hundreds who couldn't get in.

Because of this crowd and the predominantly male self-conscious aggressive attitude, the atmosphere was the most brutal and terrifying I have ever witnessed.

... it was only when Alphonse Smith read from 'Image' and the audience laughed that the audience diffused and finally became sympathetic.

In the beginning they hung on to every swear-word, every

sexual description and fantasy, but later the audience judged the material on its reading, i.e. they became more sophisticated and eventually became bored by 1½ hours of reading passages (a really good proof against censorship, Mr Chipp). The slides shocked, probably because it was the first time people had been confronted by them in a large mixed crowd...

... Radicals say that the Anti-Censorship Campaign is reformist, diversionary and safe, but this is not necessarily so.

It illuminates authoritarian bureaucratic secrecy, it is a valid issue in itself, it forces the enemy to defend itself openly and a lack of censorship is fundamental to any free society.

Item 43: CAAC leaflet, in yellow, undated. Note the Moratorium demonstrations against the American war in Vietnam occurred on 8, 9 and 10 May 1970, held to coincide with anti-war protests in the US, days after the killing of four students at Kent State. In the Moratorium demonstration in Melbourne on 8 May there were over 100 000 people; across Australia, there were 200 000 people. The second Moratorium was held in September 1970.]

CENSORSHIP IN SCHOOLS

The Campaign for Action Against Censorship strongly objects to the actions of those school principals who have prevented teachers and students from wearing Vietnam Moratorium badges and from making Moratorium information available to others.

Whether one supports the Moratorium or not, it is clear that these examples of repressive personal dealing amount to political censorship...

... In general, the authoritarian insistence on short hair and a grey uniformity is an attempt to prevent any diversity in styles of personality and social behaviour... to be forcibly kept unaware of any other values, experience, life-styles or political beliefs.

Such paternalism is both insulting and relies on a strict system of censorship.

... The individual has the right to see, read, hear or discuss anything he [hhhmmm, 'he': no impact here of contemporary feminist movement] wants to, whether inside or outside school.

Item 44: *Arena*, Macquarie University student paper, 28 April 1970, article by John Docker, School of English:

> RED PLUS BLUE EQUALS CHANGE – J. Docker
> ... Modern radicals can see that the record of socialism concerning censorship has been disastrous, but they are unable to relate this realization to an understanding of Australian society. While it is readily seen that opposition to the Vietnam War involves one in a wider analysis of capitalist society in general, it seems radicals in Australia still work on a strict hierarchy of political importance. Insufficient allowance is made for the diversity of fronts on which to attack Australian capitalism, so as to establish a necessary and vital pluralism which could then continue after the desired revolution.
>
> Their dismissal indicates that Australian radicals look only to America for revolutionary concerns and methods. Anti-Vietnam [war] interest, in Australia, for instance, is obviously dependent on a high level of anti-Vietnam activism in America. Women's Liberation is another movement taken over as a blue-print from the American example. Australian radicals tend to be derivative: yet American radicals are so absorbing because their radicalism depends on very specific analyses of American society and history. The anti-corporate attack, black and white relations, the history of American liberalism and its associated expansionism, the examinations of the American Dream and its related ideals of personality and social life (the Liberal emptiness, the western myth, the concept of the American male as motherfucker)

– all these analyses are so new and inclusive because they are so specifically American.

If censorship is not a key concern in America, radicals here aren't interested in it. However, if specific analyses were made by radicals of Australian cultural patterns, of our own particular liberal and frontier myths and the ideals of personality entailed by them, then censorship would be seen as fundamental to Australian history.

Australian society is made up of an isolationist community of predominantly Anglo-Saxon whites. Historically it has been obsessed with preserving its European ideals and institutions intact; these ideals and institutions are habitually defined against those of other races and cultures which either surround Australia or, like the Aborigines, were once meaningfully in it. Racism is inherent in Australia's idea of itself.

In insisting on a single identity for the community as against other cultures, Australia has never encouraged any kind of pluralism of ideas, or any effective liberal tradition of the individual's right to anything he [!] wants to see and read…

… Just as the White Australia policy physically keeps out people who offend against the Australian ideal of racial purity, the role of censorship is to keep out ideas and ideologies which might establish for the individual in Australia a plurality of values and life-styles from which to choose. These ideals are kept out because they are considered politically subversive, or because they deal with sex and violence, potentially anarchic forces.

Australian censorship, then, is directly political. To break this censorship must be part of any general aim to break the paternalistic style of government, to lessen nationalism as a political force, and to establish a great individualism in social behaviour.

… Much of this came out at the recent Festival of Banned Works at Sydney University (April 8). In many ways the evening must have been educative. The audience consisted mainly of men, many of them non-students...

... In the main the audience were too over-excited to listen for the first half-hour. After that [they] settled down, became attentive, began to applaud and laugh with the readers. This must also have been educative: it became clear during the evening that there were varied kinds of pornography and sexual fantasy, and that a lot of it, heard freely... was simply funny and enjoyable in its own right. The free pornography created a normalizing situation, so much so that within an hour and a half the audience was bored with the readings, and demanded the slides. But with these, too, they became bored; the shock-value of porno for the audience was measurably low.

In some of the porno, the actual style of sexual relationship described cut across the stereotype of sexual relationship implied by the sub-culture. [By sub-culture, J Docker meant, described before in the article, a 'whole sub-culture' of conventional Australian men that included distribution of pornographic material and a network of blue movies.] In Australian cultural patterns the dominant, aggressive role of the male is emphasized, with a corresponding role of sexual passivity for the women. The end result of such passivity is that the woman becomes a sexual object. However, the Victorian porno from *The Pearl*, for example, suggested that the woman... was hugely enjoying herself, and that her sexual role was quite active.

Item 45: *Pix* 2 May 1970, The Jim Oram Column, 'Packed in For Pornography'; *Pix* was a large-format popular magazine with stories accompanied by lots of photos. For this article there was a photo of two policemen with an organiser discussing the event. Another photo was captioned: 'Photographs of obscene slides, too shocking to print, were destroyed in the offices of *Pix*, the photo of cut-up prints, or purported cut up prints:

We were waiting for the start of Australia's first Festival of Pornography. For the sake of future historians, it began at 8.03 pm...

The show promised us such erotica as readings from banned books, excursions into hardcore pornography, blasphemy, sadism and masochism and, as a finale, a collection of colour slides showing adventurous and imaginative sexual acts.

The show... worked as its organisers hoped it would. It showed pornography to be a joke but mostly a bore.

... A piece of sado-masochistic hard-core pornography from France called 'Image'.

The Pearl was next. This was an underground paper printed in the Victorian era and recently reprinted by Grove Press.

Item 46: Commemoration Day *Honi Soit* 6 May 1970, a three-page spread. Members of the Sydney University Campaign for Action Against Censorship have compiled the following information explaining all aspects of film censorship. Head and first sentence:

> CLICK GO THE SCISSORS
> A GUIDE TO FILM CENSORSHIP IN AUSTRALIA

During the first three months of this year, 27 of 35 feature films released in Sydney theatres have been cut by the censor. It is estimated that approximately three in four films imported into Australia are censor-cut. [A select list of banned and cut films follows.]

Item 47: In her scrap book Ann includes a special supplement to *Tharunka*, the University of New South Wales student newspaper, focusing on anti-censorship, which included writers and critics such as Frank Moorhouse, who introduced the supplement, as well as Michael Dransfield, Thomas Keneally, Thomas Shapcott, J

Riviere Morris, Michael Wilding, A D Hope, Frank Hardy, Buzo, Robert Adamson and Peter Mathers.

Item 48: [*Sydney Morning Herald* 12 May 1970, '"Blue" show at university':]

> A Festival of Banned Works is to be held on the library lawn of the University of N.S.W. tonight.
>
> 'The police have threatened to arrest everyone concerned', a spokesman for the Campaign for Action Against Censorship, which is arranging for the free festival, said yesterday.

Item 49: CAAC leaflet concerning *Three in an Attic*, plus general reflections on censorship:

> The film you are about to see has been cut by just over 15 minutes. This is an extraordinary amount of viewing time to lose.
>
> The cuts are almost too numerous to list.
>
> They involve:
> 1. Extensive cuts of dialogue throughout the film.
> 2. A love-scene between a black woman and the white hero. This sequence between black and white people has been especially heavily censored: the cuts represent a clear example of racism by the Australian censors.
>
> *Three in an Attic* is the worst cut film ever to enter Australia. The film is so badly cut it would be useless to see it.

Item 50: *Daily Telegraph*, 16 May 1970:

> CHURCH DECISION ON CENSORSHIP
>
> The General Assembly of the Presbyterian Church decided last night that Australia's censoring authorities should be made to justify any decision to cut a book or film.

Item 51: *The Australian* Saturday, 10 May 1970:

> CUTS GO BACK IN CENSORED FILMS
> Two overseas experimental films bought by the National Library and cut by Australian censors, have had the cuts restored.
> The Minister for Customs, Mr Chipp, decided to overrule his department's decision after talks with library officers.
> … Mr Chipp wrote to Mr Cantrill yesterday advising him of his decision.

Item 52: Front page *Sydney Morning Herald*, 6 June 1970:

> Police were called to Ibrox Park Boys' High School at Leichhardt [in inner western Sydney] yesterday when teachers clashed with representatives of the teachers' Moratorium group handing out leaflets to students.
> For the past month, Ibrox Park School has been a centre of controversy over the right of its students to wear Moratorium badges.
> One of the leaflet distributors, Miss Cathy McDonald, a Teachers' Federation official, said later she had not expected such a violent reaction.

[Three teachers, including a Mr Bradford Caffrey, a mathematics teacher, snatched the leaflets and tore them up.]

Item 53-: *Sydney Morning Herald*, 9 June 1970:

> 'MPS TO SEE BANNED FILMS'
> The Minister for Customs, Mr D. L. Chipp, said tonight he had arranged a special showing of two films banned from screening at the Sydney Film Festival.

'CORRECT'

> The films are *Like Night and Day*, from Sweden... and *A Married Couple* from Canada...
>
> Mr David J. Stratton, director of the Festival, said last night he understood 'A Married Couple' had been rejected solely because of strong language.
>
> ... Mr Chipp said tonight he believed the board's decisions were correct.
>
> ... Mr Chipp said the board had not banned the films outright but festival authorities had said they would not show a film which been cut in any way.

Item 54: *The Australian*, 9 June 1970, concerning two festival films banned by the censor:

> ... Mr Stratton said before last night's session of the festival it was ludicrous to prevent an adult audience from seeing films of quality uncut.

Item 55: *The Australian*, 9 June 1970, Michael Thornhill, 'Reactionary forces joining to hound the innocent':

> ... On duty outside the Century cinema the Melbourne Campaign for Action Against Censorship... was protesting against the 648 ft, or 7 min 12 sec missing from Frank Perry's new film, *Last Summer*.
>
> ... If, as Mr Chipp's department suggested recently, the Press has published inaccurate information about the censor cuts, this has been entirely due to the fact that such information was withheld by the censors, the distributors and the exhibitors.

Item 56: *Sydney Morning Herald* 10 June 1970, 'Leaflet protest again at High school:

> Supporters of the Teachers' Moratorium group yesterday handed out leaflets at Ibrox Park Boys High School in another protest at the policies of the headmaster, Mr E. Smith.
>
> … As the school broke up for the day, several students rushed out holding placards. They were called into the office by the headmaster.
>
> [There were two accompanying photos of boys holding up placards, reading 'Freedom of choice does not exist in this school' and 'Down with fascism at Ibrox Park'.]

Item 57: CAAC leaflet – I have a dim memory of handing this out in front of Ibrox Park school:

> Political Debate in Schools
>
> The incident at Ibrox Park High School on Friday (June 6), when a maths teacher was reported to have torn up leaflets, raises crucial questions about social freedoms. The teacher, Mr B Caffrey, reportedly stated:
>
>> Everyone is entitled to their opinion, but no one should be allowed to hand out this trash to influence the minds of kids.
>>
>> [See Item 51 above.]
>
> This is clearly contradictory. Mr Caffrey first comes out with the liberal belief that every individual can hold and express his own views. But as soon as he disagrees with someone's views, Caffrey drops his liberalism. His attitude becomes immediately repressive, and his thinking and language authoritarian. The view he disagrees with becomes 'trash', and 'should' be suppressed.
>
> Suppressed by whom? Caffrey obviously believes the state – or arms of the state, like the N.S.W. Education Dept. – should decide on what is to be considered acceptable views, and suppress those it doesn't like. If the state won't do it, Mr Caffrey will employ his own brand of vigilante violence …

...Mr Caffrey's views are, clearly, very representative Australian ones...

Overall, Australia physically prevents other ideas from coming into the country by censoring books, films and pop music. Australia physically prevents the entry of visitors, like Dr Ernest Mandel, who have different ideas and ideologies. [I return to the banning of Dr Mandel from Australia in the next chapter concerning the 1970 Socialist Scholars Conference.] And Australia physically preserves its social and racial uniformity by preventing other races from coming in.

What Australia needs is cultural diversity: the diversity which might break down Australia's racism; its absurd nationalism about its own social ideals; and its paternalistic style of government and education with their 'authorities' who tell people and 'kids' what are and are not the right views and style of behaviour.

CAAC

Item 58: Julie Rigg, Point of View, *The Australian* 11 June 1970 has some fun at Chipp's expense, saying his constant vacillating makes her feel mildly nauseous:

> Not only does he want to be Censor, but he wants us all to like him as well... he has begun to believe that it is possible to be both a censor and be Understood. Even Appreciated.

Item 59: *Sydney Morning Herald* 12 June 1970 'Second group backs Ibrox principal' reports that Mr Smith, the headmaster of Ibrox Park Boys High School, has been defended by the Council of Metropolitan High Schools' Headmasters:

> ...There have been demonstrations at the school and members of the Campaign for Action Against Censorship plan to distribute leaflets there this morning.

Item 60: *Sydney Morning Herald* 12 June 1970:

> A full-scale revision of film censorship regulations is under way.
>
> The Minister for Customs and Excise, Mr D. L. Chipp, announced this in the House of Representatives today in a major statement of the Government's attitude to censorship.
>
> Mr Chipp announced two immediate steps to change film censorship procedures:
>
> He is inviting the States to discuss a system of restricted classifications that would enable films to be shown to adults only.
>
> Beginning next week, the Chief Film Censor will issue a monthly bulletin listing rejected feature films and the length and nature of cuts in feature films.
>
> [Chipp then vacillates as usual:] Mr Chipp said that censorship ('undesirable, but necessary') should be open to public scrutiny, and should be as little as possible – within the limits set by community standards.

Item 61: [*The Australian* 12 June 1970 'Regulations on films are being revised, says Chipp':

> Mr Chipp was making what he said was the first major statement on censorship to be given in the House of Representatives since 1938.
>
> Mr Chipp said the concept of censorship was abhorrent to all who believed in the basic freedoms.
>
> As a philosophy, censorship was evil and to be condemned – but censorship was a necessary evil.

Item 62: CAAC leaflet expressing irritation at film festivals:

> The Festival of Censorship
> [CAAC.] protests against the elitism of the Festival's policy on

censorship [presumably the Sydney Film Festival; neither Ann nor I can recall what prompted this CAAC leaflet.]

That is, the policy whereby festivals, instead of taking a stand against all film censorship, seek special treatment for themselves and other non-commercial film-exhibiting bodies, such as the national film theatre and film societies.

Whatever the views of individual members of the Festival Committee, the Festival's policy is a stand taken on the basis of self-interest and not as a matter of principle.

... Despite the workings of self-interest, the elitism of the Festivals would seem to have got them nowhere, since Festival entries continue to be banned.

... Total lack of censorship must be the open goal of anyone who insists on basic individual freedoms.

⁓❦⁓

Here the CAAC archive, compiled by Ann in a blue school project scrap book comes to an end. I sit here thinking about it. I think the scrap book (minus all my square bracket interpolations!) is a brilliant montage; it reminds me of an ideal of Walter Benjamin, to display quotations without any commentary, so effecting a break with history conceived as continuity, acknowledging that in modernity there can no longer be any unifying tradition of interpretation.

The Campaign for Action Against Censorship brought together anti-censorship people, then young, who would later become prominent in various fields, such as Phil Noyce in film, Jill Roe and Ann Curthoys in history, Frank Moorhouse in experimental writing, Michael Thornhill in film criticism and film-making, George Molnar in Sydney Libertarian philosophy.

The leaflets and newspaper cuttings Ann assembled gathered a kind of momentum, from early to mid-1970, suggesting an insurrection across the society to oppose secret bureaucratic censorship and replace it with a straightforward and sensible A or X certificates system; an insurrection that by mid-year had brought success, or at least the promise of film-classification certificates that critics of censorship had been calling for. By January 1971, a Film Board of Review was established, and in November 1971 compulsory R-ratings were introduced.

CAAC, as far as I remember, from mid-year of 1970 simply faded away, at least in Sydney, though I don't think there was any meeting to discuss this. It just sort of happened.

Historical interest in the anti-censorship campaigns of 1970 and beyond has sporadically continued, and is perhaps intensifying. Early on, Wendy Bacon mused about anti-censorship and the wonderfully way-out-there anarchist actions of her *Tharunka* group at the University of New South Wales in 'Sex and Censorship', *Lot's Wife*, 18 March 1971 (available on the Anarchism in Australia website), and later in her essay 'Being Free by Acting Free', *Overland* 202, 2011. In 2012 Nicole Moore's *The Censor's Library: Uncovering the lost history of Australia's banned books* appeared. In the same year an honours thesis in the Department of History, Sydney University, 2012, by Dominic Bowes, Exposing Indecency: Censorship and Sydney's Alternative Press 1963–1973, refers to CAAC and the Festival; in his acknowledgements, Dominic Bowes writes: 'My thanks go particularly to my supervisor Ann Curthoys who not only sparked my interest in the history of "sixties" activism, but provided invaluable guidance, support, and access to her personal archive.' In 2014 Lisa Featherstone (ed.) published *Acts of Love and Lust: Sexuality in Australia from 1945–2010*.

Ann kept in her office at Sydney University in the years 2008–13 a large box of documents of all kinds, which she freely permitted honours students to go through for their research: old *MeJanes*, the very early Sydney feminist newspaper, Ann on the cover of the first issue in 1971; and many documents arising from student radicalism, libertarianism, the New Left and the antiwar movement.

I think it's fitting that at this point of musing on CAAC and its contribution to the 1970 anti-censorship campaigns, that Ann gives her experience of attending in Wallace Theatre the Festival of Banned Works, which I know she found deeply disturbing and upsetting.

> ANN: I enjoyed being part of CAAC, demonstrating against film censorship and supporting the idea of film classification so that adults could see material not appropriate for children. It brought together the techniques of student radicalism with a libertarian ethos. I did not, however, at all enjoy the Festival of Banned Works. It seemed like a good idea at the time, confronting Australia's outdated and excessive censorship laws, and perhaps a bit of fun too, but it didn't turn out that way for me. John was in the organizing group and up on the stage, while I was in the body of Wallace Theatre on my own. All around me were young men, no women, and, it seemed, they hated my presence, they were angry, hostile, abusive, and physically aggressive. The man behind me stuck his knee or foot firmly in my back for the entire time, it really hurt and however much I shifted and tried to get out of his way, I couldn't. So, I saw the whole thing in a state of physical pain, and a realisation that I should never have come. I don't remember much about what was shown, only the sense of male entitlement and aggression around me. I was unbelievably relieved when it was all over, and I could get that knee/foot out of my back and regain my sense of self. Sometimes I wonder if I

should have shouted or even asked for the perpetrator to move his knee/foot, so strongly pressed into my back, but I was too afraid to cause a scene.

Looking back, while Women's Liberation had by this time started in Sydney, and I was deeply involved and being changed by it, we had not yet connected the dots. We hadn't yet begun to ask how libertarian anti-censorship ideas might take on board feminist confrontations with violence against women, or indeed how feminism might find ways to value freedom of speech and at the same time provide trenchant critiques of then-pervasive and indeed still-pervasive misogyny. Now, almost half a century later, we are in the midst of a tide of female anger in the film industry at the exploitation and denigration of women, and the difficulties women have had and continue to have as filmmakers, actors, and indeed film viewers. On the other hand, film and television have been major sites for exploring feminist themes and concerns and I remain a regular and avid filmgoer, watching all manner of movies, some of which would once have been so censored that they barely made sense.

In an article in the online *Guardian* 26 May 2018, 'How Portnoy's Complaint made Australia a better place', David Marr wrote that when Philip Roth's 1969 'scatological masterpiece' was banned from entering Australia by the Liberal prime minister John Gorton, Penguin Books courageously printed a local edition, which was then banned for obscenity everywhere except in New South Wales. Penguin Books chose to defend the novel against the charge of obscenity in a landmark case held in a Sydney courtroom on the ground of its literary merit, with writers including the famous Patrick White appearing for the defence, pointing to *Portnoy's Complaint*'s great skill and high purpose. The jury, Marr jubilantly recalls (he had been a junior lawyer on the defence team), refused to convict the novel of obscenity, thus effectively lifting the nation-wide ban and striking a major blow against book censorship.

~·~

In the *Guardian* for Thursday 31 May 2018 I notice an article by Sari Braithwaite, '*[CENSORED]* was meant to celebrate freedom. Instead it exposes something darker'. I excitedly say to Ann, there's an article here in the *Guardian* by Sari Braithwaite. I knew Ann had the highest opinion of her former honours student at ANU and then research assistant, especially for Ann's research project on Paul and Eslanda Robeson's visit to Australia and New Zealand in 1960. Ann opens the article on her iPad. We see that *[CENSORED]* is receiving its world premiere at the Sydney Film Festival on Monday 11 June; Ann immediately goes on line and books tickets for us at the Dendy Cinema, Circular Quay. We are visiting Sydney from 5–12 June in any case, for medical appointments and to see friends and if possible, check out any Sydney Film Festival film we might want to go to: here it is!

In the *Guardian* article Sari writes that in 2014 she made a short film with David Stratton called *Smut Hounds*, about the uproar that occurred in 1969 when the Australian government censors cut a scene in a Swedish film. While making that film she found a 'huge audiovisual archive of all the clips sliced out of cinema in the period 1958 to 1971'. However, watching for months 'nearly 2,000 clips', which she thought would be a 'playful', 'irreverent' and 'cathartic' thing to do, she began to feel how 'suffocating' an experience it was, even 'deeply disturbing'. These 'stray fragments were screaming an unexpected message – and it wasn't about government censorship. I was drowning in an archive of a dominating, violent gaze: a male gaze. And I hated it.' As a feminist and female film-maker, Sari realises that 'what the censors accidently created was a distilled catalogue of the destructive patriarchal imaginary', a record of 'terrorized women and toxic men'. In *[CENSORED]*, in making 'this male gaze so visible' that it 'can no longer merely wash over us', Sari wants us to reflect on 'how this history speaks to us today', in the age of #MeToo and #TimesUp and #OscarsSoWhite, and the 2018 furore at Cannes about the dearth of female directors: 'I wanted to create space for understanding the problems of our spectatorship; to use this archive to make us better, more discerning viewers.'

Ann immediately got in touch with Sari, emails flew back and forth. Ann told her of my chapter on CAAC I was writing and that the first demonstration outside a cinema we held was to highlight the cutting of *Medium Cool*. Sari extremely generously forwarded what she knew of the cuts to that film from the censorship archive. It makes remarkable reading. Please join with me in perusing it.

Medium Cool Tully Friedman and Haskell Wexler

Spool 1. At 7 mins. Delete words underlined 'Shoot the shit out of them'.
At 18 mins. Reduce love making shots of bare breasts, groping hands and mouths.

Spool 2. Delete whole sequence from where John and Ruth strip naked and frolic around the flat ending in lovemaking on bed (i.e. to end of spool)

Spool 3. At 7 mins. Delete from dialogue the word underlined 'I got chicken-shit cameramen'.

Spool 4. From 2 mins. Delete from dialogue words underlined 'You've been out when he's needed you screwing around'. 'Tell me what kind of shit's flying around'. 'What the hell is this crap'.

At 8 mins. Delete word underlined 'What's so great about your <u>shitty</u> car'.

Spool 5. At 8 mins. Delete from dialogue word underlined 'He cuts through the bull <u>shit</u>'.
At 11 mins. Delete from dialogue words underlined 'I will love the police as they kick <u>the shit out of</u> me on the street['].

Spool 6. At 8 mins. Delete dialogue '<u>Fuck you pigs</u>' (in background as Eileen stands at traffic light).

⁓❦⁓

At the Sydney Film Festival late in the afternoon on Monday 11 June, Circular Quay, on the east side of the Quay, we walk towards the Dendy Cinema, on the way to and not far from the Opera House; there are huge crowds everywhere, it is a public holiday, Queen's Birthday, the annual Vivid lighting displays were on at the Quay, especially lighting up the sails of the Opera House (the coloured patterns rather boring, we thought, this year). We come to the Dendy, get our tickets checked, join the long queue there to see [*CENSORED*]. The session had sold out. After the film was over, in many ways a harrowing experience – especially the sequences of film cuts showing men slapping women, men raping women, women stripping for both men and women's voyeuristic gaze, men's violence towards other men – in film festival style, Sari the director and Chloë Brugale the producer, both magnificently pregnant, stand out the front and take questions from the audience. The opening question is hostile and accusatory, from someone who has positioned herself near the front. She accuses Sari of not making a proper, objective, documentary, she should have given dates and contexts, especially local contexts, for the scenes the film shows; Sari replies that she wants the film to be personal, to reveal and explore uncertainties and ambivalences she can't resolve, and that she wished to create out of the scenes the censors had cut a new text, not a conventional documentary-like reflection of the times; the questioner wouldn't let go, repeats her question, the audience becomes restive, there are cries that other people here want to ask questions too you know. Other people then ask questions.

Then it was all over and Ann went down the front to meet Sari, there were joyful hugs, and after a while we drifted along with her friends and her parents John and Val Braithwaite, who Ann knew from ANU, he in restorative justice, she in social policy, to the Opera Bar below the Opera House for complimentary champagne and delight about how well it has all gone.

✦

Ann and I say our goodbyes and as we walk back towards the cinema say to each other, why don't we go to Guylian's the Belgian chocolate café next to the Dendy and immediately write down what we think. We find a seat inside, we order hot chocolates, we start writing.

ANN: Thoughts on Sari's Film *[Censored]* 11 June 2018, Guylian, Circular Quay, 8.30pm

Sari's film and the discussion afterwards made me wonder, what do we now think about censorship? I loved her voice over – thoughtful and personal, and seeking in a quite complex way a redefining of censorship so that it refers not only to censorship by the state but also to the everyday censorship conducted by film-makers and viewers as they negotiate what is made and what is seen. Film, Sari says, involves power and power relations. Thinking over the issues, I'm left opposing censorship, especially censorship conducted secretly, as it was in Australia in the 1960s, but wanting guidelines to help me choose what I want to see.

The film clips were, as Sari said in her commentary, appallingly repetitive, and showed endless violence against women – slaps, domestic violence, and rape, as well as extreme voyeurism. The rape scenes were especially shocking, but so too were the endless face slaps, as one male character after another slaps a woman in a way suggesting this was ordinary normal acceptable behaviour. It was interesting that there were only a few clips that did not express contempt for women – one from a film made by a female director, one a film of childbirth, and another from a film by Ingmar Bergman.

Watching these film clips, nearly all from the 1960s, made me think about the specificity of that decade. As sexual mores became less puritanical, sexual cultures went through a phase of an apparent free-for-all for men, alongside extreme objectification and denigration of women. When feminism emerged at the very end of the decade and at the beginning of the 1970s, it had a hard time negotiating a pathway between ideals of sexual freedom on the one hand and seeking validation of and respect for women generally on the other. Debates over pornography, libertarianism and female sexuality were, I remember, quite heated.

JOHN: Guylian, Quay 11 June 2018

I incredibly like Sari's film. I'm left thinking that I don't know what to think.

I reach for some Walter Benjamin and Hannah Arendt. Certain images are distilled so that they become crystallisations; many are disturbing to the point of unbearability, as in the sequences showing men slapping women, men raping women, women undressing for male and female spectators. Out of discarded cuts, these crystallisations create an entirely new film, a new text.

When at the bar, when we talked to Sari, we said the sequences of images of male violence were so disturbing, so unbearable, starting with the scenes of men slapping women, Sari commented: it was that sequence that was so important to me, I knew then how to shape the film – Ann, what did Sari say exactly?

ANN: Yes, it was the women's faces in the slapping scenes that helped her know what the film would be about.

JOHN: I do have a stray thought, that Sari's confession as narrator of uncertainty, of ambivalence, of herself not knowing quite what to think, inherits a long period in intellectual thought of the importance in any historical text, including documentary, of the I-voice, of a personal vision, associated with a postmodern and poststructuralist stress on uncertainty and undecidability of meaning, even if we now question poststructuralism's lack of focus on the body and emotion. What is so, so haunting about Sari's film is how much it foregrounds the body, and race, as in the scene the censors had cut from a French film (Godard?), of black men on a train in Paris protesting French racism towards Africans.

We read what the other has written, and talk some more. We finish our hot chocolates, we pay, we join the crowds outside watching Vivid, we walk towards where we can catch a taxi back to where we are staying, on the way we see some smaller cameo-like Vivid creations we quite like, metallic birds lit up in a tree, a filigree chrysalis display where butterflies are about to come forth.
We hail a taxi.

5 July 2018: Sari Braithwaite has just sent a lovely email to Ann and me talking about the [*CENSORED*] night, and also how interesting she found the chapter on CAAC including Ann's record of leaflets and press cuttings; she was amused, as I was, by a reference in the CAAC campaign to a film being 'emasculated' by the

censors, also quite rightly pointed out the resonance between the sexual violence revealed in the cut scenes in [*CENSORED*] and Ann's horrible experience at the Festival of Banned Works; Sari also told me that the scene with the men on the train was from Godard's *Masculin Feminin* (1966).

1   There is an excellent discussion of the Free U in the PhD thesis by Megan Dymphna Jones. Its title is *Remembering Academic Feminism*, and it is available online at the University of Sydney library. See also T H Irving 2013 '"The triumph of green hearts over sere": reflections on student radicalism at Sydney University in the 1910s and the 1960s, Radical Sydney/Radical History', referred to in Terry Irving, 'Which Voice? Which Working Class?' in Dee Michell, Jacqueline Z Wilson and Verity Archer (eds), *Bread and Roses: Voices of Australian Academics from the Working Class* (Sense Publishers, Rotterdam, 2015), pp.29–37.
2   John Docker, 'The Sydney Connection: A Reflection on Arena', *Arena* 99/100, 1992, pp.141–6.
3   John Docker, *Australian Cultural Elites: Intellectual traditions in Sydney and Melbourne* (Angus and Robertson, Sydney, 1974), ch.8, 'John Anderson and the Sydney Freethought Tradition'.

34

1970: Interlude – a Socialist Scholars Conference, Without its Invited Main Speaker

In the previous '1970' chapter, in Item 57 of Ann's scrapbook collection of Campaign for Action Against Censorship material, I mention that a CAAC leaflet to be handed out in front of a Sydney high school that had banned any discussion of the American War in Vietnam and of the Moratorium protests against it, referred to another signal act of banning, this time on the world stage, the exclusion from Australia of the internationally prominent Marxist economist Dr Ernest Mandel. He had been invited to speak at the 1970 Socialist Scholars Conference to be held at Sydney University during 21–24 May.

Publicity for the event – in 2011 in Mitchell Library I looked at a folder I'd kept of Socialist Scholars Papers, I'm now staring at the notes I took – announced that the conference would cover topics such as: Australian Labour History; Counter-culture; Politics and Literature; Marxism; Power in Australia; Aborigines; and Colonialism. The Program Committee members were: Terry Irving, Geoff Hawker, Howard Morris, Hall Greenland, Col Waddy, Phil Sandford, Jenny George, Russ Darnley, Gordon Adler and Pat Aarons (Pat Healy, who had been on the 1965 Freedom

Ride with Ann). The conference's Visiting Scholar, Ernest Mandel, would be speaking on:

> The Crisis of the Capitalist Relations of Production.
> Dr Mandel is the author of *Marxist Economic Theory*, *La Formation de la Pensée Economique de Karl Marx*, and numerous articles. His most recent book is being translated as *Europe versus America? – Contradictions of Capitalism*.

As it turned brutally out, Dr Mandel was refused an entry visa by the Australian government, meaning he could neither attend the Socialist Scholars Conference in Sydney nor give lectures in Melbourne where he had been invited.

Nonetheless, despite losing Mandel their international attraction, the conference continued, and was very well attended. Rowan Cahill, for many years now a prominent scholar of Radical Sydney, recalls in a 2008 essay that he consulted ASIO reports which suggested that the 1970 Socialist Scholars Conference 'drew between 300–400 participants for each of four days (21–24 May)'.[1]

I'll list here some sessions as I noted them down in Mitchell Library in 2011. The conference was held at Sydney University, mainly in the Carslaw building, a tall blue-coloured modernist building near City Road.

Thursday 21 May, in Chemistry Theatre 1:
Janine Blackley and Dave Evans, 'Australia: a Mini – or Sub-Imperialist Power?', chairman John Playford; Mike Kahan, 'Working-class False Consciousness'; Doug Moore, 'Technological Colonialism'; John Playford, 'The Myth of the "Sixty Families"', comment by Rupert Lockwood.

Friday 22 May, Carslaw Theatre 4:
Coonie Sandford, 'Women in the Workforce'; Ian Bedford, 'Prospects for Revolution in India', chaired by Ravinder Kumar; Dick Thompson, 'Marxism and Mass Media', chaired by Sid Lovibond; Eric Aarons, 'Lenin's Theories of Revolution'.

Saturday 23 May:
Terry Irving and Baiba Berzins, 'History and the Old Left', chair Ken McNab; Humphrey McQueen, 'Towards a Revolutionary History of Australia', chair Geoff Hawker, comments by Bob Gollan, Terry Irving.

Sunday 24 May, Carslaw Theatre 4:
Dave Clark, Bruce McFarlane, and Ernest Mandel: 'Mandel's *Marxist Economic Theory*', chair Ted Wheelwright, [then parallel session] Colin Mackerras, 'The Reform of the Theatre in China', Doug Miles, 'Australian Anthropology in Sarkhan', chair Chandra Jaywardena. [Ernest Mandel's name seems here to have been kept in by mistake; elsewhere his name has been removed as part of the overall conference.]

In 2011, I found myself particularly interested in Coonie Sandford's talk entitled 'Factors Affecting Women in the Workforce'. I ask Ann about her. She was an American feminist, recently arrived from the US, who knew a lot about what was happening in the women's movement there. She was important in the very early days of Sydney Women's Liberation meeting in 67 Glebe Point Road in 1970 onwards; I recall that Ann would mention her in conversation. Her talk begins:

> There are two attitudes generally taken to the women's liberation
> movement, both of which say that struggling for the liberation

of women and fighting a class struggle against capitalism are antagonistic to one another. The 'Women's Liberation' people generally argue that all women should be liberated, regardless of their class, and the 'class' people argue that any struggle, including women's liberation, which is not directly relevant to white male blue-collar workers, is just a diversion and must be fought because it splits the anti-capitalist struggle. I feel that this idea of one struggle being superior to another is not only ludicrous, but does great harm to both parts of the movement. I would argue very strongly that the two struggles, for the liberation of women, and against capitalism, *must not* be separated. Need it be said that just as women do not constitute one class, nor does the working class constitute one sex.

I don't quite know how it came about, but some of us literary types thought, fairly or unfairly, that the conference was underplaying literary and cultural aspects of the world, and set to organising at the conference a parallel stream of talks, which I will now list. It includes Michael Wilding's 'Literature, Politics, and The University', though, from memory, he gave that to the main group.

SOCIALIST SCHOLARS' CONFERENCE

The Socialist Scholars' Conference at Sydney University on May 21–24 will include a series of related papers on 'Literature, Politics and Counter-Culture'.

> Denis Altman, '"Turn on, tune in and drop out": Political change through counter-culture'.

> Steven Knight, 'The Class War and the Recent English Novel'.

> Bill Browning, on Q. D. Leavis's *Fiction and the Reading Public*.

John Docker, 'James McAuley: Anti Liberalism from the Right'.

Ian Lennie, 'Male assumptions and the Idea of Nature in D. H. Lawrence'.

Terry Sturm, 'Raymond Williams on Literature and Politics'.

Michael Wilding, 'Literature, Politics and The University'.

When I took notes of these talks in 2011, I was particularly interested in their assessments of the Leavisite school, critiquing the way the Leavisites connected literature to life and history, as they conceived them. Bill Browning, a postgraduate in the English department at Sydney University and a friend of ours, offered a brilliant forensic analysis, highly critical of Q D Leavis's *Fiction and the Reading Public*, especially its 'group of assumptions' concerning bestsellers that inform her judgements on particular authors, from Elizabethan times to the 1930s, when she was writing her analysis. Bill sharply questioned her dismissiveness towards popular literature, including her claim that such fantasy literature leads to maladjustment in life; and her view that the Elizabethan past, in terms of the relationship between literature and society, was clearly superior to the twentieth century.

Michael Wilding, a young lecturer in the Sydney English department who had helped send off the Leavisites back to Melbourne in the mid-1960s, felt that the ongoing critical repudiation of the Leavisites, justified as it was, was nonetheless leading to unfortunate consequences. He recognised the 'failures, distortions and anti-intellectualism' of the 'Leavis-Scrutiny school of criticism' in the particular ways it insisted on the 'inseparability of life from literature'. However, in his view – and of his colleague Terry Sturm, also in the Sydney English department – the critical reaction against the Leavis-Scrutiny project strengthened hostility to 'any attempt to look at literature in the light of political, psycho-analytical, or religious positions'. This 'hostility', he continued, has become the 'prevalent mood of English studies in England and Australia at the moment'. In support, Wilding quotes approvingly from an essay by Terry Sturm, 'Literature and Politics', *Australian Highway* (July 1963), lamenting how restrictive the exclusion of possible political considerations for critical enquiry was becoming.

Wilding argued that while the Leavis-Scrutiny school had been 'contained' to one university, Melbourne, the 'reaction and recoil from it are evident in practically all the other English departments' in Australia, Britain and the Commonwealth; a rejection of the 'possibility of any approach to literature that involves extra literary values', leading to a 'retreat into a hermeticism', especially in rejecting the 'political connexions and implications of literature'. What is now happening is that literature is considered to be something that 'had to be studied in isolation of the political world – which meant that the existing political world was accepted'; to relate 'colonialism or capitalism or Vietnam to the texts for discussion was felt to be an extra-literary intrusion'. There was now no encouragement of students or teachers to 'question the accepted corpus of Eng. Lit.', to suggest adding to the syllabus such writers, for example, as the 'absurdly neglected socialist William Morris'.

Wilding points out that political themes are important in Shakespeare's *Julius Caesar* and the poetry of Marvell, Milton and Dryden, and in a long list of novelists, from Swift to Dickens, Disraeli, George Eliot, Trollope, James, Meredith, Morris, Conrad, Lawrence, Huxley and Orwell.

We can, Wilding says, envisage a new range of university courses: on imperialism as a theme in English literature, focusing on writers already considered of high literary status; on writers important for their contemporary popular acclaim, for example, Conrad, Kipling, Joyce Carey, Forster, Rider Haggard, Maugham and Graham Greene; or a course on utopian fiction, as in More, Swift, Butler, Morris, Wells, Huxley, Orwell; or a course on criticism that looks at the political affiliations, and explicit social writings, of, say, Johnson, Coleridge, Ruskin, Arnold, Eliot and Leavis.

The Socialist Scholars literary and cultural stream talks of 1970 on 'Literature, Politics and Counter-Culture' must have lodged in subsequent years in the back of my mind, in various ways foreshadowing and inspiring my later interests and writings. For example, Browning and Wilding's reflections on Leavisism resonate with my 1981 *Meanjin* frolic 'How I Became a Teenage Leavisite and Lived to Tell the Tale', while I echo Bill Browning's scalding critique of Q D Leavis's *Fiction and the Reading Public* in my 1994 *Postmodernism and Popular Culture: A Cultural History*, in chapter three, 'Modernism versus Popular Literature'.[2]

Michael Wilding's analysis and suggestions resonate with my own later interest in utopianism and anti-utopianism, history as hope or nightmare, a focus of my doctoral thesis, Literature and Social Thought: Australia in an International Context 1890–1925, which I began at ANU in 1975 and submitted in March 1980, I see in the inside cover of the huge green covered tome it became. The thesis has chapters on the varied utopias and dystopias of William Morris's *News from Nowhere*, Edward Bellamy's *Looking Backward*, Ignatius Donnelly's *Caesar's Column*, Mark Twain's *A Connecticut Yankee in King Arthur's Court*, William Dean Howells's *A Traveler from Altruria*, and William Lane's *A Workingman's Paradise*. In my *The Nervous Nineties: Australian Cultural Life in the 1890s*, published in 1991, which is a sort of free-wheeling reprise of my doctoral thesis, I have, in a section devoted to Utopias and Anti-Utopias, chapters such as 'Utopians at War: Bellamy *v.* William Morris' and

'Utopians and Anti-utopians in American Literature: Bellamy *v.* Ignatius Donnelly'. I also added a long section, not in the doctoral thesis, entitled 'Things Fall Apart', on an effervescent fantasy literature that flourished in the fin de siècle.

~~~⚜~~~

My interest, in my doctoral thesis and subsequently in *The Nervous Nineties*, in American utopian and dystopian literature, especially the rather chilling state socialist utopia of Edward Bellamy's *Looking Backward* as against the wild dystopian vision in Ignatius Donnelly's *Caesar's Column* of the Nineties as an apocalyptic period of destruction and disaster, came from the historian Bob Gollan, especially reading and thinking about two essays of his from the early 1960s: 'The Australian Impact' in Sylvia Bowman, ed., *Edward Bellamy Abroad: An American Prophet's Influence* (1962), and 'American Populism and Australian Utopianism', *Labour History* 9 (1965).

I should explain how Ann and I became friends with Bob and Anne Gollan. Much, I think, of one's life is shaped by chance and unforeseen encounters. At the end of an autobiographical chapter I wrote for *Bread and Roses* (2015), a collection devoted to essays by academics from the working class, I reflect that, as in Chaos Theory, apparently small decisions and events can have life-shaping consequences; I think of the arrival of the Leavisites at Sydney University coinciding with my student years there, or my decision to return to Sydney at the end of the 1960s after my rather sad Melbourne sojourn in 1967-8.[3] My indistinct memory is that during our stay in London during 1973 and 1974, almost certainly in 1974, in the English summer, not too long before we had to return to Australia because Ann (as my grandmother would say) had fallen pregnant, – one could not be on the plane after five months of pregnancy – we were strolling about the library in the Institute of Historical Research in the rather bizarre Senate building of University College, it was on the first floor I think, when a young woman walked towards us. We passed each other, then Ann stopped, turned and looked back, as did the young woman. They recognised each other; it was Susan Magarey, who Ann knew from Women's Liberation circles in Australia. We talked. Susan asked, why don't you come along to where Bob and Anne Gollan from ANU are staying in London, on their sabbatical leave? Susan said she will be there, it will be fun; she was doing a doctoral thesis at ANU at that time.

Reader, we went, chatted amiably with Bob and Anne and Susan, sipped wine, and Bob during the course of a sunny afternoon said something like, John, why don't you come to ANU to do a PhD, maybe in history or maybe English? As it turned out, we returned to Sydney and, after our son Ned was born and we had spent some time in Newcastle with Ann's parents, we moved in January 1975 to Canberra and I started a PhD in the English department, while a year later Ann became ANU's first lecturer in women's studies.

I've just looked again at *The Nervous Nineties*, and am pleased to see how much Bob Gollan's 1960s essays on Edward Bellamy and Ignatius Donnelly influenced my interest, as I note in my Preface, in the Nineties as a particular period in history, a liminal period (to adopt a phrase from American anthropologist Victor Turner), one that comes at the end of a century, one that is between centuries, confronting past and future. The Nineties could be viewed as (to adopt a phrase from another American anthropologist Clifford Geertz) a period of deep play, where attitudes, tensions, traumas, anxieties, resentments, passions and desires not usually permitted full expression – to do with evolution, the ideal order of society, men and women, hierarchies of humanity, the future of European empire – could be represented, played and experimented with.[4]

Bob Gollan's essays refer to the late 1880s and early 1990s

as feverish years of utopian and dystopian visions where the contrasting figures of Edward Bellamy and Ignatius Donnelly were both well known in Australia in labour and radical journalism; part of a fractious international conversation.[5] Given my affection for William Morris's *News from Nowhere*, I could, in the spirit of an essay by Ann on Chaos Theory and feminism, construct an unresolved, unstable, triangular relationship in cultural and intellectual history between Australian, British, and American literature.[6] In the Preface to *The Nervous Nineties* I also raise methodological questions, pondering how we construct historical periods; I suggest that the literary culture of the Nineties possessed no essential spirit, neither a central preoccupation nor turning on a single conflict or set of oppositions; rather, like all historical periods, it was constituted by all sorts of literary and discursive differences, conflicts, arguments, contestations, oppositions, antagonisms.[7]

I'll leave the Campaign for Action Against Censorship and the Socialist Scholars Conference here, in the first half of 1970, as the huge impact of Women's Liberation and feminism began so profoundly to challenge, to sweep across, to keep sweeping across, world consciousness.

1970: Interlude – a Socialist Scholars Conference 167

1. Rowan Cahill, 'Security Intelligence and Left Intellectuals: Australia, 1970', *International Gramsci Journal*, 1(1), 2008.
2. John Docker, *Postmodernism and Popular Culture: A Cultural History* (Cambridge University Press, Melbourne, 1994), pp.24–35.
3. John Docker, 'A Space for Self-Fashioning: An Antipodean Red-Diaper Baby Goes to University in the Sixties', in Dee Michell, Jacqueline Z. Wilson and Verity Archer (eds), *Bread and Roses: Voices of Australian Academics from the Working Class* (Sense Publishers, Rotterdam, 2015), p.67.
4. John Docker, *The Nervous Nineties: Australian Cultural Life in the 1890s* (Oxford University Press, Melbourne, 1991), Preface, p.x.
5. Docker, *The Nervous Nineties*, pp.23, 106–7, 125, 133–4, 140.
6. In her fascinating essay 'The Three Body Problem: Feminism and Chaos Theory', *Hecate*, vol.17, no.1, 1991, pp.14–21, Ann refers to the importance of the number three in Chaos Theory, creating relationships that while mutually constitutive are always inherently unstable; Ann's examples are the dimensions of race, class and gender.
7. Docker, *The Nervous Nineties*, Preface, p.xii.

35

1971–2: A Tribute to Henry Mayer – Inspiring Mentor, Intellectual Trickster, a non-Jewish Jew, a Diasporic Consciousness, the Stranger Who Stayed

In 1972 the journal *Politics*, edited by Professor Henry Mayer, of the Department of Government, University of Sydney, published my essay, 'Sydney Intellectual History and Sydney Libertarianism'. The Sydney Libertarians were a distinctive intellectual grouping in the 1950s and 1960s, that grew out of, then broke away from, the vibrant and innovative Sydney freethought tradition given shape and direction in the 1930s and 1940s by the Scottish-Australian philosopher John Anderson along with his ex-students P H Partridge and J A Passmore, important philosophers in their own right.

In returning to this essay now, I wish to do several things: reflect on Henry Mayer, evoke the essay's content, and draw attention to the Sydney Libertarians as an important presence in Sydney's intellectual and cultural history. I also have to acknowledge that I wrote the essay in a particular historical moment, when the Sydney Libertarians were being challenged in the late 1960s and early 1970s by the social movements associated with the New Left, of black liberation, women's liberation, gay liberation, the counter-culture. My essay, written in 1971, published in 1972, acknowledged the historical importance of 1950s and 1960s Sydney Libertarian ideas, yet also wished to critique them in terms of a new historical consciousness associated with these new social movements.

The ideas of the Sydney Libertarians of the 1950s and 1960s raise interesting questions about anarchist traditions, and also quite profound questions about how intellectuals relate to societies. It was Henry Mayer in particular who drew my attention to how important these questions are. During 1971, as I was preparing the essay for publication in his journal, Mayer shared with me in correspondence his disillusioning experience of the Sydney Libertarians in the early 1960s. I'll talk about, and quote from, this correspondence soon.

I evoke the article as it appeared in *Politics* (Vol.VII, no.1, May 1972), abridging as I go. Then I will talk about Henry Mayer's own personal involvement, temporary and bruising, with the Sydney Libertarians, which may help explain his hospitality to my article, why it pleased him so much to publish a critique of the group's ideas; then explore his 'world history' interest in the role of intellectuals in modernity by various European thinkers.

※

Who was Henry Mayer? I think Henry Mayer (1919–91) was many things, wished to be many things, many personae to present to the world. What particularly interests me is what I indicate in my title, that, in my view, he was, or played with, or manifested, the intellectual as trickster; a non-Jewish Jew, a secular Jew, in the tradition inspired by Spinoza in the early Enlightenment, as argued in the famous essay by Isaac Deutscher; he enjoyed the freedom of a diasporic consciousness; and in terms of another famous essay, Georg Simmel's 'The Stranger', he could partake of another freedom, of detachment and possibly scepticism towards the conforming demands of group identity and unproblematized tradition.

I'll begin by drawing hints and clues out of the *Australian Dictionary of Biography* entry on Mayer, written by political scientist Murray Goot and historian K S Inglis, published online in 2014. Here we learn that Mayer, born 4 December 1919 in Mannheim, Germany, became part of a stream of exiles, émigrés and refugees who left Germany after Hitler became chancellor in 1933; a teenager, he moved with his family to France, Switzerland and Italy, and thence to England, becoming part of his extended family's diasporic life in Britain. After high school, Mayer adopted a nom de plume, 'Henry Holmes'; in 1938, as 'Henry Holmes,' he became, he would later say, a supporter of the tiny Socialist Party of Great Britain; wrote short stories for pulp magazines and scripts for the British Broadcasting Corporation; turned his hand to interpreting and fortune-telling; and became a part-owner of a night-club and a publicist for a jazz band.

On the outbreak of World War II in September 1939, Mayer was classified as an enemy alien, and in June 1940 was transferred to the *Dunera* and transported with over 2500 others from Liverpool to Australia, a much written about voyage. Mayer disembarked in Sydney and was sent to an internment camp at Hay in NSW. To help pass the time he taught English, demonstrating his talent for teaching, and wrote poetry. From Hay he was transferred to Tatura refugee camp in Victoria. There he was keen to introduce his fellow internees to socialism, making contact with the minuscule Socialist Party of Australia; hopeless causes, Goot and Inglis observe, would always attract him. After the war, in 1947, Mayer enrolled at the University of Melbourne, completing a BA and MA; among his teachers in its department of political science was P H (Percy) Partridge. In 1950 Mayer moved from a tutorship at Melbourne to a teaching fellowship in the department of government and public administration at the University of Sydney, where Partridge was now situated; for a while Mayer became involved with the Libertarians, former pupils of or influenced by Anderson.

~~~~~

Walking beside the sea, the Indian Ocean, this morning in Perth, thinking about Henry Mayer, a stray idea occurred to me (I almost said: crossed my path). In my essay 'How I became a Teenage Leavisite and Lived to Tell the Tale' in *Meanjin* in 1981, I record that coming from Sydney to the University of Melbourne to do an MA there in its Department of English in 1967 and 1968, I felt estranged from the way, as I saw it, Melbourne intellectuals assumed that they were at the centre of society, ever ready to offer inclusive values and ideals that all could and should follow. I felt my desire to return to Sydney as a home of pluralism was purely personal, I didn't even wonder if it had occurred to anyone else. Now, looking at the *ADB* entry on Mayer and having also read the entry on P H Partridge, I realise that my journey to and away from Melbourne was not at all unique. In the *ADB* entry on Partridge (1910–88), you can see that Partridge grew up in Sydney and studied under John Anderson in the Sydney philosophy department in the 1930s and became a lecturer in philosophy there in the 1940s. In 1947 he moved to the University of Melbourne to become a senior lecturer in political science; in 1948, however, he returned to the University of Sydney to become chair of the department of government and public administration.

It very much appears that Partridge, while in Melbourne during 1947–8, had not abandoned the pluralist philosophy he shared with John Anderson and J A Passmore. Moreover, Mayer followed Partridge from Melbourne to Sydney, in 1950 moving from a tutorship at the University of Melbourne to a teaching fellowship under Partridge in the department of government and public administration at the University of Sydney; neither

Partridge nor Mayer, then, had been seduced by Melbourne intellectuals' visions of a unified society which they would intellectually lead and hopefully bring about.

I will return to Anderson, Partridge, Passmore and the Sydney freethought tradition at the end of this chapter, for, as I evoke it in my 1974 book *Australian Cultural Elites*, I admire it.

~~✤~~

Dear reader, in Goot and Inglis's *ADB* entry on Mayer I catch sight of historically effervescent figures of cultural identity that, I now will argue, helped shape his sensibility; help us try to explain his being in the theatre of the world. I'll begin my speculative journey with Mayer as possible trickster figure.

In my *Postmodernism and Popular Culture: A Cultural History* (1994) I have a chapter, 'Fool, Trickster, Social Explorer: The Detective', where I reveal my enthusiasm for Mikhail Bakhtin's portrait of the trickster as a powerful figure in the cultural history of early modern Europe; in Bakhtin's conception, the trickster is among a group of outsider figures, clowns, fools, cranks, who have the carnival right to mock and parody. Tricksters are masters of masking, masking as mystery, uncertainty, difficulty, opportunity; masking that suggests the openness of identity, the everpresent possibility of change, transformation, metamorphosis. The trickster outwits the hangman in always escaping death as it closes in on him, holding out the hope that fate does not have to be regarded and feared as that which in life and history is inescapably destined to harshness and destruction; and the trickster also parodies himself, so disestablishing any claims to absolute truth. Following Bakhtin we might say that the trickster creates a playful poetics of chaos; an irresolvable chaos of values.[1]

In sketching this portrait, I feel very happy to recognise Henry Mayer as a trickster intellectual, the intellectual as trickster, who always escapes the hangman: death by orthodoxy. He plays with identity, is 'Henry Holmes' who writes stories and poems; he is one of the unclassifiable ones (in Hannah Arendt's terms, referring to Kafka and Walter Benjamin, one 'whose work neither fits the existing order nor introduces a new genre that lends itself to future classification').[2] He takes pleasure in supporting marginal causes (including in 1970 alerting readers through his newspaper column to the activities of the Campaign for Action Against Censorship, making his own hyper-pluralist intervention); in Mikhail Bakhtin's terms, as trickster he can wear many masks; in world historian Janet Abu-Lughod's terms, he believes world history can most fruitfully be approached through a personal vision, through idiosyncrasy and eccentricity.[3]

※

There is another historical figure we can detect in Goot and Inglis's ADB entry on Mayer. Goot and Inglis note that Mayer was the son of Oscar Mayer, a lawyer and atheist who had been brought up as a non-observant Jew, and his Czech-born, Catholic-raised wife, Rosemarie, née Kleiner. They also tell us that on the outbreak of World War II, in September 1939, when Mayer was classified as an enemy alien, he gave his occupation as journalist and his religion as 'none (Jewish origin)'; an atheist, he would always insist he was not a Jew.

Hhhmm, I think, hhhmm. What if we can espy in the *ADB* entry on Mayer the figure of the non-Jewish Jew, the secular Jew, in the tradition dazzlingly, poignantly, inspired by Spinoza in the early Enlightenment.

As I relate in my Introduction, Baruch Spinoza, 1632–77, born of Portuguese Marrano parents in Amsterdam, was, in his twenty-fourth year, excommunicated from the Portuguese Jewish community there for heresy; Spinoza chose to remain outside the Jewish community after the *herem* (ban), and changed his name to Benedict, Latinising Baruch; he interrupted the writing of his most famous philosophical work the *Ethics* to write the *Tractatus Theologico-Politicus*, which was published in late 1669 or 1670, Spinoza hoping that by publishing it in Latin the *Tractatus* would be read only by those of liberal religious sentiments, given that it ventured controversial readings of the Bible, a body of writings central not only to Judaism but also to Catholicism and Protestantism. He didn't want it read by the ordinary run of theologians and preachers – priests, pastors, rabbis – who he felt were prejudiced to the point of superstition; and certainly not by the mass of people in Holland, in a time when religious hatreds and mob violence in political conflicts were all too common. The heterodoxy of the *Tractatus*, however, quickly became known not only in supposedly liberal and tolerant Holland but across Europe, provoking some of the most violent responses to any published work in the seventeenth century; it was widely perceived and denounced as blasphemous, abhorrent, subversive, atheistic, infamous and pestilential. Assuredly, wonderfully, Spinoza is one of history's great heretics.[4]

Everyone I suspect has a book they treasure, that you sometimes check in one's bookshelves to make sure it's still there. I recall also in my In Introduction, noting that I treasure Isaac Deutscher's small book of essays *The Non-Jewish Jew*, published in 1968, with a wise, affectionate and very moving introduction by Tamara Deutscher, who tells us that when Isaac Deutscher was a young boy growing up in the small Polish town of Chrzanów he took to reading the works of Goethe, Lessing, Heine and Spinoza; the precocious young Isaac was intensely drawn to 'Spinoza the rebel, the atheist, the heretic, the excommunicated Jew', leading him to abandon 'religion for good and all'.[5]

In the lead essay Isaac Deutscher argues that the 'Jewish heretic who transcends Jewry belongs to a Jewish tradition'; 'those great revolutionaries of modern thought' Spinoza, Heine, Marx, Rosa Luxemburg, Trotsky and Freud, who all went 'beyond the boundaries of Jewry'; they all 'found Jewry too narrow, too archaic, and too constricting'; they represent the 'sum and substance of much that is greatest in modern thought' in the last three centuries, in philosophy, sociology, economics and politics. Yet, Deutscher feels, in going beyond the boundaries of Jewry 'they were very Jewish indeed'.[6] I'll quote Deutscher here at his most eloquent:

> I do not believe in the exclusive genius of any race. Yet I think that in some ways they were very Jewish indeed. They had in themselves something of the quintessence of Jewish life and of the Jewish intellect. They were *a priori* exceptional in that as Jews they dwelt on the borderlines of various civilizations, religions, and national cultures. They were born and brought up on the borderlines of various epochs. Their mind matured where the most diverse cultural influences crossed and fertilized each other. They lived on the margins or in the nooks and crannies of their respective nations. Each of them was in society and yet not in it, of it and yet not of it. It was this that enabled them to rise in thought above their societies, above their nations, above their times and generations, and to strike out mentally into wide new horizons and far into the future.[7]

I think Deutscher's insights here resonate with aspects of Henry Mayer's biography, especially in relation to Spinoza. Excommunicated from the Sephardic community of Amsterdam, Spinoza changed his name from the Jewish Baruch to the Christian Benedict; Mayer, from an atheistical secular Jewish family, chose a non-Jewish nom de plume, 'Henry Holmes'. Spinoza, Deutscher writes, 'was brought up under the influences of Spain, Holland, Germany, England, and the Italy of the Renaissance'.[8] Mayer, we read in the *ADB* entry, effected a diasporic journey from Germany through France, Switzerland,

and Italy and then to Britain, his imagination, one speculates, influenced by different and contrasting societies and histories, his mind maturing where (as Deutscher has it) diverse cultural influences crossed and fertilised each other, and he lived in the nooks and crannies of these different nations and the borderlines between them; in each he was in a society and yet not in it, of it and yet not of it.

Mayer, I also think, inhabited what I refer to in my *1492: The Poetics of Diaspora* as a diasporic consciousness, which, in my Preface, I minimally define as a 'sense of belonging to more than one history, to more than time and place, more than one past and future. Diaspora suggests belonging to both here and there, now and then. Diaspora suggests the omnipresent weight of pain of displacement from a land or society, of being an outsider in a new one… yet also the possibility of new adventures of identity and the continued imagining of unconquerable countries of the mind.' In a chapter on Joyce's *Ulysses* entitled 'Strangers amongst the nations: Mr Bloom and Spinoza', in its final section 'Bloom and Central Europe', I refer to what Leopold Bloom learned from his father Rudolph Bloom who had journeyed from the Austro-Hungarian Habsburg empire, from Szombathely to Dublin, through Budapest, Vienna, Florence, Milan and London. Bloom inherited from such Central European movement between city and city a skepticism and mobility of mind and observation reminiscent of Spinoza, who Bloom admires; a depth of diasporic consciousness, an attentiveness to other and previous histories, a worldly ease of reference and multiple habitation, a lack of fear of the elsewhere; his mind and sensibility like an archipelago of many islands, where fragments of contradictory consciousness add themselves to other fragments of contradictory diasporic consciousness.[9]

We can also speculate that there are continuities between a diasporic consciousness, the non-Jewish Jew, and another intriguing historical figure I discuss in my Introduction. In *1492: The Poetics of Diaspora*, I venture that Bloom in *Ulysses* is recognisable in the German Jewish sociologist Georg Simmel's brilliant essay 'The Stranger' (1908). Here Simmel (1858–1918) argues that the stranger is a figure who, simultaneously and disturbingly, fuses features of both wandering and fixity. The stranger, says Simmel, is the wanderer who comes today and stays tomorrow. While he belongs to a spatially defined group, he always remains a potential wanderer. His position in the group is determined by the fact that he has not belonged to it from the beginning, that he imports qualities into it which do not and cannot stem from the group itself. He is an element of the group, in his interactions with it both a fully-fledged member yet outside it and confronting it. His relations with it are contingent, exhibiting a kind of abstraction. Towards the group the stranger feels a certain kind of objectivity, a particular structure of feeling composed of nearness and distance, involvement and indifference, though such is not to be confused with passivity. Such objectivity gives him a kind of freedom, in terms of perception, understanding and evaluation of what others in the group take as given.[10]

I'm trying to recall what led up to the publication of my essay in *Politics* 1972, how did it happen. Remember, dear reader, that, born in 1945, I was young, I didn't know how academic conventions worked. I remember that when I returned to Sydney in late 1968, early 1969, and began tutoring, I was both mixing in Sydney Libertarian pub life with Ann, and also tutoring, first in the Sydney English department in 1969, and then in the English department at Macquarie University from early 1970; perhaps it was at Macquarie that I began reading Australian writers such as Christopher Brennan, Kenneth Slessor, A D Hope, and Patrick White, as well as becoming interested in a manifesto by the painter and novelist Norman Lindsay (who had come from Melbourne to Sydney to join its bohemia), setting out how intellectuals should relate to Australian society.

Somehow, on my return to Sydney it began to occur to me that there was a kind of similarity between what I perceived as a Sydney literary and cultural tradition composed of these artistic and literary figures, and the ideas of the Sydney Libertarians Ann and I were socially mixing with in their bohemian Push, though on the edges, edges giving one a certain distance; one was in it, yet not in it, of it yet not of it; without quite formulating it to ourselves, we wished to preserve the outsider's inner independence, a wariness about being committed to any single set of beliefs or credo or fixed positions one had to follow.

That independence was tested on an occasion I still recall. I can record here that, perhaps because of Ann and my association with the 1970 anti-censorship campaign, at a party in East Balmain, a peninsular in (very) inner west Sydney, standing outside in the backyard, next to a back fence, drinks in hand, night sky overhead, the Bridge not too far away across the dark waters of Sydney Harbour, a Libertarian writer who we had associated with in that campaign, asked us if we wished to *join* the Libertarians. We probably said we would have to think about it, but we didn't join.

⁓⚹⁓

Having come back to Sydney in late 1968, living in Balmain with Ann, socially mixing with Libertarians at the Newcastle hotel in George Street in the city and in Balmain at the Forth and Clyde and parties afterwards, I now conceived the idea that what I regarded as a Melbourne intellectual consciousness – their assumption that whatever was important to Melbourne intellectuals was important to Australian society – was the reverse of a Sydney intellectual and literary consciousness. In both the Sydney literary tradition, and the Sydney Libertarian philosophical tradition, society was registered as indifferent or hostile; society was always to be opposed, and very different realms were to be explored in opposition to society, as alternative modes of being. Each Sydney tradition conceived a notion of what I came to think of as elite pluralism: in themselves they represented an elite of true consciousness, but they could only survive if society was conceived as a plurality of groups, where they were one group among others. I wrote a long essay making this argument, and then, foolhardy as only the young can be, hoped somehow it could be published whole, in the one place.

In Ann and my papers that I looked at in 2011 I came across a folder which contained the original whole essay, all 34 densely typed pages of it, entitled 'Sydney's Intellectual Life: Norman Lindsay, Kenneth Slessor, and Sydney Libertarianism'.

As it turned out, it couldn't be published whole, of course it couldn't, academic journals serve different specialist disciplines and readerships. In 1972 the Libertarian part was published in *Politics*, while in 1973 the literary part appeared in *Australian Literary Studies* as 'Norman Lindsay's *Creative Effort*: Manifesto for an Urban Intelligentsia' (Vol.6, no.1, May 1973, pp.24–35).

'Sydney Intellectual History and Sydney Libertarianism', the 1972 essay in *Politics* – I have the issue before me – was not very long; at the bottom of the first page it mentions that the 'author is a Tutor in the School of English, Macquarie University'. I'll summarise its argument, hopefully trimming lots, occasionally deploying an indented quotation to give the flavour of the original.

I opened by saying that I was taking up historian Manning

Clark's suggestion that where Melbourne produces historians, Sydney produces poets and philosophers.[11] I would focus, I said, on Sydney's distinctive history through a detailed 'history of ideas' analysis of Sydney Libertarianism, in particular, its pessimism about social change; the Libertarians saw themselves as permanently opposing society as a response to an historical situation of inability to influence the Sydney society around them, which became identified with Australian society and then society as such.

I reprised their history, that Sydney Libertarianism developed after a split in the Freethought Society at Sydney University in 1951, over various issues, including the anti-communist referendum, and conscription.[12] Functioning mainly in the middle and late fifties and early sixties, the Libertarians produced a regular *Broadsheet*, brought out three issues of a magazine, *The Libertarian*, and met for discussion at Sydney University and downtown in the city (sometimes, symbolically, in hotels, for example, the Royal George Hotel). They also brought out *The Sydney Line*, a selection from the first twenty-five *Broadsheets*. Their key doctrines, of permanent opposition, social pluralism, and a pluralist interpretation of the concepts of ideology and moralism, were derived, variously, from their interpretations of John Anderson, Max Nomad, Marx, Sorel, Freud and Wilhelm Reich.

From Anderson, the Libertarians derived their social pluralism, and their interest in Marx and Freud.[13] Most of them were Anderson-trained philosophers, or psychologists with philosophic training. They disagreed with Anderson over the question of his authoritarian anti-communism of the fifties, but the key theoretical difference is that Anderson stressed that culture could only continue if critical enquiry were carried on by a 'resistant' minority within the university.[14] Although earlier in his life Anderson had been a Marxist, almost a Communist, and then a Trotskyist, his position was finally one of social pessimism. In the face of an ignorant, moralistic society, a small minority had to pursue freethought and enquiry as goods in themselves, not worrying about the social ends of enquiry; in such a society, enquiry had to be defended as a good in itself against all utilitarian claims on it.

For the early, younger generation of Libertarians emergent in the fifties, I wrote, such an interest must have been too university based – too concerned with intellectual enquiry to the exclusion of a theory which could integrate cultural opposition to society with an inner urban life-style. The Libertarians added an anarchist strand to their thinking, an emphasis on opposition to all forms of authoritarianism, not only the authoritarianism which affected university-based enquiry.[15] They incorporated that aspect of anarchism which emphasised being culturally and personally free now, not waiting for a revolution which hopefully would establish a free society somewhere in the future. At this point I'll quote directly from my 1972 article:

> The Libertarians took over a strand in European anarchist thought called 'pessimistic anarchism', or 'anarchism without ends'.[16] The fusion of this pessimistic anarchism with their social pluralism was the central concept of 'permanent protest'. The term was borrowed from Max Nomad.[17] For the Libertarians, Nomad's view of history was adapted from the 'pessimistic sociologists', Pareto and Michels, using their concepts, the 'circulation of elites' and the 'iron law of oligarchy'.[18] In fact, Nomad's view derived almost entirely from Waclaw Machajski.[19] All societies, whether feudal, capitalist or socialist, are run by elites. These elites are continually being challenged by 'out-elites', the out-elites employing an ideology which claims to represent the causes of the masses. Some reforms are carried out in this struggle between elites and so the burden of the masses, particularly in terms of the standard of living, is occasionally lightened. Nomad thus agrees with the classical anarchist objection to the socialists who wanted to win state power: state power has its own dynamic, and 'in-elites'

never abolish themselves. The classical anarchists, nevertheless, in wanting to abolish the state, looked ahead to a society without conflict or ruling elites. To Nomad and the Libertarians this was clearly naïve and utopian. It was also unpluralist, since there would always be conflict in society. However, the Libertarians' dissatisfaction with Nomad was similar to their dissatisfaction with Anderson. They felt Nomad's concept of permanent protest was too narrowly conceived, in this case in economic and political terms of standards of living and struggle between elites. The Libertarians re-interpreted permanent protest to mean total cultural criticism coincident with a free style of life.[20]

The Libertarians defined ideology to mean that groups in society, attempting to gain more social control for themselves, put forward their own values and beliefs as if they were for the good of all other groups, as if they were universally desirable.[21] As against the classical anarchists like Kropotkin, the Libertarians felt that their pessimistic view of the way groups and ideologies work is politically realistic and toughminded.

This view of ideology had crucial consequences for any interest in reform, or 'meliorism'.[22] If Libertarians were to try to reform society, they would have to put their own values and beliefs across as if they applied to society as a whole. To indulge in 'meliorism' would be to subject oneself to the falsifications of ideology. Also, if one did gain power, one would be just another power-centred elite speaking for the 'common good'. With regard to political movements, Libertarians developed a marked 'cleaned hands' syndrome. Any involvement meant the manipulation of one's own beliefs to include others, which was inherently dishonest.

Reformist activity necessarily concentrated on the future, on social 'ends'. As such it not only involved a manipulative political style (by employing ideology), but ignored the enjoyment of free activities in the present. Social ends could not be achieved anyway, given the laws of history. Libertarianism, then, became a life-style with a justifying pluralist and anti-manipulative social and political theory. The emphasis was on a present oriented lifestyle, which was incompatible with worrying about meliorist ends, whether these ends were reformist or revolutionary.[23] If you were a reformer or a revolutionary, you couldn't be a Libertarian, since you would be future oriented. Future success is illusory.

Permanent opposition was the pursuit of free activities, unhampered by society or social repressions. This particularly applied to free sexual activity.

> ... free love exists in opposition to the prevailing social demand that sexuality be frustrated and, as such, it is a species of permanent protest.[24]

Sex was seen in opposition to society, as of all activities the supremely natural. Because of this, Reich was preferred to Freud as a sexual theorist.[25] Freud insisted too much that explanations of neurosis were to be found within the individual, and in the individual's failure to sublimate sexual energies into other directions of personality.[26] In Freud's view, sublimation was necessary to ensure social stability. Against Freud, Reich asserted the primacy of 'genital' (meaning primarily vaginal and penile contact) sexuality. The 'genital character' formed by this sexuality was superior to the 'neurotic character' produced by society. The most natural sex was seen as heterosexual genital sex, other modes of sexuality being considered implicitly less natural, incapable of discharging sexual energy as completely as genital sexuality:

> ... non-genital modes of discharge leave higher levels of libido in the organism, and a chronically high level of libido causes certain changes in the organism which we know as symptom formation, anxiety attacks and other neurotic activities...[27]

Thus clitoral sexuality, masturbation, lesbianism, and homosexuality were lesser forms of libido discharge, leading potentially to neurotic tensions.[28]

Libertarianism flourished at Sydney University in the 1950s and probably reached its peak of influence and theoretical cohesiveness in the early 1960s. After that time Libertarianism declined, and many former views, particularly the interest in Reich, were largely abandoned, the Sydney University philosopher George Molnar suggesting that the 'amalgam of Freud, Reich, and social pluralism is now little discussed or appreciated'.[29] In the early sixties arguments broke out about moralism, Reich, and Anderson's notion of servility. A downtown group of Libertarians tended to split away from the more theoretical university Libertarians; in 1961 the Libertarians were accused of pursuing their life style without intellectual content – there was now only 'beerhouse theorizing' or 'critical drinking'[30]. Disputes arose over the editing of the *Broadsheets*.

Libertarianism, I argued, rested on a constellation of beliefs and values, Andersonian philosophy, social pluralism, anti-authoritarianism, free activity here and now, critical interests in the early Marx, Freud and Reich, a liking for Sorel's distinction between active producers and passive consumers, and approval of working-class movements which opposed the state (for example, the Wobblies). This constellation was assumed to be internally coherent and necessary. Libertarianism flourished in the 1950s when Australian society was uniformly philistine, when Christianity was making an ideological comeback (for example, in the Newman Society at Sydney University), and when the only model of political activism was a Leninist, anti-intellectual and puritan left. In this situation the Libertarians could feel themselves the one centre of intellectual enquiry and free living. Once there was a greater degree of sexual permissiveness in society, and once the left became more counter-cultural and less exclusively

Leninist, Libertarianism began to falter. Its proponents necessarily became more introspective,[31] or more interested in changing society.[32]

With introspection, Libertarian theory disintegrated, revealing many internal inconsistencies. The hope that in an unfree society Libertarians could maintain their own freedom was seen to be itself utopian.[33] It ignored the point that Libertarians, for example, by having academic positions, were daily involved in compromising authoritarian attitudes or decisions. It ignored, too, that authoritarianism could not simply be wished away from their own social relations, as was revealed in their disputes over what should go into the *Broadsheets*, and in the tensions between the downtown 'critical drinkers' and the university Libertarians.

When a dispute broke out in the *Broadsheets* about whether 'servile' was a moralistic term, some Libertarians defended the term as merely describing an authoritarian relationship which the 'servile' individual accepted and sheltered behind. George Molnar, I thought rightly, argued that 'servile' (a highly moralistic term which Anderson borrowed from Hilaire Belloc) implied that the Libertarians, in an ideological way, thought their own values were desirable for the rest of the community.

The notion of genital sex came under increasing critique from within the Libertarians, not least by George Molnar. Molnar, 1934–99, a Hungarian Jew from Budapest, was a Holocaust survivor who had managed to migrate when young with his mother to Australia in 1951; the novelist Susan Varga, also a postwar migrant from Hungary, writes in her affectionate obituary in the *Sydney Morning Herald*, 9 August 2003, that Molnar was a man of many personae.[34] Now I'm wondering if we can see Molnar as, like Henry Mayer, a stranger in Simmel's terms, the wanderer who came today and stayed tomorrow, involving a degree of detachment from Libertarian group consciousness.[35]

In my article I argued that the need to adopt Reich involved the

Libertarians in a dogmatic and alarmingly unpluralist interpretation of what is sexually desirable. Preoccupied by opposing sexual repression, they insisted on the more real sexuality obtained by the supremely natural 'genital' mode of sex, with its moralistic and monistic focus on vaginal sex alone as the true way to sexual satisfaction, rather than being interested in a plurality of sexual satisfactions. In ignoring a sexual plurality they must have imposed a repressive psychological atmosphere that genital sex as such *had* to be enjoyed.[36]

Fundamentally, the Libertarians felt that they represented consciousness in a society without it. But it was a consciousness based on a definition of human nature which transcended society. A free sexuality would generate in one's consciousness other essential human freedoms; sex, potentially the most free of activities, was bound to generate other free activities.[37] Sexual dissidence would be followed by intellectual and political dissidence. But this was a hope based on an *a priori* definition of human nature, rather than on any certain empirical evidence. Such an incoherence was overlooked while the Libertarians defended themselves as a group against society.

Again, as Molnar suggested, Andersonianism was 'not necessary' as a basis of Libertarian thought, their social pluralism being derivable from other sources.[38] As a sociological method, the pluralism itself can now be seen as clearly inadequate. It was based on assumptions which are apriorist and ultimately anti-historical. History was seen in static terms as consisting of immutable historical laws (the law of oligarchy, the law of permanent opposition). Because they assumed these laws, the Libertarians had no interest in history, which further meant they could not be interested in historical explanation. They assumed that a plurality of groups existed in society. But they could not historically explain the origins of these groups, nor could they relate the ideologies of various groups to larger historical traditions existing before the cross section of social groups they were examining. In their insistence on groups always being plural (a plurality which guaranteed their own right to exist) they had to atomise society; they could not focus on the way groups in history can at times coalesce into larger groupings, perhaps 'classes'. There are historical blocs and continuing traditions as well as atomised social groups caught in a static picture. Also, because they ignored history, their definitions of what constituted a group were bound to be arbitrary and imprecise. They had to assume the analytic importance of the groups they were describing. It is little wonder that the early analyses of particular group conflicts in the first *Broadsheets* petered out.

The Libertarians developed a heavily sub-cultural style, which focused on inner urban living. Although insisting on rationality and consciousness, they were always in danger of anti-intellectualism, of ritualistically holding onto presumed universal natural and social laws. They could not afford to be highly individualistic, tending to hold to their group style with its dependent social pub and café life. However, with this group style went dangers of ingroup manipulation, the more or less subtle influence of power and prestige considerations, a hierarchical male status system, and a narrowness of intellectual and cultural interests.

The Libertarians can be seen as contributing to Sydney's intellectual history in many ways: in their internationalism; in an unutilitarian emphasis on the value of detached enquiry in itself; in consistent attacks on censorship; in an unpretentious, unpompous and refreshingly cynical social style; in their insistence that means should not be subordinated to ends, and their stress that intellectual values can be integrated with life styles. The life styles themselves exhibited a city-centred internationalism, exploiting the value and possibilities of inner city living.

When preparing 'Sydney Intellectual History and Sydney

Libertarianism' for *Politics*, I must have talked about the essay with Henry Mayer; my distant memory is that I visited his house, in Lane Cove, on the north side of the harbour. It was perhaps then that he gave me a copy of his pamphlet, *Mahkaeyvism: The Poverty of Permanent Protest*. He felt strongly that I should make one thing clear in my essay, that the Libertarians wrongly believed that Nomad's view of history was adapted from the 'pessimistic sociologists', Pareto and Michels, using their concepts, the 'circulation of elites' and the 'iron law of oligarchy'. Henry said this needs correcting, it needs to be pointed out that in fact Nomad's view derived almost entirely from Waclaw Machajski; I made this correction in the text and in an explanatory footnote. I'll return in a moment to Henry's interest in this late nineteenth early twentieth century Polish-Russian thinker, born in Poland in 1866, died in Moscow in 1926, skeptical, to the point of hostile, theorist of intellectuals.

When I looked at Ann and my papers in 2011, there was a folder, entitled 'Lindsay/Libertarian Article Correspondence (mainly Mayer)'. This has personal material from Henry, especially letters, that in 1971/1972 I perhaps didn't take as much notice of as I should. My main concern then was textual, to analyse a range of Libertarian writings, especially in the *Broadsheets*, Paul Reubner, a friend of ours in the Push drinking scene, had lent me all the copies he had collected over the years, I think he said he had collected all of them. But now, looking at Henry's 1971/1972 letters, I can see how impassioned they are, especially concerning his own involvement with the Libertarians and his critical assessments of their main ideas. I can now see that he had his own reasons for publishing my essay; how sharply he felt that the Libertarians had betrayed him and their own pluralist ideals; his feeling that their much heralded pluralism should have been hospitable to a wider variety of viewpoints, even viewpoints that were highly critical of their key concepts, limited cultural interests, and intellectual heroes (like Max Nomad and Wilhelm Reich); he had tested their pluralism, and instead of responding to his challenges with reflection and self-questioning they answered with repudiation, with censorship.

Henry's typos, especially in hurried notes suggesting one should read something, were famous. However, the following letter, concerning my proposed article, reads fairly smoothly, and it was certainly a pleasure for a young author to peruse it. I can't see a date on it.

> Dear John Docker,
>
> I like this very much indeed. If you've not done so yet, it might be worthwhile showing it to Ian Bedford who was always one of the most autonmous [sic] people in the group. Overall, your view is somewhat too rosy – no doubt because you look at it from a more general angle. You might also look at Doug McCallum's thing on Anderson and Libs.
>
> (I think) it was in Highway. And there was an impt. transitional paper *The Critic* (?) which might be worth looking at – Doug wd know.
>
> The Nomad thing is the only factual error to be fixed. When you're ready, give me a ring at 422055 and I will try and dig up the refs. I mentioned. As to Nomad being based on Machajski – I seem to recall I did show this in the ronoed [sic] paper I mention which, hopefully is in Mitchell. I'm sure it's crude and dreadful.
>
> I was glad to see this.
>
> Regards,
> Sincerely,
> Henry Mayer

⁓❦⁓

In Mitchell Library in 2011 I came across Henry's reflections on my essay after he had received it and while reading it; the comments, on 'John Docker's ch.', are signed 'hm' and dated 1 August 1971 and he may have sent them to me or given them to me to read over and ponder. It's clear from these notes that Henry had broken sharply with the Libertarians and he felt that at times I was being too kind to them, though he also saw that I did make some critical remarks and he responded to these with his own memories of what occurred some ten years or so before:

p.23 key doctrines of libertarians:
(a) the 'social pluralism' (a reference bottom p.24 to 'inner-urban life style' and 'being culturally and personally free now') was in fact much more restrictive than is being implied here and in the whole analysis. You rely too much on Jim Baker, who always glamorized the whole thing.

In fact there were a whole set of very strict taboos eg you must not eat in bourgeois restaurants; you must not mix (much) with non Lib circles; you must not be interested in art; you must, in literature, be mainly interested in Joyce, Dos Passos; you must not be selective at parties etc etc.

If the stress is on the contribution of Libs to Sydney, your emphasis is fair enough, at the same time (this is not unusual) the <u>internal</u> structure of the group was remarkably authoritarian and their interests, as intellectuals, very narrow. Hence, in this sense, it is very misleading to speak of '<u>total</u> cultural opposition' (24 bottom) which suggests a much greater <u>scope</u> for Lib outlook than there was.

p.25 Nomad. This is definitely false, and needs fixing. Nomad's views derive almost entirely from a Polish chap Waclaw Machajski, who (this is why impt.) wrote long <u>before</u> Michels and Pareto. M. was (in so far as one can use this concept at all) 'the father' of the view that socialism meant a new ruling class of intellectuals and (this impt. for you) that <u>knowledge</u> was a form of 'capital'. He attacked Marx and Bakunin. The 'pessimistic anarchism' was, then, a minor strand in European anarchist thought. Nomad traed on the fact that M's work was only available (allegedly) in a few onion-skin copies in Plish, he used him in the US to make a living, and never translated his master's stuff. At the time, I attacked Nomad and dug up what little there was on Machajski and his group known as Makheavites. The Libs were supposed to publish this, but when they saw it was critical of them, refused, so I published it. It is pretty crummy, I think, though have not looked at it for years. I did put a copy in Mitchell – it's called the Poverty of Makhaeyism. If you cannot find it there, I will see whether I have a copy anywhere.

As to M. there have [been] 2–3 serious pieces on him since then – my stuff was amateurish – and I could dig up ref. to these.

The main point is M's stress on intellectuals as the next ruling class, and his view of the functions of 'knowledge' neither of which, in this form, are in Pareto/Michels.

p.27 anti-manipulative theory – well, maye, but the nightly life was one of super manipulation, cliques, and more of it – the thing night by night was round 80% that, who would stab whom in the back and more manipulative than most bourgeois life styles obviously are.

p.29 bottom 'deluded into' – while I was associated with it, there were pretty constant dispues re 'scientific' most people I recall took the view that it wqs a competing moralotyl.

p.30 monistic sex. Very very true – in my last weeks with them I gve a paper debunking the concept of vaginal orgasm, there were attemps to susppres it, Baker intervened as chairman against sich heresy etc etc.

I don't want to get into a general discussion of 'pluralism'... just to point out that there is a plurality of pluralisms, that Lib. was one rather poor versoj of this, and – something you stress in the MS but not so much here – that to me its chief merit was that it took over (from Marx ?????) a <u>conflict</u> rather than consensus model. There are 2 distinct issues: a. re cpmflict/harmony b. re <u>what</u> it is that conflicts.

[At times Henry's typos did threaten clarity, though one also recalls W.H. Auden's appreciation of a printer's error in his poem 'Journey to Iceland', transforming the line 'The poets have names for the sea' into 'The ports have names for the sea', Auden writing to Christopher Isherwood that the 'mistake seems better than the original idea'.]

p.32 concscousness within you – excellent but 'impossible to conceive' ????? many 'conceived' at the level of deriving it from 'free fucking' then ratiomalized in crude Reichian terms. There was also – you ignore this enrrley – the role of the GURU – absorption by osmosis etc. Trmenedous jealousis as to who at a given occassion, a camp or party might displace or replace (f absent) – No.1. Guru. With guruhood went bootty in terms of grog and girls – and <u>obligation</u> to be sexually avaiable to 'recognized' girl stars.

hm 1 August 71

I now realise, taking a fresh look at these fascinating notes as I sit here in Perth writing in August/September 2018, how very personal was Henry's interest in my essay, he says he was censored twice by the Libertarians, they refused to publish his critique of Nomad being so derivative of Machajski, and when he gave a talk, a critique of the notion of 'vaginal orgasm' as monistic, in 'my last weeks with them' as he puts it, there were attempts to suppress it and Jim Baker as chair intervened, presumably to stop Henry speaking.

In these notes, Henry was reprising his intellectual journey through and beyond the Libertarians in the early 1960s; no wonder he was so receptive to my intellectual journey through and beyond them in the early 1970s.

※

In Mitchell in 2011, I saw in a folder, along with a copy of Henry's essay 'Makhaeyvism: The Poverty of "Permanent Protest"', which I will evoke in a moment, a large envelope addressed to me at Macquarie University, sent by HM, with the following note.

Govt. 16-8-71

Dear John,

Enclosed the 3 main things in English on M. – it will be more than you'll need.

Regards,
Sincerely,
Henry Mayer

In the envelope were three offprints: S V Utechin, 'Bolsheviks and their Allies after 1917: The Ideological Pattern', *Soviet Studies* Vol.X, No.2, October 1958 pp.113–35; Paul Avrich, 'What is "Makhaevism"?' *Soviet Studies* July '63, pp.65–75; Marshall Shatz, 'Jan Waclaw Machajski: The "Conspirac" of the Intellectuals', *Survey* Jan '67 No.62 pp.45–57.

Henry may have hoped I would discuss these in my 1972 *Politics* essay, but I probably felt my exposition of the ideas of the Libertarians would lose focus; I contented myself with a clear statement borrowed from Henry that, 'In fact, Nomad's view derived almost entirely from Waclaw Machajski', and in a footnote I listed Paul Avrich's essay and added also what Henry had told me, 'The Libertarians interpreted Nomad through the concepts of Pareto and Michels, who did not, unlike Machajski, stress that the intellectuals were to be the next ruling class.' In the same footnote, I referred to 'the critique of Nomad, and, indirectly, of Libertarian theory in Henry Mayer, *Makhaeyvism: The Poverty of Permanent Protest*, roneoed pamphlet, Sydney, n.d. (1961?).'

How I first obtained a copy of Henry's essay 'Makhaeyvism: The Poverty of "Permanent Protest"' in 1971–1972 I really can't precisely recall now. However, in Mitchell Library in 2011, when I opened the folder entitled 'Lindsay/Libertarian Article Correspondence (mainly Mayer)', there was the essay, and sitting there in Mitchell I took notes of passages I thought particularly interesting; what I present here is quite abridged. As political theory the essay reveals a penetrating mind, forensically logical.

Henry Mayer, <u>Makhaeyvism: The Poverty of 'Permanent Protest'</u>

The ideas of Waclaw Machajski have acquired a certain popularity among those who think in terms of 'permanent protest'. In this article, I shall give an exposition and criticism of Machajski's ideas, and then turn to a brief appraisal of Nomad's views.

I shall try to show that neither Machajski nor Nomad are to be taken very seriously as social theorists.

I <u>Makhaeyvism</u>

What is Makhaeyvism? It is essentially an attempt, on the basis of Marx's labour theory of value, to describe the place of the intellectuals in society, combined with some ideas which run parallel to Bakunin and syndicalism.

Its analytical theses are:
(1) 'Education' or 'Knowledge' are to be treated as a sort of 'means of production' or 'capital'.

(2) Since the possessors of this intellectual capital are the 'intellectuals' or 'intellectual workers', they are a separate social class, with its own class interests and class ideology...

...(4) In their struggle against the capitalists, the intellectuals look round for a mass-basis, an army. They find it in the unskilled workers...

I think [Mayer continues] Machajski's attraction to some people rests on their belief that he is establishing a general social theory; that he is asserting a universal connection between a particular class and the mass basis through which it gains power; between that class and its mass basis and a particular ideology; and between the criteria of that class and its power position. But, in fact, there is no <u>logical</u> connection between his points. He is not setting up a 'model' or 'ideal type', he does not try to show that the Intellectuals <u>cannot</u> assert their interests by means of a non-socialist ideology, nor that they <u>cannot</u> acquire ruling power by basing themselves on a class other than the unskilled workers, nor that the unskilled workers cannot follow a non-socialist ideology.

IV <u>Max Nomad</u>

Nomad derives most of his interesting ideas from Michels. Michels was an impressive thinker, and his 'Political Parties' should not be judged by the vulgar and shoddy summary of it in Burnham's 'The Machiavellians'.

For Nomad, 'permanent protest' is a means to an end which will never be wholly achieved, but which, in any case, has no necessary connection with opposition to authority as such.

VI <u>Conclusion</u>

So much for Machajski and Nomad. What now of the slogan of

'permanent protest' in general? Does it serve to characterize the general attitude of an anti-authoritarian group?

> ... one may say that as long as, but only so long as, there are indeed resources to be distributed, approval to be bestowed, and as long as there must be reliance on these, as they arise from within the group, there will be a permanent struggle between the permanent critics.
>
> <u>It will be a joy to behold.</u>
>
> Henry Mayer

From those final sentences, turning the notion of permanent protest back onto the Libertarians themselves, we can take it that in *Makhaeyvism: The Poverty of Permanent Protest*, Henry Mayer was saying goodbye to the Sydney Libertarians, whom he now felt deserved only contempt.

To adapt Walter Benjamin, we can say that in the Sydney Libertarians, Mayer encountered Those in History Who Would Always Betray You.

❦

I'm sure I only briefly glanced at the three articles, by S V Utechin, Paul Avrich and Marshall Shatz, that Henry sent to me on 16 August 1971. In Mitchell in 2011, looking at them, I decided to read them properly and take notes, my feeling was that here is a strand of intellectual and political history worth trying to understand, that might well relate to growing up in a Communist family. I'll summarise the three articles as quickly as I can, they tend to overlap with each other. I'll begin with S V Utechin's 'Bolsheviks and their Allies after 1917: The Ideological Pattern'.

Utechin tells us that the Petrograd coup of 17 November 1917 brought to power in Russia the Bolshevik Party, but far from being single-minded in matters of ideology as Lenin would have wished, party members exhibited a remarkable variety of views and tendencies, mostly continuations of pre-1917 ideological traditions and their sub-divisions. There were the various branches of the Marxist tree: Leninism, Bogdanovism, and Social-Democratism; there was Populism in its two main forms, radical and moderate (Neo-Populism); Anarchism was in the mix; there was the ideology of industrial managers and technicians – Technocentrism; étatist ideology in its new form of National Bolshevism; and the eccentric development of religious thought, Fyodorovism.

There was also, Utechin writes, another ideology that had for long existed on the fringes of the party, Makhayevism, given systematic form by a former Polish Social-Democrat, J W Machajski, while in banishment in Siberia in 1898–1900, though, Utechin observes, the anti-intellectual bias which was fundamental to Makhayevism had been known in Russian Social Democracy from its earliest beginnings. Utechin argues that Makhayevist theory was an attempt, starting from the basic conceptions of orthodox Marxism, to find an answer to the question of the place occupied in the social organism by the intelligentsia. In Machajski's view, knowledge is a kind of means of production, and its possession by the intelligentsia means that the latter is a separate social class. In the process of production and distribution the intelligentsia appropriates a part of the surplus value; hence, and this is the main thesis of Makhayevism, it is an exploiting class. The interests of the intelligentsia are therefore necessarily opposed to the interests of the proletariat, and the 'Socialist' phraseology of the intelligentsia is merely a device in the struggle for its own interests. It wants to use the proletariat for the socialization of the means of material production, which would then be managed by the intelligentsia without interference from the capitalists. But the intelligentsia does not want to 'socialize knowledge', the means of intellectual production; rather, they wish to preserve it for their own monopolistic possession.

Socialism, then, is the 'class ideal' of the intelligentsia, which wants to replace capitalists and to concentrate in its hands all means of domination over the proletariat.

Utechin reflects that Makhayevist ideas influenced the thinking and behaviour of a large section of the Bolshevik party after 1917. They were the core of all 'intellectual-baiting' tendencies, fashionable in the party, despite half-hearted reproofs from the party authorities, until 1936, when Stalin declared that the intellectual-baiting of the Makhayevists must no longer be applied to the new Soviet intelligentsia. The Makhayevists became victims of the Great Purge of 1937, which put an end to all remnants of organized heterodoxy, physically eliminated most heterodox thinkers, and silenced the rest.

Paul Avrich's essay, 'What is "Makhaevism?"' is more biographical in focus, relating that Jan Waclaw Machajski was born in 1866 in Busk, a small town situated near the city of Kielce in Russian Poland. He was the son of an indigent clerk, who died when Machajski was a child, leaving a large and destitute family. Machajski attended the *gimnaziye* in Kielce and helped support his brothers and sisters by tutoring the schoolmates who boarded in his mother's apartment. He began his revolutionary career in 1888 in the student circles of Warsaw University, where he had enrolled in the faculties of natural science and medicine. Two or three years later, while attending the University of Zurich, he abandoned his first political philosophy (a blend of socialism and Polish nationalism) for the revolutionary internationalism of Marx and Engels.

Machajski was arrested in May 1892 for smuggling revolutionary proclamations from Switzerland into the industrial city of Lodz, which was then in the throes of a general strike. In 1903, after a dozen years in prison and Siberian exile, he escaped to western Europe, where he remained until the outbreak of the 1906 revolution.

During his long term of banishment in the Siberian settlement of Vilyuisk (in Yakutsk province), Machajski made an intensive study of socialist literature and came to the conclusion that the Social Democrats did not really champion the cause of the manual workers, but rather a new class of 'mental workers' engendered by the rise of industrialism. In a so-called 'socialist' society, Machajski declared, private capitalists would merely be replaced by a new aristocracy of administrators, technical experts, and politicians; the manual labourers would be enslaved anew by a ruling minority whose 'capital', so to speak, was education.

To avoid this new enslavement, Machajski proposed the creation of a secret organization of revolutionaries called the Workers' Conspiracy, similar to Bakunin's 'secret society' of revolutionary conspirators. The mission of the Workers' Conspiracy was to stimulate the workers to 'direct action' – strikes, demonstrations, and the like – against the capitalists with the immediate object of winning economic improvements and jobs for the unemployed. The 'direct action' of the workers was to culminate in a general strike which, in turn, would trigger off a world-wide uprising, ushering in an era of equal income and educational opportunity. In the end, the pernicious distinction between manual and mental labour would be obliterated, together with all class divisions.

Avrich tells us that Machajski's theories provoked passionate discussions within the various groups of Russian radicals. In Siberia, his critique of Social Democracy 'had a great effect upon the exiles', as Trotsky, who was among them, recalled in his autobiography.

Avrich concludes that although neither the Workers' Conspiracy nor any other organization of Makhayevtsy reappeared in 1917, the spirit of Makhaevism was much in evidence within the labour movement, in the Bolshevik Party as well as among anarchists.

In Mitchell Libary in 2011 I took only brief notes of Marshall

Shatz's 'Jan Waclaw Machajski: The "Conspiracy" of the Intellectuals'. I must have thought then that it didn't add anything substantial to what had already been suggested by Utechin and Avrich's essays, so all I copied out was Shatz telling us that it is unlikely that Machajski in the early twenties, before his death in Moscow in February 1926, had any direct connection to such opposition groups as the Workers' Truth and the Workers' Group, which arose within the Communist Party; but their complaints against the 'new bourgeoisie' of party bureaucrats and managers bore similarities to Machajski's doctrines.

Marshall Shatz continued his interest in Machajski as a significant historical figure, publishing a biography in 1989, *Jan Waclaw Machajski: A radical critic of the Russian intelligentsia and socialism*. The Anarchist Library has placed the biography on its website. In his Preface, Shatz writes that part of the interest of Machajski is the sheer originality of the group of ideas named after him, Makhaevism, a novel synthesis of various elements of anarchism, Marxism, and syndicalism. In the biography, Shatz makes clear, he will touch on more general histories, such as the idea of the 'new class' (an idea first articulated by Bakunin as part of an anarchist critique of Marxism, but given more systematic form by Machajski), anarchism, socialism, the role of intellectuals in the modern world. But his predominant interest will be in Machajski's notions of the role of the intelligentsia in Russian life, its identity, class character, and ultimate aspirations.

Looking back on my growing up in a Communist family, I can relate Machajski's radical distrust of intellectuals as wishing to appropriate power and control for themselves, to my father's frequent asseveration that I've talked about before, that in a revolutionary situation intellectuals were not to be trusted, and his narrating with some satisfaction how he helped expell writers and intellectuals from the Communist Party like Judah Waten and Guido Baracchi (yet much later was perhaps haunted by what he did).

I also now wonder if there is a touch of Machajski's sociology of intellectuals as a new class in the Arena Project I've talked about, their view that the intellectually trained as a rising group in modern society were fatally cut off from traditional and continuing face-to-face relationships, helping to pervade modernity with a destructive spirit of abstraction.

A week or two ago, I was talking with Ann over dinner at Zenos, our favourite fish restaurant near where we live in Hillarys in northern Perth (now unhappily defunct, we visited a few nights ago, a Saturday night, the restaurant was boarded up, it happens too often in one's life, always a slightly traumatic event), about Henry Mayer and his long ago wishing me to read about Machajski; how, now, having read the essays he had sent me, I was learning a lot more about Machajski's distrust of intellectuals and wondering if this might relate to my father. Ann said her mother would say similar things about intellectuals when she was growing up in her Communist family in Newcastle. Of course, I immediately extracted a promise from Ann that she would talk about this aspect of her family history, and its complex working out.

ANN (8 August 2018): I remember when I was leaving my Newcastle home at the age of 17 to go to the University of Sydney, in early 1963, my mother saying to me to beware of intellectuals. Learn all you can, Ann, but remember to maintain your loyalty to the working class, not to intellectuals, who have their own agendas and can't be trusted. Something like that. I took her warnings to heart, for a while, and then gradually became absorbed into the university-based milieu I was now in, shifting from Communist to New Left politics, and becoming an intellectual myself. My mother never challenged my changing politics, or admonished me in any way for them; she was always supportive and interested.

Her warnings are slightly curious, on reflection, in view of the fact her parents had both been teachers, her husband was a scientist, and she both read widely and occasionally wrote for publication, such as a series of biographical essays on women in history. However, at this point, she had not herself been to university; that was something she did a little later, in the late 1960s, along with many other women of her generation. Later, she wrote several major essays on Communist history, and jointly authored a book on the history of the Union of Australian Women. Her distrust of intellectuals in 1963, I think, was absorbed as part of her Communist Party membership and loyalty, and over time, especially as in her forties she completed a BA with honours in Psychology, I suspect it faded, and eventually disappeared.

Henry's interest in, and publishing in *Politics* in 1972, my essay on the Sydney Libertarians, was not the last time Henry and I had contact. I've just plucked from my shelves a couple of issues of *Media Information Australia*. In its issue No.30 November 1983 appears my essay 'Give Them Facts – The Modern Gradgrinds'. On the contents page, it records that *Media Information Australia* is produced for the Australian Film and Television School, and that Prof. Henry Mayer is Academic Editor and Chairman of the Editorial Board. I can't remember how it came about that Henry encouraged me to write 'Give Them Facts – The Modern Gradgrinds', but he made it the opening article for the issue; I've just glanced through it; I begin by saying that, in essays recently published elsewhere, 'I have argued for the importance and value of "popular culture", particularly television'; I say how much I disagree with the 'left pessimist' view that popular culture, mass culture, 'secures mass conformity, or ideological hegemony for dominant social values', rather, I maintain, mass culture builds on and transforms 'ancient and continuing elements of popular culture'; programs like quiz shows, I instance *Sale of the Century* and *The New Price is Right*, 'incorporate "popular" attitudes that stress participation by audiences in the studio and at home', refuting the bedrock left pessimist view that audiences for mass culture are always passive; I suggest TV shows like the New York comedy *Taxi* and soaps like *Dallas*, *Knots Landing*, and *Dynasty* reveal that the 'desire for wealth and power leads to manipulativeness, coldness, distrust, disaster in relationships'; in *Prisoner*, 'we can see a stress on sharing, cooperation, loyalty, trust, however precarious, amongst the prisoners, as they resist the authority and power that tries to divide and repress them'; I suggest also that popular television culture does not confine itself to realism or naturalism, but 'explores as well fantasy, melodrama, pantomime and magic'.

I also see that I defend shows such as *I Dream of Jeannie* and *Bewitched*, involving female magic, and evoke the 'kind of mayhem, chaos, and anarchy that relates a lot of comedy to "carnival"', hence acting out the 'reversals and inversions of social order, of authority, power, status, rationality', that have been 'important for centuries' in popular culture more generally. For this argument I cite an essay by the British cultural theorist Terry Lovell ('A Genre of Social Disruption?', in Jim Cook ed., *Television Sitcom*, 1982, p.29), which I had found illuminating, and also the literary and cultural historian Ian Donaldson's 1970 book *The World Upside-Down*. I hadn't yet made my own explorations of carnival and carnivalesque in the popular culture of early modern Europe, which, with the assistance of Mikhail Bakhtin, I pursued in the middle 1980s at the Humanities Research Centre at the Australian National University, where Ian Donaldson was its director and encouraged my interest. This research eventually resulted in my 1994 book *Postmodernism and Popular Culture: A Cultural History*.

Towards the end of 'Give Them Facts – The Modern Gradgrinds', I confide that in 'the last couple of years I've taken arms against what I regard as the dominant Marxist and radical positions on popular culture', which led to almost theatrical displays of hostility towards Ann and me by our fellow cultural studies practitioners when we gave a frankly admiring paper on *Prisoner* at the Australian Communication Association conference in Sydney in July 1983, entitled '"Nothing but nasty people behaving nastily in a nasty situation": A Discussion of *Prisoner*'. We argued that *Prisoner* (known in the US as *Cell Block H*), was conspicuously sympathetic to the group of women prisoners rather than to authority, and we related such sympathy to the principle of inversion, of World Upside Down, the reversal of the usual and accepted in any society, and then related, with the assistance of Ian Donaldson's *The World Upside-Down*, such inversion to a long cultural history in early modern Europe that included seventeenth century comic drama as well as carnival and popular imagery. At the end of our talk, one prominent cultural studies practitioner rose from his seat, red in face, and shouted in true left pessimist mode how wrong we were to talk about World Upside Down and cultural inversion in that way, since, as everyone knows, popular television shows like *Prisoner* were obviously mere safety valves.[39] I also recall that at the end of the session, when we got to the tea and coffee room, not one of our cultural studies confreres would come over to talk to us, a line seemed to have been drawn across the room, instead of the usual conviviality we stood there talking to each other.

Another theatrical moment occurred at the same conference; during discussion time by another paper giver, I asked a question suggesting that the paper giver had not made a necessary distinction between as it were high culture television such as the BBC and the ABC, and popular culture programs, they were, I suggested, wrongly lumped together as mass culture. The paper giver paused for a moment, and said something like, I refuse to answer a question from someone who likes quiz shows like *The New Price is Right*.

Looking back at 'Give Them Facts – The Modern Gradgrinds',

and thinking of Machajski, there is a thread throughout the essay that too much ties mass culture and its left pessimist critics to a specific class formation of working class and professional middle class. I had begun by trumpeting that 'Australian society is divided on class cultural lines', where popular television culture is 'despised' by those who identify with the 'ABC and the Fairfax print media', purveying a 'middle class cultural continuity' of 'smug superiority'. At the end, I ringingly declare that I now see 'puritanic rationalism as not just an *intellectual* attitude that can be argued for and against intellectually. I now see it as a class assumption, an assumption shared by radical intellectuals with other, non-radical, members of their class, the professional middle class. In adults such puritanic rationalism is probably incurable. But let's try and save the children!'

It wasn't too long before I drifted away from trying to tie cultural differences to class, it was way too schematic, too restrictive, it foreclosed open thinking, its conclusions were already decided. I became more and more interested in postmodernism, with its delight in the extravagance, exuberance, parody, self-parody and excess, of popular genres from romance through detective fiction to melodrama.

As for the children, they also were saved from the puritanic rationalism of their parents' generation by growing up in a postmodern era of relaxed pleasure in popular genres.

⁕

In *Media Information Australia* No.59 February 1991, pp.7–26, Henry Mayer published a long contribution of mine as the lead essay, entitled 'Popular Culture versus the State: An Argument against Australian Content Regulations for Television'. I've just glanced at it again. I'll try to be as brief as I can in talking about it. In a preamble, I quote for an epigraph from the section on Panopticism in Foucault's *Discipline and Punish*: 'Bentham's

Panopticon is the architectural figure of this composition', where, Foucault writes, 'the inmate must never know whether he is being looked at at any one moment; but he must be sure that he may always be so'. I did have a Panopticon in view, the Australian Broadcasting Tribunal, specifically when in November 1989 the Tribunal released its television program standard 14, regulating Australian content on commercial television.

In the preamble I explain that I wrote a critical response concerning program standard 14 for the *Sydney Morning Herald* (14 December 1989), which drew on a report I had researched and written in 1988 for the Federation of Australian Commercial Television Stations (FACTS); it was appended to the submission FACTS presented to the Tribunal's public inquiry into Australian content, an inquiry that had been proceeding for much of the decade. Standard 14 required the commercial stations to operate under a points system that heavily favoured drama production and arts/intellectual programs. Further, the shorter drama is – that is, the less like long-running series or serials (serial melodrama, the soaps) – the more it will be favoured.

I then explain that my FACTS report took several months to research and write and occasioned no little trepidation on my part. I'd never heard of anyone coming from a 'left' intellectual culture, with its traditional opposition to capital and capitalism, to the world of big business, to businessmen, to media companies, the media moguls, commercial television – I knew of no one who had done such a thing. I confided that when it became known ('Docker has done a report supporting FACTS'), I gathered my intervention into the Australian content debate was felt around the radical-intellectual traps to be scandalous, incomprehensible, unconscionable, baffling, unpleasant.

I also explain that throughout the 1980s I had written essays challenging what I took to be the radical-modernist orthodoxies in media studies, in particular that there could not be long continuities between popular television and the carnivalesque culture of early modern Europe; and I welcomed 'aesthetic postmodernism', with its mixing of 'high' and 'low' genres and consequent relativising of aesthetic values and criteria.

Increasingly, I went on, it began to seem to me that a logical consequence of such relativising was that the regulation of popular culture by the state was based on highly questionable cultural judgments and theory. I also thought it was time that a long tradition of support for state surveillance and policing of popular culture was challenged.

I explained that I tried to get the FACTS report, some 35 000 words long, published as a book, but this didn't happen. I then record my thanks to Henry Mayer for inviting me to air my report and update it if need be in *Media Information Australia*, only asking me to condense it to 13 000 words. This I did, noting in the preamble that I was not opposed to state regulation of broadcasting as such; every aspect of society is subject to regulations, more or less; in this case, I considered, it should be very much less.

One alarming feature I homed in on. The public interest groups supporting Australian content regulations for commercial television, – centred on encouraging arts and drama production, where the assumption was that drama in the theatre should set the standard for all other drama, – loudly demanded that the regulations be very strictly enforced and policed. There was a repertoire of terms referring to the need to discipline, to punish; an affection for a language of compulsion, which, on New Left anarchist grounds, I felt repelled by.

In a final section, 'Is there a Common Broadcasting Good? What Do the Philosophers Say?', I suggested that the public interest groups supporting punitive Australian content regulations saw audiences in Reithian BBC/ABC terms as there to be instructed, educated, informed, enlightened. I charted an intellectual history for this moralistic and paternalist view going back to social and educational ideals associated with the development, within liberal philosophy in Britain and Australia in the late nineteenth century, of New Liberalism, a philosophical attempt to maintain social harmony, to unite society around common goals, the common good. Unlike earlier laissez-faire liberals, the New Liberals urged an expanded conception of the role of the state, which would embody the larger purposes of society that individuals should identify themselves with.

I referred to this New Liberal philosophy as altruistic elitism; everyone in society was to join together in a community of shared values, but there was no question who, ethically, intellectually, culturally, was to lead and who to follow; who were to create the values that would be shared and should constitute the common good; who were the ideal citizens that should be the model for all others. A key figure in espousing New Liberalism early in the twentieth century in Australia was the University of Sydney philosopher Francis Anderson, who had taught philosophy to ABC chairman Richard Boyer. Another New Liberal trained in Francis Anderson's philosophy, Garnet Vere Portus, director of tutorial classes at Sydney University from 1918 to 1934, was influential in the ABC in the 1930s in promoting the notion of the 'talks man', the talking radio head who informs and enlightens.

Yet, I pointed out, the notion of the common good is not at all in the history of philosophy an uncontested or uncontroversial notion. In Australia New Liberalism would, from the late 1920s on, be vigorously opposed by John Anderson, who succeeded Francis Anderson at Sydney University and was professor of philosophy from 1928 to 1958. For some three decades John Anderson was a pervasive influence in Sydney intellectual life, helping establish what became known as the Sydney freethought tradition and its offshoot the Sydney Libertarians. Anderson and fellow philosophers like P H Partridge [and J A Passmore] argued very strongly for social pluralism and just as strongly against what they considered was the chief enemy of pluralism, the notion of the common good. Writing in 1945, a highwater mark of New Liberal influenced plans for postwar reconstruction, Partridge argued that within any society there will be conflict between different interests. The state, therefore, cannot represent all interests but will be pressured to legislate on behalf of some and in opposition to others.

Partridge was not against all forms of state activity – for example, it can be useful in counteracting political and economic inequalities, or in providing free education – but he felt increasingly uneasy about plans for the state to assume ultimate responsibility for carrying on important social activities; by state planning for production, education, leisure. Such state planning will, he argued, increasingly involve the use of official 'experts' who will potentially become a new, privileged governing group of professional administrators.

John Anderson had written a couple of years before that the greatest danger to democracy was submission to experts, who shelter behind an inaccessible central political authority and become another self-interested group in society. In a time-honoured ideological way, they will put forward their own particular views and values as universal.

Can't we, I asked, apply such an analysis both to the Australian Broadcasting Tribunal, playing cultural engineer with popular television, and to the public interest groups? In inquiry after inquiry, advocate after advocate of the public interest groups put forward a New Liberal derived ideal of social and cultural betterment through broadcasting as if that ideal represented the common good, *the* public interest. Further, in inquiry after inquiry these advocates strongly argued for the necessity of 'experts' who, sheltered behind state bodies, would decide what should go on commercial TV screens, for children and adults alike – which is to say, basically what already goes on ABC TV screens. Given their fealty to the notion of the common good, it's no surprise that they exhibit an ever gnawing hunger to homogenise broadcasting, to blanket it with their own criteria.

In my Conclusion, I suggested that perhaps it was time that the tide of debate should start flowing the other way, that we more and more scrutinise the quality of argument of the public interest advocates supporting standard 14, especially their overall lack of cultural generosity, tolerance, pluralism, delight in difference. It was high time that the public interest groups defended their desire and right to be, in Foucault's terms, a panopticon imposing on popular culture a 'regime of truth'.

[29 August 2018: the epigraph from Foucault I began with concerning Bentham's Panopticon, can, I now hazard, be applied to program standard 14 and the 'experts' who were to supervise its functioning. Those in commercial television, inmates of a certain kind of prison, would constantly have before their eyes the tall outline of a central tower, standard 14, from which they are being surveilled by the tower's guards, the watchful vigilant 'experts'; the inmates must never know whether at any one moment they are being looked at, but they can be sure that they may always be so.

Thinking now about the power to be given by the state to 'experts' in deciding and enforcing a common broadcasting good, I'm tempted to recall Machajski's historical warning, his distrust of intellectuals as wishing to appropriate power and control for themselves, the 'experts' as a new class, a new rising group of the intellectually trained.]

☙ ❦ ❧

Media Information Australia 59 came out in February 1991. Only a few months later, Henry Mayer died, 4 May 1991.

A wake was held in the politics department at the University of Sydney, which I attended.

For the 1991 essay in *Media Information Australia* essay I had drawn on Chapter 8, 'John Anderson and the Sydney Freethought Tradition', of my 1974 *Australian Cultural Elites: Intellectual Traditions in Sydney and Melbourne*, where it is clear that decades before I had become very interested in Anderson and P H Partridge and J A Passmore, his students from the 1930s who by the 1940s had become his associates in building up the Sydney freethought tradition. I felt their social pluralism was and still is impressive, is relevant to our times, is certainly worthy of careful attention and contemplation; opposed to the doctrine of assimilation, they stressed the importance of the multicultural, and what we now refer to as an intersectional understanding of social being; I mentioned this to Ann, and she suggested that the Andersonians were perhaps intersectional *avant la lettre*.

In the chapter 'John Anderson and the Sydney Freethought Tradition', I begin by sketching in the long career of John Anderson; his tenure as Professor of Philosophy at Sydney University from 1927 to 1958 spanned, in political terms, an interest in the possibilities of Russia as a 'worker's state', Trotskyism, sympathy for trade union activism, and in the Cold War 1950s a turn to anti-communism and 'anti-proletarianism'. However, looking back, I moved too quickly, I should have offered biographical information about Anderson's earlier, pre-Sydney, life, which might turn out to be illuminating for his later philosophical concerns. I'll try quickly to make up for that absence now.

I've just looked up the *ADB* entry, by W M O'Neil, published in Vol.7, 1979. John Anderson (1893–1962) was born 1 November 1893, Lanarkshire, Scotland; he attended the University of Glasgow, graduating in philosophy in 1917; during 1920–26 he taught at the University of Edinburgh. He was trained in Absolute Idealism but came to reject it; of twentieth century philosophers he was interested in William James, G E Moore, and Bertrand Russell, the American new 'realists', and the Australian-born Samuel Alexander. Outside of philosophy in the narrow sense, he was interested in Freud, Marx, and the 'political pluralists' of Orage's journal *New Age*, but his interpretations of all these thinkers was often highly original and idiosyncratic. His general position was pluralistic. There are no ultimates. Everything, whether it be a physical object, a human mind, or a society, is a plurality of cooperating and competing activities, each of them in turn a complex plurality.

In his long career at Sydney University from 1927, for three decades, he was, the *ADB* entry continues, a feisty controversial provocative presence. In 1931, he gave a lunch-hour talk on patriotism to the Freethought Society, where he attacked various patriotic shibboleths as obscurantist and touched on war memorials for good measure. The local press, except for the *Labor Daily* which gave him space to reply, erupted; many State parliamentarians condemned him and the senate of the university censured him. In 1943 he addressed the New Education Fellowship as part of a series on Religion and Education, arguing that religion and education are antithetical to each other and that religious influences should be kept out of education. Again an outcry ensued in parliament, with public demands that the university senate do something about him. On this occasion, the senate replied by saying that its establishing Act provided that there be no religious test in the university and refused, perhaps uncomfortably, says the writer of the entry, to do anything; whatever the reason, it was an important assertion of university autonomy.

During World War II, Anderson, Partridge and Passmore launched crisp critiques of the Australian state, and in particular of the Ministry of Postwar Reconstruction set up by the federal Labor

Government; many of their critiques appeared in the *Australasian Journal of Psychology and Philosophy* (*A.J.P.P.*), of which from 1935 Anderson was editor. For the Labor Government as for its advisory intellectuals like Lloyd Ross and H C Coombs, I suggest in 'John Anderson and the Sydney Freethought Tradition', the Second World War was an historical opportunity; war encouraged social cohesion, a cohesion which fed their hopes of creating a society patterned around common values formulated by its intellectuals; society would ideally be a kind of organic whole, rationally planned. In the view of Anderson, Partridge and Passmore, the wartime desire for social cohesion and rational planning was profoundly wrong, historically, sociologically, and ethically. Andersonians were moved to redefine and sharpen concepts of solidarism, voluntarism, meliorism, the common good, and servility, in order to attack reconstruction policies, the Labor Government and its intellectual experts, and planning as such; they felt the Labor Government had become a centralizing party, believing in a publicly policed and guided economy and social community.[40]

Partridge opened the Andersonian campaign against centralist assumptions in 1941 in 'Some Thoughts on Planning' in the *Australasian Journal of Psychology and Philosophy*; he considered that the notion of a wholly rational society was illusory; rational planning breaks down because it is impossible to 'predict fully, or even adequately, how the institutions, social habits and interests to which a policy is directed will react'. In ethical terms, social planners do not realize that the plans and morality which they advocate are 'congenial to their own interests and ways of life', but are 'not so congenial to subordinate groups' who do not 'possess the preponderance of power'. Anderson wrote in *Australasian Journal of Psychology and Philosophy* in 1943 that the voluntarist or 'well-intentioned reformer *always* produces results which he did not anticipate, helps on tendencies to which he is avowedly opposed'; planning can never be rational, it always has unintended consequences, and people in any case often act out of unconscious motives; the doctrine of social harmony is used to conceal or suppress actual social conflicts and the expression of divergent opinion; it is, Anderson wrote, intellectually dangerous, in putting at a discount Marxist and pluralist social criticism, which sees society, in war as in any other time, as the scene of opposed and irreconcilable activities and tendencies.[41]

In 1943 in particular the Labor Government began to announce plans for postwar reconstruction, resulting in sharper and more frequent criticism from Andersonians; as a direct response, Anderson wrote in that year one of his most influential essays, 'The Servile State'. In *Australasian Journal of Psychology and Philosophy* and also in the collection *Prospects of Democracy* edited by W H.C Eddy in 1945, Andersonians provided alternative concepts of social organisation; they critically examined the role of representative government, majority rule, the state, the notion of assimilation and the rights of cultural minorities.[42]

As pluralists, Andersonians were especially attentive to social diversity, and the importance of cultural minorities, 'racial, political, or religious', retaining their independence. In his contribution to *Prospects of Democracy*, J A Passmore argued that Australian society does not 'recognize the value of diversity within a culture': 'Our tendency is to think that the growth of democracy implies an ever-increasing uniformity – not as we should think that it implies an ever-increasing variety.' The mistaken assumption in the concept of the 'will of the majority' is that cultural minorities should conform to a common way of life. In Australian society it is the 'will of the majority' concept that is the problem, in being repressive and uniformitarian: 'We say that we are determined to have no "problem of minorities" without realizing that it is often enough not the minorities but the majorities which create the problem.' This, said Passmore, has particular consequences for Australian immigration.[43]

In his *Prospects of Democracy* essay, Passmore reproduces a discussion that had occurred on the ABC between himself and Brian Penton, editor of the local Sydney newspaper the *Daily Telegraph*.

> Penton:... Australia must assimilate all migrants, with all the skills and ideas they might have to offer.
> Passmore: Yes, well you see it's just that word 'assimilate' that I'm worried about. I'm afraid of the suggestions behind it, because it seems to me that when Australians talk about 'assimilating' migrants, what they usually mean is making them conform to Australian standards of conduct; making them surrender entirely their old traditions and their old culture.[44]

Passmore added the curious, elitist touch that 'what we need here are educated and competent migrants, not dispirited peasants', presumably feeling (with little historical justification) that 'dispirited peasants' would lack the independence and confidence necessary to maintain their distinctiveness.[45] Passmore launched a pluralist attack on the cultural tendencies within Australia which supported the White Australia Policy and the notion of 'majority rule', which implied a national interest and a national way of life. What emerged from Anderson, Partridge and Passmore was that pluralism implied participatory democracy, cultural diversity, and internationalism.

In 'John Anderson and the Sydney Freethought Tradition' I also point out the interesting engagement of the pluralist Andersonians with Marxism. In his 1943 essay 'The Servile State' Anderson judged that the doctrine of history as struggle is the valuable part of Marxism, whereas the doctrine of Socialism as something to be established in a conflict-free classless society is a 'servile' notion. Marxism tended to subsume the plurality of social struggles into only one form of struggle, that of class conflict. Anderson argued that it is true that in certain crises a body of wage-workers is found solidly opposed to a body of non-wage-earners, but 'such a conflict never covers the whole of society nor does it cover all the interests even of the participants in it'. In Anderson's pluralist view it is clear that 'the individual may belong to many different institutions and movements, that even conflicting interests may be operative in him'.[46]

[Here we can think of the importance, since the late 1980s and continuing, of notions of intersectionality.][47]

***

I met Henry Mayer personally only once, in 1971, visiting his home in Sydney across the harbour. We had kept in touch over the years, and I see that in my Acknowledgements for *Australian Cultural Elites: Intellectual Traditions in Sydney and Melbourne*, I inscribe: 'I would like to acknowledge the assistance, direct and indirect, of Professor Henry Mayer, of Sydney University; Geoff and Nonie Sharp, of *Arena*; Terry Sturm, for detailed discussion of ideas and careful reading of the whole manuscript; and Ann Curthoys, who suggested that I write the book.' On the page before, I dedicate the book 'To Ann Curthoys'. And thinking of John Anderson as Scottish-Australian, I also think of Ann's Scottish family heritage, through her mother, born Barbara Lindsay McCallum.[48]

***

When I finished the above draft of this chapter, I was very concerned to send it off to our friend Judith Keene. Ann had known Judith from early days in Women's Liberation in Sydney; for many years Judith had taught European history, art, and film in the History department at Sydney University, and has only recently retired, though not before editing, with Liz Rechniewski, in the university's French studies department, *The Cold War: Seeking Meaning, Seeking Justice in a Post-Cold War World* (published by Brill, 2018); Ann contributed the opening historiographical chapter, 'Writing Australia's Cold War through History and Memoir'. Judith, I knew, had as a young research assistant worked on Henry Mayer's *Politics* before my essay appeared in 1972.

To my great pleasure, Judith wrote back on 2 October 2018 that she had very much enjoyed the chapter and then offered some very thoughtful reflections and reminiscences; I immediately wrote back to Judith asking her if I could publish an extract as a kind of coda to the chapter, and, 5 October, she generously agreed.

Judith is recalling Henry's generosity to her when she was just embarking on her own distinguished scholarly career:

> … yesterday I went off to burrow about in the boxes in my room, to no avail, in search of Henry's magic 'An Introduction to All you Need to Know about Social theory' when starting a post graduate degree in sociology at UNSW.
>
> Henry brought it in one morning after I had told him that I was accepted into postgraduate sociology at UNSW but actually had never done any sociology. He left it in my mail box: 4 closely typed foolscap pages on his funny old typewriter with all the typos and fade-outs that you show in your chapter. As I recall there were 4 sections that explained the different ways of approaching the world in social theory, among which, and I had never heard of, were Simmel and Mead which he explained at length and which I thought were amazing. I see in your analysis of Simmel's The Stranger why H focused on this take on the social world. And it connects with the non-Jewish Jew, the secular figure who is steeped in her /his own tradition, or more accurately, background but not bound by it.

My deepest thanks to Judith.

1   John Docker, *Postmodernism and Popular Culture: A Cultural History* (Cambridge University Press, Melbourne, 1994), pp.223–224, 243.

2   Walter Benjamin, *Illuminations*, edited by Hannah Arendt (1968; Schocken Books, New York, 2007), Introduction, p.3.

3   Ann Curthoys and John Docker, *Is History Fiction?* Second edition (University of Michigan Press, Ann Arbor, 2010), p.249.

4   John Docker, *1492: The Poetics of Diaspora* (Continuum, London and New York, 2001), pp.89–90, 99.

5   Tamara Deutscher, 'Introduction: The Education of a Jewish Child', in Isaac Deutscher, *The Non-Jewish Jew and other Essays* (Merlin Press, London, 1968), pp.x,17; 25.

6   Isaac Deutscher, 'The non-Jewish Jew', pp.26–7.

7   Isaac Deutscher, 'The non-Jewish Jew', p.27.

8   Isaac Deutscher, 'The non-Jewish Jew', p.28

9   Docker, *1492: The Poetics of Diaspora*, pp.vii–viii, 105–106.

10 Kurt H. Wolff (ed.), *The Sociology of Georg Simmel* (The Free Press, Glencoe, IL, 1950), pp.402–8; *1492: The Poetics of Diaspora*, pp.86–7.

11 Manning Clark, 'Faith', in Peter Coleman (ed.), *Australian Civilization* (Melbourne, 1967), p.87; cf. also Clark, 'Melbourne: An Intellectual Tradition', *Melbourne Historical Journal*, 2, 1962; Ian Turner, 'Intellectuals in Australian Life', *Overland*, 33, 1965–6.

12 D.M. McCallum, 'Anderson and Freethought', *The Australian Highway*, September 1958, pp.71–5; A J. Baker, 'John Anderson and Freethought', *The Australian Quarterly*, December 1962, pp.61–63; Ross Poole, 'The Freethought Movement', *Honi Soit*, July 27, 1967, pp.10–11. For a brief non-technical summary of Anderson's views, see John A Passmore, 'Philosophy', in A L McLeod (ed.), *The Pattern of Australian Culture* (Ithaca, 1962), pp.131–169 at 148–55.

13 A J Baker, 'Introduction', *The Sydney Line: A Selection of Libertarian Comments and Criticisms* (Sydney, 1963), p.7.

14 John Anderson, 'The Servile State', *Australian Journal of Psychology and Philosophy*, December 1943, p.131.

15 Poole, 'Freethought', p.11.

16 Baker, 'Sydney Libertarianism', *The Sydney Line*, pp.27–32; D J Ivison, 'Futilitarianism – a libertarian dilemma?', *Libertarian*, 3, January 1960, pp.21–22.

17 Max Nomad, *Aspects of Revolt* (New York, 1969).

18 Baker, 'Introduction', p.7.

19 Cf. the critique of Nomad and, indirectly, of Libertarian theory in Henry Mayer, *Makhaeyvism: The Poverty of Permanent Protest*, roneoed pamphlet, Sydney, n.d. (1961?). For Machajski: Paul Avrich, 'What is 'Makhaevism'?', *Soviet Studies*, July 1965, pp.66–75. The Libertarians interpreted Nomad through the concepts of

Pareto and Michels, who did not, unlike Machajski, stress that the intellectuals were to be the next ruling class.

20 Baker, 'Libertarianism', pp.31–2.

21 Baker, 'Ideologies', p.6.

22 Cf. Anderson, *A.J.P.P.*, 21, p.131.

23 Cf. Poole, 'Meliorism', *Broadsheet*, 51, May 1967, p.7.

24 Ray Pinkerton, 'The Ideology of Chastity', *Libertarian*, I, September 1957, pp.22–32.

25 Baker, 'Reich's Criticism of Freud', *Libertarian*, 3, January 1960, pp.19–20; D J Ivison 'A Reading List for Libertarians', *Broadsheet*, 36, March 1964, pp.5–6.

26 Cf. Anderson, 'Freudianism and Society', *A.J.P.P.*, 18, pp.50–52.

27 Ivison, 'Orgasm Theory', *Libertarian*, 3, 1960, p.18.

28 Cf. *Broadsheet*, 19, September 1961.

29 Report of paper by George Molnar, *Broadsheet*, 35, January 1964, p.7.

30 Graham Pont, 'Why I am not and never was a Libertarian', *Broadsheet*, 19, September 1961, pp.10–12.

31 Cf. report of papers by Molnar and Ian Bedford, *Broadsheet*, 35, January 1964, pp.7–8.

32 Recent Libertarian activity in *Thorunka*, *Thor*, anti-censorship and events linked to Germaine Greer's visit suggested this.

33 As Ross Poole noted in his review of *The Sydney Line*, *Honi Soit*, 30 June 1964; see also Ken Maddock, 'Pluralism and Anarchism', *Red and Black*, Winter 1966.

34 Susan Varga, 'Twice the Man', *Sydney Morning Herald*, 9 August 2003; see also her *Heddy and Me* and *Headlong*.

35 Cf. Molnar's cogent critique of Reich, 'The Sexual Revolution', *Broadsheet*, 39, September 1964, pp.1–5. Also, earlier, Cam Perry, 'Is there a genital character?', *Broadsheet*, 27, July 1962; *Broadsheet*, July 1961 and later 1961 issues.

36 It was said to me by a former Libertarian that 'Libertarian women' were subject to heavy psychological pressure to say that they experienced primarily vaginal satisfaction.

37 Anderson, 'Art and Morality', *A.J.P.P.*, 19, December 1941, pp.262.

38 'Libertarianism and Philosophy', *Broadsheet*, 35, January 1964, pp. 4–6.

39 Ann Curthoys and John Docker, 'Stuart Hall and Cultural Studies, circa 1983', *Cultural Studies Review*, Vol.23, No.2, 2017, p.166; also, John Docker, *Postmodernism and Popular Culture: A Cultural History*, p.159.

40 *Australian Cultural Elites: Intellectual Traditions in Sydney and Melbourne* (Angus and Robertson, Sydney, 1974), pp.131–2.

41 *Australian Cultural Elites*, pp.132–3.

42 *Australian Cultural Elites*, p.133.

43 *Australian Cultural Elites*, p.135.
44 *Australian Cultural Elites*, p.135.
45 *Australian Cultural Elites*, p.135.
46 *Australian Cultural Elites*, p.138.
47 See Ann Curthoys, 'The Three Body Problem: Feminism and Chaos Theory', *Hecate*, Vol.17, no.1, 1991; Kimberlé Crenshaw, 'Mapping the Margins: Intersectionality, Identity Politics, and Violence against Women of Colour', *Stanford Law Review*, Vol.43, no.6, 1991, 1241–99; Ange-Marie Hancock, *Intersectionality: An Intellectual History* (OUP, New York, 2016).
48 See Ann Curthoys, 'Scottish settlers and Indigenous people in colonial Australia', in Alison Inglis and Patricia Tryon Macdonald, curators, *For Auld Lang Syne: Images of Scottish Australia from First Fleet to Federation*, Art Gallery of Ballarat, 2014, pp.83–101, and Ann Curthoys, 'Conflicts of Interest, Crises of Conscience: Scots and Aboriginal People in Eastern Australia, 1830s-1861', in Angela McCarthy and John M MacKenzie (eds), *Global Migrations: The Scottish Diaspora since 1600* (Edinburgh University Press, Edinburgh, 2016), pp.98–117.

36

1973: Hippie Trail through South East Asia – Bali, Jogjakarta, Jakarta, Singapore, Malacca, Kuala Lumpur, Penang

❦

In the former chapter taking the narrative up to 1971–2, the tribute to Henry Mayer, memory was aided by a great deal of written material and Mayer's lively letters. In contemplating how to evoke our five months journey in 1973 through South East Asia, I felt anxious, what if I only have memory, especially my defective memory, to work with. But this turned out not to be the case. Ned Curthoys handily suggested that we might have taken photographs at the time, and this got Ann hunting through folders and she did find some invaluable photos, mostly that she had taken (whenever I try to take a photo, my hand wobbles) circa 1973–4. We recalled also that we had brought along David Jenkins' *Student Guide to Asia*; its first edition, Google tells us, was published by the Australian Union of Students in 1972, and there was another edition issued in March 1973, this is the one we would have read; we no longer have it and we can't remember what happened to it. We didn't at that point have Tony and Maureen Wheeler's *Across Asia on the Cheap*, the first of many Lonely Planet guides, which appeared in 1973. Ann has put in an interlibrary request for David Jenkins' *Student*

Guide to Asia, which should very much help us work out how we made our preparations and then set off and travelled about.

We're still wondering, however, why we went to the places that we did go to. Ann thinks that her old friend Camille Guy from Women's Liberation days in Sydney in 1970, who went on the hippie trail a year or two before we did, may have been sending letters, those blue aerograms of yore, about where she and her partner were visiting.

I will still have to try mainly to work off memories, so the anxiety remains. I'm pretty sure my memories, such as they turn out to be, could well be different from Ann's memories, which I'm confident will be both better and possibly quite different. So, I'm thinking of asking Ann to stage our memories in a kind of arabesque, memories weaving in and out of each other. Ann can add her memories and reflections whenever she likes, or whenever I make urgent appeals for assistance.

⚜

'1973' rang in some changes for the two young Sydneysiders, Ann and John. They were experiencing certain dissatisfactions. Action was needed.

⚜

Ann was tutoring in the history department at Sydney University, only four tutorials a week as a full-time tutor, even now we're astonished to think back on it; it meant, however, that Ann had plenty of time to work on her PhD thesis on mid-nineteenth century racial attitudes in relation to Aboriginal people and Chinese immigrants. We were sharing a house with our old friend Lyndall Ryan in Annandale, in the inner west, in Piper Street, off Johnston Street, next to a tiny park, where a photo was taken of Ann on a swing for the front cover of the Women's Liberation newspaper *MeJane*. Upstairs in a large and airy attic was Ann's study, every afternoon she would be joined by Smoky, our tabby, placid and affectionate, who would sit in the top drawer of her desk, waiting patiently for his dinner. The house was ideal, a Federation house, very sociable, often visited, with a large round coffee table we all put our feet up on, and chatted. But there was a shadowing anxiety, not unknown to postgraduates struggling with a thesis, Ann had done massive research but now the writing was going depressingly slowly.

John had his troubles, he had been at Macquarie University, out in the Bible belt north west of Sydney, since early 1970, teaching the same poem six times a week for three weeks in a row, then the next three weeks on another poem would start, and was frankly feeling pretty demented. My memory is that I would come home from Macquarie, complain about the teaching torture, and then wander about the house until visitors came and we put our feet up on the round table and talked about the world. Why don't you, Ann suggested, start writing a book, fill out the ideas in the long essay you wrote on the Sydney literary and philosophical traditions that you split in two and published separately; while I write my thesis, you write your book, with detailed chapters on the literary and philosophical figures you mention in the essay, what do you think? I did start writing the various chapters on a large table near the front of the house, the bay window side, but what about all this horrible teaching I have to do at Macquarie, what can I do about that? And how can we make things better for you to write your thesis?

We used to go for after-dinner strolls with Fire, our rather irritable marmalade cat, he would accompany us in his own eccentric way, dashing from beneath one car to the next, until we had walked around the block and got home again. It was perhaps during one of these excursions that the idea occurred to us, a plan, a plan in three parts, I would resign from Macquarie so I could write all the time, and we would leave our otherwise idyllic home (actually owned by an anthropologist Lyndall knew who had moved to ANU in Canberra) and rent a place somewhere else in Sydney's inner west.

We then told everyone we knew of our plan, that we were going to withdraw from the world and work as hard as we could until we had finished thesis and book.

Then, the third part of our plan, we would take off, travel the long hippie route through South East Asia and Afghanistan and Iran and finally reach London, the desired destination of so many young Australians (and New Zealanders, like Ann's friend Camille). Perhaps, we idly wondered, we might never come back.

We found a place to rent not too far away from Annandale in Glebe, closer to the city, oddly enough in a new block of flats, tucked away in a short cul de sac, Sheehy Street, why the flat, which was on the top floor, full of light, overlooking Blackwattle Bay, became available in a new apartment block we never knew, though the whole building seemed a bit shonkily constructed, weird things would go wrong. Sheehy Street was down the bottom of a very steep road, Forsyth Street. At the top of Forsyth Street, turning the corner into Glebe Point Road, was Tony's Delicatessen, this was a stroke of good fortune, or changing social history, Tony was from Central Europe, perhaps Austria, and his small delicatessen was a kind of cosmopolitan treasure trove of foods and cuisines, there were dark rye Baltic breads (maybe from distant memory Estonian or Lithuanian) which gave us a lifelong love of rye loaves, there were all sorts of cheeses and Mediterranean and Hungarian salamis, and, enticingly, a shelf of highly coloured Asian spices in little bags, near the front of the shop, next to the street. We had become interested in cooking Indian food through literary critic Bill Browning who lived nearby in Glebe, on a precarious cliff top, he said he had been introduced to Indian cuisine by a fellow student at Cambridge; we started to cook Indian dishes, Ann thinks from a book entitled something like *The Sultan's Kitchen*, maybe it was on sale in Tony's shop.

I'm reminded now of Bruce Beresford's lovingly crafted 2018 film *The Ladies in Black*, about the spreading influence of cosmopolitan Central and Eastern European migrants on Sydney life in the 1950s.

Ann has just done some google-sleuthing, we're now pretty sure the cook book was *Curries from the Sultan's Kitchen*, written by Doris Ady, we stare at the images on screen, it seems to have been published in the UK but also in the late 1960s in Wellington in New Zealand and also in Sydney, with a spiral binding, and distinctive cover, with particular colours, that we instantly recalled: this is it, this is what we used to cook from in the Sheehy Street flat, Ann you're a genius, how did you do that. Somewhere in all our moves it too dropped out of sight. Ann has ordered Doris Ady's book on interlibrary loan, hope it comes soon, we're intensely curious to know what recipes are in it. Its full title we notice is *Curries from the Sultan's Kitchen: curries from India, Pakistan, Burma and Ceylon*; illustrations by Inge Fernando; introductory note by Margaret Fulton; published in 1968 by A H and A W Reed, Wellington and Sydney.

Ann has kept folders of photos, including a folder entitled Ann and John Sydney 1969–1973; I ask Ann what photo is this, where did this happen, it shows a young John Docker, in a pink tee-shirt, with long hair and absurdly slim, like a pencil, concentrating while cooking, cutting something up on a wooden kitchen board, that's you, Ann says, in the Sheehy Street flat.

Meanwhile, while we waited it seemed interminably for the interlibrary loans to come through, David Jenkins' book had to cross the continent from Macquarie University library, Doris Ady's book had to make its way from the University of Adelaide library, I wrote most of this chapter, as best as I could.

30 October 2018: news has come through from the UWA library, both David Jenkins' *Student Guide to Asia*, 1973 edition, and Doris M Ady's *Curries from the Sultan's Kitchen*, have arrived on interlibrary loan, they're in UWA's Reid Library waiting for us to pick them up. Ann was going in a day or two later to UWA for a meeting of the humanities writing group she convenes, she collected the two books and brought them home, we stare at them, smiling. This will be fun, these will tell us lots.

Because most of this chapter was written before the Jenkins and Ady books came through, I'm not sure how to handle this, I think I'll interpolate new information from their books in square brackets, see if this works. Dear reader, please bear with me, I know it's going to be a bit clumsy.

Ann recalls that when she visited me in Melbourne in 1968, early in our relationship, in my tiny flat, she noticed I was cooking from one of Elizabeth David's books, its title something like *The Mediterranean Cook Book*. I've looked up some relevant information: Elizabeth David published in 1950 *A Book of Mediterranean Food*, her first book, based on a collection of recipes she made while living in France, Italy, the Greek islands, and Egypt. My memory is that older sister Lorraine who was then living in London had sent letters urging the family to become interested in David's books, she encouraged my mother, for example, to put garlic into a lamb joint when roasting. In the Sheehy Street flat Ann and I plundered Elizabeth David's *A Book of Mediterranean Food* as well as Doris Ady's *Curries from the Sultan's Kitchen*.

I've now read through *Curries from the Sultan's Kitchen*: *Recipes from India, Pakistan, Burma and Ceylon*. (On the outside cover, the author's name is given as Doris M Ady; on the inside title page, her name is given as Doris Ady; for consistency, and because Doris M Ady sounds a little formal, I'll use Doris Ady.)

The blurb inside the cover tells its readers why the book will be new for those becoming interested in Asian food, for example, 'the standard ready-mixed curry powders' should especially be avoided. 'This book reveals how, with the use of individual spices and other ingredients easily obtainable in Australian and New Zealand cities, you can blend and balance your curries and their accompaniments into 116 different dishes... Any enterprising housewife (and any keen amateur male chef) can, with this book at hand and a small and inexpensive repertoire of ingredients, open up a whole new world of gastronomy – for sophisticated entertaining, for meals tête-à-tête... Written by an author whose skills were learned while living in India, Burma, and Ceylon, and who has since lived ten years in Australia, this book brings you foods worthy of a "Sultan's kitchen"'.

The book must have met a demand, a yearning to learn, the publication dates on an inside page indicate that it was first published in 1968, then reprinted in 1969, 1971, 1972, 1973, and 1974.

On another inside page, there is an Introductory Note by Margaret Fulton, Cookery Editor, *Woman's Day*, who informs readers: 'This book is an important milestone in the publication of cookery books in Australia and New Zealand, for it is written by a newcomer who has brought her skills and knowledge of Asian food to our countries; who has lived with us, entertained generously and lavishly and been entertained in return, has learned our ways, and has slowly and carefully introduced many of her own ideas among her ever-increasing circle of friends... To be a guest at one of Doris Ady's curry meals is an experience one would not miss for worlds, and I speak for many of her friends when I say,

"*At last*, Doris is giving us her recipes!"' Margaret Fulton adds that Mrs Ady has been 'backed by her husband who, in order to get the best spices from the world's markets, started his own business importing – to mention only a few items – cardamoms and peppercorns from South India, cloves from Zanzibar, and cinnamon from Ceylon'. The Adys 'sell their premier goods under the brand name "Sultan's Choice"'. Margaret Fulton also adds that 'even the most modest garden can grow chillies and mint, while your milkman can deliver sour cream and yoghurt'.

Margaret Fulton's Introductory Note is followed by Doris Ady's own Foreword, where she expresses her admiration for the 'Australian and New Zealand housewife' who is 'game to tackle anything and taste everything', yet at the moment is 'a little inexperienced' in the cuisine of South-East Asia. However, says Doris Ady, this is changing because of the influx into Australia and New Zealand of 'thousands of people' from the 'former Dutch East Indies, now Indonesia', as well as from the 'former British colonial territories' when 'Britain, having given independence and a helping hand to her former Asian dominions and colonies, is now finally withdrawing her troops from the Far East'. Many of 'these European people have lived for generations in the East, and know and love Asian foods'. Her book will introduce the Australian and New Zealand housewife to the 'art of spice cooking, an art which her neighbours on the vast Asian continent have practised for centuries'.[1]

In her Foreword Doris Ady tells readers that when 'we lived in Rangoon, after World War II, we were lucky to have in our employ an Indian cook who could read and write English'; he was an 'excellent cook', and many of the 'recipes in this book are his'. She advises readers on how to start on their curry journey: 'If an initial purchase is made of, say, a jar of cumin, coriander, turmeric, chilli powder and garam masala, a bottle of tamarind sauce and a packet of frozen coconut cream', more than 'half the recipes in this book can be tackled'. Then the range of spices 'can gradually be increased'.[2]

I focus here on chapters two and three, the longest chapters in the book, on Indian and Pakistani curries and accompaniments, which we particularly wanted to learn how to do, perhaps because of our friend Bill Browning talking about his pleasure in Indian food. Doris Ady makes some observations relevant to social history, that she has included a number of vegetable curries, even though she recognises that 'New Zealanders and Australians do not appear to be greatly interested in vegetarian cooking', yet millions of Indians subsist daily on a vegetarian diet, so it is 'not surprising therefore to find to what a high state of excellence they have brought the cooking of vegetables', which are never 'just plain boiled', spices or fried onions or garlic or yoghurt are always added.[3]

For a long time now, when I try out a new recipe book, I apply a preliminary rule, I look at the chicken recipes first (when the book is not vegetables only, like Yotam Ottolenghi's 2010 *Plenty*) to see if I will enjoy cooking from it. I may well have applied this rough-and-ready rule to Doris Ady's *Curries from the Sultan's Kitchen* when Ann and I first read it somewhere between 1968 and 1973. In the Indian and Pakistani chapters, I espy a recipe for 'Country Captain', a 'spicy version of fried chicken', its ingredients: 1 small chicken; 2 oz ghee or cooking oil; 4 large onions; 2 cloves garlic; 1 teaspoon turmeric; half a teaspoon of chilli powder (optional); 1 teaspoon salt; half a cup of water, with 1 chicken soup cube added. Serve with 'mashed potatoes and vegetables'.[4]

Hhhhmmm, Ann and I may well have cooked from this recipe, adapting as we went along like cooks do, though I wouldn't have used a 'chicken soup cube' nor served the dish with 'mashed potatoes', I'm a lifelong steamed white rice addict.

We would have been keen to cook meat curries such as 'Spiced Stewed Lamb', which details cooking lamb cutlets with garlic, green ginger, turmeric, carrots, potatoes, capsicum, 'frozen peas' (we would have used fresh peas), garam masala, and 'tamarind sauce' (not sure if we could buy tamarind sauce then). There is also 'Lamb Curry (North Indian)' which includes 'chopped almonds', and 'Kashmir Lamb Curry', this recipe including sultanas and dried apricots, Doris Addy glossing here that in the 'lovely valley of Kashmir good fruit is grown and the Kashmiris and Pakistanis do occasionally add fruit to their curries'.[5]

I catch sight of vegetable recipes, for example, 'Sambal of Green Beans', its ingredients: 1 packet of frozen beans; 1 small onion; 2 cloves garlic; 3 fresh red chillies (optional); bay leaf; 1 teaspoon turmeric; half a teaspoon garam masala; 2 oz ghee. We might have cooked something like this, though not sure why Doris Ady used a packet of frozen beans rather than fresh beans, or a 'packet of frozen peas' rather than fresh peas in another recipe, 'Potato Curry with Green Peas'. (I know packets of snap frozen peas are available now in supermarkets now, and indeed we buy them, have for many years, but when did these start becoming available?) We might have also tried her eggplant recipes, given our lifelong love of eggplant dishes, though I doubt we would have used 'frozen coconut cream'.[6]

I've looked ahead to chapters VII and VIII concerning 'Ceylonese Cookery' and 'Ceylonese Curry Accompaniments', an exciting cuisine we came much later in our lives to explore. In her introductory note to 'Ceylonese Cookery' Doris Ady talks about her family background, that though she herself has never actually resided in Ceylon, her 'parents were both born there, descendants of the Dutch settlers who came to the island in the sixteenth century'. She has visited Colombo frequently, and 'on every occasion my palate has been assailed by new and exotic flavours', including 'cinnamon and cloves in savoury dishes instead of in sweet ones'. Doris Ady also comments that Ceylon is well-known for its coconut growing industry, and it is therefore not surprising to find that 'coconut milk is used with a lavish hand in all their food preparations, whether they be curries, rice dishes, *sambols* or sweets'; the 'main difference between Ceylonese curries and those of central and north India, and Burma', is that 'coconut milk provides the stock in which the curries are cooked'. She also notes that 'canned coconut milk' is available in the cities in Australia.[7]

(Ann and my very distant, and possibly very wrong, memory is that we have always used canned coconut milk or cream, for example in Malay or Nonya cooking; perhaps we could buy it in Tony's Delicatessen in Glebe).

Altogether, it would have been an exhilarating experience to cook from the Indian and Pakistani chapter of Doris Ady's *Curries from the Sultan's Kitchen*!

Bruce Beresford's *Ladies in Black* evokes the spreading influence of cosmopolitan Central and Eastern European migrants in the 1950s; perhaps we can also think that the European ex-colonials who left the newly independent nations of Asia to settle in New Zealand and Australia may have contributed to a non-European cuisinary cosmopolitanism, a broadening and widening, which is always more than cuisinary.

Ann tells me that our particular interest in the Indian recipes in Doris Ady's book resonates with our subsequent lifelong interest in India culturally and intellectually, up to and including your 2008 *Origins of Violence* book, where in your 'Conclusion: Can There Be an End to Violence?' you declare (I've just got the book down from my bookshelves to have a look) that Gandhi's ideas of non-violence 'remain the key alternative to the endless recourse to violence in history and the contemporary era': 'for Gandhi non-violence is a way of life, a mode of spirit and being, a kind of ensoulment, a *Bildung*, a mode of moral reflection'.[8]

Ann and I recall that in the late 1960s and early 1970s we were enjoying a fairly cosmopolitan range of cafés, becoming increasingly characteristic of postwar Sydney; in Chinatown in the Haymarket there was a particular Chinese restaurant we went to, upstairs, maybe it was the Tai Yuen (before it moved and became the New Tai Yuen, not sure of this); there was a long established Greek café, Diethnes, in the city, in the south end of Pitt Street, downstairs; there were Lebanese cafés at the corner of Elizabeth Street and Cleveland Street; in Taylor's Square, there was 'The Balkan'; in George Street, not far from Railway Square, there was the legendary Malaya, with its Nonya cuisine, very hot sambals and an eggplant dish I still mourn, and its dedicated regulars, we went there every Friday night after drinking at the bohemian hotel The Newcastle in George Street near the Quay; there was also a regional Italian café in Glebe, in Bridge Road, down the hill from the intersection with Ross Street, on a kind of raised corner, serving we think northern Italian food, veal with cheese on top, it could have been called The Siena, Siena in Tuscany, we can't quite recall now, it's in my mind's eye, a café with French windows, looking north, light streaming in.

~~※~~

In the Sheehy Street flat Ann the historian took over one of the two bedrooms for a study, surrounded by books, I'm looking now at another photo from the 1973–74 folder showing Ann, with long hair and very slim, working at her desk; her study overlooked an old warehouse and then beyond the warehouse, concealing where Blackwattle Bay would have been, the city to the east.

I got to writing chapters on the dining room table, reminding me of doing homework in the Bondi flat when I was growing up, we ate our dinners on the beautiful small coffee table my father had made for us, in front of the TV, we hardly saw anyone, hardly anyone dared visit the recluses, we wrote and wrote, Ann completed her thesis and handed it in to Sydney University to be examined, I wrote the various chapters for *Australian Cultural Elites: Intellectual traditions in Sydney and Melbourne*, and then a stroke of good fortune, Ann noticed that the venerable Sydney publishers Angus and Robertson were running a competition for new writers, the Vogel Award for an unpublished manuscript. Not too long after we found ourselves entertaining two young publishers from Angus and Robertson, the poet John Tranter and the versatile Bob Debus (later an ABC journalist and then politician, once we heard him say on air to an interviewee, I think it was Basil Davidson the well-known British imperial historian of Africa, 'you can say that again with knobs on', Ann and I looked at each other, did he actually say that). They sat in our only two armchairs, talking at the same time, but we were able to gather that while my book certainly had not won the competition they were nonetheless interested, they wanted to publish it. I said, Ann and I are just about to go to London via the hippie route, but when we get there I can make any changes you might care to suggest, if that's OK.

As it turned out, in London I did do further work on the Conclusion, in particular taking notice of the *Nation Review* as a sign in journalism of the greater fluidity and unpredictability encouraged by the new movements which arose during the sixties and early seventies in the wake of the Vietnam War, in the counter-culture, women's liberation, black liberation, gay liberation; I noted that *Nation Review*'s publisher Richard Walsh conceived his weekly magazine in terms derived from Sydney freethought traditions as pluralist, while also acknowledging an interest in social change and so also coming close to Melbourne traditions; *Nation Review*, I commented, was enabling greater interaction between the Sydney and Melbourne intellectual and cultural worlds.[9]

Ann travelled through Asia not knowing if her thesis had been passed, though once we got to London good news did come through after a few weeks, for Dr Ann Curthoys. We decided to celebrate by having lunch in an English café we had walked by in the centre of London somewhere, maybe near Kingsway, which boasted cold eel, this was a truly monumental mistake, we both reeled afterwards, it ranks as the worst meal we've ever had. I may say that for the rest of our lives as the cook I have tried to make up for that frightening experience of English food by adding to Elizabeth David's *A Book of Mediterranean Food* and Doris Ady's *Curries from the Sultan's Kitchen* further cookbooks of non-English cuisines and continuing to try out a varied palette of recipes, the spicier and more piquant the better.

As I record in the opening chapter, 'His slave, my tattoo: romancing a lost world', of my *1492: The Poetics of Diaspora*, after we returned from London to Sydney in late 1974 we assembled over time a cache of cookbooks that we could journey around. Encouraged by Ann, who was always on the look-out for new cookbooks, I have absorbed myself in cooking Italian, Indian, Singaporean (my treasured copy of Wendy Hutton's *Singapore Food* has telltale food stains all over favoured pages), Malaysian, Indonesian, and Thai recipes. I search for the necessary spices and condiments: ground coriander, cumin, ginger, paprika, turmeric, cayenne pepper, cardamom, cloves, cinnamon sticks, whole nutmeg; fresh ginger, galangal, tamarind, blachan, lime leaves, kaffir limes, lemon grass. I love cooking aubergine and okra; at some stage I realise I have become addicted to chillis, I'm a chillihead, I feel part of a wider movement, the chillification of the world. I came to realise that Persian food, so subtle and delicate, is a kind of ur-cuisine, that historically spread and enriched and interacted with cuisines from Moorish Spain and Morocco to Venice and the eastern Mediterranean, thence to India and beyond in the East; in this vast cuisinary crescent, India and South-East Asia remain connected to the Mediterranean, past and present.[10]

I increasingly absorbed myself in exploring – this is well before the appearance of Yotam Ottolenghi and Sami Tamimi's superb books – the historical adventure that is Mediterranean cuisine. A great find was Barbara Santich's *The Original Mediterranean Cuisine: Medieval Recipes for Today*; Jeannette Nance Nordio's *Taste of Venice: Traditional Venetian Cooking*; Paula Wolfert's *Good Food from Morocco*. I keep adding to my kitchen stores of pomegranate syrup, sumac, preserved lemons, pickled turnips, rose water, orange water. I return over and over to the Sephardi section of Claudia Roden's *The Book of Jewish Food: An Odyssey from Samarkand and Vilna to the Present Day*.

In London in 1982 for Ann's study leave, with our son Ned, then seven going on eight, we acquired *Madhur Jaffrey's Indian Cookery*, based on a BBC series we saw on TV; we must have immediately sent away for it; this slim volume is still a mainstay of our cooking, I have it in my hand now, it says, 'This book accompanies the BBC Television series *Indian Cookery*, first broadcast on BBC2 from October 1982'; we must have acquired it just before we returned to Australia in December 1982. In 2003, when we went to Georgetown University in Washington DC for nine months, Ann was the GO8 Professor in its Australian Studies program, we took Madhur Jaffrey's book along with us, even though it was already starting to fall apart, we felt we needed her recipes, spicy, homely, to cook with, I still turn to her book wherever we live in Australia, including, currently, here in Perth.

Our journey through Indonesia, Singapore, Malaysia (with its wonderful Nonya cuisine), Thailand, Burma (Myanmar), India and Nepal became food journeys as part of travelling; later in life Ann and I have kept trying to extend our range of cuisines, including Spanish (Claudia Roden's *The Food of Spain: A Celebration*), Ottolenghi and Tamimi's books like *Jerusalem*,

Ottolenghi: The Cookbook, *Plenty* and a new work *Simple* in 2018, and Luke Nguyen's *Indochine* on French legacies and influences in Vietnamese cuisine.

Yet still the long-ago scarring image of that cold eel in a graceless English café has never entirely gone away, even though we have also come to appreciate robust British food like Shepherd's Pie or a roast with baked vegetables, as well as British cheeses, and in deep winter, a Lancashire hotpot. (We also know there are spicy and attractive South East Asian ways of presenting cooked eel, as in John Mitchell's *The Best of Asian Cooking*, a store house of interesting recipes Ann once found in an airport bookshop.)

Now when we visit London we go to an Ottolenghi/Tamimi restaurant as soon as we can.

In 1973 Ann and I had never travelled overseas before, we were both 27, quite late in contemporary terms when people now travel from a young age; it wasn't that long before that during the 1950s and 1960s young Australians were travelling to Britain and Europe by ship, my older sister included. In preparation, we had got married in 1971, we were worried by stories about Singapore frowning on young westerners with long hair; we had kept our separate surnames on our passports, but the passport authorities had insisted that Ann's passport include, in parenthesis just after her name, the statement 'formerly (or was it formally?) known as Ann Docker', which in either case was untrue. Ann also brought along a copy of our marriage certificate in case we needed to prove we were married while travelling in Asia. I had my hair cut quite short.

Having now carefully read David Jenkins' *Student Guide to Asia*, I was pleased to see that it provides information and details we must have heeded or that influenced us in our travelling choices. In the Introduction, Jenkins advises that, as well as obtaining visas for various countries where they are needed, a 'health card' is essential, stamped and signed by the doctor who gives one the necessary inoculations, for smallpox, typhoid, cholera, with anti-tetanus shots also strongly recommended; proof of inoculation against smallpox is required by every country in the region, and cholera shots are necessary for all but a few; the 'series of injections', Jenkins adds, 'usually takes at least three weeks', and must be recorded in a yellow International Health Certificate, which should be carried with you wherever you go. Also, Jenkins advises, because malaria is present in most Asian countries, anti-malaria tablets are a good idea, start taking the tablets a week before you arrive in Asia and keep taking them there and don't stop taking them for six weeks afterwards.[11]

Ann and my memory is that we went to a friendly Indian doctor in Darling Street, Balmain, and he effected the inoculations, choosing a certain place on the tops of our arms, and then stamped the health cards for us. We both feel that the place of the inoculations was visible on our arms for a long time.

Ann's memory is that we did take anti-malarial tablets with us but didn't use them, not sure why we made that decision.[12]

We must have been alerted to the problem of long hair in Singapore and elsewhere by a particularly spirited protest by Jenkins, when he writes, surprisingly scornfully perhaps for a travel book, that

> a number of Asian nations have recently been cracking down on so-called 'hippies' who, with their long hair and suspect moral standards, ae seen as a dire threat to the Wholesomeness and Goodliness of the average Asian teenager. The attack on the long-hairs has been bravely spearheaded by Prime Minister Lee Kuan Yew of Singapore but now half a dozen other Asian States, no doubt angered by the leech-like excesses of some particularly odious Western freeloaders, have fallen into line behind him. The result is that those of hippie demeanour are no longer welcome

in Singapore, Indonesia, Malaysia, Thailand, Taiwan, Sri Lanka (Ceylon) or, God forbid, Nepal. So if you wish to enter these lands, it may be necessary to trim your tangled locks and change out of your kaftan before applying for a visa.[13]

Elsewhere in the Introduction Jenkins writes that a 'pullover is important for the cooler regions', it's 'not just places like Nepal and Japan' that get cold, it can be 'pretty chilly in the mountains of Indonesia at night'. I'm not sure if we heeded this general reminder enough, especially in Malaysia.

In terms of clothing, Jenkins includes suggestions for what women might wear in Asia.[14]

In his Preface to the *Student Guide to Asia*, Jenkins tells us that the 'very comprehensive chapter on Indonesia was written by Ann Hawker, an Australian journalist who has lived in Jakarta for more than a year and travelled widely throughout the Indonesian archipelago'. This must have proved most useful to us as we set off for Indonesia.

One day recently, that is, in December 2018, Ann suddenly said that she remembers now how we flew from Sydney to Bali, the first leg of our hippie trail journey, it was by Pan Am. Ann googled and came up with the following rather unsettling information. There was a Pan Am Flight 811 that each Wednesday flew from Sydney to Denpasar airport in Bali, where we got off, 811 continuing on to Hong Kong. We must have flown on this flight one Wednesday in May 1973.

However, disaster struck the airline the following year. Pan Am Flight 812, its route from Hong Kong to Denpasar to Sydney, crashed in a mountainous region just outside Denpasar on 22 April 1974 with 107 people on board; everyone died. (*New York Times* report, 23 April 1974.)

Captain Donald Zinke, in command of Pan Am Flight 812 when it crashed on 22 April 1974, had touched down in Denpasar on 16 May 1973 on Flight PA 811. It is likely that this was the Pan Am flight we took from Sydney to Denpasar.

In the aftermath of the crash on 22 April 1974, Pan Am stopped their flights between Hong Kong and Sydney via Bali. There were also three other Pan Am crashes that year.

Pan Am, it would appear, was at its peak as a world-circling airline in the 1960s and 1970s, declining after the 1974 oil crisis. On 21 December 1988, Pan Am Flight 103 from London to New York was destroyed by a bomb in its hold, while flying over the Scottish town of Lockerbie. On 4 December 1991, the airline folded.

We first flew to Bali, landing at Denpasar airport and then making our way to Kuta to stay in a *losmen*, somewhat inland from the beach, I don't know how we knew of this particular *losmen*, but it was quite beautiful, indeed easily the most beautiful of any place we stayed in. My memory is that we were in a small room with a little deck, overlooking a flowery garden; here we spent a lot of time, I'm sure we brought books to read though I can't at this moment recall what they were; every afternoon, towards evening, a lady of the house walked around the garden laying out a small portion of rice on a leaf, as a gift to the gods, followed by an attentive dog, who immediately ate the rice; in the centre of the garden was a shower, it had high walls, people took it in turns to wash, only one's head showed; in the morning we went out to little cafés for a sort of European-style breakfast, toast with egg, we must have eaten lunch and dinner in cafés as well, maybe we enjoyed very spicy dishes from Sumatra (I've just googled: perhaps this was Padangese cuisine, replete with chilli, lemongrass, ginger, garlic, and coriander).

[In *Student Guide to Asia* Anne Hawker suggested some restaurants to go to at Kuta Beach, which offered European food, but none of the names of the restaurants stir any memory, maybe we never went to them; Hawker adds that 'Javanese kopi tobruk (coffee) is good', but, unfortunately, we weren't into coffee then, that particular obsession was in the future.][15]

Sometimes we walked to the beach, and there, our first experience of bartering, we purchased two batiks, one with golden colours, the other with a sort of dark blue pattern, which we wore for years until they lost themselves in the drift of time, though Ann has kept photos of us wearing them in South East Asia here and there, in a folder entitled Overseas and London 1973–4. Bemos would come past our *losmen* in the morning, checking to see if anyone needed to go into Denpasar.

Bali was fascinating because it was part of a surviving Hindu history in Indonesia; in the cafés travellers would sit around swapping information, word would go around of what to do, where to go to see something that day or night; I recall Ann and I watching a funeral procession. I also have a distant memory of hearing about a cock fight, we went along, sat in the stands with the locals; a young girl was selling nuts, maybe peanuts, and I saw a man grab her behind, she scowled at him; perhaps Bali was not so idyllic after all. Once we went to Ubud in the hills, which we never forgot, we visited there again, in 2018, a few short weeks ago.

Reading Ann Hawker's chapter on Indonesia now, Ann and I realise how *Student Guide to Asia* might have prompted us to look for certain things in Bali and Java; there is a photo, opposite p.109, of a cock fight, with villagers looking on, this may have encouraged us to attend one in Bali. In a section on Culture, Hawker refers to Indonesia's popular wayang puppet shows, usually drawing on the great Hindu epic the Ramayana, the leading figure is Dalang, who manipulates the puppets and speaks the words for the shadow theatre. Yes, we agree, we did seek out shadow puppet shows in Bali. Hawker reminds us of other things we saw there, such as a cremation ceremony; there were also the remarkable dancers (opposite p.121 there is a photo of a young woman dancing, with highly stylized hand movements).[16]

Ann Hawker explains why Bali is so culturally rich. The great empire of Majapahit (1294–1500) was based in East Java, its Hindu-Buddhist religion blending in with traditional Javanese animism; however, Majapahit was abandoned as the influence of Islam moved into Java around 1500. The leading artisans and court officials moved to Bali; this forced migration of courtly architects, sculptors and painters established Bali as a centre of Hinduism while Islam triumphed in Java.[17]

Ann and I suddenly remember the novels we may have been reading while we travelled about, from Bali onwards. Ann, I murmur, a vague vague memory has come back, a novel written somehow in terms of different colours. Ann's vastly superior memory fills in the rest: yes, *The Golden Notebook*, Ann recalls, four different colours for different sections on aspects of her life, maybe one to do with politics, another the personal, and a gold section which was supposed to bring them all together. Who wrote it, we can't remember the author, I say let's have a look at Wikipedia, which tells us that *The Golden Notebook* was by Doris Lessing and was published in 1962. Wikipedia relates that *The Golden Notebook* presents the story of a writer, Anna Wulf, constituted in four notebooks in which she records her life and consciousness: black, referring to Southern Rhodesia before and during World War II; red, evoking her experiences as a member of the Communist Party; yellow, recording love and its disappointments; blue, Anna's personal journal where she sifts through her memories, dreams, and emotional life; and the fifth, gold-coloured notebook, where Anna tries to tie these fragments together.

Ann thinks she read *The Golden Notebook* in Sydney, before we left; I think I was reading it in Bali. Also, Ann remembers reading *War and Peace* in Indonesia, probably Jogjakarta, and being drawn into the novel's suspense of what would happen to Natasha, and also reading George Orwell's *Burmese Days* in Burma, in preparation for going to Mandalay.

⁂

We did experience a certain uneasiness in Bali. Thinking back on it, Ann reflects that 1973 was not that long after the 1965–6 mass killings in Indonesia of Communists, or those designated as Communists. We would have read the following passage in Anne Hawker's chapter:

> The Indonesian Communist Party, which had a membership of three million before the *coup* attempt on September 1965, has been destroyed and most of its leading members either killed, imprisoned or driven underground. Some 300,000 Communists are reported to have been murdered by irate Indonesians (mainly hard-line Moslems who went about their butchering work in Java and Bali while the army stood by either unable or unwilling to stop them) and another 32,000 are still in rather grim jails across the archipelago. Despite pleas from bodies like the International Commission of Jurists, the present [Soeharto] government is not overwilling to treat these people more leniently. The prevalent attitude is: 'Why should we? They would have killed ten times as many of us had they been successful.'[18]

Knowledge of the mass killings in Indonesia of 1965–6 of between 400 000 and 500 000 people has increased over the decades, in intensifying historical research, powerful documentaries, harrowing survivor testimony; the mass killings are now internationally recognised as genocide and crimes against humanity;

they occurred in conjunction with torture, unjustifiable imprisonment, forced labour amounting to slavery, systematic sexual violence, political persecution and exiling, and disappearance of many thousands.

What of Bali? There didn't seem to be any visible trace of the mass killings when we were in Bali in 1973. On one occasion, however, a traveller in one of the cafés we frequented said, don't be fooled by how quiet and peaceful Bali looks, in the mid-1960s 'the rivers ran with blood', a phrase we still remember. According to Wikipedia, massacres in Bali occurred with special ferocity. Between December 1965 and early 1966, an estimated 80 000 Balinese were killed throughout Balinese villages by militia death squads, while in the towns Chinese stores were destroyed and their owners killed; eventually the Indonesian army, having perpetrated mass death in Java and then providing logistic support in Bali, decided to rein in the Balinese death squads, to prevent chaos.

———❀———

In conversation in the cafés in Bali travellers would often offer advice of where to stay in a town or city: so you want to go next to Jogkjakarta in Java, well, you could stay in a place we stayed in; you're going to Bangkok, well, stay in a place we know there. We also heeded Anne Hawker's advice on eating etiquette in Indonesia – 'One must always eat with the right hand if using fingers' – and remembered it for the rest of our travels.[19]

We were in Bali for two or three weeks, then set off for Jogjakarta, or Yogyakarta, I'm confused here about spelling; we stayed in a room in some kind of lodging house, perhaps for a week. In my scattered memory, one night there was a knock on our flimsy door, we opened it to be greeted by soldiers with guns, not smiling, who are you, where are you from, show us your passports; it appears that next day a princess was visiting Jogjakarta and all the foreigners were being checked out.

We visited a famous Hindu ruin, Borobudur, and looked at its carvings of gods and goddesses; one night there was a performance of an Indian epic in a kind of open field, we went along to watch, I can't remember if it was the Ramayana or Mahabharata. We visited an art gallery, and bought batiks for friends back home, I'm not sure of this memory. I feel as if there is more to remember about Jogjakarta, I'll see what Ann recalls. (Ann: help!)

> ANN: My main memory of our stay in Yogyakarta were the streets of silversmiths, making silver jewelry and other items as one watched. It was the first time I had ever seen traditional craftsmanship like this up close.

Somehow we got from Jogja to Jakarta, not sure how, Ann thinks it was by bus and that the bus stopped at Bandung, where we had lunch; that stirs a distant memory, so I Wikipedia and it tells us that in 1955, as part of the rise of the Non-Aligned Movement, an Asia-African or Afro-Asian Conference was held to promote Afro-Asian economic and cultural cooperation and to oppose colonialism and neo-colonialism; it was organised by Indonesia, Burma, Pakistan, Ceylon (Sri Lanka), and India.

I have no memory at all of our stay in Jakarta; Ann says we stayed in some sort of hostel with bunks, men and women in different quarters.

I don't think we were in Jakarta for very long, and then we flew to Singapore. Nothing unsettling happened at customs at the airport, though maybe they took a second look at Ann's passport information. We stayed in a small Chinese hotel. My initial memory is that we didn't do anything much in Singapore except eat. For breakfast we found a café near the water, I think it was Indian, we remembered the eating etiquette, take care to only eat with one hand, not the toiletry hand. At night we went to the Orchard Street market, then in a car park, and, yes, relished Singapore chilli crab, I recall at one stall we sat on stools and ate so uninhibitedly, biting into and sucking claws, that the stall holder complimented us, young westerners eating with such gusto, we were chuffed. In another market I remember seeing Australian Packham pears being sold, freshly cut up and dipped in cold water, that began an unlikely long romance with crisp Packham pears that persists, I still often cut them up in that Singaporean way, as a mouth freshener while eating or just after, with a squeeze of lime juice.

Still, thinking about it, we did more than enjoy Singapore as a vibrant food experience. We branched out. We caught some kind of cable car to the top of a hill; googling, this may have been the cable car to Faber Peak. Also, this memory just came back, one day we visited Raffles hotel, we sat there in the huge armchairs on the verandah, in the cool shade, sipping tea.

In Ann's folder of photos entitled Overseas and London 1973–4, there is a photo of a pond, with pink flamingos it looks like standing on one leg, this could have been in Singapore; I've just googled, we may have been visiting Singapore's Zoo Park, which appears to have a pond with lots of pink flamingos.

Dear reader I hope you will indulge me here, if I refer to the cover of my *Australian Cultural Elites*; the back of the book records that the 'cover illustration is a detail from Sydney Long's etching *The Spirit of the Plains* reproduced by permission of the Australian National Gallery'. I'm grateful to the publishers for having chosen this illustration. Sydney Long was known as Australia's foremost Art Nouveau artist; the painting has Pan playing his flute with flamingos swaying sensuously to the music, and dates from 1902.

David Jenkins' chapter on Singapore offered helpful information that may have influenced what we did there. For Accommodation, Jenkins says that 'Chinese hotels provide the cheapest and, generally, the best accommodation for money', I look down the list of hotels, maybe we stayed at the Shang Oun Hotel, 'Very clean. Asian-style lavatory. Highly recommended,' or the Tong Ah, both in Beach Road.[20]

Jenkins mentions, under Places to See, the Kranji War Memorial on Bukit Timah Road, which 'commemorates 24,000 men and women who died during the Japanese attack on Singapore, Malaya and the Netherlands East Indies in 1942'.[21] I say to Ann, I'm pretty sure that we didn't go to see this, and we reflect that on the journey through South-East Asia we weren't interested in looking at historical memorials and visiting museums, yet at some time that lack of interest thankfully changed, we came to our senses, now when we travel we visit museums as much as we can.

❧

Ann reminds me that something we looked forward to in the five months of our journey was that the Watergate revelations and arrests were occurring as we travelled from city to city. Just before we left in May 1973, Nixon had dismissed John Dean, and Haldeman and Erlichman had resigned; Nixon, who had ordered the cover-up, was still insisting he knew nothing. The public senate hearings were under way, with Dean testifying against Nixon in June, and knowledge becoming public in July that there were White House tapes that might incriminate Nixon. By August, when we would have been somewhere in India, a judge ordered Nixon to hand over the tapes and he refused. Every time we got to a city we would buy a *Newsweek* to see who had fallen since our last stop. It would take another year of drama before Nixon resigned, in August 1974.

❧

Memory is very hazy here. How did we get from Singapore to

Malacca? In his chapter on Singapore, Jenkins refers to the 'famous Causeway' connecting Singapore to the Malay Peninsula, there are daily bus services from Singapore to Malacca, this is something I later clearly completely forgot about, so maybe we simply caught the Singapore-Malacca bus.[22] I do have a memory that at some stage in Malaysia we hitched a ride with a middle-class Indian man in a Mercedes I think, at one point he stopped, said wait here, got out, and walked across the road to a stall selling durian, when he returned he said the durian here are especially good.

In Malacca I can't remember where we stayed or where we might have eaten or how long we stayed. I do remember that Ann and I visited a Portuguese fort, or its ruins, looking out to sea. I've just chatted with Ann, she recalls how still and glassy the sea looked.

In his comments on Malacca in his chapter on Malaysia, Jenkins writes that Malacca, which comes from the Arab word *Malakat* (market), is 155 miles north of Singapore and 96 miles south of Kuala Lumpur, and was 'once the greatest city in all South East Asia', tracing its history back unbroken to the 15th century. The 'famous Chinese eunuch admiral Cheng Ho', envoy of the Ming Emperor Yung Lo, visited the port in 1409 and forged important trading links between Malacca and the powerful Middle Kingdom. In 1511 Malacca fell to the Portuguese, who in their 130-year rule turned the early Malaysian city-state into 'one of the mightiest fortresses in the Orient'. The Dutch seized Malacca in 1641, and held it for another century and a half before exchanging it for a British outpost in Sumatra. Today, Jenkins continues, this 'multi-national past' is reflected in Malacca's architecture. For an idea of early Chinese settlement, he advises a visit to the Cheng Hoon Teng Temple (1704), the oldest Chinese temple in Malaysia, while Bukit China (Chinese Hill) has, behind the Poh San Teng Temple, one of the largest Chinese cemeteries outside China, with many graves dating from the Ming Dynasty (1368–1644). The only surviving vestiges of the Portuguese occupation are the 'great Portuguese fortress', the 'gateway of Porta De Santiago'; St Paul's Church (1521), which once held the 'body of St Francis Xavier', while the Church of St Peter (1710) also shows the influence of Portuguese architecture. The best expression of Dutch architecture is the 'salmon-pink Christ Church' (1753), now an Anglican church; the Stadthuys (Town Hall, 1641–1660) is thought to be the 'oldest Dutch building in the East'; the influence of the former Dutch occupiers of Malacca is also reflected in the '312-year old Malacca Museum building'.[23]

Despite Jenkins' eloquent urgings, neither Ann nor I can remember visiting any of these sights and places.

༄༅༄

Why did the Portuguese have to have a fort, later to be occupied by the Dutch? Only much later in life, as I record in my *1492: The Poetics of Diaspora*, did I become interested in this question. The opening chapter 'His slave, my tattoo: romancing a lost world', is a series of reflections on Amitav Ghosh's great book *In an Antique Land* (1992), a wonderfully unclassifiable text composed of many forms and genres: autobiographical memoir, anthropological treatise, apprentice's woes, travellers' tales, comedy, romance, detective, mystery, utopia, dystopia, and anguished conversation with history.[24] *In an Antique Land* engages with and draws on S D Goitein's *Letters of Medieval Jewish Traders* (1974) as well as his monumental multi-volume study, *A Mediterranean Society: The Jewish Communities of the Arab World as Portrayed in the Documents of the Cairo Geniza*, published from 1967 onwards, which evokes the thousand-year-old interactions between Europeans and Jews and Arabs and Indians in the mercantile world of North Africa, the Mediterranean, Arabia and the Indian Ocean.[25] From where I sit here in my study, I can see on my book shelves the large volumes of Goitein's *A Mediterranean Society*, I write about them in *1492: The Poetics of Diaspora*.

What happened to this trading seafaring adventurous ethnically and religiously plural world that, as world historian Janet L Abu-Lughod writes in her wonderful *Before European Hegemony: The World System A.D. 1250–1350* (1989), stretched through the 'Mediterranean into the Red Sea and Persian Gulf and on into the Indian Ocean and through the Strait of Malacca to reach China'? Abu-Lughod notes that Europe came late, very late, to the international networks of trade and exchange already long established in the Islamic world, and for a lengthy period it was but a minor player that had everything to gain from the association.[26]

In *In an Antique Land* Amitav Ghosh writes scathingly that the inclusivity of the medieval Indian Ocean was a signal achievement for humanity, but it was ended, quickly and brutally, by colonising Europe, in particular by Portugal; Vasco da Gama landed on the west coast of India on 17 May 1498; two years later a Portuguese fleet arrived on the Malabar coast, demanded that the Hindu ruler of Calicut expel all Muslims, and then bombarded the city-state for two days; another year on and Vasco da Gama returned with a much larger fleet. *In an Antique Land* reflects that in all the centuries when trade and contact between India and East Africa and southern Arabia and the Middle East flourished, no state or king or ruling power had ever tried to control the Indian Ocean by force of arms, in part because, the narrator speculates, the influential Gujarati traders were pacifist in their beliefs and customs.[27]

After Malacca we somehow made our way to Kuala Lumpur, we didn't want to stay there for more than a few days, our aim was to keep going north and get to Penang and stay there for a couple of weeks. David Jenkins evokes in Kuala Lumpur sights and places that we should have gone to, but I have no memory of doing so: the National Mosque, the National Museum, the Masjid Mosque (Old Mosque), the Batu Caves, and the University of Malaysia, 'in the Pantai Valley 8 miles out of town, [it] has a man-made lake and rolling green lawns and is one of the most attractive campuses in South East Asia'.[28]

Ann and I recall that from Kuala Lumpur we made an overnight visit to the Cameron Highlands; Ann took some photos while we were there, they are in the cache of photos entitled Overseas and London 1973–4, I'm looking at them now. This visit turned out to be a minor disaster; we hadn't realised how cold it was in the Highlands, we only wore light clothes, when night came it was so cold we couldn't sleep, we went round to the office of the hotel we were staying in and asked if they had a blanket, they said no, they didn't, so we went back to our room and lay on one double bed mattress and put another double bed mattress that was in the room over us; we survived the night, though not without a slightly traumatic memory of the absurdity of having a mattress on top of one.

'Nights can be cool', David Jenkins writes in the Malaysia section of *Student Guide to Asia*, 'especially in places like the Cameron Highlands.' We had obviously failed to heed this sensible warning. Jenkins also lists three hotels to stay in in the Cameron Highlands, in the same street, Tanah Rata; looking at the list now, Ann feels sure it was the Cameron Hotel that we tried to go to sleep in.[29]

We also remember in the Highlands seeing Malay Indigenous people; we wondered about their history.

We returned to Kuala Lumpur.

✦

We both remember that we visited the home of Marian Aveling (Marian Quartly, historian and feminist) and Harry Aveling, I thought in Kuala Lumpur, but Ann wonders whether it was in fact in Penang.

Ann tells me that the Sydney University English department figure Michael Wilding had suggested we look up Harry Aveling, he's somewhere in Malaysia, indeed, as we would happily come to know, he was teaching at the Universiti Sains Malaysia, in Penang. About Marian Aveling, I garner information from the *Encyclopedia of Women and Leadership in Twentieth Century Australia*, entry by Judith Smart: Marian was also teaching courses at the Universiti Sains Malaysia in Penang, in Historical Method and Malay history.

> ANN: I remember visiting Marian quite well. She had two young children, and was teaching history part time at the university. But the main thing we talked about was her research into Hindu temples of the Tamils of Penang, which she visited frequently, and in fact I now find she published an academic article entitled 'Ritual change in the Hindu Temples of Penang' in 1978.[30] I still remember her enthusiasm for her subject, so different from anything else she had done.

Uncertain as to where Harry and Marian lived, on Friday, 12 October 2018, I emailed Marian: 'We both remember visiting you in Malaysia in about June or early July 1973, and I would like to mention our visit in my memoir. But here's the question. Were you living in KL or Penang? Neither of us can quite remember. It's 45 years ago, so we have an excuse, I suppose. But it would be nice to get it right… Best wishes, John.'

On 14 October 2018, Marian, we were delighted to see, replied:

> Hi John, hi Ann. It was Penang where we were living. I do remember your visit. You both looked real, dyed in the wool (ti-dyed?) hippies. I guess we all did at that point… Harry

remembers that we all went to the Penang Swimming Club, the expatriate hang out, and John felt a bit underdressed.

Marian

Marian posted a lovely photo of her and Harry and children looking, she says, a 'bit alternative'; now I would think, we all looked impossibly young.

I have to confess to feeling rather shaken that I don't remember that it was in Penang that we saw Marian and Harry, that we went to a club and so on. I'm also beginning to wonder how attentively I read the chapter in *Student Guide to Asia* on Malaysia. In a section on Penang, David Jenkins writes: 'The University Sains (Science) Malaysia (formerly the University of Penang), which opened in June 1969, is housed in the old Garrison Headquarters at Minden Barracks and set amid 250 lush green acres on a hill overlooking the Glugor Sea.'[31] Why I thought Marian and Harry lived in Kuala Lumpur rather than Penang I don't know.

⚘

I vaguely recall catching a ferry across to the island of Penang. We stayed in a room in a hotel in a village, and rested; we read a lot. Every morning we walked outside where we ate breakfast at a stall, maybe an omelette, Ann retains an image of a man cooking it in a wok, throwing in bean sprouts and maybe some greens. For lunch, we would go into town to a Chinese café and enjoy steamed chicken, sliced, with rice.

> ANN: My memories are similar to yours; I think we stayed mainly in and near the hotel, which was close to the water, and we had an upstairs room and a nice view of the sea. We read a lot, as you say, and rested, though I do remember also plenty of walks along the sea shore, in the late afternoon or early evening.

By this time, we had worked out our philosophy of travel: after journeying from somewhere, stop and rest, maybe for a week or two or more, then travel again.

⚜

From Penang, we caught a train to Bangkok. I sit here thinking: I can't remember anything at all about Bangkok, except we must have read another *Newsweek* story about Watergate. We stayed in a hotel someone must have told us about, rather dingy and dismal. I do have in my mind's eye the image of one guy there, I recognised him as someone I used to play tennis with in Bondi when we were kids; I said, we used to play tennis together, at the courts off Wellington Street, Don was the coach, do you remember, but he was so bonged out he could barely talk. In *Student Guide to Asia*, in in the chapter on Thailand, section on Accommodation, David Jenkins writes of one particular hotel in Bangkok, which sounds like the one we stayed in: 'Thai Song Creet Hotel, 247 Rama IV Rd… is one of the most popular hotels for shoestring sojourners. It is pretty rowdy and grubby (some say it has gone right off in recent years) but still an excellent place to meet other travellers and pick up on travelling tips. The Thai Song Creet has a very reasonable restaurant on the ground floor.'[32]

I recall us going on a boat trip, not too far, something unpleasant happened, I can't remember what, then back to the hotel. Ann, over to you, I'm bereft, this is appalling.

> ANN: We misunderstood the currency conversion and as a result were unknowingly grossly overcharged for the boat trip; when we realised we asked for our money back, the ticket collector refused, but then a Thai man on the boat came to our assistance, argued with the ticket collector, and our money was returned. It was unpleasant, though actually I also remember that gliding by the houses and people along the river was quite stunning.

Ann has a sudden memory, that Bangkok felt politically tense, there were frequent student protests, with female university students wearing a kind of uniform. We've looked this up, and learn that 14 October 1973, just three months or so after we were there, there was a popular uprising involving students and others that led to the end of the ruling military dictatorship in Thailand and had long-term effects on the country's political system.

From Bangkok we flew to Burma. India and Nepal were beckoning.

1   Doris M. Ady, *Curries from the Sultan's Kitchen: Recipes from India, Pakistan, Burma and Ceylon* (A.H. and A.W. Reed, Wellington Sydney London, maybe 1973), p.9.
2   Doris M. Ady, *Curries from the Sultan's Kitchen*, p.10.
3   Doris M. Ady, *Curries from the Sultan's Kitchen*, p.20.
4   Doris M. Ady, *Curries from the Sultan's Kitchen*, p.45.
5   Doris M. Ady, *Curries from the Sultan's Kitchen*, pp.26, 28, 43.
6   Doris M. Ady, *Curries from the Sultan's Kitchen*, pp.35, 46–7, 54, 55, 57.
7   Doris M. Ady, *Curries from the Sultan's Kitchen*, p.85.
8   John Docker, *The Origins of Violence: Religion, History and Genocide* (Pluto Press and UNSW Press, London and Sydney, 2008), pp.217–8.
9   John Docker, *Australian Cultural Elites: Intellectual traditions in Sydney and Melbourne* (Angus and Robertson, Sydney, 1974), Conclusion, pp.159–160.
10 John Docker, *1492: The Poetics of Diaspora* (Continuum, London and New York, 2001), pp.15–17.
11 David Jenkins (ed.), *Student Guide to Asia*, published by the Australian Union of Students on behalf of the International Student Travel Conference (Globe Press, Melbourne, 1973), pp.6, 9.
12 David Jenkins (ed.), *Student Guide to Asia*, p.10.
13 David Jenkins (ed.), *Student Guide to Asia*, p.12.
14 David Jenkins (ed.), *Student Guide to Asia*, p.15.
15 David Jenkins (ed.), *Student Guide to Asia*, Ann Hawker chapter on Indonesia, p.134.

16 David Jenkins (ed.), *Student Guide to Asia*, Ann Hawker chapter on Indonesia, pp.109, 113–4, 120, 121.

17 *Student Guide to Asia*, Ann Hawker chapter on Indonesia, p.108.

18 *Student Guide to Asia*, Ann Hawker chapter on Indonesia, p.111.

19 *Student Guide to Asia*, Ann Hawker chapter on Indonesia, p.133.

20 *Student Guide to Asia*, chapter on Singapore by David Jenkins, pp.261, 265.

21 *Student Guide to Asia*, chapter on Singapore by David Jenkins, p.263.

22 *Student Guide to Asia*, chapter on Singapore by David Jenkins, pp.260, 262.

23 *Student Guide to Asia*, chapter on Malaysia by David Jenkins, p.205.

24 Amitav Ghosh, *In an Antique Land* (Granta/Penguin, London, 1994); Docker, *1492: The Poetics of Diaspora*, p.2.

25 Docker, *1492: The Poetics of Diaspora*, pp.1–2, 8.

26 Janet L. Abu-Lughod, *Before European Hegemony: The World System A.D. 1250–1350* (Oxford University Press, New York, 1989), pp.6, 11–12, 15–16, 33; Docker, *1492: The Poetics of Diaspora*, p.12.

27 Amitav Ghosh, *In an Antique Land*, p.287; Docker, *1492: The Poetics of Diaspora*, pp.12–13. Concerning Janet L. Abu-Lughod's *Before European Hegemony* and her 1995 essay 'The World-System Perspective in the Construction of Economic History' in relation to historiography, see Ann Curthoys and John Docker, *Is History Fiction?* Second Edition (UNSW Press, Sydney, 2010), pp.247–9.

28 *Student Guide to Asia*, chapter on Malaysia by David Jenkins, pp.203–204.

29 David Jenkins, *Student Guide to Asia*, pp.192, 213.

30 Marian Aveling, 'Ritual change in the Hindu temples of Penang', *Contributions to Indian Sociology* (NS), vol. 12, no. 2, 1978.

31 David Jenkins, *Student Guide to Asia*, p.202.

32 David Jenkins, *Student Guide to Asia*, p.331.

37

1973: Hippie Trail through Burma, India, Kathmandu

~~~✤~~~

From Bangkok we flew to Rangoon. Ann says that she remembers at Bangkok airport while waiting to catch our flight, hearing a flight number being called repeatedly, accompanied by a sound something like *sop sop sop*. We think they are Thai numbers. Ann has just now googled and it appears that what we were hearing was Thai for two, so Flight 222.

We knew that travelers then only had seven days to be in Burma. We had to keep moving, to stay a short time in Rangoon and then travel to Mandalay. My memory of Rangoon is how run-down it was, how poor, with grass growing out of the buildings. The first night, we sat eating at a stall in near darkness, there seemed to be barely any light in the city. However, during the day we also visited the astonishing golden temples. Then we must have set off for Mandalay, Ann thinks by train. Ann recalls that when we queued for tickets, someone insisted that we as Europeans be taken to the head of the queue, Ann is not sure we did but it felt uncomfortable.

In his chapter on Burma, David Jenkins writes that Mandalay is the 'second city of Burma' and lies '439 miles' north of Rangoon. It was founded in 1856, 'at the foot of the 775-ft Mandalay Hill', and is of 'enormous sentimental significance to the Burmese people as this was the capital of their last monarch, King Thibaw. Energetic visitors who struggle up the 1729 steps to the top of Mandalay Hill will be rewarded with a magnificent panorama.'[1] In Mandalay we climbed those steps, and looked over a vast expanse of rice fields to the distant horizon, one of the most transcendentally beautiful sights I have ever experienced. Thinking about it now, the rice fields, product of remarkable agricultural engineering, seemed to blur the boundaries of art and nature, or better, makes one think of art as nature and nature as art. (Is there here a distant confused vague memory, or mis-memory, of a particular Enlightenment neoclassical ideal, articulated somewhere in Alexander Pope's poetry, maybe.) Ann's memory is that the rice fields were like a vast quilt.

Ann remembers that we returned to Rangoon first by boat along the Irrawaddy, to Pagan, and then by train. On the boat I was wretchedly ill in a way travellers may recall all too clearly.

> ANN: We were on the boat for about a day, and I walked around it on my own, while John was ill. It was quite crowded, people had mats to sit and lie on and as you walked around everyone cautioned you not to step on the monk's mat. I remember the sight of golden pagodas along the river, and wondering about the contrast between the evident poverty I had seen around me in Burma and the wealth embedded in those pagodas, covered in gold. The boat trip was quite magical, but the train trip to follow was anything but. On leaving the boat at Pagan (now called Bagan), we bought our tickets for the train to Rangoon, and boarded the train. It was full, and it did not move for at least eight hours, overnight. It finally started moving ever so slowly when the light came, and took many hours. We finally arrived, exhausted.

We didn't eat or go to the toilet all that time, it was as if our bodies shrank into a kind of death-like stillness.

Earlier in 2018, in Ubud in Bali, Ann and I climbed a short hill and came to the Sweet Orange café, where with other travellers we ate tasty local food and sipped coffee while looking mesmerised for a couple of hours at the rice fields. I thought of being on Mandalay Hill, though, as Ann reminds me, at the Sweet Orange café we were very close to the rice fields, amidst them, and we could see up close the remarkable engineering channeling water at the sides of the rice paddies.

It may be considered ridiculous, perverse, absurd, to say, but for me the view from Mandalay Hill ranks with the Taj Mahal we saw later on our 1973 journey, and many years afterwards in Spain when visiting those wondrous legacies of Moorish Spain, the Alhambra of Granada and the Great Mosque of Cordoba, their so moving beauty so important to humanity.

⁂

From Rangoon we flew to Calcutta, and here we met up with Soumyen Mukherjee, who was teaching Indian history in the history department at Sydney University when Ann was there as a tutor, until we left for Bali in 1973. Ann was tutoring in Australian history, the lecturers were James Waldersee and Heather Radi; another tutor was a friend of ours, Mary Murnane, who at that time was doing a thesis in Indian history, and tutoring in Soumyen's courses. We used to talk to Soumyen in the University Staff Club, have lunch together, laugh a lot, when we told him we would be going to Calcutta he said he would be there at the same time, and we arranged to meet. Soumyen showed us around, a genial and thoughtful host. In my mind's eye I can see us in the garden of a hotel somewhere in Calcutta. Soumyen introduced us to his friends, fellow Bengali intellectuals, and we enjoyed the conversation. At some point, Soumyen asked if we didn't mind if he and his friends spoke Bengali for a while, he hadn't had a chance to talk Bengali for some time, he missed it. Soumyen invited us to his mother's house for lunch, a very beautiful meal, this was a highlight of being in Calcutta, a highlight of our lives, to be invited into his mother's house, how kindly and gracious she was. It taught us a life lesson, how much people traveling, who spend so much time in hotels, appreciate being invited to one's home, and we have tried to practise that life lesson wherever we have lived or stayed for any period in the world, inviting people for lunch or dinner.

In Calcutta Soumyen took us to meet an elderly man, a Communist of the old school, he reminded Ann and me of my father, utterly dogmatic in his pronouncements about the state of the world. We were very touched to meet him.

When I mention this memory to Ann, she suddenly exclaimed, Dilip Bose, she said the name suddenly popped out.

Ann set to and did some of her expert google-sleuthing. Dilip Bose, it would appear, was a Communist historian, who wrote books including *The World Communist Movement: Third Communist International 1919–1943*, published by CPI, New Delhi, 1975, *May Day and the Indian Working Class*, published by the People's Publisher, 1979, and *1942 August Struggle and the Communist Party of India*, CPI 1984. He also published articles on Rajan Palme Dutt, Palme Dutt being very high up in the British Communist Party (and admired by my father).

We catch a glimpse of Dilip Bose in the autobiography of Zarina Bhatty, *Purdah to Piccadilly: A Muslim Woman's Struggle for Identity* (2016). Here, Zarina Bhatty, a Muslim woman born and brought up in pre-Partition India, chronicles her life over 80 years; she went to the UK and studied sociology and political science at the London School of Economics, taught at the University of Delhi, and is a former President of the Indian Association for Women's Studies. In a section entitled 'Political Involvements in London', Zarina Bhatty recalls that LSE was 'very politically active in the 1950s because of Harold Joseph Laski's legacy', as he had 'left-wing leanings'; most Indian students in Britain had grown up during the 'Indian Independence Movement and were politically conscious'; they had formed an association called the London Majlis, very active in 'articulating India's aspiration for political freedom'. In the 1950s the Indian student population in England was 'dominated by Bengalis', and a large number of Bengali students had joined the Communist Party of Great Britain. Among the more prominent communists during her stay in London 'were Taruna and Dilip Bose', who went to London to study and stayed on for several years, becoming 'more politically than academically involved'; they lived on the same street as Zarina and her husband Hayat. Zarina used to 'meet Taruna and Dilip at the Finchley Road Tube Station', and they would take the train into the city together for meetings. When London Majlis called a meeting to discuss the newly-framed Indian Constitution they invited Palme Dutt, then Vice President of the British Communist Party, to be the chair; at the meeting Taruna asked Zarina to give a floral bouquet to Palme Dutt. Soon Zarina became part of the left-wing Indian students' group, and on Taruna's suggestion she took 'some lessons in Marxism'. Zarina recalls that it was a very exciting time in England; after many years the Labour Party came back into power, and 'a new Left movement was emerging, welcoming students from newly independent countries'. Along with other Indians, Zarina 'felt proud of having come from an independent country', but she and her friends also wished to 'get the benefits of British citizens': 'In all official forms, there used to be a column "Origin of Birth" where we would fill in "British." There used to be another column, "Race", where we would write "Homo sapiens".'[2]

It would appear that Soumyen Mukherjee had been supervised by Eric Hobsbawm at Birkbeck College in the University of

London from 1956 for his doctorate, and arrived in Sydney from London in 1971. Perhaps he knew Dilip Bose from the time they were both studying in London.

> ANN: I remember meeting Soumyen's friends in Calcutta, at a bar or restaurant and a table setting alongside a lovely green lawn. The women all seemed so gracious and witty, speaking rapidly and excitedly. My other memory of Calcutta is quite different; we were walking somewhere, looking for a consulate to get a visa, perhaps for Nepal, and took a wrong turn, ending up in a very poor part of the city, and felt like intruders.

From Calcutta we took a train up to Darjeeling, the old Raj hill station. Soumyen Mukherjee had told us of his pride in the railway, it was created by Indian engineers. My memory fails me completely with Darjeeling, where we stayed, what we saw.

Actually, not quite. As I later explain, when writing about our later visit to Nepal's border with China, or rather, Tibet, I had a sudden flash of memory that while visiting Darjeeling we had made an excursion to a nearby Tibetan refugee centre. Wikipedia tells me that there is indeed a Tibetan Refugee Self Help Centre in Darjeeling, which initially provided emergency relief for Tibetan refugees who had come through a hazardous trek over the Himalayas into India, a consequence of the Chinese Communist government led by Mao Tsetung invading Tibet in October 1959, with the aim of incorporating Tibet into the People's Republic of China. From 1959 the main activity of the Tibetan Refugee Self Help Centre became the production of Tibetan handicrafts. One accompanying photo of the 'Hill Top Shop in Darjeeling, India', shows a building with a sign on its front: 'Home for the Orphans. Tibetan Refugee Self Help Centre, Darjeeling'.

The Hill Top had a special significance for Tibetans, because the Thirteenth Dalai Lama had spent his exile in India from 1910 to 1912 following the invasion of Tibet in early 1910 by a Qing dynasty military expedition, which occupied Lhasa on February 12 and officially deposed the 13th Dalai Lama 13 days later; however, all Chinese forces left Tibet by the end of 1912.

1910 was not the first time China asserted control over Tibet; the Qing dynasty invaded Tibet in 1720, establishing it as a protectorate rather than ruling directly.

> ANN: the only memory I can add to this is that in the evening after we arrived, we went to a local restaurant, looked at the menu and ordered some food. We were told they didn't have what we ordered at the moment, so we looked and ordered something else. They didn't have that either. So we asked what did they have, and they said nothing. One of those bizarre travel experiences you remember for no particular reason.

From Darjeeling, we made a long train journey across India to the holy city of Varanasi. I recall spending a lot of time at the sacred Ganges River where people were bathing, we saw a Hindu cremation, one could still see the body amid the flames. Ann adds: I remember the moment of realising the object in the fire was actually a body, it was quite a shock.

These were remarkable sights, I can't recall anything else about Varanasi, the sacred river was fascinating enough.

From Varanasi, we continued by train to Delhi. Whenever it stopped, sellers would come to the windows and we could buy sugar cane, suck its juice, or chai in little clay cups to be thrown out the window after drinking the tea.:

Throwing the clay cups out of the train to be broken reminds me now of William Morris's view, that art should be used for a while then discarded and replaced by new art to be used and then discarded. In the chapter, 'Utopians at War: Bellamy v. William Morris' in my 1991 *The Nervous Nineties: Australian cultural life in the 1890s*, I relate that when *Looking Backward*, the state socialist utopian novel by the American writer Edward Bellamy was published in 1888, William Morris in Britain, ex-Pre-Raphaelite, medievalist, poet, novelist, artist, designer, printer, cook, environmentalist, urban conservationist, libertarian and communitarian socialist, Marxist, was incensed. He feared that Bellamy's *Looking Backward* might be acclaimed as the only future for socialists to consider and if possible install; yet in Morris's view what *Looking Backward* was offering was a vision of a rigidly controlled, highly bureaucratic and hierarchical state-centred industrial society, with a comprehensive division of labour where every individual is confined to one specialised and graded task.

During 1889 and 1990 Morris expressed his irritation in letters and commentaries on *Looking Backward*. Morris urged socialists to make a fundamental break with industrial society, and search the past for alternative forms. In 1990 he decided to confront *Looking Backward* directly by writing *News from Nowhere*, wittily recreating England as a utopia that is the very reverse of *Looking Backward*'s authoritarian state socialism. In this utopia, a plurality of interests and diversity of lifestyles are encouraged; much of the vigour and alertness of its social life results from the residential and seasonal mobility of its inhabitants; people move about the island visiting each other; they're always welcome to stay in the communal houses; they exchange information and ideas; they enjoy helping in harvesting, and so on. London has become ruralised, full of meadows, woods, forests and the Thames teems with salmon. A key difference from Bellamy's *Looking Backward* is that in *News from Nowhere* art and pleasure are integrated with daily work; as in the medieval fourteenth century, work is pleasure and pleasure is work.[3]

In 'Utopians at War: Bellamy v. William Morris' I note that the associated notions of work as pleasure and art as participatory in *News from Nowhere* look back to the mid-Victorian art and architecture theorist John Ruskin, in particular his essay 'The Nature of Gothic' in *The Stones of Venice* (1853); Morris had Ruskin's essay reprinted by itself at his Kelmscott Press in 1892, with a preface admiring Ruskin for possessing the key to the problem of human happiness. In Ruskin's view medieval Gothic architecture derives from the tribes of the north of Europe and is to be distinguished from the art originating from south of the Alps, from the Greek and Roman styles of architecture, which exhibit an aesthetic that Ruskin disliked because it demands perfection, an exact finish; in being finished and complete, it is divorced from nature, because nature is always in a state of becoming, of change, growth and decay, and then new growth. Gothic architecture features imperfection and redundance, and hence closeness to natural forms, to the changeability and unpredictable richness of vegetation and foliage. The Gothic medieval cathedral would grow like the inventiveness of nature itself; furthermore, the large element of the grotesque in Gothic, Ruskin argued, doesn't reflect the supposed barbarism of the Middle Ages, but the imagination of the workmen, a delight in imagery that is fantastic and ludicrous as well as sublime. The very imperfection of Gothic art allows the participation and inventiveness of the workmen involved; they possess a creative freedom of thought denied to the nineteenth century's industrial slaves, who have been dehumanised by the division of labour. It is because Gothic is 'rude and wild' that it enables the creation of wholeness, of unity of humanity and nature, art and daily life, mind and sense, intellect and feeling.[4]

Somewhere in my mind a little voice is saying, John, John, don't forget it's 1973 and you're on a train going from Varanasi westwards towards Delhi. Come back!

I will return to the Varanasi-to-Delhi train journey, but I've thought of something else, which has just occurred to me. In 'Utopians at War: Bellamy v. William Morris', what if I transpose the Bellamy v. Morris opposition to Nehru and Gandhi, and their separate and opposed visions for an independent India, Nehru sort of aligned with Bellamy, Gandhi sort of aligned with Morris (and Ruskin)? I have in mind an essay, 'Homespun Wisdom: Gandhi, Technology and Nationalism' by the literary critic Anjali Roy, in a book of essays, *Rethinking Gandhi and Nonviolent Relationality: Global Perspectives*, that Debjani Ganguly and I edited and was published by Orient BlackSwan in Hyderabad in 2009. This collection came out of a conference Debjani and I convened on the theme of 'Gandhi, Nonviolence and Modernity' at the Humanities Research Centre at ANU in September 2004.

I remember that Anjali Roy's essay counterposes Nehru and Gandhi, so I thought I'd reread it and draw out her comparison of these two great figures in twentieth-century Indian history. But first, I thought, I'd better see if a connection between Gandhi and nineteenth-century cultural theorists like William Morris and John Ruskin has already appeared, is even perhaps a commonplace. So I googled, and immediately up came an essay by Patrick Brantlinger, 'A Postindustrial Prelude to Postcolonialism: John Ruskin, William Morris, and Gandhism', in *Critical Inquiry* in 1996. I've downloaded the essay and, sure enough and no surprise, Brantlinger says excellent and very relevant things. He opens with twinned epigraphs suggesting what Anjali Roy would also later explore, that there was a historic conflict between Gandhi and Nehru over what should be the place of 'machinery' in post-Raj India. In the first epigraph Brantlinger quotes Gandhi from his famous 1909 manifesto *Hind Swaraj*: 'It is machinery that has impoverished India'. The second epigraph quotes Gandhi writing in a letter to Jawaharlal Nehru in 1945, with independence imminent: 'We can realise truth and non-violence only in the simplicity of village life.'⁵

Brantlinger's argument is that there are clear connections in terms of conceptions of the ideal society between Gandhi, Ruskin, and Morris; Gandhi from early in the twentieth century admired Ruskin's 'anti-industrial utopianism', a vision of pre-capitalist communalism that Gandhi identified with traditional Indian village life; Morris also admired and was influenced by Ruskin's ideas and conceptions, as is evident, Brantlinger notes, in *News from Nowhere*. Brantlinger observes that it is not certain that Gandhi ever read Morris, but what he wishes to stress is the intellectual kinship between Gandhi, Ruskin and Morris which endures in world thought far beyond Ruskin (1819–1900) and Morris (1834–1896) in the nineteenth century and *fin de siècle*, and beyond Gandhi's death in 1948, a year after India achieved independence. Nonetheless, he finds irony in Gandhi's liking for Ruskin and Morris-like ideas in the British arts and craft movement, because it ignored how much Ruskin was a Tory imperialist and that his views on India were thoroughly Orientalist, and we must not forget as well that while Morris was critical of imperialism and more sympathetic to India than Ruskin, he never advocated Indian independence or escaped from some version of Orientalism.⁶

Brantlinger draws attention to the vicissitudes after his death of some key ideas Gandhi advocated throughout his life, as in prizing *khaddar*, or home-spun cloth, and *swadeshi*, which involved his rejection of British manufactures and his urging the necessity of the restoration of a flourishing village culture, based on guilds and handicraft. These ideas were kept alive by Gandhi's disciple the Anglo-Sinhalese philosopher and art historian Ananda Coomaraswamy, who coined the term 'post-industrial' to suggest Gandhi's desire that industrial society should become a past phase of history in a return to ecologically sustainable pre-capitalist village and craft-based life. However, Gandhi's ideas, Brantlinger tells us, were in succeeding generations after his death derided by theorists such as Aijaz Ahmad and Partha Chatterjee as naïve, essentialist, and romantic, while in contemporary times post-industrialism has come to mean the decline of heavy industry accompanied by a turn to computerization, robotics, and transnational corporations. As well, from Nehru onwards, the Congress Party leadership steered India towards centralization and big technology, as in Tata Steel, Air India, and nuclear power.[7]

Nonetheless, Brantlinger also points to the interesting journeys ideas make in world history, ideas can resurge; this is especially the case with Gandhi. Gandhi's vision of a new India, indeed a new world, based on ecologically sustainable craft-based lifeways, would influence E F Schumacher's alternative economics in *Small is Beautiful: Economics As If People Mattered* (1973), concerning appropriate technologies. Gandhian ideals also persist in the environmentalist movement and among the Greens, both within and beyond India. Brantlinger concludes on a very pro-Gandhi note, that the world still needs Gandhi's critique of industrial society, and the kind of thinking Gandhi drew out of certain Ruskin texts that resonates with what William Morris also drew out of *his* reading of Ruskin texts, as well as the power of Marx's thought: 'We still need Gandhi; we still need Morris and Ruskin; we still need Marx, only more so.'[8]

After evoking Brantlinger's very helpful essay, I had a sudden thought, what about the Anthropocene, what if Gandhi's ideas and ideals have resurfaced there, or rather, here, since we are in the calamitous midst of it? It was the end of the day, and I quickly made a scribbled note, google 'Gandhi Anthropocene', in the notebook that sits in the corner of my desk, then closed the computer. Except I quickly re-opened it, I was too curious, and up came lots of references to Gandhi in the Anthropocene literature. After a quick glance, I closed it again. I'm the cook, I'd better start making dinner, darkness outside was closing in, a glass of wine beckoned, I will turn on some music while I slice and cook. At dinner Ann told me how the essay she was writing on the legacies of Caribbean slavery in nineteenth-century British colonies in Australia was going – an ego histoire essay we often talk about on our morning walks, where she evokes her family history of a daughter of a political prisoner from Yorkshire who marries the mixed race son of a Caribbean slave-owner on the Victorian goldfields in the 1850s.⁹ I told her how I was going writing about the Brantlinger essay, and also that I was thinking of hazarding an idea about Gandhi and the Anthropocene, that there might be a connection, what do you think. I said I'd already sneaked a look, and it looks promising. After dinner, clearing a space among disordered plates, haphazard knives and forks, glasses of water, wine glasses, salt and pepper shakers, Ann opened her iPad and we looked together at the plethora of references, Gandhi's ideas were again being appealed to in this time of crisis for the planet, we looked at each other, this is pretty incredible.

It's now the next morning, and I've opened again the web entries on Gandhi and the Anthropocene. There are UNESCO reports, reports of conferences by study centres around the world, and academic articles, one in particular that caught my eye, an essay by Karen C Sokol, 'Rethinking Rights in the Age of the "Anthropocene": The Potential of a Gandhian-informed Jurisprudence for Forging Robust Environmental and Public Health Protections', which refers to the importance of Gandhi's notion of *ahimsa* as the interconnectedness of all beings and the Earth.

Dear Reader, I invite you to google and glance at this expanding literature.

I'd like now to report on Anjali Roy's 2009 essay, 'Homespun

Wisdom: Gandhi, Technology and Nationalism', in *Rethinking Gandhi and Nonviolent Relationality: Global Perspectives*. Roy argues that it was Nehru, the first Prime Minister, rather than Gandhi, who triumphed in shaping post-independence India. Nehru established the Indian Institute of Technology Kharagpur as the model for the 'higher technical institutions' which would bring into being the 'Nehruvian vision of a modern industrialized nation'. Gandhi, the Father of the Nation and author of *Hind Swaraj*, was silenced, so much so that the Report of the Sarkar Committee that in 1948 laid the blueprint for the IITs – Nehru's 'temples of modern India' – does not acknowledge him as part of India's 'nation-building dream'. The silence over Gandhi continues over the decades in the sporadic reports that celebrate the strength and achievements of the IITs, that has culminated in Bill Gates hailing the IITs as Microsoft partners. Roy tells us that since 1951 the IITs have produced 'nearly a hundred thousand graduates' who have supplied the 'technical manpower' not only for India's development but also for the West: 'Every year, many of these graduates migrate to the US and Europe', to the point that the 'Golden Jubilee celebrations of the IITs' in the Silicon Valley substantiates the claim about the IITs 'having become a global brand' and Bill Gates hailing them as an 'incredible institution'.[10]

Even when, Roy points out, the 'ecological rediscoveries of Gandhi' have been welcomed in the new social movements of recent decades, and when the IITs themselves have come to talk of appropriate technologies, Gandhi remains occluded in the national acclamation of the Nehruvian vision of modernity that continues to inspire the ideological imperatives of the IITs, dictating their teaching and research priorities. Gandhi, Roy suggests, has to be repressed because he represents a whole range of alternatives that were rejected in India after independence. The 'Nehruvian model' continues as if it has never been, and never could be, challenged, for acknowledgement of Gandhi's perspectives would threaten Nehru's and the Sarkar Committee's 'nationalist dream of an industrialized India based on the Western developmental model'.[11]

Nonetheless, Roy feels that the Sarkar Committee Report remains 'haunted' by the issues Gandhi raised in *Hind Swaraj*, which had been reprinted in 1938. The meaning of the Sarkar Report, she argues, can only be constructed by that to which 'it does not refer', the 'Gandhian alternative'. The terms reiterated throughout the Sarkar Report, such as industrial, development, machinery, education, technical and technology, acquire added resonance when 'read through the traces of the absent querulous Gandhi'. The Sarkar Report admired Manchester as a desired Western model of 'capital-intensive industrialization and urbanization'; yet that model invokes its absent opposite as espoused by Gandhi, 'rural, decentralized, low cost cottage industry', with its ideals of artisanship and 'the "homegrown" and "handmade"' that Gandhi saw as the bedrock of *swadeshi*.[12]

What was crucial for Gandhi, Roy observes, was that India should possess a 'decolonizing purpose', which involved eschewing Western models of development that worked to destroy indigenous crafts. Gandhi warned against reproducing the heavy industry model of Manchester in India; in Gandhi's words, 'Our very moral being will be sapped'.[13]

I'll leave Anjali Roy's fascinating essay at this point, the essay itself continuing to explore the many ramifications for India, and for world history, of the clash between Nehru and Gandhi's competing visions of modernity, a clash we can contemplate ever more urgently in the Anthropocene and the frightening threats to the planet of climate change.

※

Ann had remembered, as I had not, that in Jogjakarta we saw silversmiths at work. I google and gather that tourists seek out the silversmiths now, take classes in making silver jewelery; the history of the silversmiths reaches back many centuries to the Mataram Kingdom, a once powerful Hindu-Buddhist kingdom in Java and beyond. Ann also reminds me that in 1999 we visited Vietnam on a Gourmet Food Tour run by Intrepid Tours, which started in the north and ended in the south; in Hanoi, we saw a street of silversmiths, while when we got to the Mekong delta and moved about by boat we saw rice paper being made and a pottery kiln with many pots.

Once more I think of Gandhi.

Gandhi's cosmopolitanism came to the fore in an anguished way during the disaster of the Indian partition in 1947 which he strenuously, desperately, opposed.

In 2010 in *Holy Land Studies*, I published an essay 'The Two-State Solution and Partition: World History Perspectives on Palestine and India' lamenting the ubiquity of partition in the twentieth century and into the twentyfirst in Ireland, India, Palestine, Germany, Vietnam, Korea and Cyprus. Thinkers such as Martin Buber and Walid Khalidi regarded the partition of Palestine in 1947 as a tragic mistake, as does Gyanendra Pandey in relation to India in *Remembering Partition: Violence, Nationalism and History in India* (2001). In August 1947 with undignified haste, the British imperial government represented by Louis and Edwina Mountbatten decided to partition and quit India, even though partition was opposed by such major figures as Gandhi and Nehru. Auden would later write a satirical poem ridiculing a British judge the British sent, Cyril Radcliffe, who notoriously arrived in India on 8 July 1947 to divide, in a matter of weeks, the subcontinent into two states. Radcliffe had never been to India before, and he did not visit or inspect the land, villages, and communities to be so summarily sundered.[14]

Historian Ian Talbot observes that the exact number of people killed will never be known, but is conventionally reckoned at around 1 million. Gyanendra Pandey in particular questions conventional nationalist Indian historiography which, he points out, continues to celebrate the Independence of 1947 that came as a result of partition. In the nationalist view, Pandey observes, the violence of partition is seen as incidental to the national narrative, aberrant, possessing no profound effect on life, history and consciousness. To the contrary, Pandey contends that violence was constitutive of the partition; it created new identities and new consciousness, and led to militarisation and continuing conflict, war and the threat of war. The forced exchange of populations in the partition turned into one of the greatest mass migrations in history; and partition created a dangerous binarism. Where before there had been a long history in India of heterogeneity composed of richly diverse communities, cultures, languages, religions, peoples, ethnicities, classes and occupations, partition posed the ever-present threat of nationalist groups attempting to forge a single bloc. Because of partition, a majority population would now view those different in religion as minorities, whose claims to true citizenship would always be suspect. Partition produces extreme distrust, uncertainty, unease and fear of not belonging.[15]

While, Pandey writes, we associate Gandhi with *satyagraha*, with non-violence as ethics, philosophy and sensibility, we should also associate the Mahatma with upholding the idea of cosmopolitan cultural histories and hybridised societies; a point also made by Debjani Ganguly in her illuminating essay 'Vernacular cosmopolitanism: world historical readings of Gandhi and Ambedkar' in Ganguly and Docker's collection *Rethinking Gandhi and Nonviolent Relationality: Global Perspectives*.[16]

Pandey calls attention to Gandhi's impassioned opposition to the cultural death, the memoricide, he believed would inevitably occur in a partitioned India, for example, if the long and remarkable Muslim history of architecture and all it signified in terms of mixed communities were to be removed and obliterated. In speech after speech in September 1947 and afterwards opposing partition, Pandey tells us, Gandhi asked what would Delhi be like without its Muslim heritage and its Muslim inhabitants? 'Delhi has a long history behind it', Gandhi said in one of his prayer speeches in October 1947. 'It would be madness even to try to erase that history.' What, Gandhi asked, would then be left of its mosaic of buildings and unique complex of cultures? What would Delhi be like if the Jama Masjid or Great Mosque, built in the time of Shah Jahan, was removed from the city?[17]

⁓⁕⁓

Intrigued by this reference to the Mughul history of Delhi, I google and see that Shah Jahan shifted his capital from Agra to Delhi in 1639, naming it Shahjahanabad, where he created, in what came to be called Old Delhi, wonderful architectural monuments, including the Red Fort, which Ann and I feel we visited in 1973, as well as the Juma Masjid, the Humayun Tomb and more, many more, monuments. And in Old Delhi is the Raj Ghat, the memorial to Mahatma Gandhi on the site of his cremation after he was assassinated on 30 January 1948.

⁓⁕⁓

According to the web, there are over 70 countries with Gandhi statues.

Of those we have seen ourselves, our favourite must be the statue of Gandhi in Tavistock Square in Bloomsbury, opposite the London hotel the Tavistock we sometimes stay in. In the square, as so many visitors who come from everywhere would know, is a statue of Virginia Woolf, the Japanese peace tree, and, in the centre, in pride of place, the statue of Gandhi. (Later, in the course of her research on Paul and Eslanda Robeson's visit to Australia in 1960, Ann discovered that the statue had been sculpted in 1968 by Fredda Brilliant, a Polish-born friend of the Robesons who had lived in Melbourne in the 1920s before moving to New York, then Moscow, and finally London in 1937.)

In Canberra, there is a statue of Gandhi near the city centre, in Glebe Park, which we occasionally strolled along to admire when we lived there from 1995 to 2008. When we lived in Georgetown in Washington DC for nine months in 2003-4, we would occasionally catch the bus to Dupont Circle and could catch sight of a Gandhi statue in a small triangular park as the bus rattled past. When we holidayed in Mumbai in 2007 we visited the Mani Bhavan Gandhi Museum, Gandhi's headquarters in Mumbai for some 17 years, from 1917 to 1934, there is a Gandhi statue in the library.

Gandhi, and Gandhi statues, are, however, not universally admired in the world, certainly not in Africa, as our friend Alan Lester, the British imperial historian, has reminded us, suggesting we google Ghana and Gandhi, which we do. *Aljazera*, accessed 15 December 2018, reports that a statue of Indian independence leader Mahatma Gandhi, installed in 2016, has been removed from Ghana's most prestigious university, the University of Ghana, in the capital Accra, following protests from students and faculty that Gandhi was racist towards black Africans. Soon after the statue was installed, professors at the university launched a petition, citing passages written by Gandhi during his time in South Africa 1893-1915, depicting Indians as 'infinitely superior' to black Africans and using the racist pejorative 'kaffirs' to describe them. One of Gandhi's writings cited in the petition reads: 'Ours is one continual struggle against a degradation sought to be inflicted upon us by the Europeans, who desire to degrade us to the level of the raw Kaffir whose occupation is hunting, and whose sole ambition is to collect a certain number of cattle to buy a wife with and, then, pass his life in indolence and nakedness.' Obadele Kambon, the head of language, literature and drama at the Institute of African Studies, said the removal was an issue of 'self-respect': 'If we indeed don't show any self-respect for our heroes, how can the world respect us? This is a victory for black dignity and self-respect.'

The protest against the Gandhi statue in Ghana was one of a number on university campuses in Africa and beyond about the enduring symbols of the continent's colonial past.

Campaigners in Malawi are trying to stop a statue of Gandhi being constructed in the capital, Blantyre. According to *BBC News* accessed 31 October 2018, in a report entitled 'Malawi court halts work on Gandhi statue after critics brand him a racist', more than 3000 Malawians have signed a petition against the statue.

―❦―

I'm reminded here of other occasions when European intellectuals one might very much admire in other contexts have been egregiously racist towards Africa, Africans and African Americans, including Raphaël Lemkin, Hannah Arendt and Adorno and Horkheimer. I've written about this deeply disturbing history before. In an essay 'Raphaël Lemkin, creator of the concept of genocide: a world history perspective', in a volume of essays edited by Ned Curthoys entitled *Key Thinkers and their Contemporary Legacy*, I relate that the genocide scholar Dominik J Schaller, analysing Lemkin's unpublished manuscripts, expresses dismay at Lemkin's views on Africa, and that Lemkin swayed between condemnation of and admiration for European colonial rule. In terms of the German colonial war against the Herero in Namibia, Schaller feels that there can be no doubt that Lemkin 'regarded his concept of genocide' as 'perfectly applicable to the events of 1904–1908'. Yet Lemkin also, he points out, fell in with a myth that the Herero, unable to reconcile themselves to subjection and loss of independence, chose to kill themselves in a kind of national suicide, with particular blame being attached to the Herero women. Lemkin also, Schaller argues, considered that the imposition of Belgian colonial rule in the Congo and the forced labour of the indigenous population that accompanied it, was genocide, yet described the 'native militia' in the pay of the Belgians as 'savages' and 'cannibals'. Schaller says that Lemkin has to be recognised as an 'enthusiastic advocate of colonialism' by European powers in Africa, seeing it as a necessary task that Europeans bring 'civilisation' to the continent. The ways Lemkin perceived Africans, Schaller concludes, 'can only be described as racist': 'Africans are portrayed as either weak-willed and helpless victims or as bloodthirsty cannibals'.[18]

In this essay I also point out that Hannah Arendt's attitudes towards African Americans and Africa are proving increasingly controversial, especially after the publication in 1995 of a highly critical essay by Anne Norton, who devastatingly critiqued Arendt's 1969 book *On Violence*. Arendt, Norton points out, follows Hegel in regarding Africans and African Americans as outside world history.[19] Ned Curthoys has suggested that Arendt 'adjudges the real tragedy of colonialism as its abrogation of European humanism and republican values, rather than its invasion and displacement of existing indigenous cultures', and that, unlike Sartre in relation to Algeria, Arendt refuses to acknowledge 'those dimensions of colonialism and imperialism that constituted physical and cultural genocide'; Arendt consistently fails to acknowledge the 'dignity and complexity of non-Western societies' and the 'subjectivity of non-Western peoples'.[20]

In relation to other exiled European intellectuals in the US, we might also think of Adorno and Horkheimer's notorious judgment in *Dialectic of Enlightenment* that jazz is a mere manifestation of nature – nature interacting with the demands of the American mass-entertainment industries. Adorno and Horkheimer refer to jazz as stylised barbarity and non-culture. In these terms, Adorno and Horkheimer, along with their contemporaries and fellow exiles Arendt and Lemkin, were conforming to a long tradition of European superiority and contempt towards Africa.[21]

Dear reader, I've kept my promise, my mind has returned to 1973 just as Ann and John's train from Varanasi is arriving in Agra. We find ourselves standing before the Taj Mahal, intensely white, which, I've read somewhere, as you look at it its transcendental beauty hovers between heaven and earth. Wikipedia tells me that the Taj Mahal was built from ivory-white marble, unlike the red usually favoured by Mughul rulers. It was commissioned in 1632 by the emperor Shah Jahan, who reigned from 1628 to 1658, to house the tomb of his favourite wife, Mumtaz Mahal, a Persian princess who had died during child birth. The complex was completed in its entirety in 1653; the construction project employed some 2000 artisans under the guidance of a board of architects led by the court architect Ustad Ahmad Lahauri; the Taj Mahal incorporates and expands on design traditions of Persian and Mughal architecture.

Ann and John now journey towards Delhi.

I can't remember very much about Delhi at all. I'm pretty certain we explored Old Delhi, it sounded much more interesting than New Delhi, though I think we stayed in a hotel in New Delhi. Ann has a memory of sitting in the hotel at a table of beautiful red wood, with light streaming in, where we read news of the overthrow of the Chilean leader Allende in a coup backed by the Americans against his elected government by a military figure, Pinochet.

I don't think we stayed long in Delhi, our aim was to go from Delhi to Kathmandu, though we're not sure how we got there, we both think it was by bus rather than flying.

I can't remember much at all about Khatmandu, where we stayed, what we saw. In *Student Guide to Asia*, David Jenkins writes that Durbar (Palace) Square is the 'heart of Kathmandu' and many of the city's main attractions are clustered there, including a temple dedicated to erotica. The Hanuman Doka, the old Royal Palace, must be visited, Jenkins urged; it contains some of the 'world's all-time great erotic art', some of the 'most beautifully carved and painted erotica imaginable'; no-one, he adds, 'should be shocked by the scenes depicted on such temples', for the Nepalese, who blend Hindu and Buddhist thoughts, 'look on the sex act as a symbol of creation' and thus a 'challenge to death and decay'. Also in this part of Kathmandu is the Jagannath Temple, 'another erotic-art temple', which depicts 'countless copulating couples'.[22] I have no memory at all of visiting these temples in Khatmandu, or maybe any temples, my only distinct memory is when eating at cafés I took to ordering a lassi and still enjoy them when we visit a Nepalese restaurant, usually asking for the mango lassi.

> ANN: I remember we walked around Khatmandu quite a lot, and that there were some very persistent street children, seeking attention, begging and touching, which was rather disturbing. Some googling now tells me that street children, mainly homeless boys, have been a feature of Khatmandu for a long time and still are.

I have a far clearer memory of excursions beyond Kathmandu. We took a bus to visit a small town or village, Ann remembers the name, Dhulikhel, and there, maybe at a tea house, we got talking to a young American about the same age as we were, and somehow the conversation got round to us all saying we grew up in Communist families; he said he was part of a young radical doctors group working in poorer parts of New York, they all decided to wear jeans and loose shirts, but their patients didn't like it, they wanted doctors to wear what doctors usually wear, be neat, maybe don white coats. He said he was about to leave Nepal, he had some kind of traumatic moment in Kathmandu, something about wandering into a temple and seeing some kind of what he thought was an animal sacrifice going on, he couldn't take it, I'm freaking out, I want to go home to New York.

On another excursion we took a bus to Nepal's border with China, we'd never been to China, we wanted to look over the border and think to ourselves we've now seen China. At the border post we also bought a little red book, *Quotations from Chairman Mao Tsetung*, pocket-sized, I've still got it, I've kept it through all our moves, though I don't think I've ever read a word. I look at it now. On an inside page, below 'Workers of all countries, Unite!', Ann wrote: 'John Docker Ann Curthoys Bought 1 September 1973 in Nepal near Chinese border'. On a further inside page, the name of the publisher is inscribed, 'Foreign Languages Press, Peking, 1972'. I've been chatting with Ann about it, and Ann points out that the border was really between Nepal and Tibet.

⁌✻⁍

From Kathmandu we went back to Delhi. John wasn't feeling very well, he was sick with fever, starting to shiver, have hot flushes, this wasn't good. I don't think I sufficiently heeded David Jenkins' general advice in his introductory notes on Health in *Student Guide to Asia* that 'various heating disorders' may 'cause trouble', I don't think I was drinking enough fluids, though here were lots of difficulties. Jenkins stressed that travelers should be 'careful with unboiled water, ice blocks, cream, unbottled drinks, cold meat and cold food dishes like salads'; try to eat unpeeled fruit only, and 'take care with fresh orange and lemon juice'; especially in India,

Nepal or Afghanistan, it is 'not safe to drink unboiled water'. One should 'stick to tea, coffee, hot orange or lemon drinks or reputable soft drinks'.[23]

Ann suggested we abandon our original idea of keeping going on the hippie trail through Afghanistan and Iran, let's fly straight to London. Yes, John nodded weakly.

⁕

On a morning walk in December 2018, nearing the new year, we agree that we should try to reflect on what the five months' journey through South East Asia, Burma, India and Nepal might have meant for us, then as we travelled about, and now in the present as we try to evoke it. I'll go first, though I'm sure Ann's reflections will be far more acute.

JOHN: we've discussed this, we didn't seem to have been interested at all in cities, not in Jakarta, or Malacca, or Kuala Lumpur, or Rangoon, or Bangkok, or New Delhi, or Khatmandu. It looks like we hurried out of them as soon as we could. Singapore, however, we found interesting, for the exciting food certainly, which featured different cuisines, Chinese, Indian, Malay, Singapore as a multicultural city, a port city. We also very much enjoyed our time in Calcutta, but that was because we met up with Soumyen Mukerjee, who introduced us to Bengali intellectuals and we met his gracious mother; something else I remember is that we went with Soumyen to a quite swish air-conditioned restaurant, styled in something like black marble, Soumyen went over to the waiters and had a conversation with them, which he reported to us: he said he tried to order the food in Bengali, but they said no, speak English, as if to emphasise that they knew he was only visiting Calcutta, he didn't live here anymore.

What is memorable, too, was a signal absence, we never visited museums in any of these cities. Ann, years later, when teaching

Applied History at the University of Technology, Sydney, became very interested in museums as one of the institutions communicating ideas about and knowledge of history, and some of the students she taught in Applied History worked in museums. With a young child, we didn't go overseas for many years, until 1999, when we went on a food tour to Vietnam that I think I mentioned before somewhere in this ego histoire; when we got to Ho Chi Minh City, we visited a museum, called, Ann remembers, the War Remnants Museum, that referred not to the 'Vietnam War' but to 'the American War in Vietnam', a phrase I had never seen used before and now always use; there were photos on the walls of westerners, Australian and New Zealand, protesting against the American war, including protestors in a Sydney street trying to block the cavalcade of American president Johnson, one showing Ann's younger sister Jean lying on the road, surrounded by the police.

After the Vietnam trip, visiting museums, often situated in cities, has become a mainstay of our travelling wherever we go.

Another reflection: I have a vague distant memory of reading when a young teenager a book by Maxim Gorky on the university of life. I've looked it up: Gorky, who spent many years living in exile from Russia in Italy, in Capri and later Sorrento, wrote an autobiography in three volumes, *The Childhood of Maxim Gorky*, *My Apprenticeship*, and, the final volume, *My Universities*, an ironic title since he had never been to one.

Maybe, I'm venturing, the hippie trail through South-East Asia was for Ann and me a varied and surprising and intriguing university of life: not just charming and curious, but introducing us to other histories, of genocide, catastrophe, and terror; histories we knew of from afar but now were learning about closer up. We already knew of genocide, catastrophe and terror from Australian settler coloniser history, especially Ann, who had been on the 1965 Freedom Ride and for her doctorate had researched racial attitudes in relation to Indigenous peoples and Chinese immigrants, and we both had joined in protests in Sydney against the rugby tour in 1972 by an apartheid South African team; our travels helped us see Australian history as part of world history.

ANN: We had not traveled overseas ever before, and indeed had rarely caught a plane before this long journey through Asia, involving flights to Bali, Singapore, Burma, Calcutta, and then from Delhi to London. Our knowledge of the world came from many sources, including our studies, friends who might have come from elsewhere, the media and political involvements, but until this point not from travel. When I think how often our grandson, now seven, has flown, to Sydney, Brisbane, Adelaide, Bali, Malaysia, Singapore, London, I realise how much the world, and Australia's place in it, has changed from the one in which we grew up. Again and again, I got a little shock, in India at the number of people in the streets, the extreme poverty, the cremation, along with moments of delight, such as a huge red sky at dusk in India over bright green rice fields, or the lush green gardens and fields in Bali, or the friendliness of so many people we met as we traveled. Though I am conscious of how much I've forgotten, I'm also surprised at how strong some of my memories are of a trip taken 45 years ago.

286 Growing Up Communist and Jewish in Bondi

1   David Jenkins (ed.) *Student Guide to Asia*, published by the Australian Union of Students on behalf of the International Student Travel Conference (Globe Press, Melbourne, 1973), p.39.

2   Zarina Bhatty, *Purdah to Piccadilly: A Muslim Woman's Struggle for Identity* (Sage, London, 2016), pp.90-91.

3   John Docker, *The Nervous Nineties: Australian cultural life in the 1890s* (Oxford University Press, Melbourne, 1991), pp.82-95.

4   Docker, *The Nervous Nineties*, p.88.

5   Patrick Brantlinger, 'A Postindustrial Prelude to Postcolonialism: John Ruskin, William Morris, and Gandhism', *Critical Inquiry*, Vol.22, no.3, 1996, pp.466-485, here p.466.

6   Brantlinger, 'A Postindustrial Prelude to Postcolonialism', pp.467-68.

7   Brantlinger, 'A Postindustrial Prelude to Postcolonialism', pp.468, 479-82.

8   Brantlinger, 'A Postindustrial Prelude to Postcolonialism', pp.482-5.

9   Ann Curthoys, 'From Montserrat to Settler-Colonial Australia: the intersecting histories of Caribbean slave-owning families, transported British radicals, and Indigenous peoples', *History Workshop Journal* (2020).

10 Anjali Roy, 'Homespun Wisdom: Gandhi, Technology and Nationalism', in Debjani Ganguly and John Docker (eds), *Rethinking Gandhi and Nonviolent Relationality: Global Perspectives* (Orient BlackSwan, Hyderabad, 2009), pp.280, 291.

11 Anjali Roy, 'Homespun Wisdom: Gandhi, Technology and Nationalism', pp.281-3.

12 Anjali Roy, 'Homespun Wisdom: Gandhi, Technology and Nationalism', pp.283-4, 288-9.

13 Anjali Roy, 'Homespun Wisdom: Gandhi, Technology and Nationalism', p.289.

14 John Docker, 'The Two-State Solution and Partition: World History Perspectives on Palestine and India', *Holy Land Studies*, Vol.9, No.2, 2010, pp.147-168, here at pp.148-150.

15 Docker, 'The Two-State Solution and Partition', pp.150, 162-4.

16 Debjani Ganguly, 'Vernacular Cosmopolitanism: World Historical Readings of Gandhi and Ambedkar', in Debjani Ganguly and John Docker (eds), *Rethinking Gandhi and Nonviolent Relationality: Global Perspectives*, pp.309-333.

17 Docker, 'The Two-State Solution and Partition', pp.162-3.

18 John Docker, 'Raphael Lemkin, creator of the concept of genocide: a world history perspective', in Ned Curthoys (ed.), *Key Thinkers and their Contemporary Legacy, Humanities Research*, Vol.XVI, No.2, 2010, pp.65-6; Dominik J. Schaller, 'Raphael Lemkin's view of European colonial rule in Africa: between condemnation and admiration', *Journal of Genocide Research*, vol.7, no.4, pp.531-8.

19 Anne Norton, 'Heart of Darkness: Africa and African Americans in the writings of Hannah Arendt', in Bonnie Honig (ed.), *Feminist Interpretations of Hannah Arendt* (Pennsylvania State University Press, University Park, 1995), pp.247–61.

20 Ned Curthoys, 'The Refractory legacy of Algerian decolonisation: revisiting Arendt on violence', in Richard H. King and Dan Stone (eds), *Hannah Arendt and the Uses of History: Imperialism, nation, race, and genocide* (Berghahn, New York, 2007), p.125; John Docker, 'Raphaël Lemkin, creator of the concept of genocide: a world history perspective', pp.70–71.

21 See Theodor Adorno and Max Horkheimer, *Dialectic of Enlightenment* (Verso, London, 1979), pp.127–8; Docker, 'Raphaël Lemkin, creator of the concept of genocide: a world history perspective', p.71.

22 David Jenkins, *Student Guide to Asia*, chapter on Nepal, pp.221–2.

23 David Jenkins, Introduction, *Student Guide to Asia*, p.9.

38

1973–4: Ann and John in London

>⚘<

We flew to London from Delhi not long after the democratically-elected Chilean president Salvador Allende was violently overthrown on 11 September 1973 by General Pinochet with the support of the US, causing a world outcry.[1]

We first stayed in some sort of hostel for backpackers like us, women and men in bunks in separate quarters, and pretty well the first thing we did was to go on a march to protest against the coup, starting in Hyde Park and proceeding to Trafalgar Square. The autumn weather must have been quite warm; we only had the clothes we'd worn on our hippie trail travels through Asia; only later did we buy cold weather clothes. I've got a nagging feeling that I've written about this march elsewhere, but, still, I'll evoke the images in my mind's eye. The theatre or dramaturgy of the London demonstration was completely surprising. In Australian demonstrations for example, at the continuing American war in Vietnam with Australian involvement or the apartheid-era Springbok football tour of Australia people of various political hues or simply broadly New Left, with its anarchist dislike of organisation, would stroll along together chatting with friends while someone would occasionally roar out a protest.

We were rather flummoxed by the sight of the London demonstration. When it set off, it divided itself into blocs, each bloc representing some sort of left political grouping, with a space in between; here didn't seem to be anyone simply walking along. We wondered what to do, and decided to insert ourselves in the middle between two groups and just walk between them. This was a revelation. Instead of spending their time decrying Pinochet's brutality and the United States' perfidy, each group occupied itself with noisily deriding the one in front of it and the one behind it for various contemptible ideological tendencies. What they made of us we had no idea. We kept walking along as verbal missiles flew over our heads until we got to Trafalgar Square.

On a later visit to London in 1982, Ann and I purchased a lively pamphlet entitled *Go Fourth and Multiply: The Political Anatomy of the British Left Groups* (publisher Dialogue of the Deaf, Full Marks Bookshop, Bristol, 50p), which helps illuminate this curious feature of the British left. On the front cover, the author is given as Prunella Kaur, but a little googling by Ann suggests that Prunella Kaur was the byline of John Sullivan. The pamphlet is written in a satirical spirit, a little reminiscent of Marx's *Eighteenth Brumaire*, as a guide to the ever-multiplying groups and sub-groups of the British left, the British fissiparous (a word I rather like) left. The front cover directly addresses the reader:

> You are at a party and someone calls you a workerist – how do you reply? Could it be true? Yet your boyfriend says you are an ultra-left while your sister claims you have Pabloite tendencies so you don't really know what to say. Such social embarrassment can now be avoided with the aid of this guide. Now you can hold your own in the sub-world of the left. Who knows, one of the groups might suit you. You might even spot a gap in the market coverage and form your own group.

The guide doesn't claim to be comprehensive, but includes and has notes on the following groups: the Militants, who speak with a 'fake Liverpool accent'; the Socialist Workers' Party (SWP); International Marxist Group, its defining feature being that 'it is the British section of the Fourth International (Mandel Tendency)'; The Workers' Socialist League (WSL) – Deceased; Spartacus League ('The Sparts' main energy is devoted to slagging off other groups which claim to be Trotskyist'); Revolutionary Communist Group; Revolutionary Communist Party; The Revolutionary Workers' Party (RWP) Posadas; The New Communist Party (NCP); The Communist Party of Britain (Marxist-Leninist); Big Flame; and the Socialist Party of Great Britain (SPGB). Especially important is the Workers' Revolutionary Party (WRP), whose best-known member was Vanessa Redgrave, and principal figure Gerry Healy: 'Laurence Olivier's shot at portraying him in the play "The Party" was generally acclaimed as a brave try but not really up to the histrionic standards of the original.'

[Wikipedia notes that *The Party* was put on at the Old Vic between 18 December 1973 and 21 March 1974, Ann and I recall that we went to see the play and liked it.]

The front cover also has a cartoon with a Trotsky father figure pushing a pram full of little children, representing the various groups, fighting with each other with baby bottles and toys.

Trafalgar Square was a kind of node we got to know, it gave us bearings. Not too far away, a little to the north, was Gerard Street with its Chinese restaurants reminding us of Sydney's China Town, and then a bit further north was Soho, reminding us of inner city Sydney places like Glebe and Newtown, with its maze of narrow streets and its quirky shops and cafés, a quarter which we quickly came very much to like, indeed Soho is still one of my favourite parts of London; to the east of Trafalgar Square was the Strand, which we would walk along till we got to the Australian High Commission, where we could collect blue aerogram mail from Australia.

The other early demonstrations we went on were to oppose continuing Portuguese colonialism in Africa in countries like Mozambique, Guinea-Bissau, and Cape Verde, and to support the liberation movements against it. I particularly remember Cape Verde, not sure why, perhaps because I'd never heard of it before. (I've just googled; the Portuguese Colonial War involving liberation movements went from 1961 to 1974; on 25 April 1974 there was an army revolt which led to the overthrow of Portugal's authoritarian government and withdrawal of Portugal from its African colonies.) Here we met some Australians, somewhat older than us, they had been in London for some time working, maybe as lawyers or medical people, who were trying to help in practical ways the African resistance to Portugal; They were part of an Australian and New Zealand diaspora we increasingly came to relate to. Ann recalls that we immediately assented to an offer from an Australian couple there who said we could stay with them for a few days until we found somewhere to live; the very nice and helpful group advised us to sign up with a temp agency, you'll need to start earning money as soon as you can, and may also have suggested we get *Time Out* to see what's going on in terms of meetings to go to or films to see. They may have written much needed references for us. Maybe also they told us of the *Guardian* as the daily paper to read, with all its different sections, which we immediately took pleasure in doing.

Somehow we secured a small upstairs flat in a large house in Willesden Green, just north of Kilburn, on the Jubilee Line; we heard that Kilburn was reputed to be a lively 'Irish area', while, we soon realized, Willesden Green with its free standing homes was pure suburbia. One memory of living in the Willesden Green house: I'd read an article in the *Guardian* by its correspondent in Australia, which I thought was derisory towards Indigenous people; I sent a short letter of protest to the *Guardian*.

I've just looked through my 2010 notes I took in Mitchell Library, and see I have transcribed the letter I sent to the *Guardian*, dated 22 December 1973, from 130 Chatsworth Road, London NW2. The letter was published in the *Guardian* on 29 December 1973, p.10, and given the title 'Clubbing the assumptions about modern Stone Age Man'. It's too long to reproduce in full, so I've shortened it somewhat.

> SIR, – From Terry Coleman's report of his visit to Ballarat in Australia (December 22) a couple of things stand out. Of Australian aborigines he says: 'In fact the aborigines are a tiny problem there being only about 120,000 of them in all Australia, and most of these you see around are evidently the local representatives of the Stone Age.'
>
> It's interesting to see in the one sentence the association of evolutionism and racist contempt that led the British in Australia in the nineteenth century to think nothing of destroying aboriginal societies and of reducing their numbers to a 'tiny problem'...
>
> Leaving aside his offensive dismissal of 120,000 people, Coleman could consider that it is the repressive attitudes and actions of Australia's white population, past and present, which constitute the real 'problem'...

Soon after a letter arrived at 130 Chatsworth Road, London, NW2, in the morning post, advising me to go back to 'tree-climbing'. Hmm, Ann and I thought, English racism, let's not forget that in our sojourn here. (We wondered how they knew where I lived, maybe in the early 1970s a letter writer's home address was shown.)

Quite quickly, our lives acquired a kind of rhythm. We hooked up with a temp agency somewhere in the centre of London; I vaguely recall they asked me if I had a skill of any kind, and I confidently said, yes, I can type; Ann also said she could type, which she was called upon to do at various places, though I wasn't. Ann and I have just enjoyed an after – dinner chat about what we remember of our temping experiences. Ann's memories are bountiful:

> ANN: I had a series of clerical jobs. First at the London office of UNICEF, the United Nations International Children's Emergency Fund, assisting in the mailing of their annual Christmas cards. Next was a clerical position in late 1973 at the London School of Economics. The only thing I remember there is that one day Anthony Forge, a specialist on New Guinea and Bali and then a Senior Lecturer in Anthropology at LSE, came into the office to sort something out, and talked with the office supervisor. He was arranging something to do with his imminent relocation to Australia, to take up the inaugural professorship of Anthropology at ANU. I didn't say a word, just kept doing my filing and listening in with interest. I later met Forge and his wife Jane in Canberra, when I was lecturer for Women's Studies at ANU, but never mentioned the LSE.
>
> Perhaps the job I remember best is the next one, a clerical assistant at the *Daily Mail*, a conservative tabloid newspaper. I had many odd jobs, but one was to compile a scrapbook of the newspaper's coverage of the election held on 28 February 1974. I clipped all the items as requested and pasted them in the book in chronological order. I then added something I hadn't been asked to do, which was a contents page listing which items covered which political party; this showed a huge coverage of Edward Heath's Conservative Party and much less of Labour. What my index couldn't show was just how strongly the *Daily Mail* (along with most other papers, according to Wikipedia) supported Heath and opposed Labour. Despite the *Mail*'s best

efforts, Labour's Harold Wilson became prime minister, in a minority government.

The last temporary job I held before we returned to Australia was at Guy's Hospital, to deal with the mail and clerical duties of one of its doctors, who in fact was away most of the time I was there. I remember once he asked me to purchase his vouchers for a holiday abroad; I had no idea what he meant, but eventually realised he meant I was to book his flights. I can't remember if I actually did that, but I do remember the feeling that perhaps this was not my job.

My memories are sparser. I do recall also working in Guys Hospital, maybe in the basement, filing large heavy yellow envelopes (I think yellow) containing x-rays onto shelves. Another memory is of working in an office somewhere, on a higher floor, with no lighting in London's buildings and darkness setting in from about 3pm onwards; I've looked this up, on 13 December 1973 the British Prime Minister Edward Heath announced the introduction of a Three Day Week because of the threat of a miners' strike, and it ended 7 March 1974. Another memory is of temping in the office of something like a National Medical Association, one day when news came through that a particular African nation was making world headlines, a middle-aged lady in the office said with great authority, that nation is 'one of ours'. In all these places I said not a word; Ann also says she would sit quietly saying nothing. Perhaps Gorky, when he talked of the university of life, urged the value of silent observation.

In Guys Hospital, Ann and I would meet for lunch and swap stories about what it was like where we were. When we worked at different places, we would meet after work; sometimes we would go for dinner in a particular tiny Italian café we liked in Soho. On Friday nights we would collect our wages and we took to going to a restaurant, Jimmy's, downstairs in one of the main Soho streets, it reminded us of Diethnes in Sydney, we always seemed to have people there we knew to eat Greek food with and fearfully sip ouzo from little glasses, could we handle ouzo, would I get pissed immediately and stagger about, best to look like an old hand; in our group were other diaspora Australians, and sometimes Englishmen who had been at Sydney University in the 1960s as young lecturers or postgraduates doing theses, stories of past times were swapped, babble ensued, we had a whole week's silence to make up for. I've just googled to see if there's any record of Jimmy's, it appears that Jimmy's opened in 1948 in Frith Street, round the corner from Old Compton Street, it no longer exists but is fondly remembered.

Time Out was utterly invaluable for us, it gave shape to our nine or ten months stay in London; we would carefully go over each new issue, working out what night time talks and lectures we would like to go to, and every week, with the boundless energy of the young, we spent several nights going to talks and lectures.

On one of these occasions, having gone by the Tube to a talk somewhere, we went afterwards to a nearby pub and found ourselves standing next to someone we felt we knew from the English department at Sydney University and more generally the Libertarian bohemian push in its pub the Forth and Clyde in Balmain and parties afterwards. We looked at each other: you're Charles Ross, you're Ann and John!

Charles was a medievalist, he'd been to Oxford, he'd been recruited to the Sydney University English department as a young lecturer in the 1960s, and later had gone back to London. Charles, with his upper-class voice that he always used ironically, quickly became part of our diasporic circle, I'm sure he must have joined us at Jimmy's on Friday nights. We went on weekend excursions with Charles, one was to a seaside place, Ann and I toss names around,

Blackpool, Brighton, Margate, Ann thinks Margate, we would go to an arcade and Ann and Charles would play some kind of driving game trying to guide a ball around, we can't remember its name, I say a pinball machine, Ann says no, it has a different name, you sit down as if driving a car; Charles was very impressed by Ann's skill.

Another time we journeyed to Paris, Charles spoke fluent French, it was winter and cold, we went to the prominent art museums and, we recall, to a small market and bought baguettes, salami, cheese, tomatoes and sat huddled on a park bench and ate the delicious food.

Charles became a lifelong friend; he went to Italy and taught English as a foreign language, once we visited him in Bologna, he arranged for a little hotel for us to stay in and he himself lived in a tiny flat, he kept his cooking pots and pans in the shower, he cooked a curry for us, he knew we liked curries. He introduced us to his women friends from England who also taught English at the university in Bologna.

When after several years he came back to London he again taught English to foreign students; he sang in a choir, and played classical music on the piano to a high level. We would go with Charles to somewhere in Kent to visit other friends from 1960s Sydney days, Bill Browning and Vicki Browning, they taught in a local school in what looked like an old castle. In London, Charles lived mostly in or near Soho, in tiny apartments, he could just manage to get his piano into them, and every time we came to London we would do fun things together. Each time he would wistfully say, 'I should go back to Sydney for a visit', Sydney was where he broke out from his middle-class English upbringing into parties and sensuousness.

Sadly, Charles died in 2017.

Christmas of 1973 was the first Christmas we ever spent outside

Australia. Here we were helped by Camille, Ann's New Zealand friend from Women's Liberation days in Sydney. We were building up a considerable cumulative life debt to Camille. It was Camille who suggested that if you get married you can keep your unmarried name, you're not legally bound to give it up; her and her then partner's going on the hippy trail through Asia before us gave us the idea that we also could do it; and she introduced us to Gay Simpkin a long-standing friend of hers from Auckland who was then living in London. We became friends with warm quietly spoken Gay, and enjoyed Christmas with her and a male friend of hers in her bed-sit, Ann thinks it was in Hampstead, Gay had managed to roast a leg of lamb.

Camille and Gay became lifelong friends of ours, and we took to visiting them in Auckland and at Gay's shared holiday house (*bach*) in Tinopai; we also met up with them when they separately visited Sydney. One distressing day, Camille rang us from Auckland, Gay had died on 7 February 2016 after a long illness from Crohn's Disease.

While Gorky enjoins the traveller to experience the university of life, we did come into contact with para or outreach or marginal university offerings, from early in 1974 onwards. In *Time Out* we saw that in the new year courses were being put on in various places, we scanned them to see which might prove interesting. We tried out a course concerning Art and Politics in twentieth-century Russia, the course was to go for seven weeks, but I only have notes for weeks two and three listed on the course outline, these must have been the only lectures we attended. I can't see from the notes where in London the course was put on and who was the lecturer:

2. Socio-political background to 1932.
    Class structure and state in Russia 1861–1917.

Russian Social-Democratic Labour Party 1898–1917.
International Context of Russian Revolution.
Revolution Feb.1917-April 1918.
Economic Development 1918–1932: Civil War – expediency;
NEP – reconstruction; first 5-year plan 1928–32;
collectivization.
Political Developments 1918–1932: Nationalities policy;
international policy; Kronstadt and the Workers Opposition;
death of Lenin and the manoeuvring of the interregnum;
defeat of Left Opposition; defeat of Right Deviation.

3. Institutions (here I see I have hastily scribbled handwritten comments, perhaps I found this section of the course more interesting, more cultural, less political).

Narkompros and Lunarcharsky (Narkompros contained, I scribble, a lot of futurists, who resisted occupational drive in education; Narkompros was fucked, I scrawl, by NEP because of lack of money/increasing state control in twenties; Lunacharsky defended theatres as transitional academies).

Proletkult as an organisation 1917–21 (hostile to futurists).

In the booklist for the course I see Sheila Fitzpatrick, *The Commissariat of the Enlightenment, Soviet Organization of Education and the Arts under Lunacharsky, October 1917–1921*, Cambridge University Press, 1970. Decades later, Ann would have an office just along the corridor from Sheila at the University of Sydney, where both held research positions.

It was, however, the courses on aspects of Africa that we were particularly drawn to in those early months of 1974. Ann recalls the seminar she went to that was conducted by Shula Marks as a remarkable experience:

ANN: I arrived in London having recently completed a PhD on race relations in colonial New South Wales, comparing settler responses to both Aboriginal people and Chinese immigrants. In London, the closest seminar I could find to my interests was Shula Marks' series on The Societies of Southern Africa in the Nineteenth and Twentieth Centuries at the Institute of Commonwealth Studies, I think in Russell Square. Most of those who attended were postgraduate students studying African history; I am sure I was the only Australian there. In my own research, I had encountered debates by Marxist scholars over the relationship between capitalism and racial segregation and wanted to learn more. In a memoir of the seminar series, written in 2012 on the occasion of the digitalising of all 239 seminar papers given during the series' long 25-year life from 1969, Shula Marks remarks that the seminar tradition at the Institute was begun by its first director, Keith Hancock, and has continued ever since. She notes that at her series, regular participants and contributors included Martin Legassick, Harold Wolpe and Stanley Trapido.

I remember attending a paper by Wolpe on the theory of internal colonialism and hearing intense discussions of Legassick's work over the relationship between capitalism and apartheid. I don't remember Stanley Trapido, though in fact his work on colonial liberalism has in the long run been the most important for me, when trying to understand the ways in which the moves towards settler self-government were influenced by the nature of race relations in Australia. I attended the seminars for some time, but never said one word in discussion. When I returned to Australia, what I learnt at Shula Marks's seminars influenced my publications from my PhD thesis, and my thinking about the strengths and limitations of Marxist understandings of questions of race and class.

Shula Marks, one of the most exciting historians of Africa, was an effective and very democratic chair of discussion. What a contrast she was to another seminar chair I heard at this time, at the Institute of Historical Studies in Senate House in London. The paper was by leading labour historian, Raphael Samuel, on flitting, that is of working-class people quickly moving out when their rent was overdue and they could not pay. The room was full and the paper quirky and insightful. The chair was Eric Hobsbawm, that doyen of British Marxist historians, indeed of British historians generally, much revered and valued in the profession. His method of chairing I thought extremely arrogant, controlling, and tending to suppress rather than encourage discussion. Eric Hobsbawm had been one of my heroes, but I never quite recovered from hearing him chair that seminar.

We also saw that in the new year a course on African Literature as part of African Studies was being offered, Ann and I enrolled; we remember this course well, it turned out to be profoundly influential on my subsequent intellectual life in terms of literary and cultural theory and envisaging new approaches to university teaching of literature.

In my notes taken in 2010 of Ann and my papers, I write that the African Literature course was put on at the Polytechnic of Central London, Centre for Extra Mural Studies. Here is the course outline as I transcribed it:

> This course of seven lectures given by a Nigerian critic aims to provide both a detailed study of important texts and a coherent framework for understanding African literature. It will explore those areas of African literature that touch on general human concerns such as the problems of human suffering, the relation of political parties to the people, the role of intellectuals in society, the search for self-understanding and the nature of Love.
>
> Acquaintance with set texts will be indispensable and a

reading of some supplementary books very helpful. No previous knowledge of Africa or its literature will be presupposed. These lectures will be followed by a study weekend.

Mondays beginning January 21st 1974. 6.30–8.30 pm.
First floor 104–108 Bolsover St.
Course fee: £1.00 (including study weekend)

Lecture Programme

Jan 21st Nationalism, Alienation and the crisis of ideology: the historical context of African Literature

Jan 28th A World of Symbols: technology, literacy and the ambiguity of texts

Feb 4th People's Action: on the social meaning of African liberation

Feb 11th The Myth of Culture-Conflict: religion, intellectuals, elites and masses

Feb 18th On the Purity of Self: mystical parables of self-understanding

Feb 25th Love and Suffering: on the irrationality of human suffering and the elusiveness of Love

Mar 4th The Politics of Despair and Renewal: cynicism, scepticism and messianismMar 8th and 9th Study Weekend with poetry and lectures on George Jackson and Amilcar Cabral

Reading List

Lecture 1 Basil Davidson 'Which Way Africa?' 2nd ed., E. Mondlane 'The Struggle for Mozambique' 1973

Lecture 2 E. Obiechne 'On African Popular Literature' 1973; Vansina 'Oral Tradition'

Lecture 3 Sembene Ousmane 'God's Bits of Wood'

Lecture 4 Chinua Achebe 'Things Fall Apart'; J. Ngugi, 'The River Between'

Lecture 5 Wole Soyinka 'The Interpreters', 'The Road'
Lecture 6 T. U'tamsi 'Selected Poems'; Dennis Brutus 'A Simple Lust'
Lecture 7 T.M. Aluko 'Chief, the Honourable Minister'; A.K. Amah 'The Beautiful Ones Are Not Yet Born'

Supplementary Reading List
F. Fanon 'The Wretched of the Earth'
A. Cesaire 'Discourse on Colonialism'
Ngugi 'Homecoming'
Soyinka 'Collected Plays, Vol.I'
B. Davidson 'The Africans'

Course Tutors: O. A. Ladimeji (the lecturer, Clare College, Cambridge); Lewis Nkosi

[On back of course outline I noted: SOAS 7.15 Tues Ousmane film 'The Money Order'. I did take down some notes of a highly critical analysis by the lecturer of Achebe's 'Things Fall Apart':

Things Fall Apart
Systematic distortions by Achebe:
1) Ibo religion presented as if basically similar to Christianity, not as different... cf. Ngugi... thinks Ngugi much better and subtler –
2) twin-killing: presented as if son of Okwandu [?] and women in village have Christian-like dislike of it – against anthropological evidence that only one twin killed (weaker) because of mother's shortage of milk.

Achebe's position in novel is a reconciliation of nationalist (e.g. at end) position with Christian-bourgeois (pro good missionary).

Achebe is basically patronising to traditional culture. Unlike Ousmane, doesn't give sense of characters – central character Okwonku [sp?] is in Western Greek tragedy tradition.

Ann tells me that I asked questions of the lecturer, she recalls a discussion of colonialism, could Australian literature be counted as a post-colonial literature when it is the literature of a settler colonial nation.

⚜

I also recorded another course outline, entitled 'Black Culture and Political Liberation', a study week of lectures/seminars to be held at PCL Staff and Student Centre 104/108 Bolsover Street, nearest tube Great Portland Street. This course looks extraordinarily interesting, it would have followed directly on from 'African Literature', but Ann and I can't remember going to it, nothing comes to mind. I list here the lectures:

> Tuesday March 12th 6.30pm The Nigerian writer WOLE SOYINKA on AMILCAR CABRAL
> Friday March 15th 6.30pm DAPO LADIMEJI – George Jackson on Political Liberation
> Saturday March 16th 2.30pm Adekunle AJALA on Pan-Africanism
> 4.00 Louis Gates on Bessie Smith and the Harlem Renaissance
>
> Reading List
> Amilcar Cabral Revolution in Guinea Stage One
> Basil Davidson The Liberation of Guinea
> George Jackson Soledad Brother. The Prison
> Letters of George Jackson
> Blood in my Eye
> Adekunle Ajala Pan-Africanism

On the back of the course outline, there is a note in Ann's handwriting:

76 Stroud Green Road. N4
New Beacon Bookshop
Blood in my Eye
Account of Jackson's death

⁓⚜⁓

I'll now trace the more than considerable influence on my thinking of the early 1974 'African Literature' course, and then I will return to Ann and my 1973–4 doings, including travel to Cornwall and Ireland.

Ann and I returned to Australia in July 1974, our son Ned being born 27 November that year. In early 1975, we moved to Canberra, where I began a PhD at the Australian National University on Australian literature of the 1890s in international contexts, and Ann worked first as a research assistant on Kay Daniels' National Research Program, funded by the Australian government as part of International Women's Year, and then as a sessional tutor in Australian history at the Canberra College of Advanced Education. In our second and third years there, Ann was a full-time lecturer in Women's Studies at ANU.

However, while I was working on my thesis on the *fin de siècle* (later, transmogrified, to become *The Nervous Nineties: Australian Cultural Life in the 1890s*, published in 1991), I was still intensely interested in the contemporary perspectives opened up by the African Literature course and the reading I did for it. In the notes I took in 2010, I see that I wrote a long paper in the mid-1970s, perhaps in 1977, called 'Toward a comparative sociology of literature: Ferdinand Tönnies, Patrick White, and Wole Soyinka', it was for, I see, a 'colloquium in comparative sociology' (perhaps held by Doug Miles, in anthropology at ANU).

I never published this essay, perhaps it wasn't publishable in any single-discipline journal, but I fondly remember it, and I hope the reader will bear with me while I explain its interests. In the essay I sketch out possible relationships between a particular European sociological theory, and what I take to be significantly similar ideas, expressed in non-sociological form, in Australian and Nigerian literature. [In relation to Nigeria I refer to Soyinka's 1973 novel *Season of Anomy* and his book of essays *Myth, Literature and the African World*, published in 1976.] The German sociological tradition, I ventured, in figures like Tönnies, Max Weber, and Simmel, as well as many concepts and attitudes in Marx, was preoccupied with problems raised by the development of industrial capitalism, in particular by what was viewed as the sweeping rationalisation of all human activity. Such sociology developed as a response to the new industrial society of the nineteenth century, and the breakdown of pre-capitalist social formations. Industrial society was held to be destructive of everything that had previously made human life worth while.

I suggested that Soyinka's novel *Season of Anomy* and his essays in *Myth, Literature and the African World* represent a response to the same commercial and industrial incursion into rural society that prompted European romanticism. Like the European, Soyinka's 'romantic' mode dwells in major oppositions and dualities: in particular the opposition between the false allure of 'neon-cities' and a desired universal rural community; between a society based on the cash-nexus, the 'unholy God, Mammon', and an opposing way of life based on sharing, kinship, and communality; between the divisiveness, alienation, and suspicion bred by urban existence, and the solidarity and harmony of the ideal village. Soyinka's 'romantic' criticism explores its oppositions of ideal rural community, close to the natural world, and alienated urban society, not in the sociological form of categories, concepts and ideal-types, but in primarily literary modes, in terms of symbol, myth, and metaphor.

Medievalism can be seen as a shaping influence on Ferdinand Tönnies' major sociological constructs, *Gemeinschaft* and *Gesellschaft*. Tönnies admires the European Middle Ages as a time of organic community, where social relationships were based on kinship and neighbourly-type bonds. In general, *Gemeinschaft* refers to idyllic pre-industrial organic community, while *Gesellschaft* corresponds to modern capitalist mechanical society. As well, these two ideal-types correspond to two types of personalities, those who express organic or natural will (*Wesenwille*) and those who express *Willkür*, rational will.

Tönnies considered that the Middle Ages were a feminine epoch, whereas the modern period was more masculine, with its trade and war.

> All the women's activity is more inward than outward. The end of this activity lies in itself and not in some outside aim... Also, many tasks in agriculture befit the woman and have always in the soundest cultures been put, often, however, to the point of excess, on her shoulders, for farming is labour unconscious of itself, drawing strength from the heavenly breezes. Farming can be conceived as a service to nature, close to the household and immediately bearing fruit.
>
> Ferdinand Tönnies, *Gemeinschaft und Gesellschaft* (1887), translated as *Community and Association* by Charles P Loomis, London, 1955, p.187

Ideally, then, women exhibit *Wesenwille*, they are like nature itself, unconscious activity, ever passionate, creative and growing like 'vegetative life', Tönnies says at one point (p.179). When, however, a woman, Tönnies avers, takes to earning her own living, as a trader or in factories, she develops 'her rational will, enabling her to think in a calculating way.... The woman becomes enlightened, cold hearted, conscious'. 'Nothing,' Tönnies shudders, 'is more foreign and terrible to her original inborn nature...' (pp.189, 191).

Tönnies' contrast between the natural will – the spontaneous, creative, instinctive powers, as against rational, calculating, dominating, emotion-denying will-power – strikes me as amazingly close to the drama of personality and sensibility in Patrick White's novels. The equation of women with unconscious nature can be seen in White's female characters such as Miss Hare and Mrs Godbold in *Riders in the Chariot*, and like Tönnies, White portrays women as being destroyed by will, consciousness, and rationality.

In Tönnies' view, men are usually overtaken by *Willkür*, calculating rational will, but some men are more admirably feminine, more receptive to natural will, than others. In this sliding scale, businessmen, scientists, people in authority, and the upper classes are more impaired by cold, calculating, rational will; natural, organic will, however, is more evident in the peasant, the artist, the artisan, the hunter, and the common people. (Tönnies pp.177 ff.)

In Australian literature Aboriginal society offered to white thinkers and writers an image of *Gemeinschaft*, an organic community tied to the natural world, harmonious, rich in myth and legend. When Katharine Susannah Prichard in *Coonardoo* says Aboriginal people represent emotion, feeling, instinctive vitality, the unconsciousness of being at one with nature – as against the whites who are trapped in reason and intellect – then she is proposing a dichotomy that is analogous to Third World, particularly African, notions of Negritude: indeed, it is this very dichotomy of black instinct and white reason that Wole Soyinka has attacked as inverted racism. Soyinka suggests that traditional African community before the European incursion, and before the Islamic as well, represented modes of thought and feeling which transcended the dualities and disunities that people suffer under commercial and industrial *Gesellschaft*-type societies; the splitting asunder of mind and body, imagination and reason, thought and feeing, art and work.

[I appended to the essay a range of references, including: John Docker, 'Wole Soyinka as Novelist: *The Interpreters* and *Season of Anomy*', *New Literature Review*, No. 2, 1977; 'The Organicist Fallacy: Jack Lindsay, Romanticism and Marxist Aesthetics', *Arena* 47–48, 1977. I see also that in preparation for writing the essay I took extensive notes from Arthur Mitzman, *Sociology and Estrangement* (Alfred A Knopf, New York, 1973) as well as from Tönnies' book on *Gemeinschaft* and *Gesellschaft*.]

At ANU in 1975, talking with my fellow postgraduates Satendra Nandan, Bill Ashcroft and Michael Cotter, it soon became clear that, whatever the topics of our doctoral theses, we shared a similar interest in new literatures in English, and a similar desire to act on this interest, to question, to turn upside down, to upend, to propose far-reaching alternatives to, the aesthetic and pedagogical hierarchy that structured conventional English literature courses and modes of teaching. Perhaps because in our life histories we were somewhat older as postgraduates, we confidently launched ourselves into a wide range of activities, approaching other critics we knew at ANU or in other universities also interested in African or other new literatures in English, like Barry Andrews teaching literature at Duntroon Military College in Canberra.

Looking back, I'm strangely reminded of the anarchists and syndicalists of old, reincarnated in the New Left of the late 1960s and into the 1970s who felt history should begin again; we felt that literary criticism should start anew.

Something in the zeitgeist was moving. We were propelled along. There was no time to lose. We hit the ground running.

During 1976–7 we postgraduates organised our own seminar

series in the English department and gave a series of talks largely based on our seminar presentations on the local Canberra community radio station 2XX.

In Mitchell Library in 2010 I took notes from a folder on these radio talks in a series entitled New Literary Landscapes which, thinking about it now, may, at least on my part, have been inspired by the 'African Literature' and 'Black Culture and Political Liberation' courses of early 1974 in London. Here are my notes on the 1976/77 radio talks:

11.30 Fri 1. Introductory discussion [I don't note who took part in this discussion]: themes, patterns, preoccupations of Commonwealth literature.

> 9.30 Wed 2. Mike Cotter: 'The explosion of Prospero's old myth: George Lamming's Natives of My Person' (Satendra, Sue, John D.)
> 10.30 Wed 3 Satendra Nandan: 'The Talented Individual Without a Tradition: V. S. Naipaul' (Mike, Bill, John)
> 10.30 Fri 4. Bill Ashcroft: Janet Frame (New Zealand) (Mike, John, Sue)
> 11.30 Wed 5. Sue Edgar: Olive Schreiner's The Story of an African Farm (South Africa) (Mike, Greg, John, Bill)
> 9.30 Thurs 6. Greg Kratzman: Doris Lessing (Rhodesia) (Bill, Barry, Satendra)
> 9.30 Fri 7. Rabia Abbas: Poetry in English in Pakistan [no discussants?]
> 11.30 Thurs 8. John Docker: Wole Soyinka as Novelist (Nigeria) (Mike, Barry, Satendra)
> 10.30 Thurs 9. Barry Andrews: James Ngugi (Kenya) (Sue, John, Mike)
> Concluding discussion: Commonwealth literature and university English departments
> 2–4 March, 1977

1973-4: Ann and John in London

Chifley Library, Media Facilities, 9.30 to 12.30 each morning
Pilot taping: 22 February (Tuesday), 10-11, Satendra Nandan on V S Naipaul

Provisional format for each half hour tape:
1. Biographical/Critical Introduction, approx.1000 words (about ten minutes)
2. A reading of a poem or a passage from the novel [this has been crossed out]
3. A break for 15 minutes, then discussion involving 3 people (main speaker +2) (or 3)

Lunch on the Friday Italian? (Kingston) (Santa Lucia)
    Mike Cotter 3376
    John Docker 3376
    Satendra Nandan 3245
Perhaps also: Ann Curthoys, Ruth Prawer Jhabvala (India) (this might be taped later…)

[Neither Ann nor I remember what happened to this last suggestion; at the time we were both very interested in Jhabvala's novels.]

As well as our own postgraduate seminar series and the related radio talks, a new journal was clearly needed.

I've kept all these years on my shelves a copy of *new literature review, special issue: post-colonial literature 1977* in an ochre-yellow cover. On the inside of the cover, I see that the Editor is W D Ashcroft, and the Editorial Collective is composed of Satendra Nandan, Michael Cotter and John Docker. The contents are listed as: W D Ashcroft, Introduction; John Docker, Commonwealth Literature and the Universities; Susan Gardiner, For Love and Money: Early Writings of Beatrice Grimshaw, Colonial Papua's

Woman of Letters; Satendra Nandan, A Study in Context: V S Naipaul's *A House for Mr Biswas*; Michael Cotter, Identity and Compulsion: George Lamming's *Natives of My Person*; Barry Andrews, The Novelist and History: The Development of Ngugi wa Thiong'o; John Docker, Wole Soyinka as Novelist: *The Interpreters* and *Season of Anomy*; Kristine Riding, Australian Commitment in the South Pacific.

I can't see that we provided any information about where it was printed, nor any Notes on Contributors, which always interest the later explorer of past journals.

⁂

A new journal requires a manifesto, an urgent call to action.

In his Introduction, W D (Bill) Ashcroft points out that imperialism and colonialism have been historically met by colonial and subjected peoples in Asia, Africa, the Pacific, with a 'process of rejection, liberation, appropriation and condemnation'; in 'world literature in English' we see the assertion of 'individual freedom: feminism, racism [and] class struggle, and sometimes (Janet Frame and Doris Lessing) the kind of *psychological* freedom of which R D Laing is the best known expositor'; we can now seize the historical opportunity to bring 'world literature in English' into 'dialogue' with 'Western Eurocentric notions of aesthetic evaluation' whereby such notions 'may have to be changed': 'Readers today have an opportunity to step beyond anglocentric canons of taste and explore a field of literature which could prove the richest, most complex and rewarding in history.' (pp.3–4)

Docker added to Bill Ashcroft's Introduction a short note with some additional information, that during 1976, as the year went on, we realised our seminar talks were being 'dismissed by some in the Department as a hobby, [a] merely private interest: a dismissal that is the structural equivalent of removing courses in Australian, American and "Commonwealth" Literature into occasional options'; colonial and post-colonial literature, however, 'presents a challenge to the intellectual affiliations, power structures and systems of reward of traditional departments of English which they will find increasingly difficult to ignore'; accordingly, as well as essays on particular writers, this issue will discuss 'wider cultural and educational issues'. (p.4)

Then followed a mildly inflammatory manifesto by Docker, 'Commonwealth Literature and the Universities' (pp.5-9), observing that 'modern literature in English has seen the continuous entry and challenge of both non-English and non-European writers', in figures like Yeats, James, Eliot and Pound. The emergence, then, into international attention of 'Canadian, New Zealand, Australian, South African, and more recently of African, Caribbean and Pacific writers is part of a continuous broadening of literary tradition in nineteenth and twentieth century literature'. Such a broadening coincides with the areas of the world 'affected by British colonialism and imperialism, from colonised Ireland within Europe to ex-European post-colonial societies like the United States, Canada, South Africa, New Zealand, and Australia, to non-European post-colonial societies in Africa, the West Indies, Nuigini, and Fiji'.

Such worldwide broadening of literature, Docker continues, challenges bedrock assumptions held by English departments, that any new work can only be 'explicated, judged and valued if it is measured against the tradition of great works thrown up by the English literary past, from Chaucer on'; students of literature 'will have no moorings unless they gain a firm knowledge of English literature'; until armed with this knowledge, 'students cannot judge the quality of Australian literature, and by extension the quality of other non-English literatures'. Necessarily, then, 'courses in English literature, where the students' standards are formed', will be the core of a department's teaching, for the 'standards, values and monuments of English literary traditions and conventions are true of all art and of human nature as it embodies itself in art'; they are 'truly literary and universal, rather than regional and historical and sociological' as is the case with non-English literatures, which are always 'inferior' and hence not susceptible to 'purely *literary* study'.

Docker also felt that the 'anglocentric assumption in university teaching of literature in Australia' has clear implications for the 'hierarchical structure of departments' and for 'recruitment policies in the hiring of academic staff'. The 'anglocentric assumption can only be defeated historically if the god-professor system is ended', particularly in so far as the 'god-professor has sole, or almost sole, determination of hiring policy', for the 'god-professor maintains the domination of English literature by hiring, in the main, people whose first interests are in English literature'; crucial courses, as in 'first year introductory or fourth year honours courses, are often entrusted to senior staff nurtured on the god-professor's ruling anglocentric assumptions'. (It must be admitted, reading over the manifesto, that Docker gives the terms 'Anglocentric' or 'Anglocentric assumption' something of a bashing.)

> For the anglocentric domination to be defeated, there must be a radical equalisation of status and teaching power among staff. No one staff person would have the power or status to enforce the centrality of English literature, and the equality of power among the staff would correspond to the ideal plurality of courses offered. This is not of course to say that English literature should be abolished, but to argue that it should be no more important than Australian and Commonwealth literature. In terms of staff and intellectual plurality, all courses would be optional.

Perhaps in memory of the Italian futurists declaring war on pasta, or Dada attacking ossified art museums, Docker then announced that the 'challenge of Commonwealth literature can now be formulated as an immediate set of demands', which he lists in italics:

1. *the ending of the assumption that 'standards' can only be formed by studying English literature as the 'core' subject of a department;*
2. *the ending of the authoritarian notion of 'core' courses;*
3. *the abolition of the god-professor and of all academic hierarchy;*
4. *the hiring of staff on the basis of intellectual plurality, rather than as part of the continuation of the anglocentric domination (this could be accompanied by the abolition of tenured positions, so that there can be a greater movement of new people with new interests);*
5. *the ending of the Cultural Cringe assumption that English degrees are better or sounder than corresponding Australian degrees, and so the hiring of more Australians (this should be of general application to all Australian university departments);*
6. *the universal institution of options, so that students can indicate what courses interest them, rather than being forced to study English literature as central and necessary to their critical education.*

In an endnote, I added, citing James Ngugi, 'On the Abolition of the English Department', the appendix to his *Homecoming*, 1972, that East African critics are also opposing anglocentrism by fighting to restructure departments of English as centring on African literatures.

It does occur to me that my (repeated) emphasis on plurality may well have been influenced by the thinking that went into my chapter 'John Anderson and the Sydney Freethought Tradition' in my *Australian Cultural Elites: Intellectual Traditions in Sydney and Melbourne* published not long before, in 1974. I've talked earlier in this ego histoire about my liking for Andersonian notions of pluralism, now I wish to float some new reflections. In the section of the chapter on 'Social Pluralism', Andersonian philosophers J A Passmore and P H Partridge stress the danger of centralisation, which can only weaken democracy because when things are managed more and more from the centre, the tendency is that they will be increasingly controlled by the same persons; there is the accompanying repressive and uniformitarian assumption of a common good, where certain interests impose themselves on others in the name of all. By contrast, Anderson, Partridge and Passmore valued a pluralism that implied participatory democracy, cultural diversity, and internationalism.[2]

Now I wonder: perhaps in my manifesto I was translating these Andersonian arguments into a critique of departments of English. The department of English attempts always to weaken or forestall participatory democracy, literary diversity and the internationalism and cosmopolitanism of world literature, by insisting that the English department is a core, a centre, always to be controlled by the same person, the god-professor, proclaiming a common good, English literature, hence imposing its narrow, parochial and provincial interests on others in the name of all.

※

Something else speculative: it may have struck some readers as an odd, even perilous thing to do, to be so insouciant towards the very English department that housed one: how would one ever get a teaching position in that department, or anywhere else? Here we must reflect on the peculiarity of the Australian humanities doctoral system, that a thesis is not necessarily examined within a department the student is in, on the contrary, the examiners may be external, and the choice may be influenced, at least informally, by the supervisor asking the student what external examiners she or he may prefer as the most knowledgeable in terms of their research.

My understanding of the American university system is that doctoral students are always examined within a department, which means the student is henceforth dependent on that department for references and support in possible future employment. Such a system I think is infantalising for the student, requiring a lifetime dependence and subservience to the department; furthermore, supervisory staff in the department, by a time-honoured logic, can accrue too much power, with all the dangers imposed by power/absolute power. In the Australian system of external examiners, by contrast, the student can look to examiners both nationally and internationally; it offers relative independence and freedom, it is empowering, the student can be a subject in her or his own history.

Suffice it say that the editors of *new literature review 1977* flourished in their future careers. Mike Cotter secured a junior academic position at the University of New England, Armidale NSW; after that, I'm afraid we lost touch. Bill Ashcroft became a stellar figure in post-colonial studies, including studies of Edward Said. Satendra Nandan, writer, academic, parliamentarian, exile, published his first book of poems the impassioned and poignant *Faces in a Village* in New Delhi in 1976, he gave a signed copy to Ann and me dated 28.5.76, I am holding it in my hand now, with its remarkable cover of an old Indian lady; Ann and I became friends with Satendra and his wife Jhoti, and later visited them in Fiji; other books on my shelves by Satendra are *The Wounded Sea* (1991), *Lines Across Black Waters* (1997), *Fiji: Paradise in Pieces* (2000), *Requiem for a Rainbow: A Fijian Indian Story* (2001), and *Sea-Shells on the Sea-shore* (2011). As for myself, this ego histoire has been charting how I have simply followed new interests wherever they have led, writing on literature and cultural history, moving into media and popular culture studies, explorations of diaspora, reflections on monotheism and polytheism, and finally genocide studies in relation to religion, the Enlightenment and settler colonialism, via teaching in various institutions and gaining literary grants and visiting fellowships (including a long association with the Humanities Research Centre at ANU) and a five-year Australian Research Council fellowship.

Nonetheless, in 1977 it must have been, the then drone-professor of the ANU English department chose to put a stop to such effervescent and outreaching activity by a group of postgraduates: we can't have people so interested in varied kinds of literature in a department of literature; postgraduates henceforth are to confine themselves to one literature; we were to give no more seminar papers except directly on our thesis topics. This authoritarian act by this particular drone-professor denied what was obvious, that being interested in postcolonial literatures as well as one's thesis was enriching in terms of a multiplicity of ideas and perspectives. Furthermore, Commonwealth literature or new literatures in English or world literature were in the mid-1970s rapidly becoming a world-wide movement, in organisations, conferences, new journals. In Australia there was our *new literature review 1977*; at Flinders University in Adelaide, in 1977, Syd Harrex set up CRNLE, the Centre for Research in the New Literatures in English; also in 1977 the South Pacific Association for Commonwealth Literature and Language Studies held its first conference at the University of Queensland, and papers from it (as well as an essay by Vijay Mishra) were selected to be in a volume, *South Pacific Images*, edited by Chris Tiffin; running an eye now over its Contents, I see that the ANU Dadaists were well represented, with Satendra Nandan, 'Beyond Colonialism: the artist as healer', Michael Cotter, 'Fragmentation, Reconstitution and the Colonial Experience: the Aborigine in Patrick White's fiction', and John Docker, 'The Neocolonial Assumption in University Teaching of English'.

The drone-professor fell unresistingly onto the wrong side

of history, consigning his department to a mediocrity it would prove hard to shake off.

I'll return to my fascination with Wole Soyinka that was inspired by the 1974 London African Literature course, and try as quickly as I can to evoke my somewhat dense essay in *new literature review* 1977, entitled 'Wole Soyinka as Novelist: *The Interpreters* and *Season of Anomy*' (pp.44–53). I begin by calling attention to Soyinka's book of essays *Myth, Literature and the African World*, it had just been published, in 1976, and I read it with great interest as soon as I got hold of a copy. Soyinka argues that European colonialism is only an interlude in the self-development of African society and history: 'the white presence' is 'irrelevant to the deeper processes of a people's history and the reformulation of their interrupted identity'. Modern literature should not be seen as a fundamental conflict between the old African ways and the new white ways, but rather as dramatising conflicts between forces internal to Africa itself.

Soyinka feels that his notorious 'anti-Negritudinous' stand has been twisted to deny the 'existence of an African world', whereas his objection to the notion of Negritude, as expounded by Francophone writers like Senghor, is that it is a form of inverted racism. Negritude assumes that European culture has a monopoly of reason, intellect, and 'analytical thought'; on the other hand, European culture lacks what the African possesses: instinct, intuition, feeling, emotion. The task of the Negritudinist writer is to evoke and celebrate the African's non-rational qualities, so that African culture – its very existence previously denied – can regain a place in history, as a complement to European culture.

By contrast, Soyinka suggests that the African 'world-view' is organic: unlike Negritude and Western thought, it does not separate the 'creative spirit' into 'watertight categories' of thought and feeling, emotion and reason, a 'compartmentalising' assumption about knowledge and creativity that is 'foreign to the African world-view'.

Yoruba history reveals a rich and continuous civilisation, whose mythological systems Soyinka compares to the pagan Greeks. A great deal of *Myth, Literature and the African World* is devoted to explicating in detail the relationship between various Yoruba gods and mythological figures, and how they form part of a total world-view, a fully worked out metaphysical system. Soyinka relates that he explored the living quality of Yoruba traditions when he returned to Africa after five years in England; he toured around Nigeria for months observing, for example, the rituals performed for the god Ogun, the god of war and hunters, of iron and of the crafts, the god both of destruction and creativity. In these rituals Soyinka recognised an ongoing tradition of drama and performance, and could feel that his own plays were based not on European models but on an indigenous history of dramatic forms. For Soyinka, mythology involves the whole community in a ritual of disintegration and renewal; at the same time it offers ways by which the society can question itself, can work out in mythic form its deepest problems and dilemmas.

But if Soyinka in *Myth, Literature and the African World* identifies with traditional Yoruba society and sees in its forms of community and in its mythology a continuing vitality, this does not mean that he thinks modern African society or literature should be a simple reflection of the African past. In *The Man Died: Prison Notes of Wole Soyinka* (1972, p.12), Soyinka refers to the 'revolutionary changes to which I have become more than ever dedicated'. For Soyinka, the task for African intellectuals is to explore and define Africa as it is now, in terms of what might be authentic in the past and still recoverable, even if submerged under more recent guises; what is to be rejected from the past; and what is valuable or not in contemporary society.

After my opening discussion of *Myth, Literature and the African World*, I arrange a critical conversation between *The Interpreters* (1972) and *Season of Anomy* (1973), suggesting there are profound differences between these powerful novels, that, indeed, they are antithetical.

Like the novel its title recalls, Simone de Beauvoir's *The Mandarins*, *The Interpreters* explores the situations and dilemmas of an urban intelligentsia in modern society. The novel focuses on a group of articulate and highly self-conscious intellectuals, who are structurally part of the Nigerian elite by their education and position; Bandele is a university teacher, Kola an artist, Sagoe a journalist, Egbo works in the Foreign Office, Dehinwa is a highly placed private secretary, Sekoni is an engineer and then a sculptor. Yet at the same time they are alienated from the 'new order' that the ruling elite has helped to establish. Throughout the novel the interpreters attempt to define their own values, theories and philosophies, for the purpose of self-understanding and self-awareness, and in opposition to the society which they feel surrounds and oppresses them. The friends enjoy an inner-urban lifestyle, in their regular meetings in nightclubs and their visits to each other in Lagos or at the university in Ibadan. While friends, the interpreters are frequently abrasive and challenging with each other.

The novel does not suggest that any easy answers are available to the interpreters' dilemmas. For example, Egbo attempts to recover continuity with traditional Nigerian life by a search that is at once sexual and mythological. When he first makes love, it is to a woman he envisages as Simi, the Yoruba goddess of serenity; with Simi, Egbo feels that he recovers the masculine virility of traditional life, he becomes like Ogun, the Yoruba god of creativity, at one with Simi, the female earth; he is reborn and renewed, at one with nature, with the gods, with his ancestors. But Egbo also finds himself attracted to a young student, the 'new woman' of Nigeria, articulate, outspoken, and independent. Egbo hurts Simi, when he unthinkingly allows her to see his liking for the young undergraduate, though he also fails in his relationship with her, losing sight of her and never finding out her name. As it turns out, Egbo can commit himself neither to traditional nor modern Nigeria.

In the novel, Egbo's way of subsuming people for symbolic and mythological purposes – Simi as an 'impersonal symbol', the female singer at the nightclub as representing a mythological essence, the 'Black Immanent' – is revealed to be a disguised form of egocentrism, presenting one's own needs as universally necessary.

In general the Nigerian intellectuals in the novel reject the philosophy of Negritude as inverse racism, an attempt to subsume all Africans into the one, quintessential African. Yet when they themselves at first attempt to dismiss the African-American Joe Golder's search for Negritude and reject Golder's homosexuality as un-African, they come to realise that his sexuality challenges their former fixed notions of African masculinity.

The art of *The Interpreters*, I conclude, is fast-moving and often superbly funny. [If I was writing this analysis now I would probably say that *The Interpreters* is in the great tradition of Plato's philosophical novel *The Symposium*.][3]

My essay then moves on to analysing *Season of Anomy*. Where, I suggest, *The Interpreters* focusses on a play of different viewpoints in an urban intelligentsia, characters in *Season of Anomy* search for a desired community in African rural society. Where in *The Interpreters* the rural community was primarily Egbo's personal concern, an object of curiosity to his friends, in *Season of Anomy* sharp conflicts and dichotomies are introduced between urban and rural life, dichotomies which become politically and ideologically central to the novel's structure of ideas.

Season of Anomy dramatises a key conflict between rival forces, Aiyéró as the ideal community, and the Cartel, the Corporation which runs the country's cocoa monopoly, in league with the military government and private armies. The Cartel's only social 'plan' is the creation of 'commercial cities', where the sources of finance and decisions are controlled by a corrupt bureaucracy, leading to the spiritual death of the people, divided among themselves, fearful of the power-holders, and ready to join in any persecution and terror the Cartel brings on, otherwise they will appear enemies of the Cartel and so liable to be victims themselves of torture, mutilation, and death. At the same time as the Cartel creates urban alienation and divisiveness, even in intellectuals committed to the 'humanistic will' like Ofeyi the chief protagonist, it also acts to conserve tribalism, with its suspicion of 'aliens' and outsiders. The Cartel symbolises both the excrescence of the commercial cities, and the worst features of traditional tribal organisation.

Aiyéró, on the other hand, signifies the best of both the African present and past. In Aiyéró the traditional African rural community lives on, in harmony with the natural environment, with earth and water. Its social unity is carefully nurtured by its elders, like Ahime, who also functions as a priest, and so custodian of Aiyéró's religious and ritual practices, derived from Yoruba mythology. Aiyéró is a society at one with its ancestors, a unity symbolised in its 'Founder', the 'Custodian of the Grain'. At the heart of Aiyéró are 'pristine balances', between men and women in their different roles, between the people and their ancestors, and between the people and nature, constituting a 'philosophy' and 'way of life'. When the Founder dies, Ahime offers the position of Custodian of the Grain to Ofeyi, who works as the chief promotions officer for the Corporation and is an outsider to the community. For Ofeyi, 'jaded', in 'despair', 'defeated by life' in the city, Aiyéró appears as the one hope left for restoring 'our sense of wholeness'.

Ofeyi had once shared in the amusement directed at Aiyéró as a mere 'pocket' or 'comic Utopia', quaint and contemptible and certainly not a threat to the hegemonic values of the new elite. Ofeyi senses, however, that the elite's hegemonic control is shaky, and that against it, throughout the society and particularly in the rural areas, is a continuing resistance, an 'old eternal community of feeling'. Ofeyi sees in Aiyéró a 'microcosm' of 'this community of feeling', containing within itself the 'secret of a living harmony'. The Aiyéró ideal will create human relationships based on universal values of neighbourliness and community; the communal strength of traditional African rural society, expressed in the closeness of its kinship relations, will be recreated in new forms, shorn of the 'tribal' suspicion of the 'alien'.

Where *The Interpreters* raises questions, doubts, distance, about a mythological desire to see women as symbols, *Season of Anomy* wishes to see women, as in Iriyise the singer, as representing a oneness with nature, embodying the 'living harmony' of the Aiyéró ideal; her urban personality becomes a mere surface that can be discarded, as she recovers her 'essential nature' in the female 'Mysteries' of traditional women's village life; she becomes an earth goddess. Ofeyi, by joining his male intellectual vision to her female union with nature, can glimpse a final goal of wholeness for himself and for the wider society. *Season of Anomy* does record Ofeyi's self-questioning, his sense of possibly using and manipulating Iriyise and other characters in his campaign of subversive poetry, and his doubts about embracing insurrectionary violence, but they are perfunctorily entertained only as stages in his own reconstruction. Ofeyi has to cease being an alienated urban consciousness, the outsider, the intruder, and attain his 'wholeness' in a struggle that is both intellectual and violent. In contrast to *The Interpreters*, *Season of Anomy*, I argue, is over-generalised and schematic.

[Here I think of my essay on Ferdinand Tönnies' notions of rural *Gemeinschaft* and urban *Gesellshaft*, how they might relate to *Season of Anomy*, of *Gemeinschaft* as Aiyéró ('the dream of mankind all through the ages') in opposition to *Gesellschaft* as urban alienation, based only on money, the cash-nexus. I think too of Tönnies' advocacy that women should eschew rationality and consciousness, they should identify themselves with nature and rural life as their essential being. Where *The Interpreters* continuously questions Tönnies-like oppositions and his absolutist thinking about gender, *Season of Anomy* embraces, in my view unfortunately, such ideals; to put this another way, in contrasting the two novels, I very much prefer *The Interpreters*.]

Dear reader, here I will leave my participation in *new literature review 1977*, and the story, as I now see it, of how I was inspired in my thinking about literature, criticism, and teaching, by the African Literature course that Ann and I attended with such interest in early 1974 in London.

❧

It's time, it's past time, to return to our time in London in 1973–4.

During these months, either late 1973 or early 1974 we had moved from staid Willesden Green in the west to the east of London, to an apartment in a large house in a line of row houses as Americans would call them in Stoke Newington,. We'd been told there was an empty apartment there by Vivienne Brodsky, an historian we had met up with in London, she had done history at Sydney University a year or two behind Ann; she and her partner said the apartment was just below theirs. Instead of being on the Jubilee Line to and from Willesden Green, we now would catch Bus 73 that for us went to and from Stoke Newington to Tottenham Court Road (the redoubtable Bus 73, I see, has its own Wikipedia page). Stoke Newington had its own run-down character; walking to the bus stop on the high street we would see many empty houses, and on the high street quite a few boarded-up shops. Setting off in another direction from our place, we would come to a park and then the River Lea, which we would walk along, enjoying the magic of water for thinking and talking.

In April 1974 my mother had flown from Sydney to stay with us in London. In the Concluding Mosaic of my *1492: The Poetics of Diaspora* I've recorded her excited tracing of places she associated with her childhood: going to the East End's Petticoat Lane to buy smoked salmon (one of her aunts, she said, would say of the salmon on offer, 'Eyes of diamonds and sides of silver! Eyes of diamonds and sides of silver!'); she loved being in a Jewish area, going into the local delicatessens with their jars and jars of different kinds of pickled cucumbers; buying a huge black-and-white TV to watch the BBC; trying to locate the family house in Alfred Street in the East End only to find that neither the house nor the street existed any more, because of the Blitz; reminiscing about London's pea-soup fogs; walking along the Roman Road where she used to go as a child to the library; finding the pedestrian tunnel under the railway line known as Tom Thumb's Arch; finding Bow Street station and seeking out its darkened platform where East Londoners sheltered from bombing during the First World War; going to Blooms to taste 'Jewish food'; arriving at Malmsbury Road School where my mother shouted '47 years! 47 years ago I was here' and rushed inside, until emerging after quite a while, a teacher had invited her to tell the class of her childhood experiences in the school.[4]

In these months we travelled more outside London. I've mentioned before our trip to Paris with Charles. Ann became pregnant, we calculate in late March or in April. We set off for Cornwall where we met up with our New Zealand friend Gay and stayed with her for a few days (Ann remembers that Gay was staying with a New Zealand friend of hers, and both were avidly reading Georgette Heyer), then hitch hiked round to Holyhead in Wales, where you catch the ferry to Ireland, my father in one of his letters had mentioned that he would like us to visit County Clare and especially Kilrush where his mother Susan Nash had lived and migrated from in the early 1880s, and that his two brothers in World War I when on leave had visited Kilrush.

We caught the ferry and then took a train to Ennis, the main town of County Clare, we were wondering if we could find any trace of the Nash family name in its telephone book, but there weren't any Nashes in its pages. Then we went by bus to Kilrush where we found there was no hotel we could stay in; we caught a bus to the nearby seaside town of Kilkee, but it must have been off season, it was still too cold, all the seaside holiday places were closed. We went into one, and the women there kindly said the hotel was closed for repairs and painting, but, yes, you can stay in a room upstairs. Ann was not feeling very well, she couldn't leave the room; she said she'd like fresh fruit, and I bought some oranges from a shop across the road. When it was time for dinner, I went downstairs, the women said come into the kitchen, is your wife coming down, I said, no, she's not feeling well; oh, they said, well, here's some potatoes we've cooked for you – some boiled, some baked – they watched as I greedily ate.

Apart from my unfeeling perfidy in the Kilkee hotel, gorging on potatoes as Ann rested ill in our room, my memories are hazy. I think we caught the bus back to Kilrush to wander around, to wonder about a Protestant family called Nash living there in the nineteenth century, then we somehow hitch hiked along the coast, getting a ride with a young man who said he'd never heard of Australia, and then caught a train across Ireland to Dublin then returned to London. Ann remembers arriving back in London, perhaps Euston Station, early in the morning, too early for the 73 bus, so we walked all the way to Stoke Newington.

Coda: Ann's reflections on our 1973–4 London sojourn

Our 10 months in London were life-changing. We had both been straight through school and university, first undergraduate and then postgraduate, and our work experience, apart from some mundane summer jobs, had been as university tutors. Now, after five months travelling through Asia, we were in London, about which we knew a lot in theory and nothing in practice. Looking back, and reading John's account of this time, I'm struck by how much we learnt through a mix of attending courses, lectures, and seminars and travelling within southern England and to Paris and Ireland, all the while getting to know London pubs, cafés, meeting places, parks, canals, and landscapes. Since we had no scholarships or academic positions, and were supporting ourselves through temporary clerical jobs, we were free to explore new ideas, politics, and intellectual approaches at will. On reflection, it was a pretty magical time.

1973–4: Ann and John in London 329

1 Some months after this chapter was written, I received a Christmas present from Ned Curthoys of Ariel Dorfman's *Heading South, Looking North* (first published in the US in 1998). Ann and I had seen an article in the *Guardian* dated 3 December 2018 – I've just looked it up and read it again – by Ariel Dorfman about staying in a hotel in Sydney with his wife Angélica in October 2001. In late 2018 former US president George HW Bush had just died. In the *Guardian* article, a kind of critical obituary, 'George HW Bush thought the world belonged to his family. How wrong he was', Dorfman recalls that he and Angélica refused to give in to pressure to vacate their hotel room because it was near Bush's: 'My close encounter with Bush at a Sydney hotel revealed a patrician arrogance whose days were numbered.' Dorfman ponders with some bitterness that George HW Bush had been head of the CIA from January 1976 to January 1977 not long after Pichochet's regime had been launched in Chile with its disappearances, concentration camps, and torture. I had never read anything by Dorfman though had heard the name. I've now read *Heading South, Looking North* which is indeed a fascinating autobiography of his early childhood, his bilingualism in English and Spanish, his narration of the Pinochet coup, his life in Chile as part of the Allendistas, his managing to escape to Argentina and then to the US, and his insightful reflections on exile, the New Left in 1968 in Berkeley, and the achievements yet also failings of the Allende movement in Chile. I'm very glad I've read it.

2 John Docker, *Australian Cultural Elites: Intellectual Traditions in Sydney and Melbourne* (Angus and Robertson, Sydney, 1974), pp.134–6.

3 John Docker, *The Origins of Violence: The Origins of Violence: Religion, History and Genocide* (UNSW Press, Sydney, 2008), pp.94–5.

4 John Docker, *1492: The Poetics of Diaspora* (Continuum, London, 2001), pp.250–52.

39

Men and Women's Liberation 1974

This is the first chapter I wrote for *Growing Up Communist and Jewish in Bondi*. (Ann tells me that J K Rowling wrote her final chapter of the Harry Potter series first.) In 2019, I added some additional touches here and there, and am especially pleased that Ann contributed a Coda with thoughtful reflections.

It began as a talk I felt honoured to give to the Sydney Feminist History Group in beautiful sandstone History House in Macquarie Street, Sydney, opposite the Botanic Gardens, on the evening of 25 August 2011, before we all tumbled next door to have dinner at Aesop's Greek restaurant. I must thank Zora Simic for asking me; Zora said that every year they invite a man to speak, and happily in 2011 I was chosen. The evening, which went gratifyingly well, given my overriding fear that no-one would turn up and if any did they would not be amused by my attempts to amuse, was my first tentative try-out of a chapter for my ego histoire.

I focus on two episodes in the late 1960s and early 1970s, the first leading up to and including the impact of Women's Liberation; this episode features the reading of Mette Ejlersen's *I Accuse* protesting at the myth of the female orgasm, which challenged me personally but also assisted in my critique of Sydney Libertarianism and its fealty to Wilhelm Reich's theory of sexuality.

The second engages with my being in a Men Against Sexism

group in London for some months in the first half of 1974.

I must begin, however, by invoking the literary figure of the romance.

A Modern Romance

Romance as a modern literary form, its primary progenitor Jane Austen's *Pride and Prejudice*, can be defined as a love relationship with obstacles, sometimes severe obstacles. It always begins in conflict, the haughty arrogance of a Mr Darcy clashing with the lively independence of an Elizabeth Bennett; in the drama of their differing attitudes, the main characters reveal themselves capable of change and hopefully transformation, even metamorphosis. On 2 May 1967, in our conferring of degrees ceremony in the Great Hall of Sydney University, Ann Curthoys and I found ourselves sitting next to each other for alphabetical reasons, C followed by D. I was in a suit I had gone with my mother to buy at Fletcher Jones in the city, Ann like all the other young female graduates was in a white dress. I was at the time a haughty arrogant young Leavisite literary critic, confident of my superior sensibility in all matters of literature and life. I turned to Ann and said, 'Miss Curthoys, you look quite becoming in your white dress'. This searingly patronising comment put back any possibility of a relationship for some considerable time.

In 1966 Ann had done her fourth-year history honours year while I had done English honours. We faintly knew of each other because our parents were in the Communist Party, though in different cities, and indeed, we had both been in a tiny Communist Party branch at Sydney University which involved various miniscule factions. During 1967–8 I had ventured to Melbourne to do an MA in the University of Melbourne English department, its professor then Sam Goldberg, who himself not long before had returned to Melbourne after he led a kind of failed Leavisite assault on a refractory Sydney English department, which resulted in a split in the department in time-honoured Sydney University style; such splits, as in the later split in the philosophy department, remind me of the vogue for political partitions enforced by Western powers across the world in the twentieth century, partitions in my view always being a disaster, since they force heterogeneous communities into homogeneous blocs invariably accompanied by bitter dislikes and hatreds. In any case, the Leavisites were excellent haters. In Melbourne in 1967 – I've noted this before in my chapter 'How I Became a Teenage Leavisite and Lived to Tell the Tale' – I lived in Carlton near the cemetery, sharing the house with another ex-Sydney Leavisite who annoyed me by his capacity to remember and recite huge slabs of verse, while I couldn't remember a line of poetry, even of the poem, T S Eliot's *Four Quartets*, I was studying for my MA thesis. We also did no housework whatsoever, so that by the end of a few months the hallway of the semi-detached we were living in had clouds of dust floating up to our knees as we tried to walk through it. Not surprisingly, no-one ever visited.

In this house of dust I did nonetheless begin my lifelong obsession with food, having asked my mother in our Bondi flat to show me how to cook in the months before I left for Melbourne to join the Goldbergites. Carlton shopping centre was then from memory a small Italian precinct, with a great butcher shop, and I would buy slices of veal to cook with wine from recipes in a couple of Elizabeth David cook books I had heard about from a sister living in London. That was the extent of my domestic skills.

During 1967 I became increasingly discontented with the whole Leavisite project as absurdly elitist and quite fantastical in its historical view that the societies and cultures of the pre-industrial English past were somehow finer in sensibility than anything in modernity. By then I was living in Albert Park on Port Phillip Bay, in a back room of the historian Noel McLachlan's terrace, walking out on a pier to stare at the grey water of the bay with vaguely suicidal longuers, getting drunk often, and desperate to return to Sydney during vacation periods to drink at pubs – the Forth and Clyde in Balmain, and the Newcastle in the city in George Street near the Quay – frequented by the Libertarians. The Libertarians were a distinctive Sydney phenomenon, who combined a Bohemian inner-city lifestyle centred in particular hotels with certain philosophical stances influenced by the longtime Sydney University philosophy professor John Anderson (though they had split with him in the early 1950s because of his Cold War lurch towards conservatism). Here, gulping beer, I would theatrically tell anyone who would listen how bored I was with Melbourne intellectuals, they were jejunely fervent about their beliefs, they lacked Sydney skepticism and cynicism, they… and I would gulp some more. How odd this drinking looks now, in this age of coffee and coffee shops.

Ann must have detected a distant spark of humanity in me, because in 1968 we met at the Forth and Clyde in more cordial circumstances, two ex-Communists, myself also an ex-Leavisite, both now part of the New Left, both 22 though Ann was five weeks older. Ann did say, however, that there would be no relationship at all until the next time we met I was both on time and not drunk. While this was eventually accomplished, I had to keep going back to Melbourne to write my thesis and do tutoring.

I did have two close friends there, I'll call them Jane and Robert, who also had come down as Leavisites from Sydney and were becoming equally disenchanted with Leavisitism, and with whom I discussed many of the ideas I was talking about with Ann in Sydney or in our letters once I'd forlornly returned to Melbourne. One of these ideas must have concerned Women's Rights, for in Mitchell Library in 2010 while researching Ann and my papers I came across a 1968 letter of mine to Ann, on University of Melbourne letterhead, which told her how we three Sydney friends were worrying at feminist issues to do with male behaviour, for example, opening doors. I'll quote from this letter:

> Jane and Robert are well. Re Women's Rights, I must ask your view on one matter. Robert and I have been saying we see no reason why we should open doors for her [Jane], and then when we, say, go into a restaurant, she should open the door for us, and hold it while we pass through. Jane won't do it (yet). What do you think? Jane says she's becoming annoyed because Robert and I 'defer' to your every opinion, both on these and political matters…

I moved back to Sydney in late 1968 and in early 1969 Ann and I moved in together in a house in Balmain, actually an old corner shop, its chief tenant an historian, Ken McNab, his previous co-tenants historians Terry Irving and Baiba Berzins having moved to another part of Balmain. Ann was only moving a couple of streets from where she had been living. I was moving from Bondi via Melbourne. Now, acutely, questions of housework and gender presented themselves. Ann soon realised that I didn't have a clue. I tried to explain that I had done no housework when I was growing up, and indeed was accounted a mother's boy, fearfully spoilt; at our wedding some years later, my elder sister told the assembled guests that I was so spoilt as a child I had my own strawberry jam which no-one else was allowed to touch. Ann said, look, sit on the stairs, and I'll show you: this is a broom, this is how you hold it, then you use it like this… Ann taught me how to thread a needle, how to sew buttons on, how to iron shirts and blouses, and insisted I had to do my share of cleaning toilets. Whether or not I ever achieved domestic proficiency I will leave to others to judge. I certainly don't think I have. For example, I sometimes say to young people that I keep Ann company while she irons, including ironing for me, because she is better at it than I am, and I'm quite rightly met with derisory laughter. (2019 update by Ann, that she now irons so rarely herself that no company is needed.)

Clitoris Envy, or the Myth of the Female Orgasm

The effervescent New Left of the late 1960s, early 1970s was imbued with a strange kind of carnivalesque consciousness that time and history had started again, that everything and anything was open to thinking about and changing. Ann thinks it was in 1970 that we read with great interest a publication on the myth of the vaginal orgasm, which we once owned but had lost, and we couldn't now remember the name of. When we say this to people now, they usually say, oh that must have been Anne Koedt's classic essay of 1970 with that title, but we say no, we're sure it was a book. We googled it recently to find it was Mette Ejlersen's *I Accuse*, which was written in Danish in 1967 and published in English in 1969, and is praised in Anne Koedt's essay. Let's recall what Mette Ejlersen argues in *I Accuse*. She tells us that, from talking to women of her acquaintance of their unhappy sexual experiences, she has concluded that 'woman's vaginal orgasm is pure fiction, created and described by men' for their own advantage through the ages. A further male fantasy, Ejlersen notes, is that the woman in what is considered to be natural sexuality will achieve a vaginal orgasm at the same time as the man, the fantasy of simultaneous orgasm that I have observed in almost any Hollywood film or TV show that has a sex scene, except for a particular Jane Fonda Vietnam War film *Coming Home* where the male hero played by Jon Voigt is, because of his war injury, bereft of his penis. On the contrary, Ejlersen contends, the 'seat of woman's sexual sensations is in quite a different place from where it is normally proclaimed to be'. A woman's orgasm, she wrote, is a clitoral orgasm.[1]

Reading this book affected me profoundly, both intimately and in my intellectual life in terms of disengaging from the Sydney Libertarians in whose outer circles we at times moved. I knew of the Libertarians as an undergraduate; they regularly gave papers expounding their conceptions in the philosophy room at Sydney

University, near the jacaranda tree in a corner of the quadrangle, and I had gone to some of these. I came to see, after reading through the issues of their publications, especially the *Broadsheet*, that their key positions were constituted in a combination of elite pluralism and pessimistic anarchism. The Libertarians considered themselves an isolated and always threatened elite, whose best hope of survival was to exist in the interstices of mainstream society, which was to be permanently opposed. Permanent opposition was buttressed with ideas drawn from Reich, a former member of Freud's psychoanalytic circle who had drifted away towards his own theories of society and sexuality.

When in 1972 I published an essay 'Sydney Intellectual History and Sydney Libertarianism' in Henry Mayer's *Politics* journal, I questioned the claims to pluralism of the Libertarians, especially in the arena of gender relations. Looking back, I now feel that reading and talking about Mette Ejlersen's *I Accuse* very much informed this critique. I point out in the *Politics* essay that during their heyday in the 1950s and 1960s the Libertarian male theorists valued Reich's distinction between an admired 'genital character' and an inferior 'neurotic character' produced by mainstream society. The consequence of this Reichian view, I felt, was that a wide range of sexual activities, clitoral sexuality, masturbation, lesbianism, homosexuality, were regarded as lesser forms of libido discharge, leading to neurosis. For Reich and the Libertarians, heterosexual genital sex was prescribed as the most natural sex.[2]

I'll conclude this section by suggesting that in the early 1970s feminism had a devastating impact on Libertarian theory, particularly when the male theorists attempted to dismiss it, for example, in their hostility to Germaine Greer's *The Female Eunuch*, Greer herself having been part of the Libertarians while she was in Sydney. I recall that at Macquarie University the Libertarian anthropologist Les Hiatt gave a critical paper on Greer, and in question time I rather pompously accused him of lack of knowledge of feminist theory. My Mitchell Library notes record that a series of Red and Black Meetings were held around this time – I think 1971 – above Bob Gould's Third World Bookshop, 20A Goulburn Street in downtown Sydney, including talks by Wendy Bacon 'Emma Goldman and Women's Liberation' (13 May), Liz Fell 'Wilhelm Reich and Sexual Theory' (17 June), and Dennis Altman 'Gay Liberation' (8 July). Theory, we might say, was on the move.

The male Libertarian philosophers who had so dominated in the 1950s and 1960s earned their own 'I Accuse' in the pages of *Broadsheet*, inspired by their attempted belittling of Greer's book. *Broadsheet* No.67, January 1972, opened with an electrifying two-page article by Sue Robertson entitled 'Maze's Misinterpretation of Greer'. Robertson suggested that what Maze, a prominent Freudian in Sydney University's psychology department, and the other male Libertarian theorists miss is that in the psychoanalytic field 'much of the theory has the justifying qualities of myth', and that what feminists are urging is that women should free themselves from the 'guilt that Freudian theory has induced', especially the guilt brought by being frequently accused of penis envy. I'll quote Sue Robertson's eloquent and passionate denunciation of the male Libertarians here:

> To my knowledge, Greer is the first woman with Libertarian associations to commit herself in public and in print to a position on sexual relationships. How many women writers does one see in the pages of the *Broadsheet*? Are some interests being threatened?... I am wondering how it is that the Libertarian community, with its apparently egalitarian sexual ideals, has for so long failed to produce significant numbers of women with the confidence and energy to contribute formally to the formulation of Libertarian ideology, on anything, let alone sexuality.

Robertson says she is tempted to 'inquire about the sex of the current typist of the *Broadsheet*', given that 'there are so many women who have done only this as their formal contribution to the movement'. Libertarian ideology, she writes, has 'never helped women achieve the confidence to do anything other than shitwork'. She angrily asks why is it that no-one in the Libertarian community has seen fit to reply to Maze's article on Greer, and then launches into a sharp critique of Maze's charge that Greer had misinterpreted Freud by falsely accusing him of sexism. She reminds the Libertarians that not only Freud's disciple Erich Fromm, but also 'numerous feminist psychologists and psychiatrists' – she refers in particular to an essay by Natalie Shainess, 'A psychiatrist's view: images of women, past and present, overt and obscured', *American Journal of Psychotherapy*, January 1969 – also argue that Freud saw women as inherently defective because they were born without a penis, and that women were 'naturally passive, masochistic, and had weaker superegos than men'.

Robertson says Maze objects to Germaine Greer's view that Freud 'proscribed the clitoris'. In turn, Robertson says Freud and Maze following him indicate something about themselves when they refer to 'the clitoric zone [refusing] to give up its excitability'. 'Are men', Robertson scornfully asks, in the spirit of Mette Ejlersen's *I Accuse* and Anne Koedt's essay 'The Myth of the Vaginal Orgasm', 'concerned that if women get off too well on their clitorises there will be no place left for the poor old penis?' Robertson concludes by suggesting Freud's 'psychoanalytic emphasis on the vagina' indicates a certain 'clitoris envy'.

In the early 1970s the male Libertarian theorists were, it would appear, in a tattered state, unable simply to dismiss the challenge of feminism. The last page of *Broadsheet* No.70, October 1972, p.12, advertised that at a Libertarian Conference at Minto, 1–3 December, Maggi Wilson and Gillian Leahy would talk about 'Radical Feminism', which would be followed by a group discussion by Liz Fell and others on 'Male Chauvinism in the Push'. I'll leave the Libertarians there except for a final revealing anecdote. On p.12 there was an amusing item, based on a report in the 30 September issue of *Freedom*, presumably a British anarchist publication, concerning the trial in London of two anarchists, the Reverend Father Bill Dwyer, formerly of Sydney, and his colleague the Reverend Father Fuck, who were leading figures in the establishment of the Church of Aphrodite, and had publicly let it be known that marijuana was the sacrament of the Church. The outcome of the trial was that Dwyer received a suspended sentence for possessing a large quantity of LSD, and was now 'contemplating retirement to Ireland to write a book'. Father Fuck was given a suspended sentence for cultivating cannabis at their Church. The anecdote suggests, I think, that such figures as these were much more funny and wild and publicly out there than the dry rationalist Libertarian men, at least as revealed in their dour and ponderous philosophising in *Broadsheet* and other rather fugitive publications. The Libertarians of the 1950s and 1960s had wished to conceal themselves, to evade the gaze of a moralistic, puritanic and censorious postwar society. The early 1970s, by contrast, was revealing a world increasingly challenged by the theories and theatricality of the New Left, the counter culture, women's liberation and gay liberation, their marches and demonstrations drawing on an inheritance of Dadaist visuality and carnivalesque irreverence.

The London Men Against Sexism Scene

In my chapter on Ann and I arriving in London in September 1973 when we soon after joined a demonstration against General Pinochet's putsch in Chile against Allende's government, I record how surprised we were to see that the whole march had organised itself into different and competing groups; the British left, it seemed to us, couldn't conceive of life without being in a group.

One group, however, was not divided along such political groupuscule lines, as I found when I joined a Men Against Sexism group. We'd seen in *Time Out* an ad for a new group being formed in north London near where we lived in Stoke Newington. At first, I refused to go, it would be too embarrassing, I'd die first; but Ann was unforgiving, and I consoled myself by thinking that in London I would be oceans away from anyone who knew me. As it turned out, I hugely enjoyed my Men Against Sexism group; later, when we returned to Sydney in the middle of 1974, Ann then pregnant with Ned, I perhaps unfortunately wrote some reflections on the particular thinking and interactions of my men's group. I'll return to this minor fiasco in a moment.

Reading our papers in Mitchell I found that I had actually brought back lots of material on the UK Men Against Sexism scene, including three newsletters. I'll quickly try and pick out some of their most interesting features. 'Brothers: A Men's Liberation Newsletter', 8p, was produced in 1973, and had been prepared, so the introductory page said, by the Birmingham men's liberation group, delegated by the 'Men against Sexism' conference held in London in June of that year: 'This is the first (as far as we know) national men's liberation newsletter.' They apologise for the bad typing, remarking that 'one aspect of the sexist culture we inherit is that none of us is particularly good at typing stencils'. The contents include a manifesto from the US (by Jack Sawyer), a report of the London conference, personal accounts and impressions of groups in relation to the Birmingham men's liberation conference, news of a London radical psychology group, and an article on pornography.

In his essay entitled 'On the Politics of Male Liberation', Jack Sawyer urged non-violent action in order to win peace and freedom; male liberation could help undermine values basic to capitalism, which oppresses people in many ways, including those who are 'female or non-white'. The 'sex role' of the 'white American heterosexual male' leads men to 'accept a competitive system' and to 'deny their own emotional life'; in order to overcome the 'taboo on emotionality', men must realise that 'the personal is political'. There is a connection between conventional masculinity and war, in particular the American war in Vietnam: '"Big boys don't cry", and neither do President Nixon… or Lieutenant Calley.' The next item was a report by Geoff Barker on the 'First British Conference of Men Against Sexism', a one-day discussion on Sunday, 10 June 1973, called by a north London group which for more than a year had been discussing the 'implications for radical men of the issues raised by Women's Liberation'.

Despite very little advance publicity, the conference was attended by more than 30 men who talked about issues for seven and a half hours; the event had, it was agreed by those who attended, undoubtedly been a 'stimulating, worthwhile and seminal occasion'. Geoff Barker felt the success of the conference suggested there was a need in Britain to challenge the 'male tendency to objectivize and depersonalize political issues'; those engaged in an 'anti-sexist politics' have to 'learn the lessons of consciousness-raising that the women in Women's Liberation are learning'. There should be a full-scale national conference under the rubric of Men Against Sexism, rather than the term Men's Liberation, which was 'felt by some people to be a bad one'. In terms of future action, Geoff Barker recalled that the final session of the London conference urged anti-sexist men to challenge sexism among men.

A report on the Birmingham group, by Andrew, relates that it was formed when a future member wrote a short article for the Birmingham Women's Liberation newsletter asking for interested men to contact him; seven men turned up for the first meeting. That number, with occasional drop-outs and replacements, remained constant; it turned out to be ideal for an 'effective consciousness-raising group', which met regularly, once a week. At first there was some conflict about what kind of group it should be, with some men, referred to as the academics, primarily interested in a 'high degree of theoretical selfconsciousness', while others felt it should be concerned with personal experience and consciousness raising; this latter tendency won, and 'two of the theorists left the group'. The decision, then, was to 'focus on ourselves', though this focus raised problems in terms of a lack of a 'coherent political perspective'. Initially, it appears, the men there 'found it difficult even to account for their presence in the group, other than a common acquaintance with women in Women's Liberation'. The Birmingham group were, however, united in their distrust for 'much traditional left-wing theory and politics', which they termed a 'post-Marxist economism' that identified revolutionary potential with the industrial working class and so excluded 'most of us, with our decidedly "bourgeois" backgrounds and outlooks'. In a reprise of Gandhian notions about creating now the future one wished to be – and we know from Sean Scalmer's *Gandhi in the West* (2011) what a powerful tradition Gandhian non-violence and *satyagraha* was in Britain[3] – they hoped to find a 'politics which changes ourselves as part of the society we wish to change'. They were developing a 'strong group solidarity', and had talked about problems of work in terms of notions of careers, ambition, competitiveness, and families, for example, the role of the authoritarian father.

One of the Birmingham group, Rob, had thrown up his job as an engineer so that he could be at home more often. In a section written by Pete and entitled Media Note, the newsletter reported that the local TV news team had contacted Rob asking for an interview; while he did not definitely agree, they turned up anyway outside his door and set their cameras up, then filmed Rob 'giving the kids lunch' and asking him questions about house-work and wage earning: 'They were not interested in our story', Pete comments, 'they wanted *their* story – a man being a "housewife" etc.'

The second issue of October 1973 was produced by a north London group to go along with the Birmingham Men's Conference of 3-4 November 1973. Its presentation is more varied and visual, mixing short essays with cartoons and poems. Yet, composed mainly by leftwing men who were 'either communists or at least marxists of one sort or another', the issue was rather gloomy and dispirited. One of their number, Martin Smith, had been involved with a dozen or so other men in looking after some 30 kids for two days at the September 'Women's Liberation and Socialism' conference. But apart from organising all-male crèches, the group couldn't think of much else to do in terms of anti-sexist activity: 'there has, as yet, been a lack of inspiration…' Another contributor, Dan M, in his article 'Looking at Women', was particularly anguished; he felt he could not resolve his outwardly correct anti-sexist attitudes with his sexist inner thoughts. He writes that his wife is involved in various women's projects. When he meets her colleagues in these projects, he finds himself speaking 'rationally and coolly with them': 'I act externally so as to snivellingly ingratiate myself with them so they think I'm O.K.'; but inwardly he is a 'lecherous fucking animal peering out from behind his eye-balls'. At such times his head 'feels split down the middle', and he wonders if he's made 'any *emotional* progress *at all*' since Women's Liberation began, or simply learnt a 'new set of external appearances and behaviours'.

Another contributor, Marshall Harris, in an essay entitled 'scrub your filthy mouth out', challenged Men against Sexism groups not to refer to themselves as 'Men's Liberation', since men's '"oppression" does not parallel that which is suffered by women, or colonised people, or racial minorities'. What men can do is change their sexist language, and be conscious that they have been trained in 'the male system', which decreed 'thinking things out in terms of logic divorced and detached from feeling'. Clearly, this concern was a common feature of Men Against

Sexism groups in attempting to challenge themselves as men. It was certainly a repeated refrain in my own group.

The third newsletter, 'Brothers Against Sexism', Spring 1974, 10p, put together by the South London Men Against Sexism, was I think by far the most interesting and dramatic, indeed contrapuntal and polyphonic. Much of the issue was composed of reflections inspired by the 3–4 November 1973 Birmingham conference. The editors left off 'all signatures from articles to discourage any "personalities" from emerging'. There was a concern that Men Against Sexism men were turning into man-haters: 'Yes, it's easy to hate men – we are unpleasant, sexist, vicious, cruel, aggressive – we do exploit and oppress women.' But we can't, say the editors in thinking about where to go from here, give in to guilt and negativity, 'we must… begin to change ourselves and other men'. A lot of the writing in the issue is very personal, self-questioning, tortured and introspective. In the midst of a three-page article, 'Lib or Sexism', it was revealed that the essay was typed by the man's female partner, who writes in a box on its second page: 'Some brothers and sisters have asked why I as a woman helped to type the *men's* newsletter?' She explains that her partner has a flexible job and does lots of 'house-husband' errands for her during the day when she is stuck in an office, so that it seemed 'fair to reciprocate and help him'; also, her partner has 'started to learn to type; I wouldn't have helped otherwise. But he's very slow.' She warns, however, that unless more men in the group learn to type, then she will be unlikely to help next time. On the other side of the same page there is another box: 'Hi! This is your typist.' She writes that the article she is typing has become insultingly sexist, and she cannot continue to 'type mutely', and then she adds her own critical comments. So, as in a montage, the man's article was laid out in one as it were penis-like column, while on both sides were highly critical comments by the female typist.

There was also an essay, 'A Gay View of the Men's Movement.

December 1973', highly critical of Men Against Sexism. It sarcastically notes that the heterosexual men involved, by liberating themselves 'from some of their personal oppression', can now cope with 'liberated, independent females'; they can now continue to be 'sexist males though as somewhat smarter oppressors'. Gay Liberation people feel that 'exclusively heterosexual males' are 'not prepared to put their masculinity at risk', which can only be done if such men would involve themselves in sexual relationships with other men. In continuing to 'repress their homosexual desires', men's liberation men are 'incapable of much contribution against sexism'.

From my Mitchell notes I conclude that the Men against Sexism movement had in the US and the UK become in the first part of the 1970s a vibrant and expanding, yet also uncertain and perhaps fragile, movement. In Mitchell I came across a copy I had kept of *Peace News* Friday, 2 November 1973 7p, which reported on the development of 'personalist politics' exemplified in Women's Liberation, Gay Liberation, and 'now Men Against Sexism'. The journal, which was devoted to 'nonviolent revolution', gives an abridged version of an essay by an American theorist of men against sexism, Joseph Pleck, which had been circulated to participants in the Birmingham conference. Pleck suggests men's groups – 'or men's consciousness-raising, or men's liberation groups' – are a 'new social form' in which issues raised by feminist women can be discussed: 'Just as many women now feel a need to remove themselves, temporarily or indefinitely, from relating to men, so too some men feel the need to pull back from relating to women, to spend some time with themselves to find out what their needs with women are.' As men related more to other men, Pleck thought, an increasingly important issue is homosexuality, with some in men's liberation believing that 'developing relationships with other men has consciously and deliberately included gay sexuality'.

In my Mitchell notes, I came across a 'Men's News-sheet – No.1, April 1974', produced by a group based in Stoke Newington, who wished to facilitate contact between groups and provide information about coming events, by bringing out a list of groups they knew about. The list included groups in South London, Islington (two groups), Tufnell Park (three), East London/Brixton, East London, Birmingham (four, including a group composed of men, women and gays), Manchester, Leeds, Cambridge and Dublin.

In my Mitchell notes I have an essay, 'Burn your jock straps' by Paul Harrison, in *New Society*, 15 May 1975 (vol.32, no.658, pp.398-9), which offered a short history of the 'emerging men's movement', which he saw as first rising in the US. 'around 1970': 'Ironically enough, it sprang from a feminist group, the National Organisation of Women. NOW set up a working paper to study the "male mystique"'. The head of this working party was Warren Farrell, who in meetings inspired into existence many of the estimated 300 men's groups in America; Farrell became a lecturer in sexual politics, and in 1974 published a book, *Beyond Masculinity*. Harrison observes that the men's groups in the U.S. join in demonstrations concerning different aspects of sex role stereotyping: 'There have been demos outside toy departments, for example, demanding dolls for boys.' Harrison comments that the British movement, like the American, was largely drawn from the husbands and boyfriends of women in women's liberation. The British movement has so far held five national conferences, and there are now 20-30 groups. However, he feels that the movement in Britain has been much weaker and 'more disorganized' than in America. It is fragmented and 'very confused' about the direction it should take: 'Generally the relation to the women's and gay movements has been highly problematical for the men's groups: are they strictly there to change men so they don't oppress women any more (Men Against Sexism) or are they aiming at liberating men (men's lib)?'

I'm not sure how this 1975 essay came to be in with my London Men Against Sexism documents, for by then Ann and I had left London to make the long plane journey back to the antipodes.

Fiasco: The Return to Sydney

> The good Odysseus now awoke from sleep [in Ithaca]... After so long an absence he failed to recognise it...
> *The Odyssey*, chapter 13

It is a truth universally acknowledged that homecomings are not necessarily satisfying. Certainly Odysseus found it so when he finally arrived home. In London, Ann became pregnant. We had been told that Ann couldn't be pregnant more than a certain number of months when journeying on a plane. In terms of the Men Against Sexism strand of my story, coming back to Sydney featured for me a risible Kafkaesque episode of failure. Let me dolefully explain. Soon after we arrived back and were living in Rozelle with a friend from our para-Libertarian days, unemployed, not much to do, I wrote an essay, simply entitled 'Men Against Sexism', where I reported on my experience in the London Men Against Sexism scene.

I won't reproduce the essay here, though it does have an arresting beginning, mentioning that some 500 men attended the Leeds Men Against Sexism conference in March 1974, and that also in Leeds a Radical Drag group had formed, hoping to break down social pre-definitions of what is 'masculine' and 'feminine' in dress and appearance; the men don't disguise that they are men, but might wear makeup and dresses. I will quote passages that refer to particular aspects of my north London group, of eight men, in a consciousness-raising format.

> The men in my own group were in their mid-twenties, were almost

all university graduates, but had rejected the security of post-university 'careers'. Most of them were either on unemployed relief, or living off money earned when they were highly paid in their career jobs, or were doing casual teaching, or 'craft' activities like carpentering.... Most of the men in the group were middle-class, and had known or were in relationships with, people in women's liberation. Many felt that they had come to sexual awareness quite late (in their twenties), and some part of the group's discussions were given to analyzing their sexual fears and their fear of their own bodies – some felt they were too thin and had been made to feel inadequate in terms of the male stereotype of bigness and prominent muscle; one felt on the contrary that his thighs were too bulky because of playing football, and also that his knees were ugly, so that he would only wear long trousers at the beach; other fears were of not being hairy enough, or, on the contrary, of being too monkey-like and hairy. Most of the men were coming to terms with a slimness they felt had earlier in their lives been culturally despised. Masturbation was discussed, particularly whether or not men had fantasies when masturbating and/or fucking, and if the masturbatory fantasies were sexist and objectifying, even if they felt their actual sexual activity with women was not. The one working class member in the group was, as against the middle-class men, highly sexually self-confident, and also bi-sexual, whereas the middle-class men were heterosexual and gingerly moving towards discovering gayness, but very aware of their own virginity and not wanting to use gays for 'experience'. Some discussions centred on heterosexual fear of gayness, of what the physical act might entail, and of breaking barriers of touching other men.

The experience of sharing fears and doubts of their own bodies did work – the men became very affectionate, non-aggressive and supportive of each other, would freely touch each other (particularly in greetings and partings)... The closeness of the men in the group may in part be related to the peculiarity of living in a very large city like London; it could be in reaction against the alienating atomization of life in a large city that the men all became close friends very quickly. At the same time, because they had never met prior to joining the group, the men could reveal intimate details of their lives because they knew none of the other men were acquainted with their friends or the people with whom they were having relationships…

[In my group] the predominance of 'consciousness raising' discussions concerned the problems of breaking down the attitudes which separated men from men. One danger of this approach is that of establishing another form of male exclusivism – while men in groups may attain with each other supportive, unaggressive and warm relationships, they may feel this to be so absorbing that women still don't 'exist' in social situations. Men Against Sexism could become a higher form of male bonding… if it be true that in many women's liberation groups women spend a lot of time discussing men, their oppressive attitudes and actions, the men's group rarely talked about women. The emphasis was clearly on opposing sexism as it related to men liberating themselves from restrictive notions of 'masculinity', discovering their bodies, touching, learning how to relate to each other more intimately and 'personally', and possibly discovering their gayness. The other direction of Men Against Sexism, fighting sexism in so far as it related to men-women relationships, was more a matter of assumption and indirect effect than of immediate 'consciousness raising' interest.

From various letters in my Mitchell folders, I can piece together something of what occurred in trying to get this essay published. I tried to get it printed in several places, including *Digger* and the feminist journal *Refractory Girl*. The most farcical attempt involved sending the essay to *Digger*, a kind of funky uber-cool newspaper that friends in Sydney told me about, but which I'd never read myself. I have a copy of a letter I sent while Ann and I were living in 71 Smith Street, Balmain, in Terry Irving's house, in the latter part of 1974, before our son was born on 27 November 1974, asking the *Digger* collective to see if it was worth publishing. There is another letter to someone else, Warren Osmond, a friend of ours, who had suggested sending it to *Digger*, which had collectives both in Melbourne and Sydney. In this letter to Warren I wrote:

> I looked at a couple of back issues, and thought it was fairly unreadable counter-cultural journalism, but might be the only place for it. So I sent it off to their Sydney end in Glebe, and was rung up by Hall Greenland, who said they liked it and to come over in the morning, say at eleven, and talk about it. Warren, who was visiting that morning, said it wasn't cool to arrive on time for a Digger interview, and to make sure I was late. I arrived about 11.15, but Greenland was so cool he didn't arrive at all.

I never heard anything after that. I finally rang someone in *Digger*, who said the men in the group all liked it and wanted to publish it, but some of the women in the collective thought the tone wasn't questioning enough. After more months passed, I forlornly requested the essay be returned to me, which it finally was. As I wrote in a letter, with perhaps a little exaggeration: 'The condition of the returned manuscript gave an unexpected insight into the beverage-consuming habits of the *Digger* collective. The pages were hard to prize apart, because of the massive quantities of tea and/or coffee spilt on them, there was a massive tea and/or coffee stain on the back of it, and the manuscript's final page was missing.'

The concern of the women in the *Digger* collective that the essay was self-indulgent and uncritical was, it turned out, shared by the *Refractory Girl* collective. In the Mitchell notes I have a handwritten draft of a letter I wrote to them, though it's undated, so I'm not sure when I sent it.

> Dear Collective,
> I would like your permission to withdraw my article on Men Against Sexism.
> I would not like the article to be the occasion of possible divisiveness within your collective. Ideally, of course, I should not have submitted it to *RG* in the first place. I did so because there is no Men Against Sexism movement in Australia (at least that I know about), with its own newsletter, where the article would have its natural place. I hoped the article would do a little at least to stimulate thinking in readers of *RG*, some of whom must be men, about such a movement. The mild disturbance it has caused in the *RG* collective suggests, however, that there probably are more appropriate places to do this at this stage.

So, that was it, no publication. At the end of my talk to the Sydney Feminist History Group, I said I don't blame anyone for not publishing the essay; publication, I thought, would have come if there was a large and active Men Against Sexism movement in Australia in the mid-1970s comparable to the movements in Britain and the US, which could have roused people's interest in the issue. I then said, I'm mystified why there was such a difference between Australia and the UK and US. In the question time, my friend Rosemary Pringle, a sociologist who has lived and taught in the UK, suggested that the large group houses in Britain may have facilitated male group interactions and conversations not possible in the much smaller households in Sydney. Maybe! I don't know. Given that Women's Liberation and Gay Liberation were such vigorous presences in Australia, why not Men Against Sexism as well? I'm still puzzled. We might call it the antipodean Men Against Sexism conundrum.

Coda: Ann's reflections

I remember John going to his Men against Sexism meetings. When he got home, I would ask, 'What did they say about women?', thinking of my earlier women's liberation groups in Sydney which had talked a lot about men. 'We didn't talk about women at all', John would reply, 'we talked about men'.

While John was enjoying his Men against Sexism group, I was having something of a hard time with British feminism. Despite attending various feminist groups, both local and history groups, I didn't at that time make friends with any British feminists; people were just not very welcoming. I made some good British feminist friends on later London visits, so perhaps in 1973–4 I was just unlucky, or maybe just so thoroughly unconnected that I couldn't find a way into the right British feminist circles for me. I was delighted when John didn't have the same experience with the Men against Sexism group.

Above all, this chapter is a reminder that Women's Liberation posed huge challenges for both men and women, generating significant changes in ideas, ethics, and behaviour in a comparatively short time. When John gave this chapter as a paper in Sydney in 2011, the almost entirely female audience there really enjoyed it – it reminded the older women there of the anxieties and uncertainties of an earlier time, while for the younger women, it was something of a revelation.

---

1 Mette Ejlersen, *I Accuse* Translated by Marianne Kold Madsen (1968; Tandem, London, 1970), pp.7, 11, 38–40, 50, 71.

2 John Docker, 'Sydney Intellectual History and Sydney Libertarianism', *Politics*, Vol.VII, No.1, May 1972, pp.44, 47,

3 See Sean Scalmer, 'Globalising Gandhi: Translation, Reinvention, Application, Transformation', in Debjani Ganguly and John Docker (eds), *Rethinking Gandhi and Nonviolent Relationality: Global Perspectives* (Orient BlackSwan, New Delhi, 2009), pp.177–204.

40

The Chorizo and Genocide: Travel Notes on Barcelona, Granada, Cordoba, and Portbou, June-July 2005

These reflections were first published in *Sephardic Heritage Update* 176: 25 September 2005; I remain grateful to its editor, David Shasha. I've trimmed a little here and there, especially concerning Walter Benjamin's death in Portbou on the Spanish border in 1940, which I referred to in my Introduction.

Melancholy reminders of a lost medieval Moorish-Sephardic world are everywhere in modern-day Spain, in its great monuments, in the arrangement of its cities especially in the old al-Andalus, and in everyday eating. That's what I decided while Ann and I were travelling in Spain in late June, early July 2005 before attending a conference in Marseille.

23–25 June:
We fly the long long flight from Canberra to Sydney to Bangkok to London to Barcelona, taking some 30 hours. We like Barcelona very much as a cosmopolitan and legendary city by the sea. We enjoy the usual things, catching the underground and coming up at La Rambla (I walked along checking various locations with buildings mentioned in Orwell's *Homage to Catalonia*, which I'd

been reading), Gaudi's art nouveau creations, the labyrinth of narrow streets of the old quarter, the surprise of coming across buildings like the Palace of Music. We eat Basque style tapas. We think about art nouveau and modernism, why architectural modernism is usually thought of as severe, functional, and geometric, while art nouveau in Barcelona, part of the modernista shaping of the city, is so extravagant and fantastical. I think, too, of the philistinism of Australian politicians, of how, in my home city of Sydney, while it has the Opera House, politicians come and go and rarely leave monuments of beauty.

We visit the Picasso museum, and I have a heretical thought: at a certain stage Picasso stood still, began to repeat himself or run out of aesthetic ideas; I thought, he didn't travel enough, didn't see enough of the world, didn't get far away enough from Barcelona and Paris. Maybe that's ridiculous. One day Ann and I search for the Sinagoga Major. Our excellent Lonely Planet guidebook gives an address, but even though Ann is an uncannily good map reader (I'm completely hopeless), we only find it almost by accident. The museum is small, consisting of various excavations, and even the museum guide suggests a certain hovering doubt that it was a synagogue: they think it was. The Lonely Planet in its notes says that it was 'one of four synagogues in the city, but after the pogroms of 1391 it stopped being used for religious purposes', and Jews, who had lived in the city's medieval Jewish quarter and had to wear a special identifying mark on their garments, were expelled from Barcelona in the late fifteenth century.

We learn a lot about how the Catalans prize their distinctiveness, talk about independence, insist on a dual public use of Catalan and Spanish, fly the Catalan flag on public buildings, are proud of their internationalism, their openness to Europe and a wider world. I finish reading Montalban's detective novel *Murder in the Central Committee* I'd started in Canberra and had been reading on the plane from Australia. I also read not only Orwell's fascinating book but Colm Toibin's *omHomage to Barcelona*, with its sad images of the exiles – intellectuals, artists, musicians – who refused ever to return to Franco's Spain while the dictator ruled. (When I return to Canberra I also read Hemingway's *For Whom the Bell Tolls*.) Spain and the pathos of exile seem to be twinned in its history.

26–30 June:
At 9pm we catch the overnight train to Granada. We are staying at a Macia hotel on the small plaza at the foot of the hill where you catch a little bus up to the Alhambra. We go twice to the Alhambra, once during the day, and once at night to see the Nazaries, the palace lit by muted lighting. It's extremely hot in Granada, but the Alhambra with its gardens, pools, fountains and high ceilings, is cooling, tranquil and contemplative. It's remarkable to think that people from all over the world, as well as people from elsewhere in Spain, in a Western world that is told it should despise Islam and Arab peoples, come here to appreciate the Alhambra, not only for the buildings but also for the gardens, the *generalife*, as well as for the vista of towers and the city and plain below. People give barely a glance at the clumpy stubby Renaissance palace that the Catholic rulers plumped in the middle of the Alhambra complex, some of it still in ruins; they walk past the church that replaced the minaret without a glance.

Readers of the *Sephardic Heritage Update* don't need to be told of the transcendental beauty of the Alhambra and *generalife*. They know how overwhelming an experience it is to visit and think about the lost world of Muslim-Jewish-Christian *convivencia*, and all that has disastrously happened in world history since in terms of the triumph of the nation-state and nationalism. In my diary I confide: *He cried, that such beauty could ever be.*

28 June:
We catch an early morning bus to Cordoba. From Granada to

Cordoba the landscape appears to be endless olive trees, occasionally grape vines, sometimes orange trees. At the bus station in Cordoba we catch a local bus to the great mosque (*mesquita*), which is next to La Juderia, the old Jewish quarter, with white-painted buildings and orange trees in the streets, dark green leaves with glimpses of bright ripe oranges. Cordoba is very beautiful. From the Guadalquivir beside which the bus has stopped we walk up to the mosque and cathedral. Puzzled, we'd read in our Lonely Planet guide that you see the mosque and cathedral together. At the ticket office, we ask, where is the mosque and where is the cathedral? There, there, the young woman points, they're the same building. We walk over to the entrance and enter one of history's most extraordinary creations, the Great Mosque of Cordoba. Again, readers of the *Sephardic Heritage Update* know what it feels like to see the vastness of the mosque, the remarkable play of light, the elegance of the slim columns so that the faithful have uninterrupted vision of the whole, the extraordinary double arches with the red and white bands. What daring! How moving this medieval religious and aesthetic masterpiece is; and then one begins to notice the marring intrusions effected by Catholic rulers in the succeeding centuries. As you wander in wonder, you come across a church planted inside the mosque, then you start to see around the walls various shrines and statues – gross graven images – dedicated to Catholic potentates, until one sees the ultimate insult and monstrosity: a huge squat ugly cathedral plonked in the middle of the mosque, vulgarly celebrating Catholic Spain's sixteenth-century wealth and power. What a desecration – building within like a succubus, preying on yet depending on the Great Mosque, that people from all round the world come to admire.

At length we walk out into the hot sun and white light, have lunch in the old Jewish quarter, then using our map find another restored *sinagoga* and nearby an elegantly restored, perhaps twelfth-century, Moorish residence. Finally, exhausted, we catch the bus back to Granada and sleep the whole way.

29 June:
We rest during the day, including spending hours in the outdoor café area outside our hotel, sipping good coffee under umbrellas, talking and reading. We catch the bus up for the 9.30pm visit to the Alhambra, which is different at night, less crowded, quieter, sadder, filled with the melancholy of lost presences. We walk back down the hill to the plaza and look for a restaurant. We are now on Spanish time, eating lunch about three or four in the afternoon, having dinner at 10 or 11 at night.

30 June:
From the high hill of the Alhambra fortress you look across at Albaycin the old Muslim quarter. Today, we catch a little bus up to the top of the Albaycin, and find the hill where you can gaze at the towers of the Alhambra and the mountains behind. As in Cordoba with its Jewish quarter, the old Muslim quarter of Granada recalls the plural medieval world of vibrant communities, now attracting tourists and travelers for their historical memory while the peoples who created these quarters were banished so many centuries before, were forced to leave or become *conversos*, *marranos*, and *moriscos*.

We find a restaurant in a narrow street and enjoy some fine new-Andalusian food for lunch, and I note in my diary: *The Alhambra's eternity of beauty looks down with pity on Catholic Granada*. Then we start walking down the labyrinth, drinking bottle after bottle of water in the extreme heat and refilling from a small fountain we luckily find, until we reach our plaza and sink into the seats under the umbrellas and have cool orange drinks and more coffee. (As far as I could tell, in Spain there is a gender rule: the man has an expresso, the woman a coffee *con leche*, with milk; it reminds me of a similar practice in Vietnam.)

30 June-1 July:

At 10pm we catch the overnight train back to Barcelona. We arrive in the morning, appreciating Barcelona's relatively moderate heat compared to Andalusia. Later in the day our son Ned arrives with his friend Alex, who has been teaching English in a primary school in Nabonne not too far away in France; Ned and Alex are to stay in Barcelona for a few days, then drive around parts of Spain.

2 July:

We drive in Alex's car to the nearby market town of Vic, enjoy the crowded markets, see the Catalan folk custom of people, castellers, forming a human castle, and then look in the butcher shops, where various products of pork, especially a wide range of sausage and chorizo, are displayed with great skill and art. I admire the skill and art, but think to myself, why so much emphasis on pork? I start to think about the possible general cultural significance of the ever-present chorizo.

5 July:

Early in the morning we catch the train that goes from Granada to Montpellier (there we will catch another train to Marseille). The train moves northwards alongside the Mediterranean, and then arrives at the border town of Portbou. In the Introduction I record that I had particularly wanted to see Portbou as the place where Walter Benjamin died on 26 September 1940, almost certainly by suicide (though there is still doubt about that given that he was in poor health). As the train slowly negotiates the border, I bitterly scribble in my diary: *Tuesday 11.10 am – the train to Montpellier has stopped at Portbou. Vale Walter Benjamin. I'll see how far the French border is from here, how far you got into Spain as you tried to escape.*

Since returning to Australia, I've been cooking Spanish dishes.

I emailed Gleebooks my favourite Sydney bookshop, and they recommended and sent a large cookbook with lovely illustrations, *Spanish Food and Cooking*, by Pepita Aris. This is giving me great pleasure to cook from, though I studiously go nowhere near chorizo dishes, or I leave out the chorizo from dishes. There are obvious reasons for not wishing to cook and eat pork sausages, and specific historical reasons as well, when we recall (I think I'm remembering my reading a-right here) that *conversos* and *moriscos* could be reported to the Inquisition if they were suspected of avoiding pork. The introduction to *Spanish Food and Cooking* tells us that 'Spain's most famous foods – chorizo, cocido, gazpacho, bacalao, paella – have an encoded history'. Moorish and Sephardic dishes, ingredients and cooking methods are still, the introduction explains, omnipresent in modern-day Spanish cuisine. The Moorish presence is evident in the introducing and use of greygreen olives, rice, almonds, meatballs, oranges, lemons, sugar, spinach, aubergines, mint; meat on skewers; preserving in vinegar; grinding nuts such as almonds in a mortar and pestle; thickening chilled soups with almonds or a cream of garlic, bread and vinegar, forerunners of the gazpacho; spices like cinnamon, cumin, nutmeg and saffron; sweet and sour dishes; sweets like almond pastries, fritters in honey, milk puddings, quince paste, peaches in syrup, iced sorbets; also raisins and pine nuts used together in sauces.

Even the cocido, the Spanish national dish, says the introduction, is based on the Jewish *adafina*, the Sabbath casserole, cooked the night before. Yet there is a difference. The cocido was adopted by the Catholic Spanish, but pork and sausages were added, as proof that the eaters were neither Jewish nor Muslim. Indeed, the introduction observes, since the days of the Catholic kings Isabella and Ferdinand, pork sausages such as spicy red chorizo have become the main meat eaten in Spain: 'Eating sausages became a statement of loyalty and proof, if required, of conversion to the Catholic church'. Pork became an 'integral part of Spanish religion, and therefore of everyday life'.

Historically, ingesting the chorizo means to attempt to seal the death of the lost world of Moorish Spain: long after the formal end of the Inquisition, in the midst of a contemporary Spain proud of its tolerance and liberalism and, at least in Barcelona, of its cosmopolitanism. The chorizo signifies a kind of genocide, in Lemkin's definition, the destruction of the foundations of life of a group or society. The chorizo is an emblem of permanent loss for humanity.

Everywhere in the Spain we visited we registered traces of that lost world, of its death – yet also, perhaps, of its irrepressible continuing life.

41

Prostate Politics: A Personal Memoir, 2017

2017: on 9 October, the day after my seventy-second birthday, this memoir begins.

Memory so quickly slips away. How did I become aware of the question of men of a certain age – late sixties, early seventies – becoming vulnerable to prostate cancer? Ann Curthoys and I came back from Canberra in 2008, we had been at ANU since 1995, it was time to return to our home city of Sydney, to our apartment in north Bondi in a small block of flats which we had been renting out all these years; Canberra's near grotesque impersonality as a city had worn us down, going every day for fourteen years to the same well-known coffee shop down the hill from us in inner north O'Connor and not once the people serving showing the slightest sign of recognition; for the last couple of years I had found ANU unadventurous and boring, though I will always treasure the intellectual connections I developed there both with local colleagues and overseas scholars visiting the Humanities Research Centre where I worked as an honorary fellow.

North Bondi was its own little world, revolving around the cliff-edge golf course we walked on every morning before breakfast, sometimes dodging golf balls; we always visited and admired the Indigenous rock carving close to the precipitous cliffs, it reminded us of the Lascaux cave paintings in the Dordogne; the soaring landmark tower, somehow connected to the sanitary treatment works across the road, planted itself at the northern end of the golf course; just down from the golf course is the bus depot, where buses from the city to Bondi turn around, though one keeps going to the famous harbour, to Watson's Bay.

At the depot there was a young doctor who I mainly remember for rather shouting that people eat too many eggs, don't eat too many eggs, she said accusingly. Round the corner was a coffee shop, the Three Eggs, I used to go to every morning,; it didn't have a view of the beach, and after a year or so became defunct. After that, Ann and I would go every morning to the Depot coffee bar, which does have a comprehensive view of beach, sea and coastline to the south, drawing in north Bondi locals at all times and tourists in the summer.

The North Bondi doctor, referring me to specialists at nearby Bondi Junction for cholesterol and high blood pressure, introduced me to the eastern suburbs medical world, extremely expensive. I can't remember her saying anything about prostate. In late 2010, we decided to move to the inner west, to Glebe, near Sydney University, where Ann had transferred her ARC fellowship, and I was an adjunct professor. We very much liked Bondi, it's where I grew up, we enjoyed swimming between the flags at the northern end where the surf is usually calmer, going to the little pocket park tucked into the far north end of the promenade on Sundays, and strolling along the length of the cosmopolitan promenade, being near water somehow magically aiding reflection, different perspectives, sudden new ideas. We decided, however, while Bondi had all sorts of media types, musicians, actors, it was not for us – we had (and have) only one good friend there, and no academics we knew lived there; we felt that in Glebe it would be far easier to relate to our friends at Sydney University and engage in inner city intellectual life. Given the occurrence of this or that ailment, or when we needed a new prescription for blood pressure and cholesterol pills, we realized we must acquire a new doctor, and remembered a doctor from pre-Canberra days who practised in the inner west. After a year or so, I can't quite remember, for the first time prostate hove into sight; she took an active interest in results for prostate (the numbers) when I took routine blood tests, and after a while suggested – increasingly insistently – that I should go to a urologist, she knew of several, try this one, here's his phone number.

This is where memory becomes elusive. Had I already seen newspaper articles referring to the acrimonious conflict over prostate between oncologists, who prefer radiotherapy treatment, and urologists, who are surgeons who routinely – all too routinely, in the view of the oncologists – perform surgery on men, that is, remove the prostate altogether? I'm not sure now. In any case, I think it was in 2014, as instructed, I reluctantly made an appointment to see the urologist, an experience I found distinctly unpleasant: the urologist with bored eyes, who made what I considered was a rather brutal rectal probe. I decided never to see him again. But having seen him seemed to initiate some kind of automatic medical process, unbeknownst to me. Some weeks later, a letter came from a suburban hospital saying that I was to turn up on a certain day. I ignored the letter since I hadn't agreed to anything, I wanted to forget that the urologist ever existed; on the day, I was rung by one of the hospital's administrators saying where was I, I said I'm at home, why do you ask; she said you're supposed to be here; I said I don't know anything about it and have no intention of coming to your hospital. I also, I have to confess, and I'm not proud of this, starting shouting, in a decidedly unhinged way, down the phone at the hapless administrator that I had been reading up on what oncologists think of urologists, and the last thing I would now do is go anywhere near them.

My imprecise memory is that after seeing the bored robotic urologist, I had sent away for and received in the post a booklet I had noticed had been talked about in a newspaper article when a public controversy about prostate treatment had blown up: Simon Chapman, Alexandra Barratt and Martin Stockler, *Let sleeping dogs lie? What men should know before getting tested for prostate cancer*, published by Sydney University Press in 2010. Good, I thought, these are Sydney University people, my colleagues sort of, in an admittedly very distant way, humanities and science, and of course I knew of Simon Chapman because of his anti-smoking campaigns. (Actually, to be honest, I think the blank-eyed urologist belonged to Sydney University as well.) I quickly turned to their bios on the back cover: at the University of Sydney, Simon Chapman is professor of public health, Alexandra Barrett is associate professor of epidemiology, and Martin Stockler is associate professor of epidemiology and oncology. I set to and read this booklet with the greatest interest; with its direct speaking voice, it wishes, I thought, to be read by the medically trained as well as those like myself who are obviously medically untrained; as a writer I appreciated how lively the writing is; I read the booklet repeatedly, and manically highlighted what I felt were key passages, in particular, those that contest what the authors considered are the urology profession's attempt to sequester prostate cancer treatment as a matter of surgical intervention, while drastically playing down the possible disastrous side effects for men of the surgical removal of the prostate (p.114).

Men, the authors of *Let sleeping dogs lie?* suggest, should resist the increasing pressure of the urology lobby to automatically subject themselves to a medical procedure that may dramatically reduce their quality of life by causing impotence and incontinence (p.10). And such resistance is occurring: many men consciously choose not to be tested, since having a PSA (Prostate Specific Antigen) test is problematic. For some men it may save their life, but it also may find many benign cancers which could have been left alone; for many men a test will result in serious, unnecessary surgery and other interventions, in a large proportion of cases resulting in enduring and often permanent after effects in the form of sexual impotence, urinary incontinence and, less commonly, faecal incontinence. Yet, they argue, the surgery will have been unnecessary because the cancer would have never caused problems in many of these men's lives (pp.10-11, 43, 63). It is indeed sobering to read that there are many thousands of men who have had their prostates removed and who, as a result, are permanently sexually impotent (pp.12, 43, 116).

Such is the absolutely central point at the heart of this book. The authors point out that the PSA test is a tool which has a very poor ability to find problematic cancers, and it finds many benign cancers which could have been left alone because prostate cancer usually grows very slowly, it can exist in the body for many years without ever becoming a problem (pp.11, 58-61, 105, 114-115). What the authors wish to emphasise is that the large majority of men who die from the disease die late in life, close to when they would have in all probability died from another cause anyway (p.11).

Men, the authors urge, in their encounter with prostate cancer should be able to choose what they consider is the rational course of action for themselves, they should become the subjects of their own history; health agencies around the world are increasingly recognizing that many people want to be involved in decisions that affect their own health. Many people no longer want their doctor or their government to decide for them (pp.93-94). In relation to PSA testing, men should be adequately informed about the pros and cons of PSA screening before going ahead with a PSA screening test; whether you think the benefit is worth the risk is a matter of personal judgement (pp.94, 118). I really like the tone, spirit, sensibility and intelligence of *Let sleeping dogs lie?* I often get it off my bookshelves and re-read certain heavily highlighted passages, while intensely aware that I am a lay reader.

At one point the authors caution that prostate cancer exhibits a spectrum of disease from slow-growing cancers through to rarer cancers that grow and spread more rapidly (p.23). This is important for my story. A huge unknown: where am I on the spectrum?

―❦―

Things did go awry for me; what has happened is exactly what I didn't want to happen.

It turned out in the last year or so that carrying out the booklet's advice – beware of taking a PSA test because it may mean getting caught up in a whirlwind of unnecessary medical intervention from which it is difficult to withdraw (p.11) – is not an easy thing to do, especially as in my individual experience GPs are usually not at all interested in explaining the pros and cons of PSA testing. Rather, they see their routine role as prescribing a PSA test then funneling you straight into a path that leads from a biopsy, which is always done by a urologist, to surgical removal of one's prostate.

But I tried. I tried. When I next went to see my doctor in the inner-western suburbs I brought along the booklet tucked away in my manbag. She said she was concerned by the latest blood test and what it showed about my prostate. I reached into my manbag and got the booklet out and showed it to her, and also said I found the experience with the particular urologist she had sent me to, to be very unpleasant. She leafed quickly through the booklet with its many highlighted passages, put it down again without comment or interest, and said she was now sending me to another urologist, here is his phone number, I want you to go to him. I said OK, smiled, walked slowly out, and decided never to see her again; we live in a democracy I thought, one doesn't have to see any particular GP. I then contacted the Glebe medical centre we used to walk past every day, on Glebe Point Road, near my favourite bookshop Gleebooks and a few doors along from my favourite coffee shop Badde Manors, and immediately was impressed by their bright young medical staff, with computers on their desks where they tap in shared information and actually listen to you (hmph, I scoffed to myself, the other doctor didn't even have a computer on her desk); I showed one of the young doctors the booklet and we had a long conversation and agreed that we should be watchful; he didn't urge me to any sudden action.

In July 2016 Ann and I moved across the continent to Perth, from the Pacific to the Indian Ocean, to be near our son Ned, Shino his partner and our dear friend, and our grandson Leo. Months went by, until I needed my prescription for statins and blood pressure to be renewed. How to find a doctor. The first medical centre I went to I found rather depressing; sitting in the waiting room, one could see that no interview with any of the GPs seemed to last for more than two or three minutes. The doctor sent me off for a blood test, then several days later got the staff to call me in and expressed alarm at the prostate numbers, which was, I can record, 13.2 as of 3 March 2017; have you, the doctor asked, been having prostate symptoms; what are they, I asked, and she described them; I said no, I didn't have any such symptoms at all. I also showed her my Simon Chapman, Alexandra Barratt, Martin Stockler booklet, but she wasn't interested. You'll have to have a specific PSA test, she said. I succumbed. I did the test on 11 May 2017. When the medical centre notified me that the results of the PSA test had come through, I went to see another of the doctors there. I tried to show him the booklet. He almost swept it away with contempt. Look at this number, it's 18, you'll have to do something. I said OK, but I'll see an oncologist, not a urologist. He became angry, snarled and ungraciously penned a letter to an oncologist he knew; here, have this, he said, dismissing me.

Ann and I decided to abandon this medical centre, we agreed we didn't like anything about it, it was slovenly and doesn't give one enough time. We decided to go to another medical centre we had noticed, and here our experience was very different. I say our, because the GP, genial and intelligent, didn't mind at all when I said I'd like Ann to be there with me. We talked about a wide range of things, even made jokes and laughed a lot; he said what appeared to be a recent jump from 13.2 to 18, from March to May, was worrying, and that I had best see a urologist he knew and respected, and have a biopsy done; having a biopsy didn't mean I then had to have the prostrate surgically removed; I told him that I had read of the dangers of impotence and incontinence associated with removal of the prostate, and he said, yes, these are very real possibilities. For the next step it was agreed that Ann and I would come back to see him after the biopsy and discuss alternative treatments, including oncology.

Reader, I had the biopsy on 11 September, the urologist was actually very pleasant, and Ann and I went to see him on 14 September; he told us that I had prostate cancer, and asked what did I want to do next; I said I didn't want surgery and would go down the oncology route; he said that was fine, and gave me the card of an oncologist he knew. He also arranged that during the week beginning 25 September I attend a radiological centre for a PSMA scan, which would, I was told, determine if the cancer cells had spread beyond the prostate; it was to be held at a private hospital using the most recent technology which was very accurate. The appointment was for the morning of Tuesday 26 September; Ann and Ned came with me, there were other men my age in the waiting room, which was quite small, so we repaired to the cafeteria. After a while, Ann and Ned and I were called in to the waiting room, and told that the isotope (or something similar) had not reached the required 99 per cent accuracy, and we were to come back on Thursday morning 28 September. Ann accompanied me, Ned had teaching to do, and this time the scan was ready; what I particularly remember was being required to lay still for 30 minutes under the scanner with my hands above my head held in place by a kind of belt; I was told not to move; I'm not sure what if any thoughts occurred to me for 30 minutes, except I did have an idea for the chapter I was writing for my ego histoire, *Growing Up Communist and Jewish in Bondi*. I hoped I'd be able to recall it later; towards the end I occupied myself doing eye exercises. Then it was over and some time later I could go, could rejoin Ann in the cafeteria. A few days after, the urologist rang me and said the scan showed no spread of cancer cells beyond the prostate. This surely was exceedingly good news.

On 9 October Ann and I visited the recommended oncologist at a cancer centre clinic, who said the PSMA test I had at the hospital is very advanced in its techniques of detection, they don't have anything so advanced in the US, the oncologists there are jealous. That's good, I thought. Then he startled me by saying – and here Ann has come to my rescue in terms of remembering the conversation, I was feeling rather unnerved – that my biopsy revealed a Gleeson score of 8 out of 10, which meant I was in the danger zone of aggressive cancer, I needed daily treatment which would last for several weeks. He said I was very unlucky, not all men with high scores from a PSA test (18) have a dangerous level such as mine, they can be watched; on the other hand, oncology improves all the time, and the treatment is now very specific, it lasts only a few minutes, you can drive yourself to the clinic here and then drive home, and you can keep up an active life, you should keep up an active life.

When Ann and I arrived home, Ann googled for relevant information and I looked up *Let sleeping dogs lie?* The Gleason score is named, so *Let sleeping dogs lie?* tells us, after Dr Donald Gleason, a pathologist at the Minneapolis Veterans Affairs Hospital who helped develop it in the 1960s; the Gleason score suggests how aggressively the cancer cells in the prostate are likely to behave. Most men with prostate cancer, the authors say, have a Gleason score in the middle range, 6 or 7, and such men use watchful waiting or hormone treatment. However, men with higher Gleason scores for prostate cancer have potentially more to gain from active treatment (pp.67–8).

On 19 October I am scheduled to see the oncologist again, and tattoo marks will be effected to guide the radiotherapy (so Ann and I understand what he said), which will last till Christmas. I'm quite the perennial pessimist, but I'm hoping both to be cured and to be able, during the weeks of treatment, to continue writing my ego histoire. This may be a delusion. Until the prostate thing occurred, I had planned to finish *Growing Up Communist and Jewish in Bondi* by late 2018, I have been writing it for many years now, I have written some 300 000 words, what if I cannot finish it.

Sometimes when one wakes in the early hours of the morning, with darkness outside, it's difficult not to feel a certain melancholy. Why have the gods done this to me? Which gods have I offended?

Your regulation Gothic vision: Is that Death come riding over the hill towards me, towards me.

Thursday, 19 October:
Appointment for Planning CT at the clinic. This turned out to be a topsy-turvy day, nearly derailed by a mishap concerning passing water.

Ann and I woke early on the day we were to attend the clinic for my introductory session, a simulation I think. I'd put aside the information folder I'd been given when we went to see the oncologist, though keeping it in view, near my keys and where every night I place my talismanic manbag. The night before, we opened the folder with the necessary information of what we were supposed to do in the morning. We quickly realised that I should have spent the previous few days taking a laxative. We stared at each other. Fortunately, we had a laxative in the house, Actilax, and I hastily gulped some down. The instructions also – wrongly, as it turned out – decreed that, since we were to get to the clinic by 9am, at 8 am, an hour before, I should endeavour to empty my bladder and drink 375 ml of water; also, don't drink coffee, it's a diuretic which may make you feel like emptying your bladder too quickly.

In the morning, after a quiet breakfast, at 8am I emptied my bladder and then drank the required quantity of water. At 8.40, we drove to the clinic, and at 9am we were ushered in to see a nurse, who asked me to go to the men's toilet to urinate and then when I returned she produced a plastic bottle and asked me to drink 375 ml of water, which I did, though thinking I had just drunk 375 ml of water at home before we left. The nurse said (I think she said this) the water makes the bladder rise above the level of the prostate. She explained things about the course of treatment: while the first couple of weeks will go well, after that I will probably feel increasingly tired; your skin around the target area might feel as if a little burnt, you can rub an ointment on, though not, never, oil based; we're always here to talk about any problems; she told us where to go next, up to the floor where there was a waiting room. When my name was called I was ushered into a radiotherapy room and introduced to the nurses; I was to leave my i-phone in a little change area but I didn't have to take off my clothes. All went apparently well. Three tattoo marks, little dots – I would feel a tiny bit of pain, only for a moment – were effected,

I was placed just outside the radiation arch and then sort of rolled in and then after a short while out. It soon became clear something had gone wrong. I was, said the head nurse, too hydrated, I'd drunk too much water that morning, could Ann and I come back at 2pm, let's hope the hydration level goes down. Yes, coffee would be OK, it dehydrates (good, Ann and I thought, we were already getting coffee withdrawal headaches), eat some lunch (when we got home I ate plenty of Walkers Scottish Highland oatcakes with a lot of cheese), and at 1pm drink 375 ml of water, then return to the centre at 2pm. This time, all went well; how did you dehydrate so quickly, they asked. I smiled enigmatically, thought maybe it was the oatcakes and cheese or maybe the coffee, hopefully both, though I don't have a clue; how limited my medical knowledge is. There were smiles all round. They declared I was ready for the course of treatment to start, the tattoos were in place, they would see me again at 10am on Monday 30 October, the procedure each time only takes a few minutes.

The next morning Ann and I went for a brisk walk beside the sea, hoping that we will be able to do this before all the sessions in the coming weeks.

Monday 30 October.
Ann and I drive down to the coast and do a walk we like going north, the play of colour of the vast Indian Ocean so different from the Pacific Ocean that runs alongside Sydney; we feel good, pleased about getting into a walking rhythm again after a long Perth winter of pretty well every morning raining.

Breakfast, then shower, feel that I'm tensing up a bit. At 9am I drink the required 375 ml of water, and a little later we drive to the clinic, take a lift down to some kind of underground bunker, I imagine lead-lined because of all the radiation flying around. We're to receive a weekly schedule of times for my sessions. We do some required paper work, Ann gets a coffee from a machine, I'm called in by a young man in his later thirties or early forties, he tells me he and another therapist will be my therapists this morning, and I'm taken into the radiotherapy room. Looking at my jeans, he asked me if I own trakky daks, patients find it easier to take them down; I say I haven't got any trakkies. I have to say my address, my age, and why I'm attending the clinic. The other therapist appears, of similar age, they position me, I'm to lie still, they will retire to a kind of back observation room, and then the radiotherapy will begin. I lie still, and for some reason think I'm in a space ship and maybe Dr Spock, grave as usual, is nearby. When it's over the first therapist comes in, tells me that it went well but I still have faecal matter in my bowel. I rejoin Ann, I have to see a nurse, who after a little while appears; I ask if Ann can come in to, and she says sure. The nurse and I have a long and detailed discussion of what to do about the faecal matter; I may have to have the laxative twice a day, or increase the one dose a little; she also urges me to use a special cream, QV, in the relevant private areas, especially before going to bed; I say we've already bought the cream, and that earns an approving half smile; you have to start applying it from now on, from tonight, you have to make sure your skin is in good condition for the weeks ahead.

Ann drives us to the local coffee shop near where we live, and we gratefully sip down the Perth regional speciality, a long macchiato three quarters topped up in a small glass; they start making them as soon as they see us. The waitress who started the same day we first came to the coffee shop and with whom we have friendly chats, asks us how it went.

Monday, 20 November:
I'm into the fourth week, and this Friday I will be entering the second half of the treatment program, which has settled down to

being routine; also, Ann and I went to Target a few weeks ago and we chose and bought the required trakky daks. At 11.31 am today, a rather oddly precise time, Ann and I went to see the oncologist. He greets us, we walk to his office and sit down. It's a very quick interview. The oncologist said, you're nearly half way through, and there appear to be no problems, no skin problems or tiredness? I said, no, that's all fine. And you drink the water an hour before, that's going OK? Yes, that's all working out. Ann says she has a question: when will we know if the treatment has been effective? He replies that it will not be before about three months after the treatment sessions are over, through PSA blood tests. We nod. We shake hands and walk towards the lifts.

Monday. 18 December:
I'm in the final week, this is the thirty-sixth session. I drive to the clinic, have the treatment, which only takes a few minutes, then I take the lift to see the oncologist. We shake hands. He said you don't appear to have had any problems, no problems with your skin? I say, no. Your water works OK? I say yes, though not quite sure what that means. You're OK then, he beams – 'A piece of cake'. I smile, though think to myself I'm not quite sure I'd put it that way. He says that in three month's time I'll take a PSA test, then I will be monitored for a further 12 months to see if the numbers are coming down.

Tuesday, 19 December:
The penultimate day of treatment. From various hints dropped by the staff, I gather that on their final day patients often present the staff with some kind of present, for example, I was told that a lady on her last day of her chemotherapy treatment had made some home-made biscuits. Forewarned, Ann and I had

bought some chocolates, and tonight will gift wrap them to take tomorrow, with a card. (That is to say, Ann beautifully wrapped the chocolates).

Wednesday, 20 December:
Final day. Ann and I drive to the clinic, we have to be there by 12.20 pm, I feel a little anxious about how to hand over our present to a staff member, should it be when we arrive or at the end. I'm also worried I drank too much water an hour before we left, will I be able to last; will I botch my last visit with an accidental spill as it were. (I just last.) As it turned out, it was easiest to hand over the present as soon as we arrived. After the treatment, we talk to a nurse, who tells me that in the next couple of weeks, even though the 38 treatment sessions are over, keep taking the laxative every night, your body is full of radiotherapy or radiation, I can't quite remember what she said, you don't want to be constipated, also keep putting on the QV cream to protect your skin; please ring us if anything is worrying you. We say goodbye. I walk towards the car, feeling drained and tired. Ann drives to a shopping centre near where we live and we try out a new Thai café for lunch, which turns out to be very good, oysters in spicy sauce, green papaya salad, roast duck. Then we walk through the length of the shopping centre to a coffee place, where I have two piccolos in quick succession. In the evening, we visit Ned and Shino and Leo for dinner to celebrate the end of the treatment. Everyone agrees it's been all round an exhausting year. We're all exhausted.

Thursday, 21 December.
Ann and I wake early and drive to the nearby coast, to walk along the sea, water lapping at our ankles. We return home, and I have a morning coffee for the first time for months.

Monday, 12 March 2018:
Truly excellent news. Last Wednesday I took the PSA blood test, and the results were forwarded to the clinic. This morning, Ann and I drove to the clinic for a 10.30 appointment with the oncologist, he quickly told us the result of the PSA, my reading had come down from 18 to 4.2; it should, he said, come down further in the next two years; my next appointment with him will be in six months' time.

Ann and I drove to our favourite coffee shop, then went home for lunch. I know I should have been shouting for joy, but all I felt was relief and tiredness. After lunch, I fell asleep for a couple of hours.

Tuesday, 18 September 2018:
More very good news! Today Ann and I went to see the oncologist, the last few days it's been hard not to feel anxious; but he quickly tells us the new PSA result, my reading has come down from 4.2 to 3.3, he reminds us that it has come down from 18 to 4.2 and now 3.3, by the next appointment in six months' time he expects it should come down to 2 something.

A final reflection for an unfinished story. During the weeks of treatment I did manage to keep writing *Growing Up Communist and Jewish in Bondi*, working on a chapter '1938–9: In the Shadow of the Holocaust', but I would often fall asleep in the afternoon.

Epilogue:
father and son, a conversation
with Ned Curthoys

NC: Dad, it's been an absolute pleasure to read, a monumental journey actually with all sorts of rich subject matter. I might be on the wrong track here but this feels to me a bit like a Proustian enterprise, to sift through different layers of memory and feel your way back into the past in terms of what you call its 'wider and longer perspectives' as you say in the acknowledgements. That involved thinking about your parents and their genealogies which reaches out to different nations, cultures, eras. I'm a grateful beneficiary of this extraordinary research into the sometimes elusive meaning of times past.

I'd like to begin by just asking you to tell me how you feel now about your relationship to these various pasts, both intimate in relation to your family and expansively drawn in relation to world histories. Does a dynamic reconsideration of your past help you in thinking biographically about your inspiration, creative projects, affiliations, ethical impulses?

JD: Looking back on my pasts through this ego histoire, I'm struck by two key peripeteia when I was young. The first occurred during my high school years. I think it's mysterious why at school we are 'good' at some subjects, not others. In any case, at high school I found myself doing well at 'English', this is what, increasingly, as year followed year, I found myself enjoying (though I also found high school in the main very boring). This had huge consequences for my future life. Not only was I comically inept at woodwork (my father had been a carpenter), but also in my final year I found economics opaque and alien, I risked failing in it, my parents arranged for me to be tutored and learn possible answers; this ineptitude was a worry as I needed to go well in the Leaving Certificate exams in a variety of subjects to get a scholarship to go to Sydney University. But also, being good at English and inept at economics meant that I could not really follow my father, who wished me to become a revolutionary and perhaps hoped I would be good at subjects that would be important to a revolutionary. What then occurred, without consciously thinking about it, was an abiding intellectual attraction to my mother's side of the family: I think of my mother's love of theatre, her stories of going to theatres with my grandfather Phil Levy in London when a young girl, her taking me to New Theatre plays as a young boy, and knowing that my uncles Lew and Jock had been part of the Sydney Jewish Youth Theatre in the 1930s. I admired my uncles for what I would now call their Jewish passion for ideas, the internationalism and cosmopolitanism in their choice of plays, their being in Arendt's terms 'conscious pariahs'. (I'll return to this point.)

The other turning point when young, in my early twenties, occurred in late 1968, early 1969, when I met Ann Curthoys, your mum. As I note in my Preface and Acknowledgements, we started living together in Balmain after I had returned to Sydney from doing an MA at the University of Melbourne; 1969 was the year when Ann became part of the Women's Liberation movement stationed at 67 Glebe Point Road, Glebe. Ann told me of her admiration for Simone de Beauvoir, which I quickly came to share. It became crucial to our relationship, and remains so. I was inspired by Ann to read de Beauvoir's novels like *The Mandarins* as well as the autobiographies *Prime of Life* and *Force of Circumstance*, I had to catch up as quickly as I could. We discussed the importance of walking in de Beauvoir's relationship with Sartre, especially in its early stages. In *Prime of Life* de Beauvoir recalled that she and Sartre would meet each morning and walk the streets of Paris talking until late at night, about themselves, about their future life, their yet unwritten books. Ann and I tried to work out how de Beauvoir's writings might help shape our lives as intellectuals; we talked about the importance of the art of conversation and how to practise it, and the high place of friendship. We took to long walks, reflecting on what our lives together could be. We also sought out nearness to water as always magically stimulating new ideas, new perspectives, new possibilities. We would drive to the beach at Bondi and lie on the sand talking. Ann suddenly said we should think of having a baby one day.

NC: Love that part where you try to break down some distinctions between the Old Left and the New Left and suggest that, like your anti-materialistic father, you've decided to always be unswervingly radical. Can you tell me a bit more about what that means in a contemporary context where activism often takes cultural rather than overtly political forms?

JD: One thing that always struck me as very interesting about my father's reminiscences was that during World War I in Sydney he belonged to the anarchistic IWW, the Industrial Workers of the World, and during the 1920s wrote articles, very well-written articles, in support of anarcho-syndicalist ideas of direct action in the work place. It pleases me to think that when I became part of the New Left in the late 1960s and then 1970s, its anarchism reprised the anarchism of the IWW, which was as culturally lively as directly political, with its music and satirical mockery. The state destroyed the IWW in the First World War, which had long-term effects; for radicals there was a turning towards the nascent Communist Party after the war, which meant, especially during the 1930s, the long working out of its ruinous support for the intensifying authoritarianism and totalitarianism of Stalin and the Soviet Union.

There were acute differences with my father. At university I was becoming an intellectual, but my father despised intellectuals, in his view they were not anchored in the working class, they could betray the working class in a revolutionary situation. Then as a teenager at home in our flat, I had dreadful drawn-out conversations with my father where I would denounce Stalin, and even now it pains me that I used my education against him, that I used words and concepts he didn't know, and he felt this keenly, he said so, you are using your education against me.

When I think of his life I still admire his internationalism, and the courage of his anti-racism during the 1934 Kalgoorlie anti-Yugoslav and anti-Italian riots. And writing this ego histoire I've come to appreciate his Irish family history that began in the mid-nineteenth century almost at the same time as the tragedy of the Irish Famine; the specific history of Irish Protestantism that had its own radical history in Ireland; his mother supporting Home Rule for Ireland in distant Australia (the power of diaspora to feel you still belong to far away histories); his own knowledge of and friendship with Irish radicals in Australia; feeling myself drawn into the intensity and passion of Irish history.

NC: Coming to the second book, on my grandmother Elsie Levy, tell me just a bit more about why you feel there was a real urgency required in addressing your youthful fondness for Eliot, here you are almost harsh on yourself. Given that he has been established as an icon of modernism well beyond the Leavisites, does Eliot's continuing stature (I studied him rather uncritically as an undergrad myself) say something about the way literary heroes are created in the academy?

JD: Yes, in the ego histoire I felt I had to try and understand how I could make my way to the university, which I began in 1963, from our Bondi flat, with a Jewish mother from the East End of London (she was 14 when she migrated with her family to Sydney) who would often tell me when I was growing up of how as a child she was subjected by teachers in London to anti-Semitism, they would pronounce her name Elsie Levy in a slightly sneering way, and then attend English lit tutorials where a poem like 'Gerontion' was very much favoured by the Leavisite lecturers (other canonical Eliot poems from memory were as you would expect 'Prufrock' and *The Waste Land*). In tutorials, sitting in a circle in a lecturer's room, not knowing anything about each other, we young students would be asked to subject 'Gerontion' to close textual analysis, a badge of being or learning to be a Leavisite. I would nervously participate (I used to blush a lot when I talked in those years) while seeing yet not seeing the anti-Semitic imagery with its truly egregious line about 'the jew sits on the window sill'. I didn't interject and say, my mother is Jewish, my grandparents are Jewish, why are we sitting here not referring to this vile anti-Semitic image, why aren't we discussing it? In the ego histoire I decided to take the opportunity to say what I should have said as a young student. I was also fairly appalled by Leonard Woolf, who, when asked about Eliot's anti-Semitism, said, well, when they had lunch or dinner together, Eliot showed no anti-Semitism towards him, it was all very cordial.

The Leavisites wished to create traditions and canons of great novels and poems that could be discussed with a fine sensibility, forming an elite that somehow could redeem humanity from catastrophe, the industrialism and vulgar mass culture of modernity. I did my fourth-year thesis on *The Waste Land* (and Pope's *Dunciad*) and my MA in Melbourne on *Four Quartets*, but as the years went on I more and more wished to move away from Leavisite literary criticism, one reason being because it ignored the anti-Semitic poems and would not go near Eliot's non-literary early 1930s tract *After Strange Gods*. Why, I thought, didn't the Leavisites want to bring detailed textual analysis to bear on *After Strange Gods*, discuss the violent xenophobia of its language in a tutorial, ask students what do we think of this or that notion or image.

I moved further and further away not only from Leavisite literary criticism but literary criticism as such, it was too narrow, too confining, too precious, too 'high literature'. What I now saw myself doing was to value my training in detailed textual analysis, but apply the method to any text, literary or non-literary, when pursuing 'the adventure of ideas' in cultural history and intellectual history. Detailed textual analysis as a method offers a freedom I continue to enjoy; I can take it with me into any field I'm interested in. Nevertheless, I still somehow think of myself occasionally as a literary critic, and when I have too long immersed myself in, say, study of popular culture, I enjoy returning to 'high' literary texts (like Joyce's *Ulysses*). I secretly think to myself that I would like to be like Walter Benjamin, a 'European intellectual', a kind of general intellectual who is also a writer. Arendt says a couple of times in the Introduction to *Illuminations* that Benjamin 'thought poetically'; 'without being a poet he thought poetically', he regarded 'metaphor as the greatest gift of language'. I'm looking at Arendt's reflections on Benjamin now, in the edition you gave me after my own edition of *Illuminations* fell apart. I see you write on the title page: 'So that you may converse once again with Benjamin dad, for your memoir, Love, Ned.' I know how much we both intensely value Walter Benjamin. It still saddens me to think how he died on the Spanish border in 1940.

Coming back to Eliot, I've thought of something else, I feel another perspective could be considered, we should retain an ambivalence about people we are interested in. In the ego histoire, in the volume 'My Mother, Elsie Levy', yes I am very critical of Eliot for his anti-Semitism (I think at one point I indulged a fantasy that when he visited the East End to ogle Jews, did he see my mother your grandmother when he sidled about, perving). Yet I continue to return to some of the final lines of *The Waste Land*. I've just looked up the opening sentence of the Concluding Mosaic for my *1492: The Poetics of Diaspora*: 'I'd like to shape my Concluding Mosaic in the genre of the anti-conclusion, in the spirit of the closing lines of *The Waste Land* that have haunted me and that I recount in my head and misremember (because I don't go back and check) ever since I did a thesis on Eliot's great poem in the fourth year of my undergraduate life, in 1966: these are the fragments, these are the fragments that shore up my ruins.'

In my concluding volume *I am Born* I designed the disparate final essays and diary entries about prostate cancer in similar spirit, as fragments that (impossibly) shore up ruins.

I think that in admitting to what I admire about Eliot as in *The Waste Land* I am suggesting that such ambivalence keeps history's judgements open. In the ego histoire, I tried to register a similar thought about Leonard Woolf, so many facets of his life and attitudes are questionable (there he was in Ceylon in the early twentieth century, an executioner) but not all; and similarly in talking about my father, your grandfather, so many facets of his attitudes and actions are deeply questionable, at times distressingly wrong, had destructive consequences (as in the expulsion from the Communist Party of Jack Ryan, Lyndall Ryan's father), yet not all, thinking of his internationalism and his opposing the racist Anglo-Australian rioters during the 1934 Kalgoorlie Riots.

NC: I really enjoy the way you read cultural and intellectual history through various thought figures, what I have sometimes called conceptual personae drawing on Deleuze and Guattari. Why do you think the parvenu appears so prominently in your thinking in recent times, and would you agree with Arendt about the importance of remaining a conscious pariah?

JD: I'm not quite sure now why I became so interested in the figure and sensibility of the parvenu, who appears to come from nowhere, who strives with extraordinary energy and singleness of purpose to climb to the top of a society, who believes there is a centre to a society and they can reach it, master it; I wanted to draw attention to the parvenu as somehow important or at least not uncommon; to recognise the parvenu as a force in history. And thinking about the parvenu made me realise how much I didn't wish to be a parvenu, not just because the centre is always illusory, but because striving to reach an illusory centre is the very reverse of what at crucial junctures, yet more peripeteia, I wished to do, and that became a life pattern; for example, refusing to 'join', or, if I did 'join', after a while I would disengage. When I was an undergraduate I never joined any student organisation. I became part of the Leavisites as a young student and then postgraduate for a while, then found myself disengaging, writing an essay, 'How I became a teenage Leavisite and lived to tell the tale' mocking the Leavisite historical project yet also mocking myself, for self-mockery, self-parody, self-irony I have always thought very important, the self-parody of the schlemiel. Self-parody maintains contact with what Bakhtin wrote admiringly about, Menippean satire in antiquity, satire that does not criticise from a declared fixed ideal that considers itself beyond criticism, questioning, mocking.

And that is why I became so interested – I've just looked up my Introduction – in Arendt's 1943 essay 'We Refugees' where she admires the figure of the 'conscious pariah', the 'tradition of

Heine, Rahel Varnhagen, Sholom Aleichem, of Bernard Lazare, Franz Kafka, or even Charlie Chaplin'. In her 1944 essay 'The Jew as Pariah: A Hidden Tradition' Arendt refers to Heine, Lazare, Chaplin and Kafka as 'those bold spirits who tried to make of the emancipation of the Jews that which it really should have been – an admission of Jews as *Jews* to the ranks of humanity, rather than a permit to ape the gentiles or an opportunity to play the parvenu'. As I say in the Introduction, I very much admire the figure of the conscious pariah as a kind of guide to living, as formative of consciousness.

Also I think we can see my uncles Lew and Jock, in creating the Sydney Jewish Youth Theatre, as 'bold spirits' in Arendt's terms who tried to make of the emancipation of the Jews 'that which it really should have been – an admission of Jews as *Jews* to the ranks of humanity'. So there is important family history here for us to think about, a kind of out-there dissident lineage.

There is another point Arendt makes in her 1944 essay, that out of 'their personal experience Jewish poets, writers, and artists' were able to 'evolve the concept of the pariah as a human type – a concept of supreme importance for the evaluation of mankind in our day'. Arendt is suggesting that the figure of the 'conscious pariah' is the reverse of passive: the 'conscious pariah' creates new possibilities of being in the world, possibilities, intellectual and cultural, we see in the thought of 'Heinrich Heine's schlemiel and "lord of dreams"'; Bernard Lazare's 'conscious pariah'; Charlie Chaplin's grotesque portrayal of the suspect; and Franz Kafka's 'poetic vision of the fate of the man of goodwill'.

In a related way, I talk in the Introduction of the importance of Simmel's great 1908 essay 'The Stranger' and Isaac Deutscher's essay 'The Non-Jewish Jew'.

Ned, I know we are on the same page here, in your brilliant book *The Legacy of Liberal Judaism: Ernst Cassirer and Hannah Arendt's Hidden Conversation* you admiringly evoke Arendt's 1943 and 1944 'We Refugees' and 'The Jew as Pariah' essays, Simmel's essay on the stranger, and Deutscher's Spinozan concept of the non-Jewish Jew as 'the rebel, the atheist, the heretic, the excommunicated Jew'. The title of your book subtly alludes to Arendt's 1944 essay, 'The Jew as Pariah: A Hidden Tradition'.

I feel very moved by this, our mutual liking for these essays.

NC: This really is a thorough documentation of phases of your life from the Hippy Trail tour of South-East Asia and on to London just before my birth towards your recent treatment for prostate cancer. I'm wondering what for you have been the most important formative experiences?

JD: When your mum and I were in London in 1973 and 1974, we enrolled in a course on African Literature, put on at the Polytechnic of Central London's Centre for Extra Mural Studies, its tutors O A Ladimeji and Lewis Nkosi. Pondering that course proved very influential for me for many years, and still does, it led me to break away and keep breaking away from conventional approaches to literature. At ANU in 1975, where I had begun a PhD on Australian literature of the 1890s in international contexts, talking with my fellow postgraduates Satendra Nandan, Bill Ashcroft and Michael Cotter, and Barry Andrews who was teaching literature at Duntroon Military College in Canberra, we realised that we shared a similar interest in new literatures in English, and a similar desire to propose far-reaching alternatives to the aesthetic and pedagogical hierarchies that structured conventional English literature courses and modes of teaching. During 1976–7 we organised our own seminar series in the English department, gave talks to a local community radio station, and began a new journal, launched as *new literature review, special issue: post-colonial literature 1977*, accompanied by manifesto essays by Bill Ashcroft and myself, challenging anglocentric assumptions in traditional departments of English, and calling for courses devoted to African, Caribbean and Pacific writers.

In a kind of Dadaist gesture, we felt that literary criticism should start anew.

NC: Dad, thanks for your responses here, I like your use of dramatic metaphor, life is full of peripeteia which we don't always realise at the time. Can I ask you a little bit about performance, performativity? How important is it as an intellectual or writer or activist, and you and mum have inhabited these roles in your lives, to perform and enact rather than just analyse and critique which is a default academic posture? I was struck that what you also got from de Beauvoir was the idea of walks and sharing conversation with mum, so performing certain dialogical ways of living seems important here well beyond the various appearances in the public sphere of a 'public intellectual'.

JD: I agree about the importance of performativity, and maybe, I'm just trying to think this through, performativity was part of a generational adventure, it wasn't just a personal choice, though it was that, but an aspect of the 1960s and 1970s New Left breaking away from the sober mode of critique presented to the world by left liberal intellectuals in the 1950s. I recall once writing a review of the Australian journal *Nation*, it published a selection of essays from the 1950s, and there the academics and journalists who wrote for it made very good, careful, critiques of racism, especially the White Australia policy. I reflected that the New Left in the 1960s and 1970s made very similar criticisms of racism, yet broke with the 1950s sober mode of critique: highly theatrically, in noisy protest marches with their street theatre and witty placards, in Women's Liberation carnivalising language, in Gay Liberation and Black Liberation demonstrations, in the immediacy of gestetner-ing and roneo-ing and feminist newspapers like *MeJane* that your mum was involved in, indeed appeared on the cover of, on a swing, and journals creating their own inventive kinds of presentation; and all of these in conversation with kindred movements in the rest of the world. Yet, I don't think the New Left generation made a conscious decision to affect such a break with the 1950s liberal left generation, or politely declare that it was going to make such a break, it seemed to burst out like the universe itself, centrifugally. I don't like talking like this, as if the New Left generation had a single unified consciousness, but something in the Zeitgeist was moving (actually, I don't like the term Zeitgeist either, it can be totalising), but maybe we can say a vast worldwide carnivalising wave of turbulent fissiparous consciousness swept over and through the 1960s and 1970s, with long lasting and continuing effects. Maybe through such carnivalising performativity, turning the world upside down and inside out, certain theoretical positions came alive in more general epochal historical consciousness: Bakhtin's notions like carnivalesque, Menippean, dialogic, polyphonic, and something of Bakhtin's sensibility valuing eccentricity, Katerina Clark and Michael Holquist pointing out in the Introduction to their biography that Bakhtin always 'refused to join, dominate, or even follow any movement'; Said's conception of an 'unhoused philological humanism' that you explore in your essay in your and Debjani's collection *Edward Said: The Legacy of a Public Intellectual*; Arendt's 'thinking without a banister' (in the collection of essays with that title edited by Jerome Kohn, there is an epigraph where Arendt writes that 'as you go up and down the stairs you can always hold on to the banister so that you don't fall down, but we have lost this banister. That is the way I tell it to myself. And this is indeed what I try to do.'); Judith Butler's so influential notion of performing gender (don't forget you topped the philosophy class on feminism as an undergraduate at Sydney University!).

NC: I was interested that you don't discuss your interest in postmodernism too much here because I grew up with you affirming (performing) various aspects of a postmodern sensibility including collapsing distinctions between mass culture and avant garde aesthetics, appreciating the visual exuberance of postmodern architecture and skepticism towards various grand metanarratives. How would you describe your relationship to postmodernism today, how crucial was it in helping you move beyond certain Leavisite precepts and has it run out of steam?

JD: I published my *Postmodernism and Popular Culture: A Cultural History* in 1994, it was the culmination of many years of writing essays with postmodern perspectives, and also teaching part-time courses on postmodernism, I especially remember a course I taught to visual arts students at the University of Technology, Sydney. I think after the book came out, I felt I didn't really have anything new to say, at least for a goodly while, and that in any case so many positions of postmodernism had become accepted as uncontroversial, absorbed into more general intellectual sensibility, not least the dismantling of the rather austere modernist notion of a hierarchy of genres, and the welcoming of the previously despised (not least by the Leavisites) 'lower genres' such as romance and melodrama, for as you say their exuberance and extravagance always playfully bordering on self-parody.

As the years went on, and into the new century, I made journeys into genocide studies, especially researching Lemkin's linking of genocide and settler colonialism; diaspora; monotheism and polytheism; historiography, writing with your mum *Is History Fiction?*; and the origins of violence.

However, I did begin to make journeys that reprised in new ways postmodernist-like notions figuring plurality and fluidity, in particular, taking up the challenge to write ego histoire, which your mum and I became aware of at a conference in Barcelona in

2008. Also attending were Anna Cole (your mum's former PhD student at the University of Technology, Sydney, in the 1990s, you might remember her) and her friend the French-Spanish scholar Vanessa Castejon, it was our first meeting with Vanessa and we've become friends. They asked us if we would like to become interested in ego histoire; they said the French historiographer Pierre Nora had created the term, and they as scholars located in Europe were setting about applying Nora's idea to Australian Indigenous history. Vanessa sent us a manifesto Nora had written in 2001, 'L'ego-histoire est-elle possible?', where he regards ego histoire as an intervention into writing contemporary history. For Nora, the ego historian possesses a distinctive intellectual personality of an unsettled, fragmented and contradictory kind. Ego histoire is an activity of self-reflection; it involves memory, but memory that becomes self-conscious and self-questioning. Ego histoire deploys autobiography, but ego histoire cannot be encapsulated as autobiography. Ego histoire, Nora is sure, would fail if it attempts to be a single, unified, coherent project, which would return it to conventional historical writing, which ego histoire wishes to make strange, to defamiliarise; here, in terms of literary theory and dramaturgy, I think of the Russian Formalists and Brecht. In the spirit of Nora's essay, then, I regard ego histoire as an adventure of ideas, highly personal and self-reflective, free to mix and juxtapose genres, texts, media, modes, perspectives and narratives in unpredictable and surprising ways.

Another recent journey that I think reprises postmodernism is an interest in the notion of Kunstchaos and the long tradition of fragment literature, which you first alerted me to. In my essay 'Sheer Folly and Derangement: How the Crusades Disoriented Enlightenment Historiography' in *Representing Humanity in the Age of Enlightenment* (great title!) that you edited in 2013 with Shino and Alex, I take up your point about the importance of fragment literature in the Enlightenment, Lacoue-Labarthe and Nancy in *The Literary Absolute* arguing that fragment literature is a kind of 'Kunstchaos, in other words, chaos produced by art or philosophical technique'. Elsewhere I suggest that such Kunstchaos, constellating with the extraordinarily popular Galland and post-Galland translations and new versions of *The Thousand and One Nights*, challenges how the Enlightenment has been conceived in modernity. The title of my essay referred to Said's insight and striking phrasing, in his essay 'Raymond Schwab and the Romance of Ideas' in *The World, the Text, and the Critic*, where Said admonishes Schwab for not noticing the 'sheer folly and derangement stirred up by the Orient' in Europe in the long eighteenth century. In genocide studies I critique the claim in Adorno and Horkheimer as well as Zygmunt Bauman that there is a close relationship between the Enlightenment and the Holocaust. In my 2003 essay 'The Enlightenment and Genocide' in *JNT: Journal of Narrative Theory*, I oppose the view of Bauman and Mosse that the major cultural trends of the Enlightenment denigrated passion and revealed no interest in the errant and whimsical; rather, they were obsessed with exactitude, measurement, comparison and classification, thus providing the conceptual foundations of the Holocaust. In that essay I suggest that the Enlightenment was highly contradictory; there was certainly a strong interest in exactitude and classification, prominent in the mapping and scientific investigations that were so important in European colonising, yet other modes of writing and reflection worked to derange certainty, as we can see in Kunstchaos and *The Thousand and One Nights*, exuberantly enjoying the fragmentary, fantastical, wayward, quirky, and puzzling, the unfathomably odd.

In stressing that the Enlightenment was not pervaded by a single defining spirit I was very much helped by your telling me that Arendt in her multifaceted thinking was not necessarily opposed to the Enlightenment, as in her appreciative portrait of Lessing in *Men in Dark Times*, her admiration for

Berlin's cosmopolitan salon culture of the 1790s, her interest in Jeffersonian democracy in America. You also have written very positively about the Enlightenment, in relation to Moses Mendelssohn and Lessing. I've just read again the opening chapter, '"This Man of Our Destiny": Moses Mendelssohn, *Nathan the Wise* and the Emergence of a Liberal Jewish Ethos', of your *The Legacy of Liberal Judaism: Ernst Cassirer and Hannah Arendt's Hidden Conversation*, where you argue that Mendelssohn, the key formative figure of the eighteenth-century German Jewish Enlightenment (*Haskalah*), established a kind of refractory historical consciousness that continued in Jewish intellectuals in the nineteenth century and then into the twentieth, in Cassirer and Arendt. I'm fascinated by your evocation of Mendelssohn, that he is a cosmopolitan 'world-thinker'; a close friend of and collaborator with Lessing, inspiring Lessing to defend heretics and heterodox thinkers who had been historically ignored or dismissed; he helped create a diasporic Jewish sensibility at ease with a variety of cultural spheres, especially an appreciation of the cultural and philosophical tradition of Levantine and Sephardic Jews, the 'Sephardic mystique', in a turn away from Christian Europe, Mendelssohn believing Christianity was permeated with intolerance and the spirit of persecution; the 'Sephardic mystique' drew on a rich Andalusian Judeo-Arab literary heritage that included Maimonides writing his *Guide for the Perplexed* in the twelfth century in Arabic; Mendelssohn was one of the first eighteenth-century thinkers to rehabilitate the controversial, heretical, excommunicated Marrano Spinoza; he helped inspire the Spinozan renaissance which influenced not only Lessing but also Herder and Goethe; his sympathies were with the subaltern, the outsiders in history, suggesting that true religion is to be found in the excommunicated rather than those who excommunicated them; in contrast to Lessing's concept of global moral progress, he proposed *Bildung* as a model in which individuals follow their own trajectory of self-cultivation; in Mendelssohn's view, a vigorous cosmopolitanism, counter-historical energies, sympathy for outsiders and a pluralistic conception of Judaism are congenial to individual and collective flourishing. Ned, this is great writing.

I'm starting to rave here, I suppose because I'm thinking ahead to my next project, a book – actually the revival of a book that your mum and I abandoned way back in the 1990s – I'm enthusiastic about, that takes up Said's insights, to be called *Sheer Folly and Derangement: Disorienting Europe and the West, from the Enlightenment to Modernity*. I remember we talked about it on the phone, and you were very encouraging about the idea. Hopefully, I should be able to get to it before too long.

We always planned to have a dialogic conversation, from the very beginning of conceiving *Growing up Communist and Jewish in Bondi* while sipping coffee in various cafés in Sydney. The Plague Year of 2020 has us trapped on distant sides of the continent, you in Perth, I'm in Sydney. We decided on this email conversation, which I've found very productive and enjoyable; self-reflection is not an easy art, it requires as always walks and talking with your mum. Also, I've just obtained from Gleebooks Turgenev's *Fathers and Sons* and started reading it, scribbling all over it; you've told me on the phone recently that Said has written about its portrait of Bazarov the nihilist in his Reith Lectures: Representations of the Intellectual, so I'll look that up. The conversation continues!

Sydney and Perth, September 2020

www.ingramcontent.com/pod-product-compliance
Lightning Source LLC
Chambersburg PA
CBHW041310240426
43661CB00064B/2882